Religion
in America

Religion in America

Sixth Edition

Julia Corbett-Hemeyer
Ball State University

Prentice Hall

Boston   Columbus   Indianapolis   New York   San Francisco   Upper Saddle River
Amsterdam   Cape Town   Dubai   London   Madrid   Milan   Munich   Paris
Montreal   Toronto   Delhi   Mexico City   Sao Paulo   Sydney   Hong Kong
Seoul   Singapore   Taipei   Tokyo

Library of Congress Cataloging-in-Publication Data

Hemeyer, Julia Corbett, 1945–
    Religion in America / Julia Corbett Hemeyer.—6th ed.
        p. cm.
    Includes bibliographical references and index.
    ISBN-13: 978-0-205-64520-6 (alk. paper)
    ISBN-10: 0-205-64520-8 (alk. paper)
    1. United States—Religion—1960–   I. Title.
BL2525.C67 2010
200.973—dc22

                                            2009015584

Editorial Director: Leah Jewell
Editor in Chief: Dickson Musslewhite
Publisher: Nancy Roberts
Editorial Assistant: Pat Walsh
Editorial Assistant: Nart Varoqua
Editorial Project Manager: Sarah Holle
Director of Marketing: Brandy Dawson
Marketing Manager: Laura Lee Manley
Marketing Assistant: Ashley Fallon
Senior Marketing Assistant: Craig Deming
Art Director: Jayne Conte

Cover Designer: Bruce Kenselaar
Manager, Visual Research: Beth Brenzel
Manager, Rights and Permissions: Zina Arabia
Image Permission Coordinator: Angelique Sharps
Manager, Cover Visual Research & Permissions:
    Karen Sanatar
Cover Art: Julia Corbett Hemeyer
Full-Service Project Management: Shiny Rajesh/
    Integra Software Services
Printer/Binder: RR Donnelley & Sons, Inc.

This book was set in 11/12 AGaramond.

Credits and acknowledgments borrowed from other sources and reproduced, with permission, in this
textbook appear on appropriate page within text.

Prentice Hall
is an imprint of

www.pearsonhighered.com

10 9 8 7 6 5 4 3 2 1
ISBN 13: 978-0-205-64520-6
ISBN 10:   0-205-64520-8

To my grandchildren,
Courtney Elizabeth Arbogast and
Nicholas Joseph Arbogast,

and to Mike,
whose memory continues to bless my life

For all that has been, thanks;
To all that shall be, yes.

—Dag Hammarskjöld

Contents

Preface

Far too often, when people talk about religion, the discussion becomes an unproductive and unpleasant argument about who is right and who is wrong. This does not have to be the case. The academic study of religion in the humanities offers a unique opportunity to learn about American communities of faith and practice in an atmosphere free of both judgment and partisan advocacy. It focuses on what each group does and believes and on what these practices and beliefs mean to those who participate in them. It does not evaluate whether those beliefs and practices are right or wrong nor does it make judgments about whether a religion is true or false. The academic study of religion does not judge and it does not advocate. It does not present religion as preferable to nonreligion nor does it favor secularity over religiousness. It does not attempt to make converts to or from any particular community of faith. Each community of faith is presented without its beliefs and practices being judged favorably or unfavorably.

Although religious beliefs and practices are presented impartially in this book, it is important that you know from the outset that this book is not value-free. I believe that religion is an important part of humanity's story. I also believe that nothing in the entire spectrum of human religiousness can be completely strange to any of us, because we are all human. I believe firmly in the freedom of religion that is guaranteed by our Constitution. With the religious and spiritual diversity that exists in the United States, respect for those whose beliefs and practices differ from ours is vitally important. There must be dialogue, based on respect and the acceptance of differences.

You should be aware as you begin your study of religion in the United States that there is a vast distinction between religion as it is described in books—as I describe it in *this* book—and religion as people actually live it. Many Jews and Christians do not attend corporate worship with any regularity, for example. Nor do they pray with the constancy their holy books instruct. Catholics do not necessarily follow their church's teachings about such personal matters as birth control and abortion. Some American Buddhists drink wine with dinner, in violation of a prohibition on intoxicants (which some read as a prohibition on intoxication). Muslims follow their dietary guidelines to varying extents. We choose from our religions' teachings those things that are personally meaningful to us and feel free to leave the rest alone. So when you meet actual Methodists or Hindus or Jews, they won't conform completely to what you have read. Their lives, however, *will* be informed at some level by their religious faith.

The sixth edition of *Religion in America* continues the emphasis on religious diversity in the United States that has always characterized this book. Correspondingly, there continues to be somewhat less emphasis on the religions of the majority. Attention is also given to responding to the religious diversity that surrounds us. Religious diversity makes the United States an ideal place to learn about religion, not only in books, but as it is embodied in the people with whom we come into contact every day.

As with the previous edition, this edition first introduces students to the discipline of religious studies and then describes issues and concerns that cut across a variety of communities of faith. Part Two then describes specific Christian communities of faith, recognizing that Christians make up the majority of religious people here. Part Three describes the ever-widening diversity that characterizes religion in the United States.

As with earlier editions, this is not a book about the religious history of the United States, although brief historical notes are included in places. I have chosen to focus on the diversity of what people believe and practice today. The stories of how they came to these particular beliefs and practices are important. To keep this book of reasonable length for classroom use, those stories must be told by others.[1]

I hope you will enjoy your study of religion in the United States. Religion, along with families and friends, work and creative endeavors, school and leisure time, helps to make life meaningful and good for many Americans. It is a rewarding subject for study. Fundamentally, this is a book about people, because religion is about people. For most people in the United States, religion is also about something that transcends people, such as God or another higher reality. But it is always about people, what people believe and how they act in response to those beliefs. So this is a book about us, all of us, because even if we are not personally religious, our lives are influenced by the religiousness around us.

Books are always the product of far more people than just the author. Prentice Hall editor Dave Repetto and Project Manager Sarah Holle were a pleasure to work with, as was Project Manager Shiny Rajesh. Those who reviewed the previous edition helped hone and refine this one. My former colleagues in the Department of Philosophy and Religious Studies at Ball State University have been, as always, unfailingly supportive. My colleagues at Ball Memorial Hospital have also supported my writing in many ways, as has the congregation of the Unitarian Universalist Church of Muncie, Indiana. Many times while I was writing, I was about as much company as a Pet Rock. I thank my husband, Tom, for his patience and for his willingness to think of grilled-cheese sandwiches as dinner.

WHAT'S NEW IN THE SIXTH EDITION?

There is a lot that's new in this edition. Some of the highlights include

- Updated Web references and suggested reading for each chapter
- Many online references facilitate students' quick access to primary sources

---

[1]For an interesting one-chapter survey of major historical developments in the history of religion in the United States, see Ronald L. Johnstone, *Religion in Society: A Sociology of Religion*, 8th ed. (Upper Saddle River, NJ: Prentice Hall, 2007), Chapter 12.

- Streamlined organization throughout
- Some historical material eliminated from the fifth edition has been reintegrated in this edition.
- Greater attention to popular religion in Chapter 1
- New data in "By the Numbers" in Chapter 2
- New material on civil religion and on religion after 9-11 in Chapter 2
- Discussion of the decline of the religious mainline and the rise of evangelicalism within mainstream Christianity in Chapter 4
- Discussion of the *Left Behind* book series
- Greater attention to Hispanic Catholicism
- New section on how immigration has diversified Christianity in the United States
- The chapter on Humanism and the Unitarian Universalists and the chapter on Islam have been transposed to group Islam more closely with the other two major monotheistic religions
- New material on Islam and the black community in Chapter 10
- Chapter 12 has been almost completely revised to more accurately depict the diversity and dynamics of Asian religions in the United States.
- Chapter 13 now includes material on Native American religion and the critiques of the New Age Movement and Wicca.

ACKNOWLEDGMENTS

The author thanks the following reviewers for their helpful suggestions:
Professor Timothy E. Fulop, Lakeland College, Sheboygan, WI; Professor Jeffrey J. Kripal, Rice University, Houston, TX; Professor Carolyn Schneider, Texas Lutheran University, Seguin, TX; Professor Owen Anderson, Arizona State University West, Phoenix, AZ; and Professor Crerar Douglas, California State-Northridge, Northridge, CA.

Religion
in America

Religious America: Diversity and Freedom

Before you begin to read this chapter, ask yourself what your attitude is toward those whose religious beliefs and practices are different from your own. Do you feel curious? Interested to know more about them? Defensive? As if their religion is not "true" or "right"? Would you want to convince them of your own views? Do you think your own point of view might be enriched by dialogue with them?

Religious diversity in the United States and throughout the world is increasing. All of us can expect to be part of communities, workplaces, and social groups that include people of many faiths and of none. The development and growth of this diversity is an important social phenomenon and one that extends far beyond the confines of religion:

> The radicalism of religious diversity is a fact of contemporary life and may well become the most significant feature in the development of society and culture in the twenty-first century. . . . A Muslim living in the United States today is not a Muslim only when he [or she] visits the mosque, recites *Allahu akbar*, or fasts during the sacred month of Ramadan. He is a Muslim when he votes in a local election, goes to market, visits a museum, or reads the newspaper. He is, indeed, a Muslim when he meets a Christian or a Jew in the local park.[1]

We also encounter many other kinds of diversity—racial, lifestyle, political, and sexual orientation, to name but a few. Thinking through our responses to religious diversity can help us be more conscious of how we respond to diversity of other kinds, as well. There is also a particular feature of religious diversity that we should note. Most—although certainly not all—religions make claims to absolute truth. The existence of wide-ranging religious diversity coupled with absolute truth claims poses a particularly interesting challenge for thoughtful, reflective response.

RESPONDING TO RELIGIOUS DIVERSITY

Each of the five responses described below stems from authentic human concerns. Many are grounded in the sacred writings of their proponents' religious tradition or in specific interpretations of those writings. Each has its adherents

[1]Richard Evans Wentz, *The Culture of Religious Pluralism* (Boulder, CO: Westview Press, 1998), p. 13.

within most of the religions, as well as among the different religions. Different authors who write on responses to religious diversity may use the terms differently, as well.

We first need to distinguish all of these responses from *tolerance*, which may go along with any of them. Tolerance refers to the willingness to grant basic civil liberties to members of a faith other than one's own, regardless of how one feels about that other faith. Tolerance encompasses willingness to grant freedom to gather for religious meetings or to speak publicly in the hope of winning other people to one's viewpoint, and avoiding religious discrimination in matters of employment or housing, for example. A person who is tolerant may disagree, may be convinced that the other's position is wrong, but is still willing to see the other person share these fundamental freedoms.

Exclusivism is the most clearly defined response. The exclusivist holds that, because religion deals with ultimate truth, there can be only one true or correct religion and the rest are completely wrong. Exclusivism is found within most of humankind's religions. The following statement from *Evangelical Affirmations* provides a good example:

> Without Christ and the biblical gospel, sinful humanity is without salvation. . . . Any "gospel" without the Christ of the Bible cannot be the saving gospel, and leaves sinners estranged from God. . . . We affirm that only through the work of Christ can any person be saved and resurrected to live with God forever. Unbelievers will be separated eternally from God.[2]

Although exclusivism is a prominent response within the three monotheistic religions of Judaism, Christianity, and Islam, it is not wholly confined to them. Buddhism, for example, exhibits a great deal of openness toward other faiths, but followers of Nichiren Shoshu Buddhism regard it as "the One True Way . . . whereby all the people are able to fundamentally overcome the basic universal sufferings of being born, of old age, sickness, and death as well as doubts and disillusionments that plague mankind."[3]

Relativism is at the opposite end of the response spectrum. There are different forms of relativism, but all of them share the premise that all perspectives are limited, even those that lay claim to absolute truth. There is no unlimited viewpoint from which a truth that is relevant for all times, places, and persons could ever be known or expressed. This perception may lead the relativist in one of two directions: One approach is to maintain that, because religions claim absolute truth and absolute truth cannot be known, no religion is worthy of one's commitment. This approach leads to secularism or irreligiousness. Another kind of relativism, however, holds that, in the absence of knowable absolute truth, it is simply up to individuals to pick the religion that feels right for them.

---

[2]Kenneth S. Kantzer and Carl F.H. Henry, eds., *Evangelical Affirmations* (Grand Rapids, MI: Zondervan Publishing House, 1990), pp. 30–31 and 36.

[3]Nichiren Shoshu United States Web site (www.nst.org/intro3.html).

Inclusivism is a third approach. The inclusivist holds that there is one true or best religion, one that holds within itself the fullness of religious truth and human salvation. However, inclusivists believe there is something of this truth in some other religions, as well. Most Muslims believe, for example, that the revelation of God to the Jews and the Christians was true and brought salvation to its followers, but that it had been distorted by Muhammad's time. God's revelation to Muhammad is believed to confirm the truth of earlier revelations, while eliminating the distortions. The Second Vatican Council of the Catholic Church also affirmed an inclusivist view:

> From ancient times down to the present, there has existed among diverse peoples a certain perception of that hidden power which hovers over the course of things and over the events of human life; at times, indeed, recognition can be found of a Supreme Divinity and of a Supreme Father too. Such a perception and such a recognition instills the lives of these peoples with a profound religious sense. . . . The Catholic church rejects nothing of what is true and holy in these [non-Christian] religions. . . . Yet she proclaims and is in duty bound to proclaim without fail, Christ who is the way, the truth, and the life (John 14:6). In him, in whom God reconciled all things to himself (2 Corinthians 5:18–19), men find the fullness of their religious life.[4]

The fourth viewpoint may be called *synthesis*. This view holds that all religions are essentially the same beneath a veneer of cultural particularity. Synthesis downplays the differences among religions in favor of the similarities among them. Thus, all will—or should—come together in a unity.

Hindu theologian and former president of India Sarvepalli Radhakrishnan takes this position, believing that what he calls *Sanatana Dharma* (the "eternal religion," a name often used by Hindus to describe their faith) is the one religious reality that encompasses all others and toward which all others will eventually evolve. As human beings collectively mature religiously, the various manifestations of religion will converge on "the One Spirit which takes us beyond the historical formulations," which are only "imperfect halting expressions."[5]

The relatively recent world faith of Baha'i also holds a view that humankind is evolving toward one world religion. For Baha'is, one world religion is a central aspect of a larger belief in a global civilization that will include a worldwide government, judicatory system, and currency. The authors of *The Baha'i Faith: The Emerging Global Religion* state that "in reality, there is only one religion, the religion of God."[6] Baha'u'llah, the founder of Baha'i, is quoted as saying that "all nations should become one in faith and all

---

[4]Walter Abbott, ed., *The Documents of Vatican II* (New York: Guild Press, 1966), pp. 661–663.

[5]Sarvepalli Radhakrishnan, "Religion and Religions" in *Relations Among Religions Today*, ed. Moses Jung et al. (Leiden, 1963), pp. 131–132.

[6]William S. Hatcher and J. Douglas Martin, *The Baha'i Faith: The Emerging Global Religion* (New York: Harper & Row, Publishers, 1985), p. 82.

Figure I-1 The Baha'i House of Worship, located just north of Chicago on the shore of Lake Michigan at Wilmette, Illinois. The nine-sided building symbolizes the unity of all religions. It is listed in the National Register of Historic Places. *(Photo courtesy of Baha'i Publishing Trust.)*

men as brothers; that the bonds of affection and unity between the sons of men should be strengthened; that diversity of religion should cease, and differences of race be annulled. . . ."[7]

We can describe the fifth response as the *affirmation of religious diversity*. This view holds that the different religions are simply different, not headed toward a synthesis and not subsumable under the big umbrella of inclusivism. At the same time, each is ultimately true and must be honored as such. Affirmation makes for both commitment and openness. Describing this perspective, religious studies scholar Harold Coward writes:

> It is a recognition that deep religious commitment is necessarily felt as absolute and, as such, functions as the validating criteria for all of one's personal experience. This, however, does not impose it on others or rule out the recognition that in other persons there is a similar absolute commitment to a particular experience, which . . . will be different from one's own. . . . Thus, one is able to honor one's own commitment as absolute for oneself and at the same time respect the different absolute commitments of others. . . . In a dialogue this would mean the preservation of our differences in dignity and mutual respect.[8]

[7]Quoted in J.E. Esslemont, *Baha'u'llah and the New Era: An Introduction to the Baha'i Faith* (Wilmette, IL: Baha'i Publishing Trust, 1950), pp. 117–118.
[8]Harold Coward, *Pluralism: Challenge to World Religions* (Maryknoll, NY: Orbis Books, 1985), pp. 106–107.

In discussing how such dialogue could go forward, Coward notes it requires that people have accurate information about one another's religions. In light of the fact that many persons are not well informed about their own religion, nor those of others, the academic study of religion has an important role to play. It facilitates dialogue informed throughout by accurate information and animated by a spirit of inquiry and respect for the experience of others without compromising one's own commitments.

In her thorough discussion of this stance, which she labels "pluralism," Diana Eck, Director of Harvard University's Pluralism Project, notes these five points that help to clarify what an affirming stance is, as well as how it differs from some of the other views I have described:[9]

- It is not just the fact of religious diversity but "active positive engagement with it."
- It is not simply tolerance and a commitment to insure the rights of the followers of all faith traditions but "the active effort to understand difference and commonality through dialogue."
- While relativism does not allow for commitment, affirmation assumes that members of the different communities of faith are deeply committed to their chosen paths while practicing openness toward the chosen paths of others.
- It does not expect all religions to fuse together but looks for "ways to be distinctively ourselves and yet to be in relation to one another."
- The foundation of affirmation is interreligious dialogue based on understanding rather than on agreement, holding that the understanding of difference is as important as agreement.

The attitude we hold toward those whose religion differs from our own has pragmatic ramifications as well as philosophical ones. For example, it influences our willingness to grant freedom of religious expression to them. A Christian pluralist, for example, would be more likely to *willingly* give a Muslim employee time off from work during Ramadan, Islam's holy month, than would a Christian exclusivist. A college student whose approach was pluralistic would respond differently to a roommate of another faith than would a student who was an exclusivist. Our attitude toward religions other than our own also helps determine whether we try to "convert" others to our own viewpoint.

QUESTIONS AND ACTIVITIES FOR REVIEW, DISCUSSION, AND WRITING

1. What two features make religious diversity in the United States an especially interesting issue for reflective thought?
2. Describe each of the five responses to religious diversity.
3. Describe the affirmative response in greater detail.
4. Write an essay in which you describe your own attitude toward religious diversity. Be sure that you include any ideas you may have about *why* you feel as you do.

[9]Diana Eck, *Encountering God: A Spiritual Journey from Bozeman to Benares* (Boston: Beacon Press, 1993), pp. 191–199. Professor Eck's book remains one of the best accounts of the perspective I take in this book.

5. With several classmates, role-play different ways that members of one religion might approach members of another.

6. Visit the Ontario Consultants for Religious Tolerance Web site (www.religioustolerance.org), and read one of the essays. Write a response to what you have read. Be certain to include the title of the essay that you read.

FOR FURTHER READING

In this book, we look at world religions as they are found in the United States. The following two books provide additional information on world religions.

ELLWOOD, ROBERT S., and BARBARA A. MCGRAW, *Many Peoples, Many Faiths: An Introduction to the Religious Life of Humankind*, 9th ed. Upper Saddle River, NJ: Prentice Hall, 2008. This and the Fisher book that follows are good standard introductory texts.

FISHER, MARY PAT, *Living Religions*, 7th ed. Upper Saddle River, NJ: Prentice Hall, 2008. This is an easily accessible, brief introduction that does not, however, oversimplify.

Two relatively recent books that focus on religious diversity are worthy of attention.

ECK, DIANA L., *A New Religious America: How A "Christian Country" Has Now Become the World's Most Religiously Diverse Nation*. New York: HarperCollins, 2001. Notable for its accounts of specific congregations and people.

LEON, LUIS, and GARY LADERMAN, Eds., *Religion and American Cultures: An Encyclopedia of Traditions, Diversity, and Popular Expressions*. Santa Barbara, CA: ABC-CLIO, 2003. The editors are particularly concerned to document diversity in religions and cultures in the United States. It is especially valuable for its coverage of popular religion.

RELEVANT WORLD WIDE WEB SITES

The Interfaith Alliance: www.interfaithalliance.org

The Ontario Consultants for Religious Tolerance: www.religioustolerance.org

The Pluralism Project: www.pluralism.org

CHAPTER 1

Studying and Describing Religion

Before you read this chapter, think about how and where you have learned about religion so far. What kinds of things did you study? What was the purpose of your study? Also, think about how *you* define or describe religion. All of us have some idea of what religion is. What does the word *religion* mean to you?

WHY STUDY RELIGION?

Many, perhaps most, of you reading this are studying religion to receive academic credit for a course. But there are other reasons for studying religion. Those of us who are religious study our own religion to learn more about this significant dimension of our lives. Our commitment to it matures as we base our devotion on greater knowledge and understanding.

Why study other people's religions? Doing so can help us to understand other people. Religion is an important, even essential, part of many people's lives, and by understanding and appreciating it, we come to know them better. Prejudice often results in part from a simple lack of knowledge and information. While knowledge and understanding do not guarantee freedom from prejudice, a lack of knowledge greatly increases the likelihood of prejudice.

It is also important that we understand religion because it has had an important role in history and continues to have a significant impact on contemporary events. Religion has had and continues to have an impact on cultural forms such as literature, art, and music. Finally, because all religions have deeply human roots, to understand anyone's religion helps us understand ourselves better. By understanding the similarities and differences between our own religion and those of other people, we also come to know our own better.

Statements by notable religious studies scholars highlight several important themes, including the practical applicability of religious studies, which helps to relate the study of religion to the discussion of religious diversity.

Historian of religion Martin Marty points out that faith,

> both in individually packaged and communal forms, while it may not always be deep, is so widespread that it commends itself for study by anyone who wants to understand humans.

He continues that in our diverse culture, religion both defines and links sub-cultures. For example, a person may be identified primarily as an African American *Baptist* in one setting, while being more identified as an *African American* Baptist in another. Similarly, one can be both a *Catholic* feminist and a Catholic *feminist*.[1]

Amanda Porterfield, another analyst of the role of religion in the culture of the United States, notes that the discipline of religious studies helps to stabilize the public role of religion. Religious studies

> encouraged respect for religious difference along with increased self-consciousness about how religious symbols work and a general tendency to understand religion in humanistic terms. . . . [Religious] studies contributed to greater understanding of the ways in which religion functions to divide people from one another and the ways in which it could function to promote equality and build community. . . .
>
> Through its approach to religion as a universal human phenomenon manifest in a variety of different cultural forms, religious studies has contributed to the respect for religious difference that distinguishes the United States from countries where religious difference feeds violence and civil war.[2]

STUDYING RELIGION AS A PART OF THE HUMANITIES

The study of religion has many dimensions. Studying religion as a part of a course of study in the humanities may involve attitudes and methods that are new to you.

Most of us who think about religion first learned to do so within our families and later in a religious organization or a community of faith. Maybe it was in preparation to become a member of a church or synagogue.[3] Perhaps it was learning about our own religion in Sunday school or Hebrew day school classes. For some, it was learning the prayers of our faith from our parents. This way to study religion is sometimes called *theology*. This is study undertaken by members of a community of faith when they learn or study the practices and beliefs of their own religion. Therefore, we can call it an inside perspective. It involves the personal faith commitments of both teachers and students. It is, in Saint Anselm's classic definition, "faith seeking understanding."[4] Theology uses intellectual concepts to understand a particular religious tradition and to express its relevance for the present. It takes as its beginning point the faith of the community, the givens accepted as a part of their tradition. For Christians,

---

[1]Martin E. Marty, "An Exuberant Adventure: The Academic Study and Teaching of Religion," *Religious Studies News*, vol. 12, No. 3 (September, 1997), p. 20.

[2]Amanda Porterfield, *The Transformation of American Religion: The Story of A Late-Twentieth-Century Awakening* (New York: Oxford University Press, 2001), pp. 203–204.

[3]A synagogue is a Jewish place of worship and study.

[4]Saint Anselm was a Christian theologian who lived between 1033 and 1109 C.E. The abbreviations C.E. for "Common Era" and B.C.E. for "Before the Common Era" have replaced A.D. (*Anno Domini*, the year of our Lord) and B.C. (Before Christ) in most scholarly writing.

for example, the uniqueness of Jesus and Jesus's special role in God's plan for the world is such a given. For Jews, the oneness of God has a similar role. Buddhists[5] take the early teachings of the Buddha as foundational. These starting points are often found in or derived from the group's sacred writings.

The goal of this kind of study is that those who engage in it will become more knowledgeable about and more committed to their faith. It need not involve assertions of the superiority of one's own faith, although it sometimes does. It is an important part of educating people in their faith and helping them to mature as religious persons. It is a significant aspect of the growth and development of any religion. A firm understanding of one's own faith is also one foundation for dialogue with others.

The *academic study of religion* differs from theology in that it makes no assumptions about the beliefs, or lack of beliefs, of the scholar. Religious studies teachers and students alike may be believers, nonbelievers, or agnostics (people who believe that we cannot be certain about religious matters) in their personal religious lives.

Rather than concentrating on one religion, the academic study of religion promotes a lively awareness of the diversity of religious beliefs, practices, and experiences that people have. It encourages open-minded investigation of that diversity. It investigates religions in their historical and cultural settings and examines a broad range of materials to provide the most balanced treatment possible. It distinguishes between things that most people accept as historical facts and other things that are taken as true only within the context of a particular community of faith. For example, most people in the United States would agree that the founder of Christianity was an historical person named Jesus who lived in the area of Nazareth. Non-Christians usually do not accept that Jesus was in a unique sense the Son of God.

In studying religion from an academic standpoint, we may try to *explain* religious behaviors and beliefs as well as simply *describe* them. However, such explanations should never become *reductionistic*. Reductionism is an oversimplification that claims to exhaust the meaning of a phenomenon by explaining it in terms of some other, external factor. For example, saying that people are religious because economic deprivation in their earthly lives makes "pie in the sky by-and-by" attractive is a case of reductionism. While there may be some truth to this for some persons, it does not exhaust the meaning of religion.

When we study religion academically, the study takes place in an atmosphere that is free of advocacy. It promotes neither religion nor nonreligion. It educates about all religions and neither favors nor belittles any. It is loyal first of all to the guidelines of public scholarship. Its commitments are to knowledge and understanding for their own sake and to religion as a vigorous dimension of humanity's story (Figure 1-1). It does not involve the personal beliefs of its teachers and students. It is especially important to keep the distinction between theology and the academic study of religion clear in public, tax-supported schools, colleges, and universities. An institution supported by

[5]You will learn more about Buddhism in Chapter 12.

Figure 1-1   The study of religion is an integral part of education in the humanities. *(Photo by the author.)*

taxes paid by people of all faiths and by those who are not religious cannot favor one religion over others. Nor can it favor either religion or secularity. To do so clearly violates the disestablishment clause of the First Amendment to the Constitution. Our personal religious views *might* change when we study religion academically, but, if that happens, it is a personal by-product of the study and not its goal.

One study[6] has looked at how religion is studied on four college campuses in the United States. One is a state university, two are religiously supported schools, and the fourth is an historically black college that describes itself as nondenominational. This study of four representative institutions found several common themes:

- Religious studies is a "vital and appealing" topic on all four campuses.
- In addition to religious studies classes, religion is a topic in many other classes as well.
- General education and core curriculum classes, especially, expose many students to the study of religion as a part of their educational experience.
- Even at the religiously sponsored schools, teachers do not try to convert students to their own point of view. Students at all four schools feel free to express their own views in class. Religious studies classes in the religiously affiliated schools tend to promote religion more than do their secular counterparts. Religious diversity and pluralism are freely acknowledged, and critical inquiry into religion is encouraged.
- That having been said, faculty often try to relate course content to students' own lives and spiritual journeys. Students make this connection even when faculty do not.

The 1963 U.S. Supreme Court decision in *Abington* v. *Schempp* ruled that public schools and school personnel could not mandate devotional activities in their schools and classrooms. People who favored activities such as prayer and

[6]Conrad Cherry, Betty A. DeBerg, and Amanda Porterfield, *Religion on Campus: What Religion Really Means to Today's Undergraduates* (Chapel Hill: The University of North Carolina Press, 2000).

Bible reading in the public schools charged that the Court had, in effect, supported the religion of secularism (nonreligion). Justice Clark, in replying to this charge, distinguished between the *practice* of religion, such as devotional exercises, and *study about* religion. He went on to say that study about religion as a part of human culture and the humanities is well within the guidelines established by the First Amendment to the Constitution. This Supreme Court decision allows for the academic study of religion at all levels of public education.

Religious groups cannot be barred from using public school facilities or other public buildings, however. If secular groups can use these facilities, then religious groups must have the same privilege. The *Equal Access Act* was passed by the 98th Congress in 1984 and upheld by the Supreme Court in *Board of Education of Westside Community School District* v. *Mergens* (1990). For example, if a school board permits such noncurricular clubs as a chess club or Boy or Girl Scouts to use their facilities for meetings, then a Bible study club must have the same right. Usually, interpretation holds that teachers or other school personnel may not be officially involved in such groups. If a city or county building has a public meeting room, then religious groups must be allowed to use it on the same basis as secular groups. The combined effect of *Abington* v. *Schempp* and *Mergens* is that schools cannot actively promote religious activities, but neither can they prohibit them.

You may be wondering whether religious studies is defined by having a distinctive method or a distinctive subject matter. Religious studies scholars do not agree on the answer. In my opinion, religious studies is a distinct and identifiable academic discipline because it investigates the subject of religion in all its forms. Its *subject matter* is distinctive. In its investigation of its subject, it uses many methods. Human religious behavior is a very complex phenomenon and calls for many investigative tools. There is no single best way to study religion. A variety of methods is necessary, and no one of them can claim primary authority.

Within the academic study of religion, we can distinguish two interrelated types of inquiry. The *social-scientific study of religion* focuses on observation and on data that are quantifiable. Its goal is to be as objective as possible. The data that it provides makes a crucial contribution to our understanding of religion. Psychologists and sociologists who study human religious behavior often use social-scientific methods. The widespread use of computers for data processing and analysis has greatly enhanced this branch of the academic study of religion.

People *study religion as a part of the humanities* to understand a religious group, belief, or practice from the standpoint of what it is like for those who follow it. This approach encourages students and teachers to enter empathically into the life and experience of the religious other. It seeks imaginative participation, developing what can be described as an inside–outside point of view. We can, with practice, become increasingly able to see religions other than our own *as if* from the inside, while remaining on the outside. We do not become followers, but we learn to value and appreciate the meaning that the religion has for those who are participants in it.

The academic study of religion may come under attack from either of two sides. On one side are traditional believers who are threatened by any viewpoint that refuses to judge the truth or falsity of religious beliefs. On the other side are those who refuse to take religion seriously and think that it must be explained away in terms of social, psychological, or economic factors. As the philosopher of religion Ninian Smart writes, in either case, people "forget that religions are what they are and have the power they have regardless of what we may think about their value, truth, or rationality. They also forget that . . . we have to listen to one another"[7] in a nation that is as religiously diverse as the United States.

Perhaps you have felt one of these two ways at times, or perhaps you do now. You might occasionally find yourself feeling threatened by some of the material studied, by the way it is studied, or by your classmates' comments. Remember that the study of religion from an academic viewpoint allows everyone ideological space in which to exist. All that is required is that you extend to the beliefs and practices of others the same respect that you wish for your own.

DESCRIBING RELIGION

Religion is an ambiguous word. People use it to mean various things. Even scholars in religious studies cannot agree on its meaning. We do, nonetheless, have some idea of what religion is. If someone asks, for example, "What religion do you practice?" we know how to answer the question. If someone mentions a religious service, we have a general idea of what sort of activity is meant.

By itself, this everyday, unreflective approach is inadequate. It is probably limited to our own experiences with religion. Our understanding might be biased in some way, based on what we have been taught about religion. People's everyday definitions differ, and the same person may use different definitions at different times.

For purposes of study, we must have a good working description. A *working description* is one that is useful and adequate, but it is not the only possible one, nor even the only good one.

1. *A good working description of religion is broad enough to include all religions.* It should not define religion in a way that leaves out some manifestations of religion. Nor should it leave out any specific religion. For example, if we say that religion means belief in God (having in mind God as Jews and Christians think about God), we will leave out those people who worship many deities (a general word meaning gods or goddesses) and those who worship none at all. This description also focuses on belief and excludes other important dimensions of religion.
2. At the same time, *it must be sufficiently specific to distinguish religion from other similar things*, such as a nonreligious philosophy of life or a deeply held and passionate commitment to a social or political cause.
3. *It also needs to be as free of prejudice or bias as we can make it.* Descriptions that state what true or genuine religion is often fall into the trap of imposing one person's or group's bias on the description of religion generally.

[7]Ninian Smart, *Worldviews: Crosscultural Explorations of Human Beliefs* (New York: Charles Scribner's Sons, 1983), p. 17.

Box 1-1

 WORKING DESCRIPTION OF RELIGION

A *developed religion* is an integrated system of beliefs, lifestyle, ritual activities, and social institutions by which individuals give meaning to (or find meaning in) their lives by orienting themselves to what they experience as holy, sacred, or of the highest value.

We will use the working description given in the box. It is important to know and understand this description, because it underlies everything that follows throughout the book.

Religions are also *communities of faith and practice*. They are groups of people knitted together by their shared commitment to a common worldview and their participation in shared experiences. The nature of religious commitment and experience means that it often claims its adherents' greatest, most intense loyalties. The ties within communities of faith are frequently among the strongest and most meaningful of human relationships.

Let's discuss this description of religion in greater detail. A developed religion is an *integrated system*. Ideally, all the dimensions in a religion hold together to make a comprehensive, coherent whole. Its various parts work together without conflict and with mutual support. The extent to which this is the case varies from one religion to another and from one person to another. But ideally, a religion does have coherence among its various dimensions. These dimensions include beliefs, a lifestyle, rituals, and institutions.

Belief takes many forms. Beliefs are the ideas of a religion. For example, most religions have an idea about what the purpose of human life is. Most have beliefs concerning how the world came into being and what happens to people after death. These beliefs are found in scriptures, statements of faith, creeds (official written statements), hymns, stories, and theology books, to name but a few locations. The beliefs of a community of faith also exist in what its members actually affirm as truth for themselves.

Nearly all religions have guidelines for their members' daily *lifestyle*. These include codes of conduct and standards of behavior, as well as carefully worked out ethical systems. They involve both formal requirements and customs and less formal folkways and habits. Examples include dietary regulations followed by Jews and Seventh-day Adventists and dress codes followed by certain Christian groups and many Muslims.

Religions also include *ritual activities*. These are the ceremonial actions, usually repetitive in nature, which people perform as a part of their religious behavior. Religious rituals include worship, along with prayer, chanting, meditation, the lighting of candles, pilgrimages, and the devotional reading of religious books, to name but a few examples. There are religious rituals that are public and corporate, and there are those that individual people and families do privately. For many religious people, the rhythm of regular participation in the ritual life of their religion is more important than is reflection on religious beliefs.

Finally, although religion has to do with individual people, it also includes *social institutions*. Like-minded people join together for instruction, for rituals, and for fellowship. Structures for governance and decision making are necessary. Also in this category are arrangements for admitting members to the group and expelling them from it, educational functions, and arrangements for the selection, training, and support of leaders.

Religion is one way that *people give meaning to or find meaning in their lives*. Any religion is a human creation or development. Its beliefs, lifestyle, rituals, and institutions are the products of human thought and activity. It is continuous with the many other ways that we either create or find meaning in our lives, such as through the personal relationships that are dear to us, the work that we do, and the values, ideals, and causes to which we give our loyalty. Religion is continuous with these other structures of meaning and shares their profoundly human roots.

Religion involves that which people experience as *sacred, holy, divine, or of the highest value*. Although religion is continuous with other structures of meaning, it is also unique. Most interpretations of religion hold that its uniqueness is in its reference to the sacred or to the highest value. It reaches beyond the individual and the ordinary concerns of day-to-day living. Religion puts us in touch with the sense of mystery that glimmers through the cracks of our common world. It has to do with the most comprehensive, fullest expression or embodiment of reality.

Our working description of religion has both functional and substantive elements. When functionalists describe religion, they are interested in what it does—what its functions or roles are. Our description identifies religion as something that has to do with meaning in human life. It also has a substantive element in that the distinguishing feature of religion is its core experience of the holy or sacred, in whatever way that may be experienced and labeled.

POPULAR RELIGION

Earlier in the chapter, I defined religion in a way that emphasizes religions as structured social systems, institutions, or organizations. This aspect of religion can be called *institutional religion*. The words *ecclesial* and *ecclesiastical* are sometimes used to describe this aspect of religion. There is another aspect of religion in the United States that is at least as significant: This is *popular religion*—religion that occurs outside the formal boundaries of religious institutions. These manifestations of religion are popular in two senses:

> On the one hand, they have "mass appeal," they "sell." On the other hand, they are "of the people": they are examples not of the kind of religion that is taught

by theologians in seminaries, but rather of that which appeals to a wide variety of people of no special theological sophistication outside the context of formal "Sunday-morning" worship in the churches.[8]

The existence of widespread and flourishing popular religion in the United States indicates that, as one scholar puts it, the "determination of what counts as religion is not the sole preserve of academics."[9]

Most people in the United States belong to some sort of religious community—they are Protestants within particular denominations, Catholics, Jews, or Buddhists, for example. Many, however, supplement their formal membership and participation with a variety of other religious activities that do not come directly from their community of faith—participating in revivals, watching religious television, engaging in various devotional activities such as private prayer and reading, chanting, and meditation, wearing religious jewelry, or placing religious bumper stickers on their cars and trucks. For some, these activities and others similar to them become the primary focus of their religious life.

Figure 1-2   This interstate billboard in Ohio is a good example of popular religion. *(Photo by the author.)*

[8]Peter W. Williams, *Popular Religion in America: Symbolic Change and the Modernization Process in Historical Perspective* (Englewood Cliffs, NJ: Prentice Hall, 1980), pp. 3–4.
[9]David Chidester, "The Church of Baseball, the Fetish of Coca-Cola, and the Potlatch of Rock'n'Roll: Theoretical Models for the Study of Religion in American Popular Culture," *Journal of the American Academy of Religion* 59, No. 4 (Fall, 1996), p. 760.

Popular religion is a "dimension of religious life that is elusive and difficult to describe," as one study of the phenomenon puts it.[10] There is no one agreed-upon definition of popular religion, but we can describe it.[11]

- Popular religion is the religious belief and practice of ordinary people rather than of theologians and religious leaders. It is transmitted through various channels outside of religious institutions.
- It exists alongside institutional religion as a complement to it. It is a supplement to participation in formal religion for some people and a substitute for it for others. People do not abandon formal religion for popular religiosity but use the latter to personalize their religion.
- It offers people more direct access to the sacred than they have through the mediation of formal religious groups. Formal religious organizations impose order and structure on religion. Popular religion is distinguished by a lively sense of the supernatural without the imposition of formal structure. It does not have the "conceptual coherence" of organized religion.
- It draws on the core religious institutions of the culture (in the United States, primarily Christianity) but blends the core religious attributes with other sources and traditions. It often reflects both mainstream and alternative values. It draws heavily on secular popular culture.

[For] the vast majority of Americans, a sense of the supernatural so lively that it cannot be contained in creed and doctrine permeates life. . . . [O]rdinary men and women have sought and continue to seek direct access to the realm of the supernatural in order to use its power to give them control over their lives and to endow their lives with meaning. . . . Sometimes they gain that access through religious traditions and institutions, but more often [they do so] through fusing together an array of beliefs and practices to construct personal and very private worlds of meaning. If we would understand the dynamics of being religious, American style, we must explore the phenomenon of popular religiosity.[12]

Examples of popular religion abound. Although angel popularity may have peaked, there continues to be considerable interest in them. Catalogs regularly offer angel-related articles, as do gift shops, evidence that the interest level remains at least fairly high. Near-death experiences provide what some people believe to be a glimpse into a world beyond this one. A series of billboards with snappy messages signed "God" dot the landscape. One example is "That love your neighbor business—I meant that."

The *Wall Street Journal* has reported on what it termed "Do-It-Yourself Religion." Some Americans are participating in a variety of special interest religious groups to supplement or in some instances replace participation in a more traditional community of faith. These groups may be organized around worship, prayer, discussion, or other interests of the participants. Not a new

---

[10]Charles H. Lippy, *Being Religious, American Style: A History of Popular Religiosity in the United States* (Westport, CT: Greenwood Press, 1994), p. 1.
[11]This section draws loosely on Lippy, *Being Religious, American Style*, Chap. 1.
[12]Lippy, *Being Religious*, pp. 18–19.

phenomenon, these groups are similar to the Christian "house churches" and Jewish *havurah* of the 1960s. Similar groups have come and gone at various times, and the *Journal* article notes that, although the movement is strong now, history indicates that its lifespan is limited.[13]

In the commercially oriented culture of the United States, the strength of popular religion is shown in part by how well it sells. Christian retail is a multi-billion dollar industry. Some people place statues of Jesus, Mary, Saint Francis, or the Buddha in their yards, or cross or fish symbols on their cars or trucks. Many people wear religiously themed tee shirts. There is religious music in any format people like. The musicals *Jesus Christ, Superstar*, and *Godspell* continue to attract audiences. Gift items such as religiously oriented figurines, decorative items, and greeting cards sell well in religious book and supply stores and in secular stores as well. There are religious-theme computer games and educational software to help children learn about the Bible or the Qur'an.[14]

As noted earlier, most popular religion in the United States is in at least some sense Christian. However, it is not exclusively Christian. A number of catalogs offer a variety of items for people devising their own spirituality. One such catalog has an umbrella that features the eight major symbols of Tibetan Buddhism, as well as items reflecting Native American (and other) religions. In

Figure 1-3   A Buddhist home shrine is another manifestation of popular religion. *(Photo by the author.)*

[13]Elizabeth Bernstein, "Do-It-Yourself Religion," *Wall Street Journal* (June 11, 2004), pp. W1 and W5.
[14]The Muslim sacred scripture. See Chapter 11 for more discussion of Muslims and the Qur'an.

another catalog, those of Jewish faith can choose from a vast assortment of Jewish religious items such as prayer shawls, menorahs, Passover plates, and mezuzahs (which are described in Chapter 9). Several sources exist for Buddhists to obtain statues, meditation cushions and benches, and audiotapes or videotapes. *Hinduism Today*, a magazine for North American Hindus, routinely advertises Hindu religious articles such as deity statues, beads, and incense.

Although a large part of popular religion concerns material culture, it also involves religious practices, many of which are learned and practiced in people's homes. Countless parents pass on to their children the practice of saying bedtime and mealtime prayers—often the same prayers they themselves learned as children. Parents read stories of faith to their children. College students pray for aid on exams. People wear cloth bracelets bearing the letters "WWJD?" The acronym stands for "What Would Jesus Do?" a reminder to the wearer to ask that question when they cannot figure out the answer to a moral dilemma. Many people read devotional magazines, watch religious television, and listen to religious radio programming.

QUESTIONS AND ACTIVITIES FOR REVIEW, DISCUSSION, AND WRITING

1. Write a paragraph in which you explain what you hope to gain from your study of religion in the United States. Are your goals academic, personal, or a combination of both? Compare your answer with those of other people.
2. Visit the American Academy of Religion Web site (www.aarweb.org) to learn how they answer the question, "Why study religion?" Look at the Overview and Mission Statement especially.
3. What are some classroom activities that would be prohibited under Abington v. Schempp? What activities would be allowed?
4. Do you think that religious clubs such as student Bible study clubs or prayer groups should have the same opportunities to use classroom space before or after school hours as do nonreligious groups? Why or why not?
5. Take an issue in which religion has been involved, such as the abortion controversy or recent Middle Eastern wars, and analyze it from the perspective of theology, the social–scientific study of religion, and the humanities approach to the study of religion.
6. Ask several of your friends how they describe religion, and compare their answers. How are they alike? Different?
7. Look up the definition of religion in any standard dictionary, and write an essay in which you evaluate it based on what you have learned in this chapter.
8. If you are a part of a religious group, think about how the four dimensions of religion we discussed apply to it.
9. Discuss with others in your class the manifestations of popular religion with which you are familiar. Organize a "popular religion scavenger hunt" for a day or two in which people are alert for evidence of popular religion and then report what they find.

FOR FURTHER READING

NYE, MALLORY, *Religion: The Basics*. New York, NY: Routledge, 2003. Professor Nye's book is a very accessible introduction from the perspective of religious and cultural studies.

PALS, DANIEL L., *Eight Theories of Religion*, 2nd ed. New York, NY: Oxford University Press, 2006. Pals' study of eight of the classical theorists of religion includes biographical information, exposition of the theory, and analysis and critique in a very usable format.

SEGAL, ROBERT A., *The Blackwell Companion to the Study of Religion*. Malden, MA: Blackwell Publishing, 2006. This comprehensive survey of approaches to the study of religion ranges from anthropology and phenomenology to the economics of religion.

RELEVANT WORLD WIDE WEB SITES

The American Academy of Religion: www.aarweb.org

The Society for Biblical Literature: www.sbl-site.org

The Center for the Study of Religion and American Culture: www.iupui.edu/~raac

CHAPTER 2

Religion in the Life
of the United States

The United States has become known for its freedom of religion. People decide for themselves whether they will be a part of a religious group, and, if so, which one. Before reading this chapter, stop and think about what freedom of religion means to you personally. How important is it to you? In what specific ways does it affect your life? Do you think there should be limits on religious freedom? If so, what should they be, and why do you think they are necessary?

DISESTABLISHMENT AND THE CONSTITUTION

Prior disillusionment with religious establishments worked against the continued existence of established religion in the United States, as did the presence of religious pluralism. The American experience with established churches was influenced by the experience of European settlers who were forced to flee from establishments of religion in their home countries. It was also influenced by the experiments with pluralism and freedom of religion that had been carried out in Rhode Island and Pennsylvania. Many people concluded that civil power and privilege for churches led to problems, while toleration and equality under the law was good for both the churches and society at large.[1] In addition, no single religious group had enough support throughout the original thirteen states to make its belief and practice the law of the land. Furthermore, the framers of the Constitution held several views of religion. Some were Protestant and Catholic Christians. Others were advocates of naturalistic religion based on rationality and morality and still others were nonbelievers or atheists. Freethinkers either questioned or rejected traditional Christianity, and their views helped to bring about the official separation of church and state that we have now. Still others came from those strands of Protestant Reformation thought that advocated strict separation of church and state.

[1]Henry Steele Commager, *The Empire of Reason* (Garden City, NY: Anchor Press, 1977), pp. 210–211.

Religion is addressed in three places in the Constitution: Article 6, the First Amendment, and the Fourteenth Amendment.

1. Article 6 prohibits religious requirements for holding public office: ". . . no religious Test shall ever be required as a Qualification to any Office or public Trust under the United States." A person's religion or lack of religion cannot legally be a condition for holding public office in a pluralistic culture in which religion and government are separate functions.

2. The First Amendment to the Constitution contains some of the most important religious liberty legislation in our nation's history. It is part of the Bill of Rights, prepared under the leadership of James Madison: "*Congress shall make no law respecting an establishment of religion, or prohibiting the free exercise thereof*; or abridging the freedom of speech, or of the press; or the right of the people peaceably to assemble, and to petition the Government for a redress of grievances."

The establishment clause says that the U.S. Congress cannot make any one religion the official religion of the United States. It cannot act in a way that gives preferential treatment or support to one religion above others. Nor can it support religion or nonreligion generally, one over the other. Insofar as possible, it must maintain a neutral stance toward religion.

The second clause is often called the free exercise clause. It states that the government cannot interfere with any person's religion. In *Reynolds* v. *United States* (1878), Reynolds held that a law against marriage to more than one person at the same time violated his religious freedom, because he was a member of the Latter-day Saints, who at that time advocated the practice. In a landmark opinion, the Court held that the free exercise clause applied to religious beliefs but not necessarily to the actions arising from those beliefs. It held that "actions which are in violation of social duties or subversive of good order" cannot be tolerated, even when they are done in the name of religion.

This is a dilemma that cannot be fully resolved. Because religion is an intimate joining of belief and action, it may seem odd to tell people that they may believe what they please but prevent them from acting on those beliefs. Yet clearly there are actions that cannot be condoned, such as the torture of people or animals, or random terror attacks on civilian populations. There are actions that, if permitted, would utterly disrupt the social order, such as the refusal to be bound by any laws. These sorts of actions cannot be tolerated, even in the hallowed name of religious freedom.

Freedom of speech, the press, and assembly also contributes to religious freedom. These freedoms mean that people may speak and write openly about their views on religious questions. They may gather peaceably to listen to speakers or to worship in whatever ways they choose.

The framers of the Bill of Rights could not possibly have known the range of circumstances these first 10 amendments might be required to cover. The provisions of the bill are necessarily very broad, both allowing for and requiring constant reinterpretation by the courts:

> The general principle deducible from the First Amendment and all that has been said by the Court is this: That we will not tolerate either governmentally established religion or governmental interference with religion. Short of those expressly proscribed governmental acts there is room for play in the joints productive of benevolent neutrality which will permit religious exercise to exist without sponsorship and without interference.[2]

3. The Fourteenth Amendment is the final Constitutional reference to religious liberty. The crucial point for religious liberty is in Section 1: "*No State shall make or enforce any law which shall abridge the privileges or immunities of citizens of the United States*; nor shall any State deprive any person of life, liberty, or property without due process of law; nor deny to any person within its jurisdiction the equal protection of the laws."

Both Article 6 and the religion clauses in the First Amendment deal with what the *federal* government may not do. The Fourteenth Amendment holds that the *states* as well are not to "abridge the privileges" of their citizens, including the privilege of religious freedom.

The "play in the joints" of the Constitution has also led to additional legislation and executive actions concerning religion and the role it plays in the public life of the United States. One example is the Religious Freedom Restoration Act signed into law in November 1993. In the early 1990s, freedom of religious practice for smaller and less popular religions appeared to have been jeopardized by certain U.S. Supreme Court decisions. To cite a well-known example, *Employment Division of the State of Oregon* v. *Smith* (1990) overturned the principle that the government's interest had to be "compelling" to justify restricting freedom of religion. In its majority opinion, the Court held that the free exercise of religion deserves no special protection, as long as the law applies to nonreligious groups also. This line of argument lays the groundwork for the restriction of any unpopular religious practice.

In response to the perceived threats to religious liberty, a diverse coalition of religious leaders and groups came together to support the passage of the Act. This bill sought to protect the free exercise of religion through a legislative act rather than by judicial means, enhancing protection especially for the lesser-known and less-understood religions. The Religious Freedom Restoration Act was later invalidated by the Supreme Court (*City of Bourne, Texas* v. *Flores*, 1997) on the grounds that it violated the establishment clause.

This leaves religious freedom in question, especially for smaller and less-understood groups. The government needs only demonstrate a *rational* basis for curtailing freedom of religious practice; it does not have to show a *compelling* interest in doing so.

---

[2]*Walz* v. *Tax Commission of the City of New York* (1970).

Another example of a legislated provision for religious liberty is the No Child Left Behind Act signed into law in 2001. The act mandates that in order to receive federal funds, school districts must show they do not limit student religious expression. To help clarify this, the federal Department of Education issued its *Guidance on Constitutionally Protected Prayer in Public Elementary and Secondary Schools*. This ruling allows for "student initiated" prayer at school functions and events such as assemblies and sports.

BY THE NUMBERS: DATA ON RELIGIOUS AMERICA

Data are far from telling the whole story of religion in the United States. They can, however, help us to get some sense of the religious landscape, as suggested by the title of the landmark Pew Forum's U.S. Religious Landscape Survey.[3] In general, the survey concludes that religion in America is a remarkably stable phenomenon. This apparent stability, however, obscures the constant change that is occurring. There is also tremendous diversity within religion in the United States. As you learned in the previous chapter, we can think of religions as being made up of beliefs, lifestyles, rituals, and organizational arrangements. I will use these categories to introduce the religious landscape of the United States.

First of all, American religion focuses heavily on what people believe:

- Of note, Americans tend not to be dogmatic about their religion. A majority of those who are affiliated with a religious group believe that theirs is not the only path to salvation. A majority also believe there is more than one true interpretation of the teachings of their faith community.
- More than 90 percent of American adults believe that God or a universal spirit exists. Sixty percent of those say this God is a personal being with whom one can have a relationship, but almost 25 percent identify God as an impersonal force.
- About two-thirds of adults believe their sacred scriptures are God's word. But they are split about fifty-fifty on whether it should be taken word-for-word and those who believe it should not. Over 25 percent believe their scriptures were written by people and not the word of God.
- Three-quarters believe in life after death, and about the same proportion believe in a heaven where the good are rewarded with eternal life. Just under 60 percent believe in a hell of eternal punishment for the wicked.
- About 80 percent believe miracles occur today, and nearly 70 percent believe that angels and demons are active in today's world.

The survey also includes some interesting findings about religion and lifestyle:

- Americans take religion seriously, with over half saying religion is very important to them.
- Among people who are married, 27 percent are in religiously mixed marriages (e.g., a Christian married to a Buddhist). If marriages between people in different

[3]The information in this section is summarized from the Pew Forum on Religion and Public Life's U.S. Religious Landscape Survey, 2008, available at www.pewforum.org

Protestant denominational families are included (e.g., a Methodist married to a Baptist) the proportion rises to 37 percent. Younger people are more likely than older people to be in religiously mixed marriages.

- Many religious people believe the values of modern culture conflict with those of their faith, although many do not. A significant minority (42 percent) believes that the values of the movie and entertainment industries threaten their religious and moral values. As might be anticipated, those who are most religiously engaged are more likely to feel this way.
- Interestingly, however, a very substantial minority of religiously unaffiliated adults also experience this tension, although for them it revolves around being nonreligious in a predominantly religious culture.
- Although the links are not always strong, religion does help shape people's political attitudes and views. As might be expected, religious conservatism frequently goes along with political conservatism. With these ideological leanings, the religiously conservative are more likely to be Republicans than Democrats.
- The links between religion and political or social views are strongest in the case of specific issues of personal morality such as abortion and homosexuality.
- On the other hand, there is substantial agreement across religious groups on other issues. Most believe the government needs to do more to assist needy Americans and more to protect the environment.

Americans are also religiously active as a people; most of us participate in religious rituals and activities, both public and private.

- More than 25 percent attend religious services at least a few times a year, with over half attending once or twice a month and nearly 40 percent attending weekly.
- Those who attend services also participate in other activities offered by their faith community, such as choir, social activities, working with children or volunteering. They participate in prayer groups, scripture study groups, and religious education programs. Although the extent of such participation varies widely, it is an important aspect of religion for many adherents.
- Americans also participate in private devotional practices. Almost 60 percent say they pray daily and three-fourths pray at least weekly. Many point to specific times they believe their prayers have been answered. Meditation is not as common, but a significant minority (39 percent) say they meditate at least weekly.
- Most religiously affiliated parents engage in both private and communal religious activities with their children.
- About one-third of affiliated adults report sharing their faith with others at least monthly.

Finally, what about the organizational dimension?

- Every major religious group is both gaining and losing adherents. Those that are growing gain new followers faster than they lose others, while those whose numbers are shrinking are losing more than they are gaining.
- The majority of the population is Christian (78 percent), although that proportion is declining with time. Slightly over half are Protestants (51 percent) and about one-quarter are Catholic. The Southern Baptist Convention is the largest single Protestant Christian denomination.

Figure 2-1   Many people in the United States do volunteer work through their community of faith. *(Jeff Greenberg/PhotoEdit Inc.)*

- Other religions together claim slightly less than 5 percent of the population. Jews and Muslims constitute less than 2 percent each. Hindus and Buddhists each account for less than 1 percent.
- Among Protestant Christians, Baptists are the largest group (17 percent), followed by Methodists (6 percent), Lutherans, and nondenominational Protestants (5 percent each), and Pentecostals (4 percent). The many remaining Protestant denominational families have less than 2 percent each.
- The survey findings about religiously unaffiliated people are especially interesting. About 16 percent of adults say they are currently unaffiliated with any religious group. Men are significantly less likely to be unaffiliated than are women, a trend with a long history. The unaffiliated are a diverse group. About one-quarter of the unaffiliated say they are atheists or agnostics. The remainder, or about 12 percent of the adult population, describe their religion is "nothing in particular." About half of this group say that religion is somewhat or very important in their lives, making them religious although unaffiliated. The other half is unaffiliated and effectively nonreligious or secular.
- There are substantial regional variations in American religion. The Northeast has the greatest proportion of Catholics and the fewest evangelical Protestants. The Southwest, by contrast, has the greatest proportion of evangelical Protestants, many of whom are affiliated with historically black churches. It also has the smallest proportion of Catholics and unaffiliated people. The Midwest most closely mirrors the makeup of the nation as a whole. The West has the largest proportion of unaffiliated people, the smallest proportion of mainline Protestants, and the largest number of Latter-day Saints (Mormons), mainly in Utah and the surrounding states.

Several factors correlate positively with participation in religious organizations, as well as with private religious practice. These correlations have remained relatively stable over time. Women are more religious than are men, and African Americans are more religious than are their white counterparts, at least when religiosity is measured in traditional terms. Religious practice increases with age. Protestant Christians are more observant than are Catholic Christians, and Jews as a group are less so than Christians as a whole.

RELIGION AFTER 9-11

What effect did September 11, 2001, have on religion in the United States? Was that effect long term, or did it dissipate as time went on?

Survey data from the weeks immediately following the attacks indicated that Americans had in fact attended religious services in higher numbers than usual, even discounting the special services in the aftermath of the attacks. There were thousands of such services, and the percentage of Americans who attended services on the weekend following the attacks rose by 6 percent.[4] Historical data indicate that a similar effect has followed other major crises.[5]

However, data from surveys done later indicate that there has been little, if any, long-term increase in religiosity. Increases in religious participation were of short duration and mainly affected those who were very involved with religion before 9-11. Among those who were not particularly religious, the events of 9-11 had little religious impact. Whatever effect there was had largely dissipated by the end of the year.[6]

While actual religious participation did not increase substantially, the public perception of religion's importance did. Polls since the 1990s indicated that a majority of people believed the influence of religion was lessening in the United States. Following the attacks, more than 75 percent said the influence of religion was rising. This was a broad perception, shared by the religious and the nonreligious alike and distributed across racial, regional, and socioeconomic lines. However, this too was short-lived, and 6 months later, survey results returned to pre-attack levels.[7]

Although the attacks on the United States did not change the level of religious participation, those who are religious said their faith helped them deal with the attacks and their results. Even persons who are not deeply involved in organized religion indicated that their faith helped them cope.[8]

---

[4]Andrew Walsh, "Good for What Ails Us," *Religion in the News* (Fall, 2001), vol. 4, No. 3, pp. 2–5, 26.
[5]*Public Perspective, A Roper Center Review of Public Opinion and Polling*, January/February, 2003, p. 25.
[6]Ibid., pp. 26–27.
[7]*Public Perspective, A Roper Center Review of Public Opinion and Polling*, September/October, 2002, pp. 30–31.
[8]*Religion and Ethics Newsweekly* (April 26, 2002).

An examination of news coverage of events immediately following 9-11 describes another effect as well:

> American religious diversity received a new, and perhaps decisive, level of recognition. The cast of religious leaders summoned to the White House and to lead the memorial services organized and sanctioned by the government at the National Cathedral and at Yankee Stadium offered up a showcase of world religions. Henceforth, when religion is presented to the American public, the picture will include Hindus, Muslims, Buddhists, and Sikhs, as well as Protestants, Catholics, and Jews.[9]

It does appear that there *has* been a sustained determination to include Muslims alongside Jews and Christians at civic religious events such as National Day of Prayer services. There seems, to me at least, to be much less evidence that civic religious inclusiveness has continued to extend beyond the three major Abrahamic traditions, except in rare instances.

CIVIL RELIGION AND BEYOND

Sociologist Robert Bellah brought the concept of civil religion to scholarly attention and ultimately to the American popular mind. In a 1967 essay, Bellah wrote that in the United States there "exists alongside of and rather clearly differentiated from the churches an elaborate and well-institutionalized civil religion in America. . . . This public religious dimension is expressed in a set of beliefs, symbols, and rituals that I am calling the American civil religion."[10]

Bellah cited documents such as the Declaration of Independence and the Constitution, as well as the inaugural speeches of several presidents, along with holiday observances, in support of his thesis. He included belief in God, belief in America's role in God's plans for the world, commonly accepted standards of morality and civic virtue, and routinely observed holidays among the verities of civil religion.

Bellah's seminal essay gave religious studies scholars a new way of analyzing the roles that religion plays in the public life of the United States. It moved the study of religion beyond the study of ecclesiastical institutions and laid the groundwork for recognition of the importance of popular religion. The essay also provided great insight into the ways in which civic ideals and the legitimating principles of a culture are expressed powerfully in symbols that link them to divine realities.

How we view American religious culture has changed since the time of Bellah's essay. Rather than a single voice, the United States has become a chorus

---

[9]Walsh, "Good for What Ails Us," p. 3.
[10]Robert N. Bellah, "Civil Religion in America," *Daedalus*, 117, No. 3 (Winter, 1967), pp. 1, 4. This essay is available online at http://www.robertbellah.com/articles_5.htm

of many voices. Any attempt to describe a single American voice inevitably seems sectarian and exclusive. It now seems better to focus on the diversity of religions and cultures that are present in the United States, rather than looking for a unity that many have come to doubt. Bellah's interpretation has been labeled "a vestige of the de facto religious establishment of the nineteenth century." The authors go on to note that by appealing to a set of overarching religious values, Bellah's concept of civil religion encourages us to make presumptive religious judgments about what it means to be an American. Yet, it is precisely the restraint from making such judgments that allows us to see the contributions religious diversity in America has made to social equality and to social activism.[11]

At the same time, there is a reality behind the civil religion thesis that cannot be overlooked in any discussion of the role of religion in the life of the nation. A recent study notes that there remains "a pronounced tendency to approach political issues in moral terms," turning political discussions into debates about competing moral values. Political rhetoric in the United States is "infused with religious images and symbols" and continues to "provide evidence of the existence of what has variously been called a public theology, a political religion, a religion of democracy, a public philosophy, or, most commonly today, a civil religion."[12] Debates about "hot button" issues such as legal abortion, the right of gay couples to marry, prayer in public schools, and the role of the United States as the world's military police officer continue to be bolstered by appeals to religion from all sides of the discussion. The fact that the debate over the proper role of religion in the political life of the nation continues is itself evidence of the civil religion impulse, however diffuse its content. In the previous chapter, you learned that religion helps people have meaning in their lives because it relates their lives to something transcendent. At its most basic, civil religion functions the same way for the nation.

Currently, a variety of voices try to claim the right to define what the civil religion of the United States is. They can be grouped into two types: We can label one the conservative, legitimizing, and priestly type. The other is the liberal, challenging, and prophetic type. The first was perhaps best embodied in former President George W. Bush. Dr. Martin Luther King, Jr., and former President Bill Clinton embodied the second.

The first holds that the United States has a divinely appointed role to play on the world stage. Historically and in the present time, the United States is the chosen nation and enjoys a special relationship with God. It is "one nation under God." It emphasizes traditional moral values, with a focus

[11]Phillip E. Hammond, Amanda Porterfield, James G. Moseley, and Jonathan D. Sarna, "Forum: American Civil Religion Revisited," *Religion and American Culture: A Journal of Interpretation*, vol. 4, No. 1 (Winter, 1994), pp. 9–10 and 21.

[12]Kenneth D. Wald and Allison Calhoun-Brown, *Religion and Politics in the United States*, 5th ed. (Lanham, MD: Rowman & Littlefield Publishers, Inc., 2007), p. 54

on individual, private morality. At its worst, it encourages an uncritical acceptance of the correctness of America's positions by wrapping them in the cloak of divine sanction. It becomes indistinguishable from religious nationalism. At its best, it articulates the moral and political concerns of many, many Americans.

The second, prophetic point of view puts greater emphasis on the United States' commitment to uphold broad moral values such as justice, liberty, civil rights, disarmament, and ecological responsibility. It rejects the idea that America is a nation specially chosen by God. It does understand that the United States has a special role to play in the world, but not because of divine election. It is our vast resources and our involvement in causing some of the world's problems that gives us the responsibility to help alleviate them. At its best, it provides the kind of prophetic challenge that can make a nation stretch beyond its own narrow interpretation of itself. At its worst, it can cling so tightly to its ideals that it loses sight of the political necessity of compromise and becomes identified with "knee-jerk" political and religious liberalism.

Culture Wars?

The discussion of competing civil religions in the United States is related to another thesis about the role of religion in American public life: the belief that the nation is embroiled in a "culture war" that pits liberals against conservatives across a broad spectrum of policy issues and moral choices. Culture war theorists

Figure 2-2   The conflict over abortion rights often includes a religious dimension. *(Paul Conklin/Monkmeyer Press.)*

identify two rival camps. The exact description and composition of the two camps varies somewhat from author to author, but the outlines are clear.[13]

The progressive or liberal side includes liberal religionists, secularists, humanists, modernists, and their sympathizers. They draw their inspiration from Enlightenment philosophy and very liberal religion and advocate pluralism and individual rights. They favor a strong role for the federal government in promoting equality and justice. Government and religion should remain separate. Censorship has no place in a free society, no matter how offensive the content of speech or art might be. Discrimination on any basis should be eliminated. Matters of personal morality ought not to be regulated by law. They share many of the beliefs and ideals of liberal civil religion. Organizations usually associated with this perspective include the American Civil Liberties Union, the National Organization for Women, and People for the American Way.

The conservative camp includes more traditional religionists and social conservatives. Their watchword is "traditional values," reinforced by law whenever possible. They are dismayed at the proliferation of "big government." Organizationally, this group coalesced around the Moral Majority, which was dissolved in the late 1980s.

There can be no doubt that there are dramatic differences of opinion about important issues in the United States, including those as fundamental as the kind of nation that the United States is and ought to be and the best means of enhancing civil life. But do these differences signal a "culture war"? On the whole, I think not, for several reasons.

Perhaps most important is the fact that most people occupy a position somewhere in the middle, avoiding either extreme on the issues that cut across the conservative/liberal divide. There are dedicated partisans on both sides, but they are far outnumbered by moderates. Moreover, most of us are not true ideologues. That is to say, our views on social and political issues are not wholly consistent. We tend in one direction on some issues and in another on other issues. Nor is the conservative/liberal division closely associated with demographic characteristics—such as race, socioeconomic class, or region of residence—that would make it even more culturally divisive.

The metaphor of two opposing camps arrayed against each other in a "culture war" is too extreme. It is inaccurate, first of all, and it tends to cut off genuine dialogue before it can begin. It posits a sharp "either/or" that is belied by the facts. There is also some danger that such metaphors will turn into self-fulfilling prophecies. Perhaps a better image for what is going on in the culture is that of a troupe of dancers struggling to learn the intricate dance of pluralism. Few have learned their steps thoroughly yet, and every so often, they bump headlong into each other. Toes get stepped on, and tempers flare. But the dance goes on and becomes smoother with time.

---

[13]Good discussions of the culture war thesis, which remains relevant, can be found in James Davison Hunter, *Culture Wars: The Struggle to Define America* (New York: Basic Books, 1991), the title of which brought the term to popular attention; Robert Wuthnow, *The Restructuring of American Religion* (Princeton, NJ: Princeton University Press, 1988); and Robert Wuthnow, *The Struggle for America's Soul: Evangelicals, Liberals, and Secularism* (Grand Rapids, MI: W.B. Eerdmans, 1989).

Civil Religion After 9-11

The author of a recent study on religious discourse following 9-11 writes, "Suddenly, it seemed as though God and the flag were everywhere."[14] That was certainly my experience as well. To a large extent, it holds true today.

The focus of the attacks—the World Trade Center and the Pentagon—as well as the extent of the loss of life and destruction of property, made the events of September 11 symbolically significant. It threatened the culture of the United States in a way that made it necessary to look again at the national story and reassemble its parts into a whole again. The study identifies six elements of the national story that were particularly threatened:

- Omniscience: How could something like this have happened without the United States being aware that it was coming?
- Omnipotence: How could this have happened to the world's biggest military and economic superpower?
- Impregnability and inviolability: Americans had to face the fact that war could indeed be fought on their own soil.

It is worth noting that these three characteristics are often attributed to the God of the monotheistic tradition. The remaining three elements focus directly on the relationship of the United States with this God.

- Divine election: How could God allow such evil, such terror and tragedy, to happen to this, the chosen, people?
- Supreme goodness: If the United States is in fact as morally upright as its citizens believe, why do other nations hate us so intensely?
- Salvific mission: With omniscience, omnipotence, and inviolability shaking on their foundations, can the United States carry out its mission to the world?[15]

As you will see in the discussion of religion and violence in Chapter 3, these were precisely the questions the attacks were intended to raise. Analysis of former President Bush's remarks in the two weeks following the attacks shows him specifically addressing each aspect of the undermined story. This rebuilding was further exemplified in two photographs that became especially well known following 9-11: Two steel beams salvaged from the rubble were mounted on a concrete base to become a cross. And firefighters raised the American flag atop the wreckage.[16]

This rebuilding continues. My own state of Indiana issued a new specialty license plate with the flag on a blue background and the words, "In God We Trust." Unlike other specialty plates, there is no extra fee for this one, and people have adopted it eagerly.

---

[14]Melissa M. Wilcox, "Discourse Bless America: Rebuilding the National Mythos After September 11," in *Religion, Politics, and American Identity*, eds. Davis S. Gutterman and Andrew R. Murphy (Lanham, MD: Rowman & Littlefield Publishers, Inc., 2006), p. 26.

[15]Wilcox, "Discourse Bless America," pp. 35–38.

[16]Ibid., p. 39.

Figure 2-3   Indiana's "In God We Trust" license plate. *(Jeff Greenberg/PhotoEdit Inc.)*

RELIGION ON CAMPUS

Several studies of religion on college and university campuses in the 1990s focused on the ways in which religion and its influence have waned in higher education in the United States.[17] These accounts trace the change from a situation in which religion and higher education were intimately intertwined to one in which religion, aside from the academic study of it, has been virtually evicted from campuses across the nation. Although the authors of these studies do not see this as an altogether bad thing, they do claim that important values have been lost in the process.

In 2001, three scholars in the area of American religion published a study in which they investigated what role religion actually does play in the lives of American college students.[18] They did ethnographic studies of four representative institutions: a state university in the West, an historically black university in the South, a Catholic university in the East, and a Lutheran liberal arts college in the North. The authors of the 2001 study wished to examine the role of religion empirically. We have already looked at their findings concerning the academic study of religion in Chapter 1.

---

[17]See, for example, George M. Marsden and Bradley J. Longfield, eds., *The Secularization of the Academy* (New York: Oxford University Press, 1992); George M. Marsden, *The Soul of the American University: From Protestant Establishment to Established Nonbelief* (New York: Oxford University Press, 1994); and Douglas Sloan, *Faith and Knowledge: Mainline Protestantism and American Higher Education* (Louisville, KY: Westminster John Know Press, 1994).

[18]Conrad Cherry, Betty A. DeBerg, and Amanda Porterfield, *Religion on Campus: What Religion Really Means to Today's Undergraduates* (Chapel Hill: The University of North Carolina Press, 2000). See especially Chapter 6.

While not claiming to provide "a comprehensive overview" of the state of religion on American campuses, the authors believe they have enough data to begin to draw certain generally applicable conclusions:

- Both in terms of organized religious groups and more individual spirituality, opportunities for student religious practice were widely available. Religion on campus is characterized "more by seeking, nomadic wandering and choosing among diverse options (spirituality) than by the more stable posture of dwelling in or inhabiting safe, sacred places (religion)."[19] I see this in the essays on their own religious stance that my students write at the beginning of class. However, I also read a lot of essays from students who have found a religious "home" in one or another of the campus parachurch organizations such as Campus Crusade for Christ and The Revolution.
- Personal spirituality and volunteer social service appear to go hand in hand for students.
- Students are frequently involved in small group study and worship events such as residence hall Bible studies and prayer times.
- Students and faculty alike respected religious diversity and practiced tolerance, although none of the four campuses studied was free of tensions around religious issues. On the whole, religion was respected as an important aspect of life, yet, even in the religiously supported schools, students had the freedom to not be involved with religion. Openness to religious diversity existed side-by-side with missionary enthusiasm for promoting one's own viewpoint.

On the basis of the empirical data they collected, the authors of this study concluded that, rather than disappearing, the presence of religion in American higher education has become more pluralistic and participation more optional, but no less vibrant and engaging for students. "Indeed, we found religion on the four campuses sufficiently vital and inviting to make us wonder if it had ever been more so in the past. . . . [Our] study reveals that the ethos of decentered, diverse, religiously tolerant institutions of higher education is a breeding ground for vital religious practice and teaching."[20] This seems to reflect trends taking place in the population at large (see the discussion of the results of the Pew Forum study earlier). That the culture as a whole and the culture on college campuses is moving in the same direction suggests that these trends will continue and be magnified in American culture in the future.

QUESTIONS AND ACTIVITIES FOR REVIEW, DISCUSSION, AND WRITING

1. In your opinion is government neutrality toward religion a good idea, or not? Why?
2. Is something like the Religious Freedom Restoration Act necessary in the United States? Why or why not?
3. Compare your experience of religion on your own campus with that described in this chapter.

---

[19]Cherry et al., *Religion on Campus*, p. 276.
[20]Ibid., pp. 294–295.

4. Do you believe that religious and moral differences in the United States amount to a culture war? Why do you think as you do?

5. Do you agree that the terrorist attacks of 9-11 threatened the national story of the U.S.? What evidence have you seen of the role of civil religion in helping to rebuild that story?

FOR FURTHER READING

FARNSLEY II, ARTHUR E., N.J. DEMARATH III, ETAN DIAMOND, MARY L. MAPES, AND ELFRIEDE WEDAM, *Sacred Circles, Public Squares: The Multicentering of American Religion.* Bloomington, IN: Indiana University Press, 2004. This case study of Indianapolis, Indiana, as the product of the Project on Religion and Urban Culture, an ambitious project that engaged the city in reflection on the various roles religion plays in that city. As a case study of one Midwestern American capital city, it sheds light on the evolving roles of religion in urban cultures throughout the nation.

GUTTERMAN, DAVID B., AND ANDREW R. MURPHY, eds., *Religion, Politics, and American Identity: New Directions, New Controversies.* Lanham, MD: Rowman & Littlefield Publishers, Inc., 2006. This is a multidisciplinary volume that pays particular attention to two issues: religion and politics in the wake of September 11, 2001, and the religious dimensions of political issues not usually considered directly religious.

SCHMIDT, CORWIN, ed., *Religion as Social Capital: Producing the Common Good.* Waco, TX: Baylor University Press, 2003. This edited collection of readings explores the role of religion in such aspects of American civic life as charitable giving, volunteering, and the African American community. Over all, it delineates the roles religion plays in establishing civic community and engagement.

WALD, KENNETH D., AND ALLISON CALHOUN-BROWN, *Religion and Politics in the United States*, 5th ed. Lanham, MD: Rowman & Littlefield Publishers, 2007. This is a thoroughly updated edition of a classic in the field. It offers a wealth of data and careful interpretation that does not overreach the boundaries set by the data.

RELEVANT WORLD WIDE WEB SITES

Boise Center for Religion and American Public Life at Boston College: www.bc.edu/centers/boise

Center for the Study of Religion and American Culture at Indiana University/Purdue University Indianapolis: www.iupui.edu/~raac/

The Hartford Institute for Religion Research at the Hartford Seminary: www.hirr.hartsem.edu/: This site covers research in areas such as women and religion, church growth and decline, religion and the family, religion, and the Web, plus more.

The Pew Forum on Religion in Public Life: www.pewforum.org

CHAPTER 3

Conflict and Controversy

> If a pro-life advocate shoots an abortionist doctor, it is certain to hit the front page of every newspaper in the country. Meanwhile, millions of ordinary citizens will on that day have given some thought to their souls through prayer, meditation, Bible-reading and the like—activities that reach into the depths of the soul where the switches are thrown between kindness and cruelty, hope and despair. This passes without mention.[1]

> I answered God's call to acknowledge myself as a gay man. Risking the loss of my children and the exercise of my ordained ministry in the Church was the biggest risk I've ever taken, but it left me with two unshakable things: my integrity and my God.[2]

Religion may lead to or enter into conflict and controversy in at least four ways: (1) Religion can come into conflict with itself when some of its members or leaders violate its own highest standards. (2) Controversy can also arise within communities of faith when different factions disagree sharply about what is right. (3) Religion can become a problem for individuals, or for society as a whole, when it leads to violence, terrorism, addiction, or other dysfunctional behaviors. Finally, (4) in the climate of pluralism and free religious expression that we enjoy in the United States, sometimes religious persons or groups express themselves in ways or in places that others deem inappropriate. This chapter illustrates each of these.

It is important to note two things at the outset. First, communities of faith are not the only organizations that are affected by these issues. Violations of norms, disagreements about conduct, violence and conflicting interests arise in many contexts. Second, the great majority of the time, religions do *not* lead to problems either for their adherents or for the larger society.

Conflict and controversy centering on religion are not new in the United States. Our early history is replete with accounts of religious intolerance and people who have been looked down on and sometimes killed simply because they

[1]Huston Smith, *Why Religion Matters: The Fate of the Human Spirit in an Age of Disbelief* (San Francisco: HarperSanFrancisco, 2001), p. 115.
[2]The [Episcopal] Diocese of New Hampshire, The Rev. Canon V. Gene Robinson, available at www.nhepiscopal.org/BishopSearch/The_Rev_Canon_V_Gene_Robinson.htm

were of an unaccepted faith. In more recent history, countercultural movements in the 1960s gave rise to many new religious movements whose unusual practices and members' sometimes unquestioning loyalty to their leaders frightened those outside the groups. In the 1970s, opposition to nonconventional religions coalesced as the *anti-cult* movement. The 1980s saw the religious broadcasting industry and televangelism shaken to its core by financial scandals. Jonestown and the Peoples' Temple, and more recently, Heaven's Gate, still bring to mind memories of men, women, and children following their leaders to death by suicide. Mention of the Branch Davidians in Waco, Texas, recalls horrific news footage of their compound burning as federal officers closed in.

SEXUAL MISCONDUCT BY THE CLERGY

Allegations of sexual misconduct and impropriety, whether substantiated or not, have frequently been directed at nonconventional religions. Until recently, however, people have usually not thought of these things as a problem with more common and better-understood religions. Since the mid-1980s, however, media reports of sexual abuse by mainline or mainstream clergy have become increasingly common. There is now considerable agreement that the problem is extensive. Although news coverage has focused on abuse by Catholic priests, clergy sexual abuse is not just a Catholic problem. It affects virtually all Christian denominations, as well as Jewish, Hindu, and Buddhist faith communities, among others. The dynamics of abuse are similar whatever the faith community. Most reports of the problem in the United States come from Christian churches, simply because they are such a majority. However, there have been sufficient reports from non-Christian communities of faith to support the view that this is truly an interfaith problem. In whatever context it happens, sexual abuse by clergy is a glaring example of religion's leaders acting in ways that violate the highest standards of their religion and the trust placed in them as religious leaders.

Accurate data on sexual abuse in general and sexual abuse by clergy in particular, is hard to find. Underreporting is common. Psychiatrist Thomas Plante, author of *Bless Me Father for I Have Sinned: Perspectives on Sexual Abuse Committed by Roman Catholic Priests*, estimates that between 2 and 5 percent of priests have had sexual contact with a minor under eighteen. That is consistent with the percentage of male clergy in other denominations having such contact, and less than the estimated 8 percent of males in the general population.[3] It is also consistent with other investigations that indicate about 4 percent of priests have had sexual abuse of minors allegations filed against them.[4]

Other investigations show similar findings. The report of the lay National Review Board, established as an independent agency by the Catholic Church to review and report on the crisis, indicates the problem was most severe from the

---

[3]Thomas Plante, "A Perspective on Clergy Sexual Abuse," available at www.psywww.com/psyrelig/plante.html

[4]Andrew Walsh, "Godawful Numbers," *Religion in the News*, vol. 7, No. 1 (Spring, 2004), p. 19.

1960s through the very early 1980s. About 80 percent of those who have filed charges are male, and the largest proportion was between eleven and fourteen years old at the time of the assault. The two crucial factors in how the Catholic Church dealt with the problem were found to be the failure of seminaries to screen out seminarians who were potential abusers and the failure of bishops to deal forthrightly and swiftly with those charged with abuse.[5]

Psychological evaluation is especially important. Plante's research indicates that 70 percent of the accused priests are themselves survivors of abuse. "Almost all" have serious psychological problems such as substance abuse and/or mood and personality disorders. While this in no way excuses their behavior, it may help us to understand it. Research also indicates that neither the requirement of priestly celibacy nor the presence of gay priests is a contributing factor.[6]

The Catholic Church's approach has changed. The comprehensive Charter for the Protection of Children and Young People, drawn up by the United States Conference of Catholic Bishops, notes that this is "a crisis without precedent in our time."[7]

The lengthy document contains sections that address the need for healing and reconciliation with victim/survivors and their families, guarantees rapid and effective response to all allegations of sexual abuse including the offender's permanent removal from active priesthood, a checks-and-balances system to ensure that procedures are followed and that there is full accountability, and careful safeguards to protect children and young people in the future. One specific action was the establishment of the lay National Review Board with independent authority to investigate and report on the Church's handling of abuse allegations. Another is on-site audits of all dioceses to determine the extent of their compliance with child protection standards. An initial audit in 2003 was followed by a second in 2004. At least 90 percent of U.S. dioceses are in full compliance.

It may help to put the crisis in the Catholic Church in perspective to realize that, unfortunately, we live in a culture in which the sexual abuse of children is not uncommon. A draft report on educator misconduct in the public schools, which came out at about the same time as the bishops began addressing the issue in their church, notes that between 6 and 10 percent of public school children are sexually abused or molested by school staff or employees.[8] Research also indicates that a far greater percentage of children are abused by family members than by priests.

The publicity surrounding sexual abuse by Catholic priests has raised consciousness in other communities of faith, and many have established stringent and detailed policies for ensuring the safety of children and young people. These

[5]Ibid.
[6]Thomas Plante, "A Perspective on Clergy Sexual Abuse," available at www.psywww.com/psyrelig/
   plante.html
[7]U.S. Conference of Catholic Bishops, "Charter for the Protection of Children and Young People, Revised
   Edition," available at http://www.usccb.org/ocyp/charter.shtml
[8]Patrick Novacosky, "100 Times Worse: America's Other Abuse Crisis," available at www.catholic.net/
   (April 9, 2004).

often include such things as never having a child alone in a room with an adult, an open door policy in classrooms, extensive screening and background checks on all personnel who come into contact with children, and detailed procedures for reporting suspected abuse and dealing with offenders.[9]

One of the larger organizational attempts to address the problem of sexual abuse by religious leaders is the Interfaith Sexual Trauma Institute, a project of Saint John's Abbey and Saint John's University in Minnesota. They publish a newsletter and journal, maintain a resource center, and sponsor conferences and other educational programs, as well as other activities. Unlike secular agencies, the Institute specifically addresses the religious and spiritual ramifications of sexual abuse by clergy. Their goals include working actively to:

1. educate clergy and seminary students about sexual misconduct;
2. develop models in which survivors, religious leaders, helping professionals and even offenders can work together to promote healing and restitution;
3. support the theological study of healthy sexuality and appropriate use of power;
4. publish relevant materials;
5. advance research;
6. provide accurate information about sexual misconduct;
7. work with other organizations dealing with this problem.[10]

GAYS AND LESBIANS IN COMMUNITIES OF FAITH

Issues around human sexuality have been front and center in communities of faith in two other ways. Broader cultural discussion of same-sex marriage has forced religious organizations to reconsider their stance. The appointment of an openly gay Anglican bishop has heightened the debate over the role of gays and lesbians throughout the Christian church. Both illustrate the conflicts that can come about when people in faith communities differ in their interpretation of what course of conduct is most consonant with their religious traditions.

In 2004, the state of Massachusetts began granting marriage licenses to gay and lesbian couples. While many, both gay and straight, applauded the move toward full equality under the law, others heard it as the death knell of the traditional marriage and family structure on which society is based. In religious terms, the response is often depicted as a conservative versus liberal issue, and to some extent, it is. But, as is often the case, the reality is more complex than such a simple division suggests. There are religious liberals who favor legalizing same-sex civil unions, for example, but who do not want the term *marriage* used to describe them. And there are religious conservatives who use pro-family arguments to support same-sex marriages. Neither is it simply a debate between those who favor religion and those who do not.

[9]See, for example, The United Synagogue of Conservative Judaism's "Model Guidelines for Congregational Policy Against Harassment," available at www.uscj.org/images/mgcph.PDF
[10]Interfaith Sexual Trauma Institute, available at www.csbsju.edu/isti/mission.html

Figure 3-1   Same-sex marriage has been a hotly debated issue in many religious groups for the past several years. *(Michelle Bridwell/PhotoEdit Inc.)*

Statistically, people who are "very committed" religiously are more strongly opposed to gay marriage than is any other group of Americans. According to a survey by the Pew Research Center, almost 80 percent of those who attend religious services at least weekly (one measure of religious commitment, albeit an imperfect one) oppose gay marriage, and nearly 60 percent of them are against same-sex civil unions. On the other hand, under half of those who never attend religious services oppose same-sex marriage, and less than a third oppose legalizing same-sex civil unions.[11]

Certainly opposition is more common among religious conservatives. Data from one survey, for example, indicate that only 13 percent of evangelical Protestants favor gay marriage, while more than one-third of mainline Protestants and Catholics do so.[12] Although the divide over same-sex marriage is not simply a liberal—conservative issue, there is clear preliminary indication that the issue has revitalized conservative Christian political activism, which had grown somewhat listless in recent years. Conservative activists see the defense of traditional marriage as a "lightning rod for fresh energy" and a way to "rally new troops" in the movement.[13] The Christian Coalition Web site, for example, gives a lot of attention to its goal of getting a marriage amendment added to the

[11]"The Ties that Divide: A Conversation on Gay Marriage with Andrew Sullivan and Gerard Bradley," The Pew Forum on Religion and Public Life, available at http://pewforum.org/events/
[12]"Religious Beliefs Underpin Opposition to Homosexuality," http://pewforum.org/docs/index.php?DocID=37
[13]Avery Johnson, "Christian Coalition Working for a Revival," *The Wall Street Journal* (June 21, 2004), p. A4.

Constitution. The Coalition has long supported Congresswoman Marilyn Musgrave's (R, CO) Federal Marriage Amendment, which states:

> Marriage in the United States shall consist only of the union of a man and a woman. Neither this Constitution or the constitution of any state, nor state or federal law, shall be construed to require that marital status or the legal incidents thereof be conferred upon unmarried couples or groups. The Coalition also supports the Federal Marriage Amendment sponsored by Senators Wayne Allard, Sam Brownback, and Jeff Sessions introduced in Dec. 2003.[14]

In response to the legalization of same-sex marriage in Massachusetts, supportive clergy formed a coalition, the Religious Coalition for Freedom to Marry.[15] Their Web site has contact information for clergy who perform same-sex marriages and a declaration of their support, along with other resources. All of the clergy whose contact information is listed would reasonably be described as liberal. The list of those who signed the declaration itself is a bit broader, but still overwhelmingly liberal. The site states their view in terms of civic justice and freedom of conscience. They state their opposition to the use of religion to deny the legal right of marriage to same-sex couples and affirm the right of all adults to marry and affirm complete freedom of conscience on this question. When they examine the faith traditions they share, they

> are resolved that the State should not interfere with same-gender couples who choose to marry and share fully and equally in the rights, responsibilities, and commitments of civil marriage.[16]

Most often, those who oppose gay marriage believe extending the right to marry to gays and lesbians is an attack on religion and the traditional values it has historically supported. Opponents see the Massachusetts decision as one more item in a more general trend in American culture that allows and even celebrates individual sexual license over responsibility. Proponents, on the other hand, tend to see it as a civil rights issue and the right to marry as a victory for individual civil rights. The Massachusetts "decision recognizes and codifies, social changes that have been evolving over decades. For proponents, this was why same-sex marriages should be legally recognized; for opponents, precisely why they shouldn't be."[17]

Opponents of same-sex marriage see it as part and parcel of the same attitude that has eroded marital commitment and sexual responsibility across the board. This, they say, has brought with it an increase in the divorce rate, in cohabitation, in infidelity, in the number of children born to single mothers, in sexually-transmitted diseases, and pornography, among other things.

---

[14]Christian Coalition of America, available at www.cc.org

[15]Religious Coalition for Freedom to Marry, available at www.freedomtomarry.org

[16]Massachusetts Declaration of Religious Support for the Freedom of Same-Gender Couples to Marry. A summary is available at www.glad.org/uploads/docs/cases/2002-11-08-goodridge-amicus-religion.pdf

[17]David W. Machacek, "Same-Sex Culture War," *Religion in the News*, vol. 7, No. 1 (Spring, 2004), p. 6.

Proponents, while not celebrating results such as the increased incidence of sexually transmitted diseases and infidelity, nonetheless herald the underlying attitude as a positive increase in individual freedoms and a beneficial lessening of social and governmental control over what consenting adults do with each other behind closed doors.

Speaking from a self-identified conservative viewpoint, Andrew Sullivan, a participant in the Pew Forum on the issue, described his position as "at root a very pro-family argument." Essentially, his point is that all persons should be permitted to enter into marriage and family ties, for the sake of the entire society.[18] Referring specifically to the desire for an amendment to the Constitution to ban same-sex marriage, Sullivan stated his belief that since all persons are made in God's image, all deserve the same treatment under the law. The Constitution should not forbid to one group the rights it grants to another.[19]

Most religious conservatives do not agree with this position. James Dobson's Focus on the Family organization has been outspoken in its opposition, warning that the world will become "as it was in the days of Noah" (i.e., will be destroyed by God for its sins).[20]

The Southern Baptist Convention, a large conservative/fundamentalist Protestant denomination, identifies marriage as "the foundation of the God-ordained institution of the family" and states that the "union of one man and one woman is the only form of marriage prescribed in the Bible as God's perfect design for the family." It further defines marriage as "the uniting of one man and one woman in covenant commitment."[21]

Although there is nothing in the Massachusetts decision that requires the leaders of churches or synagogues to perform same-sex marriages, the legalization of it puts the question before communities of faith collectively and individually in a way that is new and promises to intensify both discussion and debate.

In 2003, an openly gay Episcopal clergyman was elected bishop in the Episcopal Diocese of New Hampshire. Bishop Robinson, previously married and the father of two adult daughters, now lives in a committed relationship with a male partner. One source described the result as "the culmination of a three-month story that has precipitated the biggest crisis in the Anglican Communion since 1534, when Henry VIII declared that he and not the Pope would be the Supreme Head of the Church of England."[22] Interestingly enough, the 1534 crisis also concerned human sexual arrangements. Henry VIII declared himself head of the Church of England because he wanted to be able to divorce his wife and remarry without censure from his church.

For many years, communities of faith have discussed, debated, and sometimes fought over the issue of what roles homosexual persons could have in their

[18]"The Ties That Divide: A Conversation on Gay Marriage with Andrew Sullivan and Gerard Bradley," The Pew Forum on Religion and Public Life, available at http://pewforum.org/events/
[19]Ibid.
[20]Focus on the Family Web site, www.family.org. This site contains a wealth of good material on the conservative Christian opposition to same-sex marriages and civil unions.
[21]Available on the Southern Baptist Convention Web site, www.sbc.net
[22]Frank Fitzpatrick, "The Anglican Crackup," *Religion in the News*, vol. 6, No. 3 (Fall, 2003), p. 2.

faith communities. The Episcopal Church has been no exception. This faith tradition has ordained gays to the priesthood for several years and has elevated them to the status of bishop as well. What made the consecration of Bishop Gene Robinson and his election to the New Hampshire office different is that he is *openly* gay.

Reaction from those not in favor was strong and swift. Bishop Robert Duncan of Pittsburgh, Pennsylvania, spoke on behalf of those opposed, noting that they were "filled with sorrow" and felt a "grief too deep for words." He voiced concern that the assembly had "denied the plain teaching of Scripture and the moral consensus of the church throughout the ages" and had "divided itself from millions of Anglican Christians throughout the world."[23] Some Episcopalians began talking about schism and leaving the historic church, while others counseled caution and forbearance.

At this time, the debate within the Episcopal Church in the United States, as well as in the worldwide Anglican Communion, continues. The American Anglican Council, a conservative movement within the American church, has issued "A Place to Stand: A Call to Action." It repudiates the consecration of Bishop Robinson and the church's acceptance of same-sex union blessing ceremonies. It calls on the church's leaders to repent and withdraws financial support as far as possible from any church structures that support them.

Despite these initiatives in response to Bishop Robinson's election, the widely predicted schism has not happened, neither between the Episcopal Church in the United States and the worldwide Anglican Communion, nor between factions within the United States, at least not as of this writing. The traditional Episcopal approach of being able to contain within itself dramatic variations of opinion seems to be holding. Even the most distressed, angry, and vocal dissenters have not wanted to make the radical move to actual disunion. Despite very deep and heartfelt differences of opinion on homosexuality and on the consecration of Gene Robinson as a Bishop, the prevailing desire seems to be to avoid schism. There is even a (as yet, informal) movement referred to by the term *Via Media* or "Middle Way," the purpose of which is to prevent schism from happening by encouraging individual dioceses not to pursue disunion.

RELIGION AND VIOLENCE AFTER 9-11

Prior to September 11, 2001, concern about religion's potential for violence had focused largely on those religions that people often label *cults*. Satanists were often accused of acts of particularly gruesome violence. Krishna Consciousness devotees and The Way were accused of weapons stockpiling. The image of the Branch Davidian compound in Texas engulfed in flames was fresh in many peoples' minds. Christian Identity, a militantly racist and anti-Semitic movement, raised fears that their radical talk about being "soldiers in God's army," responsible for helping bring about Armageddon, might translate into violence.

[23]CNN.com, available at http://www.cnn.com/2003/US/08/05/bishop/

By the turn of the century, popular concern about religion's potentially dangerous underside had already come to focus largely on the Catholic Church, a firmly established part of mainstream religion in most peoples' minds, as it dealt with the scandal of sexual abuse by priests. Then the planes tore into the World Trade Center and the Pentagon, and life for most people in the United States changed forever. Fear about religion's potential for violence shifted abruptly to the interface of religion and nationalism and especially to the relationship between religion and violence in Islam.

A recent study of religion and violence focuses on the three closely related religions, Judaism, Christianity, and Islam, that are predominant in the United States. The study's author notes that all three exhibit a profoundly ambiguous attitude about violence:

> We look to our sacred scriptures for words of consolation and hope and we find them there pervasive, but many of the words in sacred scriptures express threat and violence. Western cultures have been shaped by religions that, at best, have sounded uncertain trumpets. Judaism, Christianity, and Islam are all forms of spirituality and religious practice that derive directly from ancient Israelite religion, and that religious tradition speaks with remarkable and disappointing ambiguity.[24]

In the current situation, there are no clear-cut "good guys" and "bad guys." Although many persons and groups both here and abroad seek to give simple answers and point fingers of unambiguous blame, doing so is dishonest and further exacerbates the problem.

Muslims Respond

Muslims, of course, lived in the United States for many decades before 9-11; the first Muslim mosque (place for prayer and worship) was built in Cedar Rapids, Iowa, in 1934. Throughout the years, their presence had become increasingly visible, especially as the numbers of Muslims in the professions—law, teaching, and medicine—grew. Muslim students have also come to American colleges to study in increasing numbers.

In the days immediately following the attacks, law enforcement agencies received hundreds of reports of incidents of harassment, discrimination, and attacks on Muslim people and places. Mosques were defaced and threatening messages left on their voice mail. Religiously based slurs and epithets were directed at Muslims and anyone who "looked Muslim." I have a number of female Muslim friends who wear the traditional Muslim head covering. Many of them were afraid to leave the safety of their homes for fear of reprisals. Muslim children stayed home from schools, and Middle Easterners who are not Muslim feared for their safety as well.

[24]J. Harold Ellens, "Introduction: The Destructive Power of Religion," in *The Destructive Power of Religion: Violence in Judaism, Christianity, and Islam*, ed. J. Harold Ellens, vol. 1, *Sacred Scriptures, Ideology, and Violence* (Westport, CT: Praeger, 2004), p. 2.

A study by The Council on American Islamic Relations (CAIR) showed a 15 percent increase in the number of incidents and experiences of anti-Muslim violence, discrimination, and harassment during 2002. Further, there was an increase in "negative results produced by government policies that target ordinary Americans based on religion, ethnicity, or national origin."[25] Hardened attitudes could be seen in the publication of books detailing the "Islamic menace" and portraying Islam as a blood-thirsty and evil religion.

American Muslims moved quickly to condemn the actions of the terrorists and acquaint non-Muslims with the peaceful aspects of Islam. Heightened public scrutiny following the attacks, while uncomfortable for most Muslims, also gave them the opportunity to provide more accurate information about mainstream Islam and to counter the actions of the few. Many pushed aside their fear of persecution in order to interact with their non-Muslim counterparts, speaking publicly, answering questions, writing newspaper pieces, and addressing church groups and interfaith associations. This was certainly the case in the city in which I live. Our small Muslim community became much more vocal and visible in the wake of 9-11. The mosque sponsored events, and Muslims as individuals reached out to those of us who are not Muslim in the attempt to build bridges of understanding and peace.

At the same time, although some non-Muslim Americans reacted with hatred, most responded differently, realizing that the terrorists did not represent mainstream Islam. At local hospitals, non-Islamic staff reached out to Muslim physicians and non-Muslim Middle Eastern staff members with concern and compassion. Students and staffs of universities and colleges made a point of reassuring Muslim students and staff members that the university was a safe place where they would be respected. There were interfaith gatherings across the country in which people of all faiths and of none pledged to stand together with Muslims and against violence in the name of religion.

In the wake of continuing incidents, those of Muslim faith still experience the hatred of their fellow Americans. Information from the Council on American Islamic Relations in 2009 documents that discrimination continues to exist. Legislation proposed in Oklahoma banning the wearing of head coverings in driver's license and other identification photos makes no exceptions for Muslim hijab, nor for head coverings worn by those of other faiths, such as Jews and Sikhs. A Muslim customer at a Navy Federal Credit Union in Maryland was told she must conduct her business in an area of the office separate from other customers. Reports of airline passenger profiling, employment discrimination, and denials of religious accommodation persist. Although the incidence of violent attacks has decreased with time, Muslims still face danger and discrimination.

Why Religious Violence?

It is important to remember that, worldwide, the last decade has seen violence perpetrated by people who claimed affiliation with religions other than Islam. Religious studies scholars Mark Juergensmeyer and Catherine Wessinger call

[25]CAIR, http://sun.cair.com

to mind the shooting of doctors who perform abortions, the bombing of abortion clinics, and the destruction of the Murrah Federal Building in Oklahoma by right-wing Christians. There was the standoff at Ruby Ridge and the suicidal events in the Solar Temple and Heaven's Gate. Violence has erupted between various Jewish groups and has been perpetrated by Jews against Palestinians as well as Palestinians against Jews. Sikhs in India have been involved in assassinations, most notably that of Indira Ghandi, and Japanese radicals who claimed affiliation with both Hinduism and Buddhism left deadly nerve gas in a Tokyo subway.[26] It is also important that we keep in mind that all religious violence has not been directed at persons and groups outside the perpetrator's own faith. There has also been violence between Muslim groups, for example, and between Jewish groups, as well as between Christians.

Recent incidents of religious violence, no matter where they have occurred, have become a part of nearly everyone's lives as they have been reported and shown in graphic detail on international television. The attacks on the World Trade Center and the Pentagon brought religious violence home to Americans in a way that we had not known before. Foreign embassies had been attacked previously, but attackers from outside the United States had not attacked on American soil. Scholars began to search for answers to the pressing question, "*Why?*" To be able to answer that question offers some comfort, making the violence seem less random and chaotic. It may also lead to better informed efforts to minimize future violence.

Given the clear diversity of religious violence, can we discern any common factors? Several authors have responded to that question. One thing that seems to predispose to violent tactics in the name of religion is a sharply dualistic worldview. This view divides the world sharply and clearly into us and them, good and evil, often put in terms of God and Satan. It makes the other the enemy. Most religious persons who hold such a view—and there are many who do—engage the conflict through prayer, faith, and worship. A small minority turn to physical, armed conflict. A belief in outside persecution and a sense that the group will be unable to achieve its goals increase the likelihood of overt violence.[27]

Dualism can lead directly to the concept of *divine or cosmic warfare*, another predisposing factor. This image is a persistent one in many religions. Again, most who believe that they are called to engage in cosmic warfare do so through nonviolent methods, while a very few take up arms in what they perceive to be the cause of God. In these instances, the divine warfare imagery places the worldly encounter in a much larger context, giving it greater importance than it would otherwise have. It becomes not just earthly warfare, but

[26]Mark Juergensmeyer, *Terror in the Mind of God: The Global Rise of Religious Violence* (Berkeley, CA: The University of California Press, 2000), Chapters 2–6, and Catherine Wessinger, *How the Millennium Comes Violently: From Jonestown to Heaven's Gate* (New York: Seven Bridges Press, 2000), Chapters 3 through 7.

[27]Wessinger, *How the Millennium Comes Violently*, pp. 17–18.

an earthly embodiment of a transcendent battle whose beginnings may reach back to the creation of the world.[28]

This divine warfare has become what one author calls the "Master Story of Western culture." He states his thesis provocatively:

> This violent metaphor . . . has settled into the center of the psyche of the communities of faith we know as Judaism, Christianity, and Islam. Through them it has shaped the unconscious psychosocial assumptions of our cultures. This set of unconscious apocalyptic assumptions forms the sources and stage set for what we find meaningful in our cultures, from the violent game machines in the arcades our teenagers frequent to the actions of the Islamic Fundamentalists who flew airplanes into the World Trade Center and the Pentagon. It is a short psychospiritual step from the vicarious forms of wishful mythic violence in the arcade machine to the mythic wishes that hurled gasoline-laden flying machines into the workplace of twenty thousand New Yorkers.[29]

Whether we agree or not with his assertion that the distance between arcade game violence and terrorist attacks is a short step, there is little doubt that much of the world lives, as do we in the United States, in cultures in which powerful images of violence abound.

The religiously motivated acts of violence that have occurred in the last decade have been what Juergensmeyer calls *performance violence*. They have been not only acts of violence, destruction, murder, and bloodshed, but acts "executed in a deliberately intense and vivid way. It is as if these acts were designed to maximize the savage nature of their violence and meant to purposely elicit anger."[30] Performance violence is symbolic in that it refers to something beyond itself. It refers to the "master story" cited earlier. These "explosive scenarios are not *tactics* directed toward an immediate, earthly, or strategic goal, but *dramatic events* [that is, performances] intended to impress for their symbolic significance."[31] This feature of religious violence made the World Trade Center an especially apt target for the 1993 bombing and later for the 2001 attack. The tallest buildings in New York City, the twin towers stood as a fitting symbol of all that the radical Muslim world had come to define as the enemy other, the tool of Satan. They also symbolized the radical secularity of American public life, and to the terrorists' minds, destroying that symbol was a gain for religion, if only for a moment. They seemed to many Americans invulnerable living monuments to American economic power and international position, and for that reason, an important part of the "performance" was to show them in their greatest vulnerability. The attack on the Pentagon was similar in that it was designed to showcase the vulnerability of the American military, the agency of what the terrorists believed to be American international domination. The attempted attack on Washington, D.C., targeted the American governmental system.

---

[28]Juergensmeyer, *Terror in the Mind of God*, Chapter 9.
[29]Ellens, "Introduction: The Destructive Power of Religion," p. 4.
[30]Juergensmeyer, *Terror in the Mind of God*, p. 119.
[31]Ibid., p. 123.

Religiously motivated warfare is portrayed as being a conflict between divine forces and the forces of Satan. Thus, it demonizes the enemy. It also produces *martyrs* and sacrificial victims, another very long-standing and powerful religious image. Especially in the context of the intense religious-political commitment many have called fanaticism, martyrs sacrifice their lives for both their religion and their political agenda, gaining as it were a "double blessing." Juergensmeyer points out that sacrifice is ritual destruction that has been found in every religious tradition at some time. The word *sacrifice* itself comes from the Latin *sacrificium, to make holy*, suggesting that the act of destroying, or in the case of martyrs, volunteering to be destroyed, is sanctifying. The struggle itself, and giving one's life for it, regardless of whether there is any realistic hope of worldly success, becomes ennobling and sanctifying.

Yet another partial explanation for religious violence lies in the fact that all of the groups that have sanctioned violence in the form of terrorism have been marginal—in varying degrees—within their own religious societies.[32] Their violence has been in part a counterbalance to their marginality, a way of empowering them within their own religious communities.

Their marginality comes from three aspects of their religious style: They reject any compromise with liberal religious or secular values, compromise that characterizes the mainstream of most religions. Second, they do not believe religion should be a private matter, but rather should direct and perhaps dictate what goes on in the public square. Finally, they espouse a demanding form of the religious tradition that often characterized its earliest days. Because this is decisively not the style of mainstream religion, these groups become marginalized within their communities of faith.[33] They see themselves as embattled defenders of "pure faith" against the compromises of the less pure and rigorous.

Violence and Islam

When religiously motivated violence arises in the context of Islam, the word *jihad* inevitably arises alongside it. Although many, perhaps most, non-Muslims routinely take it to mean aggressive holy war, it is a word with complex layers of meaning in the Qur'an (Muslim sacred scripture), in Muslim tradition, and in the understanding of ordinary Muslims. There is no single interpretation that all Muslims everywhere have ever agreed upon. It changes over time and with circumstances, and different individuals and groups give it their own interpretation. Its use and misuse by politicized extremist elements within Islam to garner support and justify their actions have encouraged its interpretation as violent holy war among non-Muslims.

Islam is a religion of action. It encourages its followers "to struggle *(jihad)* to implement their belief, to lead a good life, to defend religion, to contribute to the development of a just Islamic society throughout the world."[34] This is the

---

[32]Ibid., p. 218.
[33]Ibid., p. 221.
[34]John L. Esposito, *Unholy War: Terror in the Name of Islam* (New York: Oxford University Press, 2002), p. 5.

larger context of the term *jihad*, the propensity of Muslims to understand their religion as active struggle, as striving, in all ways, following the model provided by the earliest traditions about the life of Prophet Muhammad and his followers.

American scholar of Islam John L. Esposito calls jihad "a defining concept or belief in Islam, a key element in what it means to be a believer and follower of God's Will."[35] Although it does not have to mean violence, the concept is ready at hand for those who wish to use it in that way. Muslims often distinguish between the greater and lesser jihads. The greater jihad is the daily struggle of individual Muslims to submit their wills to Allah (God). The lesser jihad is related to doing battle for the faith.

There are a number of other meanings and nuances of meaning, as well. Jihad as literal, armed warfare may be defensive, fighting against attack and oppression from without, or offensive, a more general struggle against all unbelievers and responsibility to spread the message of Islam. There are sharp differences of opinion about the extent to which it is permissible to use jihad as a tactic for conversion, as well. Most Muslims cite Qur'anic verses that speak against the use of any force in conversion, but others cite a Muslim obligation to convert everyone by whatever means necessary. Sometimes the word is used to refer to the struggle obligatory on any Muslim society to establish a just and righteous social order based on Islamic principles.

Today, the term *jihad* has become nearly all things to all Muslims, and the traditional criteria for what constitutes valid jihad—carefully spelled out in Islamic just war theory—are ignored by many of those who use the term to inflame hearts and minds against the United States and support their own use of violence:

> Today the term jihad has become comprehensive; resistance and liberation struggles and militant jihads, holy and unholy wars, are all declared to be jihads. Jihad is waged at home not only against unjust rulers in the Muslim world but also against a broad spectrum of civilians. Jihad's scope abroad became chillingly clear in the September 11 attacks against both the World Trade Center and the Pentagon, targeting not only governments but also civilians.

> Terrorists such as bin Laden and others go beyond classical Islam's criteria for a just jihad and recognize no limits but their own, employing any weapon or means. They reject Islamic law's regulations regarding the goals and means of a valid jihad (that violence must be proportional and that only the necessary amount of force should be used to repel the enemy), that innocent civilians should not be targeted, and that jihad must be declared by the ruler or head of state. Today, individuals and groups, religious and lay, seize the right to declare and legitimate unholy wars in the name of Islam.[36]

In 1967, the combined force of Egypt, Syria, and Jordan suffered a particularly devastating defeat at the hands of Israel in the Six-Day Arab—Israeli War.

[35]Ibid., p. 26.
[36]Ibid., p. 157.

This defeat was a decisive turning point for Islam. The once-powerful Muslim world was humiliated and angered. It called for jihad against Israel, fought in 1973. An Arab oil embargo, the results of which were felt around the globe, helped restore shattered Arab pride. Internal reform and opposition movements also increased within the House of Islam. All of these things contributed to an increased potential for violence within Islam.

Internal problems in many Muslim countries also have contributed to the establishment of politicized Muslim groups:

> During the past two decades, many Muslim countries have faced a large, restless younger generation; unemployment; housing shortages; maldistribution of wealth; and corruption. At the same time, globalization and increasing Western influence are seen by many as a threat to Islamic traditions. These elements have combined to create powerful Islamic political (fundamentalist) movements. . . . [Religious] extremist organizations and movements . . . "hijack" their religion, using it to justify violence and terrorism and calling for a jihad against their own societies, America and Europe.[37]

The extremists are a small minority, but they are a volatile and dangerous one.

Like many conservative members of other religions, notably Judaism and Christianity, conservative and fundamentalist Muslims believe that the values of the highly secularized Western world are fundamentally at odds with those of Muslim faith and culture. With the globalization of Western culture, many Muslims have developed a siege mentality, feeling constantly under attack. Under these circumstances, some individuals and groups will choose to fight back violently, as do those Christians in the United States who attack abortion clinics and stockpile weapons to fight in the coming "God's war."

Whether the United States dominates and exploits Muslim nations and the rest of the world, or seeks to do so, is a matter of spirited intellectual and popular debate in the United States and overseas. What *is* certain is that a substantial segment of the world's people, including some in traditionally Muslim nations, *believe* that it does. Within the Muslim world, as well, some groups perceive themselves deeply oppressed by other groups or individuals. This situation sets off a "virtually inevitable spiral of violence," according to one author. This spiral can be described in four stages: First, structural violence in the form of injustice and abuse of persons arises from the social order imposed by exploitive and predatory domineering forces. Second, protest and resistance to injustice arises. Third, the domineering group or individual uses whatever additional repression they deem necessary to put down the rebellion. The destruction continues, fourth, in an ever-increasing spiral of rebellion and repression.[38]

The prevalence of both the theme and the occurrence of violence throughout many of humankind's religions, including Christianity and Judaism as well

[37]John L. Esposito, "Islam in the World and in America," in *World Religions in America, Third Edition*, ed. Jacob Neusner (Louisville, KY: Westminster John Knox Press, 2003), p. 183.
[38]R.A. Horsley, *Jesus and Empire: The Kingdom of God and the New World Disorder* (Minneapolis, MN: Fortress Press, 2003).

as Islam, and extending to the Asian religious paths as well, strongly suggests to me that both the reaction "Islam is a bloody and militaristic religion" and the counterreaction, "Islam is all about peace" are both far too simple. Most of our religious traditions and faith communities have elements of both in their history, and most have been involved in overt violence, either in the past or currently. This may indeed be one of the rare instances in which saying *all*, rather than *most* is not specious overgeneralization.

RELIGIOUS EXPRESSION IN A RELIGIOUSLY DIVERSE CULTURE

The United States is one of the most religiously diverse, if not *the* most religiously diverse, country in the world. In such a setting, it is perhaps inevitable that the ways in which some religious organizations and individuals choose to express their religiousness will offend others. As a result, those who have taken offense may attempt to curtail that expression. What ties the following otherwise disparate items together is that they all center conflicts over religious expression in our religiously diverse culture. All of them also have to do with the principles of disestablishment and the free exercise of religion that are guaranteed in the Constitution of the United States (see Chapter 2).

The Ten Commandments in Alabama

One of the highest-profile incidents in recent years has been the furor ignited by the installation in the rotunda of the building that houses the Alabama Supreme Court of a 5280 pound granite monument with the Ten Commandments inscribed on it. The stone also contains quotations supporting the Decalogue, a part of both Jewish and Christian moral teaching, as the foundation of the American system of justice. Alabama Chief Justice Roy Moore had the monument placed in the rotunda late in the summer of 2001. It was placed at night, and no one had been notified that it would be installed. Justice Moore had earlier had a wooden Ten Commandments plaque in his circuit court courtroom. His fight against a lawsuit seeking the removal of that plaque led to his campaign and election as Alabama's Chief Justice, running as the "Ten Commandments Judge."[39]

In fall, 2001, the American Civil Liberties Union and Americans United for the Separation of Church and State filed suit to have the monument removed on the grounds that its presence in the Supreme Court building sent a clear message of government support for the Judeo-Christian religious tradition and thus violated the disestablishment clause of the First Amendment. The initial ruling was in favor of the plaintiffs. Demonstrations both for and against the monument followed in short order.

Justice Moore, as would be expected, appealed the ruling. In the summer of 2003, the Eleventh Circuit Court of Appeals again ruled in favor of the plaintiffs.

[39]www.CNN.com (November 14, 2003).

Figure 3-2 Alabama's controversial Ten Commandments monument. *(AP Wide World Photos.)*

They ordered the monument removed. Justice Moore refused and appealed to the U.S. Supreme Court to intervene. The Court rejected his appeal. The Appeals court had ordered removal by midnight August 20. On August 22, Justice Moore was suspended as Chief Justice for refusing to obey a court order. Workers removed the monument from its place in the rotunda several days later, placing it in a locked closet in another part of the building. That fall, the U.S. Supreme Court rejected an appeal by Justice Moore that the monument be allowed to be displayed in another part of the building. Moore, for his part, rejected a proposal that the Ten Commandments be displayed alongside other, secular historical documents that form the foundation of American law. Such displays have been judged constitutional in the past. In November, 2003, Justice Moore was permanently removed from his office.

Moore, as expected, fought to have himself reinstated. In Spring, 2004, however, a seven-member special review court upheld his removal from office. In a unanimous ruling, the review court held that Moore's removal from office was "proper" on the grounds that he had violated state ethics codes when he refused to comply with the federal court order requiring removal of the monument. Although this ruling appeared to be his last opportunity for an appeal, Moore has indicated he may appeal again to the U.S. Supreme Court.

More often than not, disestablishment issues and free exercise of religion issues are two sides of the same coin, or seem so in the protagonists' minds. Moore and his supporters, including several conservative Christian organizations, see the courts' decision as a violation of the free exercise of religion. The Reverend Barry Lynn, executive director of Americans United for Separation of Church and State, however, called it "a tremendous victory for the rule of law and respect for religious diversity."[40]

"Under God" in the Pledge of Allegiance

Cases involving the Pledge of Allegiance have been heard in the Supreme Court a number of times. The most recent case dealt with the inclusion of the phrase "under God" in the Pledge. *Elk Grove Unified School District* v. *Newdow* was brought by a California atheist who challenged the inclusion of the Pledge as part of the daily ritual in his daughter's public school classroom. As an atheist, he believed that his daughter's reciting "under God" in the Pledge amounted to government coercion of religion. Children are not required to participate in reciting the Pledge, but Dr. Newdow believed that his daughter's presence while it was being recited violated his religious convictions. Although the government did not rule on the church—state issue posed by Dr. Newdow's suit, its ruling leaves the words "under God" in the Pledge.

The Court ruled that Dr. Newdow did not have legal standing to speak for his daughter since he is the noncustodial parent. Although in agreement that Newdow did not have legal standing to bring the case, Justices William Rhenquist, Sandra Day O'Connor, and Clarence Thomas wrote separately to note that the recitation of the Pledge with "under God" included does not violate the separation of religion and government. In this case, the Supreme Court's ruling overturned a two-year-old ruling that had deemed it unconstitutional for teachers to lead students in the Pledge.

Response from both sides of the issue again indicates the close relationship between establishment and free exercise. Barry Lynn of Americans United commented, "The justices ducked this issue today, but it is likely to come back in the future. Students should not feel compelled by school officials to subscribe to a particular religious belief in order to show love of country." On the other side, a representative of the American Center for Law and Justice, a conservative

[40]Ibid.

Christian organization, noted that "[while] the court did not address the merits of the case, it is clear that the Pledge of Allegiance and the words 'under God' can continue to be recited by students across America." Not originally a part of the Pledge, the phrase "under God" was added in 1954. Those who supported the addition of the phrase stated that the words distinguished the United States from "godless communism."[41]

Religion Exemptions and Hiring for Tax-Funded Positions

The question of whether religious organizations may choose to hire only those of their own faith for programs for which they receive tax funding has led to controversy as well. The House of Representatives recently rejected by a 232-to-183 vote an attempt to prevent religious organizations from doing so.

The Community Services Block Grant Act (H.R. 3030) contains a provision which permits religious groups that receive funds under the program to hire only those of their own faith. This differs from hiring by other employers, who are forbidden by law to discriminate based on religion (as well as on the basis of several other things):

> Federal civil rights laws from the 1960s prevent employers from discriminating on the basis of religion but contain special exemptions that allow churches and similar religious organizations to hire only adherents of their own faith. However, several federal programs deny government contracts and funding to groups that practice job discrimination, including on religious grounds.[42]

Language is important here. The connotations of exemption and discrimination are rather different. The Act simply provides an exemption that allows religious organizations to hire based on the religious affiliation of the applicant. It becomes discrimination in the eyes of those who see it as a negative thing.

This matter concerns jobs that are not directly related to religion, and jobs for which there is at least some federal funding. There has never been any attempt to restrict the hiring practices of communities of faith for religiously sensitive positions or for which they were not receiving tax money. Presbyterians for example, are quite free to hire only Presbyterians as ministers of congregations, choir directors, or church educators. Jewish preschools and day-care centers may hire only Jewish teachers legally, so long as they are not government-funded. The concern comes in when religious organizations receive part of their funding from tax monies for social services programs. The following two comments illustrate the dilemma:

> Why should it be legal for a group to accept a $5 million Head Start or job-training grant from the taxpayers and say we are not going to hire Jews or Catholics? [Representative Chet Edwards, a Democrat from Texas].

---

[41]Anne Gearen for the Associated Press, "Supreme Court Preserves 'God' in Pledge," available at www.comcast.net/news (June 14, 2004).

[42]"House approves another bill allowing religious discrimination," Baptist Joint Committee, *Report from the Capital*, vol. 59, No. 2 (February, 2004), p. 1.

Why should a faith-based organization that is providing tremendous community services give up the protections granted to them under the 1964 Civil Rights Act just because they accept federal dollars in their mission to help low-income people? [Representative John Boehner, an Ohio Republican].[43]

These types of questions can be expected to continue and to increase as religious organizations participate in faith-based initiatives to provide social services. The interface of funding and hiring is one of the ongoing concerns of people who oppose faith-based initiatives.

No Hats, No Caps . . . No *Hijab*?

Hijab is the Arabic term for the head covering worn by many Muslim girls and women. Technically, hijab is a scarf that covers the head and neck and extends down around the shoulders. Many choose to wear it in obedience to scripture and tradition and as a symbol of their identification with Islam. Other Muslim women and girls choose to wear a scarf wound around the head and knotted at the nape of the neck.

Nashala Hearn, an eleven-year-old school girl in Oklahoma, was suspended from school twice for wearing her hijab. School officials said that her head covering violated the school policy against students wearing "hats, caps, bandannas, plastic caps or hoods on jackets" in the building. She and her family sued for her right to cover her head. The Department of Justice intervened in support of the family. Nashala was granted the right to wear her hijab to school, and the school district was required to rewrite its dress code to allow for religious exemptions.[44]

Similar questions have arisen in employment settings, not only about Muslim hijabs but about Jewish males, for example, who wear a *kippah* or head covering, or female members of some Christian groups who may not want to wear a uniform with slacks or short sleeves rather than a skirt and long sleeves. As a general rule, the courts have held that employers and school officials need to accommodate religiously-based requests for exemptions to dress codes and that employees and students must be allowed to wear religiously symbolic items such as hijabs, crosses, or wrist malas (a bracelet of prayer beads worn by some Hindus and Buddhists). They may, however, require modifications based on safety or other considerations. For example, if a Muslim woman wearing hijab will be operating machinery, the loose ends of her scarf need to be tucked in. An employer may tell a Jewish man that the color of his kippah may not clash with the color of his uniform.

It appears that controversy around religious issues, both within communities of faith and between faith groups and the larger culture, will continue, and perhaps even intensify in coming years. Both culture and religion in the United States are dynamic and evolving, and in that situation,

---

[43]Cited in "House approves another bill allowing religious discrimination," Baptist Joint Committee, *Report from the Capital*, vol. 59, No. 2 (February, 2004), p. 1.

[44]Reported in Baptist Joint Committee, *Report from the Capital*, vol. 59, No. 5 (May, 2004).

conflicts are bound to occur. It also appears that religiously motivated violence will remain a factor both here and abroad.

Religious Rights in Prisons

The Religious Land Use and Institutionalized Persons Act (passed in 2000)[45] holds in part that government may not

- impose a substantial burden on the religious exercise of a person residing in or confined to an institution, unless doing so
- furthers a compelling government interest and
- is the least restrictive means to further that compelling interest.

The act specifically forbids discrimination on the basis of religious denomination, requiring that all be treated equally.

In 2005, under this act the U.S. Supreme Court ruled that the law required prisons to provide chaplains for members of Satanic or white supremacist groups as well as for more mainstream religious groups (*Cutter* v. *Wilkinson*, 2005).[46] The plaintiffs in the case—members of Satanist, Wiccan, and Asatru faiths and the Church of Jesus Christ Christian—alleged that the prison system had denied them access to religious literature pertaining to their faith and opportunities for congregational worship, forbidden them to follow the dress and appearance guidelines of their religion, withheld ceremonial items, and failed to provide a chaplain trained in their faith.[47]

In addition to chaplains, the federal prison system provides religious books to incarcerated persons through prison chapels. In 2004, the Office of the Inspector General in the Justice Department recommended that prisons should bar prisoner access to materials that might radicalize prisoners or advocate violence. The Standardized Chapel Library project involved the development of a list of approved reading materials for each of 20 religions and religious categories.[48] Prison chaplains were ordered to remove any and all books not on this list. In 2007, books were removed and packed away. Prayer books and other worship materials were not affected and remained available.

Very soon, there was pressure from members of Congress, public outrage from both religious liberals and religious conservatives as well as from civil libertarians and advocates of First Amendment religious freedoms, and a class action lawsuit filed by several prisoners. The Federal Bureau of Prisons decided to return the books removed from prison libraries. The idea of developing a list of approved books has not been abandoned, but while the details are being worked out, books will remain available.

---

[45]The Act is available online at http://www.usdoj.gov/crt/housing/housing_rluipa.htm

[46]A synopsis of this case with a link to the full written opinion and other sources is at www.oyez.org/cases/2000-2009/2004/2004_03_9877/

[47]www.law.cornell.edu/supct/html/03-9877.ZO.html

[48]The list was not made public. One copy of the list can be found at www.nytimes.com/2007/09/21/us/21prison.html, with the notation that it may not be a current listing.

QUESTIONS AND ACTIVITIES FOR REVIEW, DISCUSSION, AND WRITING

1. Read the Charter for the Protection of Children and Young People (http://www. usccb.org/ocyp/charter.shtml). Write an essay in which you respond to its provisions.
2. Similarly, write an essay in which you respond to the work of the Interfaith Sexual Trauma Institute.
3. In your own opinion, should communities of faith bless or recognize in some other way marriages or commitments between partners of the same sex? What reasons can you give for your position?
4. If possible, have a representative of the Muslim faith come and speak to your class about the Muslim response to the events of September 11, 2001.
5. Summarize each of the reasons given in this chapter for religiously motivated violence.
6. What restrictions, if any, do you believe should apply to religious expression in our culture?
7. Should religious organizations be able to hire only those of their own faith for programs for which they receive government funding? Why or why not?

FOR FURTHER READING

AVALOS, HECTOR, *Fighting Words: The Origins of Religious Violence*. Amherst, NY: Prometheus Books, 2006. Avalos' intriguing thesis is that religious violence arises from a perceived scarcity of four key religious "resources:" sacred space (sites), exclusive revelations (scriptures), group privilege (the chosen or elect), and salvation (exclusive claims). He believes such violence could be dramatically reduced by the recognition that these are not in fact scarce, but available to all.

THOMAS G. PLANTE, *Sins Against the Innocents: Sexual Abuse by Priests and the Role of the Catholic Church*. Westport, CT: Praeger, 2004. As in the Ellens books, a team of scholars from a variety of disciplines give a very thorough analysis.

SELENQUT, CHARLES, *Sacred Fury: Understanding Religious Violence*. Lanham, MD: Altamira Press, 2007. Selenqut explores religious violence from five perspectives: the holy war, social psychology, apocalypticism, violence as a response to perceived threats to a religious culture, and violence as a response to the call for religious adherents to show their devotion through physical commitment (e.g., martyrdom).

RELEVANT WORLD WIDE WEB SITES

Churches for Middle East Peace: www.cmep.org/

Interfaith Sexual Trauma Institute: http://www.csbsju.edu/isti/

Ontario Consultants on Religious Tolerance page on religious violence: http://www. religioustolerance.org/relviol.htm

CHAPTER 4

The Waning Influence of Mainline Protestantism and the New Evangelical Majority

What do you think of when you think about "ordinary" religion in the United States? It is probably at least similar to the styles of religion described below. It is the religion of the majority of the population of the United States and has been so for nearly all of the nation's history.

As you learned in Chapter 2, Christians are the majority religion in the United States, accounting for about 80 percent of the population. In this section, we investigate the many forms Christianity takes in the United States. After describing Christian faith and practice in broad strokes, we will focus first on Protestants, who make up the majority of Christians in America. In later chapters, we will look in turn at Catholic Christianity, African American and Eastern Orthodox Christianity, and several forms of Christianity that began in the United States. Because they share a common heritage of Christian practices and beliefs, they are more alike than they are different. At the same time, each gives this common heritage its own distinctive stamp.

CHRISTIAN FAITH AND PRACTICE: OVERVIEW

Belief

In introducing Christianity, we'll follow the description of religion introduced in Chapter 1. Thus, we begin with basic Christian *beliefs*. Christian beliefs are based on the Bible—both the Old Testament and the New Testament—and on the tradition of the church. The emphasis given to either varies from group to group.

Like Jews and Muslims, Christians are monotheists, people who believe in one God. The religious life of Christians—Protestants, Catholic, Eastern Orthodox, and others as well—centers on the person, life, death, and resurrection of Jesus. *Christians are those people who are defined by their faith in Jesus as their Lord and Savior.*

57

Two classical creeds of the early Christian church form the basis for our discussion of the beliefs and practices that are shared by most Christians. A creed is an official, written statement of the beliefs of a particular religious group. There are certainly variations in interpretation, but, with a few exceptions, most members of this largest community of faith in the United States could affirm what is contained in the Apostles' and Nicene creeds.[1]

The *Apostles' Creed* (Figure 4-1) is so named because it is a summary of essential Christian beliefs as held by the Church at the time of the Apostles. It was not written by the Apostles, as legend has it, but goes back to the very old Roman Creed. In its current form, it probably dates from the seventh century, C.E.

The *Nicene Creed* (Figure 4-2) was written at the Council of Nicaea in 325 C.E. and revised at the Council of Constantinople in 381 C.E. It is somewhat longer than the Apostles' Creed. Both, however, contain much the same material.

Both the Apostles' and the Nicene creeds cover four basic topics: God the Father, Jesus Christ, the Holy Spirit, and a paragraph of miscellaneous affirmations. Christians, following Jesus's example, believe that God is a loving parent who cares deeply for humankind and for the rest of creation, as well. God is also the creator who brings everything "seen and unseen" into being. Nothing, in other words, came or comes into being except by God's will and power, which also sustains all things.

Figure 4-1

THE APOSTLES' CREED

I believe in God, the Father Almighty,
Creator of heaven and earth.

And in Jesus Christ, his only son, our Lord,
Who was conceived of the Holy Ghost,
And born of the Virgin Mary.
He Suffered under Pontius Pilate,
Was crucified, dead, and buried.
He descended into Hell.
[Alt: "He descended to the dead." Some omit completely.]
On the third day he rose again from the dead.
He ascended into Heaven
And sits at the right hand of God the Father almighty,
From whence he will come
To judge the living and the dead.

I believe in the Holy Spirit, the holy catholic church,
The communion of saints, the forgiveness of sins,
The resurrection of the body, and the life everlasting.

---

[1] A large collection of classical creeds, along with some more recent ones, can be found at www.creeds.net

Figure 4-2

THE NICENE CREED

We believe in one God, the Father, the Almighty, maker of heaven and earth, of all that is, seen and unseen.

We believe in one Lord, Jesus Christ, the only Son of God, eternally begotten of the Father, God from God, Light from Light, true God from true God, begotten, not made, of one Being with the Father. Through him all things were made. For us and for our salvation he came down from heaven: by the power of the Holy Spirit he became incarnate from the Virgin Mary, and was made man. For our sake he was crucified under Pontius Pilate; he suffered death and was buried. On the third day he rose again according to the Scriptures; he ascended into heaven and is seated at the right hand of the Father. He will come again in glory to judge the living and the dead, and his kingdom will have no end.

We believe in the Holy Spirit, the Lord, the giver of life, who proceeds from the Father [some add, "and the Son"]. With the Father and the son he is worshiped and glorified. He has spoken through the prophets.

We believe in one holy catholic and apostolic Church. We acknowledge on baptism for the forgiveness of sins. We look for the resurrection of the dead, and the life of the world to come.

Of Jesus Christ, it is stated that he is the only Son of God, who came into being through the power of the Holy Spirit and was born to a virgin. Whether these affirmations are taken literally or not, the intent is clear. Jesus was not simply a human being, although Christians believe that he was fully human. He is somehow special, related to God in a way that makes him unique. According to most Christians, Jesus was God incarnate. The church's beliefs about the most relevant points of Jesus's career are summarized: his birth, his suffering and death, his resurrection, and his future return to Earth. According to the Nicene Creed, all of this took place for the salvation of humanity. One of the most striking elements of Christian belief is the affirmation that the one God became fully human (i.e., incarnate) in order to save human beings from the results of sin. Because Christians believe that the God of Abraham, Isaac, and Jacob became fully human in Jesus, they are drawn into an especially intimate relationship with him. It is also stated that Jesus will return to earth to judge both the living and the dead. When he returns, Christians believe, those who have put their faith and trust in him will live eternally with him.

These and other classic creeds of Christianity reflect the teachings that are found in the Christian Bible. Although Protestant and Catholic versions of the Bible are very similar, the Catholic Church had not until recently given its approval to any of the translations of the Bible commonly used by Protestant Christians. In late 1991, the U.S. Council of Catholic Bishops gave their Church's official approval to the *New Revised Standard Version* (often abbreviated NRSV) of the Christian Bible. This means that Catholic and Protestant Christians (as well as

Eastern Orthodox Christians, whose leadership had approved the new translation earlier) now have a translation of the Bible that all can use.

Along with the Father and the Son, Christians believe in the Holy Spirit or Holy Ghost as the third person of the Trinity. To say that God is a Trinity means that most, though not all, Christians believe that God is best understood as three persons who are one and yet distinguishable. This doctrine itself is not found in the Bible (although it is supported by certain passages in the New Testament such as Matthew 28:19 and 2 Corinthians 13:14), but it was defined very early in the history of the Christian church, especially in these two creeds. Most Christians believe that this is something about God that people could not have known on their own but that can be known because God revealed it. The doctrine points to the centrality of relationship, not just in how God relates to human beings but within God as well.

Finally, most Christians do not believe that earthly death is the end of life. The faithful will be resurrected at the end of time and will live eternally with God. Some Christians believe that heaven is an actual place. Others describe eternal life as simply life with God.

Ritual

The worship of God is the principal *ritual* act of Christians. Christian worship has a dual focus, Word and Sacrament. *Word* refers not only to the Word of God in the Bible, which is read as a part of the service, but to other aspects of worship as well: responsive readings, hymns and prayers, repeating a creed, and the sermon given by the pastor, minister, or priest. Sacraments are special ritual acts performed in worship. Different Christians understand their meaning in differing ways and recognize different numbers of sacraments, but in any case, they help enact and make present the grace of God.

Communion, also known as Holy Communion, the Last Supper, or the Eucharist (thanksgiving) is a central sacrament. Bread and wine or unfermented grape juice are shared among believers in a ritual that ranges from the celebratory to the solemn. It is a ritual that brings the faithful into intimate contact with the central truths of their faith. Interpretations of the exact meaning of Communion vary among Christians. Some believe that the bread and wine actually become the body and blood of Christ. Others teach that Jesus is present symbolically in the elements, while some understand Communion simply as a way of remembering Jesus's death and resurrection.

The ritual of baptism is the rite of incorporation into the Christian community of faith. It is also a public witness of commitment to Christ. Some Christians believe that it is necessary for the forgiveness of sin, as well. Water is nearly always used. Specific practices vary from full immersion into water to a sprinkle of water on the head of the person being baptized. Some churches baptize people of all ages, including infants. Others believe that people who are being baptized must be old enough to understand its meaning. Most Christians are baptized in the name of the Father, Son, and Holy Spirit, although some churches baptize in Jesus's name only.

Lifestyle

There is variation in *lifestyle* among different Christians. The majority live quite similarly to others in their culture. Most believe that the material, physical world, created by God, is good, and can be affirmed and enjoyed within the boundaries of morality. God's love is seen as completely altruistic, without self-interest, and Christians believe they are called to embody that type of love in their lives. Some express their understanding of the moral life in terms of doing what Jesus would do were he alive now. Bracelets and tee shirts with the acronym WWJD, "What would Jesus do?" remind their wearers to keep this question in mind.

When the creeds refer to "one holy catholic church," the word *catholic* is being used to mean universal, rather than "Catholic" as a distinct branch of Christianity. In spite of the many divisions within Christianity, it is understood to be one Church, having one Lord, and continuing back to the time of the 12 Apostles whom the Christian New Testament says that Jesus gathered around himself during his earthly life. The followers of Jesus the Christ are called into a community, the church. The church is not simply a human community, although it is that. It is a community called into being by God and sustained in its life by its relationship with God.

Organization

Organizationally, the Christian church has three major branches. Protestant Christianity and several of the major Protestant denominations are described in this chapter. The Catholic Church and the Eastern Orthodox churches are described in Chapters 6 and 7. All its branches have their roots in the Christian community of faith that came together following Jesus's death and resurrection. Eastern Orthodox and Catholic Christianity divided over religious, social, and political issues in 1054. The Protestant Reformation of 1517 led to the formation of the many Protestant denominations. In addition to these three groups, there are other Christians who do not trace their heritage to any of these three branches. Some of these are described in Chapter 8.

PROTESTANT CHRISTIANITY

The term *Protestant* in most people's minds calls up the image of German reformer Martin Luther protesting against certain practices of the Catholic Church in his time. But the word also goes back to an earlier meaning of the term *protest*: It means to testify or witness to what one believes. Protestants are those Christians who affirm an interpretation of Christianity that goes back more than half a millennium. Its beginnings are usually linked with the life and work of Martin Luther in Germany, but the forces that led to reform had been at work centuries before him.

Belief and practice vary somewhat among Protestant denominations, and even among congregations within a denomination. Despite this diversity, there were, and still are, certain beliefs and practices that, although with modifications, have been a part of Protestantism since Reformation times. We will use the now-familiar four elements of religion to organize our thinking about what most Protestants hold in common.

Beliefs

We have already touched on some of Protestantism's core beliefs when we discussed the beliefs that most Christians have in common. First, *the Bible plays an absolutely central role for Protestants*. Protestants, along with other Christians, Jews, and Muslims are a "people of the Book," and this theme is highly developed in Protestantism. Martin Luther's classic phrase was *Sola Scriptura*, the authority of the Bible only. With this, he pointed out the sharp contrast between the new faith and Catholicism.[2] Catholics recognize two sources of religious authority: the Bible and the long record of the Church's teaching and interpretation. The Church is, in effect, the guardian and official interpreter of the Bible. Protestants, on the other hand, go directly to the Bible, using the church's interpretations of its meaning only in an advisory capacity. John Calvin, for example, emphasized the need to check one's own private interpretation against that of the community of faith in the interest of preserving good order.

It was this need for some statement of the church's belief to counterbalance a too-individualistic view that led some of the Reformation churches to formulate creeds. For Protestants, the authority of any creed or confession of faith is subordinate to that of the Bible, and any such document is valid only insofar as it is an accurate representation of what the Bible teaches. Creedal groups use written creeds or statements of faith to express the essence of their beliefs. The Presbyterians developed the Westminster Confession of Faith and the Episcopalians retained much of the Church of England's theology in their Thirty-Nine Articles of Religion. Lutherans use the Augsburg Confession as one standard statement of faith. There are also more recent statements, such as the Presbyterian Confession developed following the 1983 merger and the Barmen Declaration. Some groups require that candidates for membership affirm that a particular creed or confession of faith embodies biblical teaching. Congregational repetition of a creed is usually a regular feature of worship, and the study of the creed in an important part of religious education.

Other communities of faith do not have a formal creed as such, although some of them may make occasional use of creeds, especially of the early ones. Adherence to a creed is not a prerequisite to membership in these groups. Communities of faith that do not have a formal creed take this position for a

---

[2]The Catholicism of Luther and Calvin's time was vastly different from Catholicism in the United States now. Significant changes came about with the Second Vatican Council in the early 1960s. In particular, the differences between the two types of Christianity were much larger than they now are. Chapter 6 provides more information on contemporary American Catholicism.

variety of reasons. Some believe that formal creeds are too restrictive and violate the right of individual conscience in religious matters. Others fear that acceptance of a creed can too easily become a substitute for faith in Jesus.

What is important for Protestants is not the Bible itself but the Word of God contained in it. This has two meanings. First, the Bible is the direct access to the Word made flesh in Jesus: "In the beginning," writes the author of the Gospel according to John, "was the Word, and the Word was with God, and Word was God . . . And the Word became flesh and lived among us, and we have seen his glory, the glory as of a father's only son, full of grace and truth." (John 1:1, 14, New Revised Standard Version). The only mediator between God and humankind, according to Protestants, is revealed to be the eternal Word made flesh, and this all-important story is told in the pages of the Bible. The term *Word of God* also has a second layer of meaning in Protestant thought. Whether objectively or through the action and influence of the Holy Spirit, the words of the Bible are God's direct and personal communication to each and every individual.

It was the prominence given to the Word contained in the Bible that led to the Protestant enthusiasm for translating the Bible into the language of the people. Having only Latin Bibles reinforced the Church's position as the only interpreter and official custodian of biblical truth, because only the priests and higher officials of the Church could read and understand Latin. Even though illiteracy was high—few people could read even in their own language—having Bibles available in the common language of a people meant that people could hear the Bible read in the language they understood and could come to their own interpretation. It is perhaps difficult to imagine the thrill some of these people must have felt upon hearing the Bible read in their own language for the first time. It was as if God were speaking directly to them, rather than addressing them through a translator or interpreter.

Protestants believe that *salvation is a gift from God*, an effect of grace and grace alone. There is nothing that people can do to earn salvation. All are equally guilty, equally subject to death due to sin. People cannot possibly make themselves worthy before God. At the same time, there is nothing that people need to do to earn salvation, because God has made it a gift of his grace in and through Jesus, who for this reason is known by Christians as Savior (see, for example, Ephesians 2:8-9).

Protestants believe that *the church is the gathered fellowship of believers*. It is the people meeting together to hear the Word preached, to participate in the sacraments of baptism and communion, and to encourage and help each other. It is the people, rather than the institution or the hierarchy. In a very real sense for Protestants, the church is not an institution but an *event* that *happens* each time and place that believers gather. Prior to the Reformation, the church had functioned as a complex system of two-way mediation between God and people. Through the Church's teaching (including but not limited to the Bible), hierarchy, and sacraments, God's will and grace became available to people. People reached God by following those teachings and participating in the means of grace the Church made available. The reformers simplified this structure of mediation, teaching instead that God relates to people through their trust and faith, on a model analogous to human relationships. This relationship then calls people into the church, the community of the faithful.

This gathered fellowship, Protestants say, *is a priesthood of all believers*. Protestants find support for this belief in the New Testament and in the writings of the Reformers. In the first letter to Peter, the faithful are called a "chosen people, a royal priesthood" (1 Peter 2:9).

The priesthood of all believers means shared responsibility, shared worship, and shared authority. Each Christian has the responsibility to pray for, teach, and encourage every other Christian and to tell God's story to nonbelievers. The responsibility for a shared ministry belongs to all equally; it is not reserved for those who are ordained as priests or ministers. Each person offers his or her own worship to God and is a priest in that sense also. Corporate worship is the collectivity of the worship of each and every individual, not a common act of the church's worship in which individual worshippers are overshadowed. And each Christian shares with all others the same authority. No one has an inside track, and no one is relegated to outsider status in matters of religious authority. All are equal, because all have equal access to the Word.

Protestants, in other words, distinguish between priesthood and ministry. Baptism makes all Christians priests, some of whom are then called to preach, administer the sacraments, and govern as ministers. The minister is one who is chosen to serve a congregation, rather than one given special powers by God or special authority by the institution.

Lifestyle

What of *Protestant lifestyle*? This is not as easy to identify as are the specific beliefs, and we must make some distinctions. Most Protestants feel that their faith directs them squarely into the middle of the world. Martin Luther entered a monastery early in his life, believing that to be the surest way to salvation. He later left the monastery. Christian faith, say most followers of its Protestant branch, must be lived out in the midst of the world, not in retreat from it. God provides all the various arenas of human activity, such as marriage and family, vocation and work, civil government and politics, leisure and play. Each in its place is equally good, equally capable of being transformed by grace. People are called to live in the world, glorifying and obeying God in all things.

For Luther and his followers and for those who were a part of the English reformation, enjoying life and one another and the good things the earth had to offer was a way of praising God, although moderation was important. The Calvinists, on the other hand, were stricter. Restraint and sobriety were the hallmarks of their way of life. Too much enjoyment might lead one away from the proper path, and a certain sternness pervaded all they did. Some Protestants who believe that the world is saturated with evil and temptation separate themselves from it insofar as possible. Contact with the world and its pleasures brings with it the danger of spiritual contamination and should be avoided. This attitude remains today in some of the holiness churches.

For all Protestants, living morally, charity toward others, upholding the law, and being faithful in one's commitment to God and to the community of God's people are important virtues. Freed from its role in bringing about salvation, morality became a central feature of Protestants' lifestyle, as a joyful and obedient response to God's freely given gift of salvation.

Ritual

Two things stand out when we look at the *specific religious acts* of Protestants. Whereas the earlier church had observed seven sacraments (a practice which continues in the Catholic, Episcopal, and Orthodox Churches today), most Protestants have only two. *Baptism* and the *Lord's Supper*, or *Communion*, are the only two acts that Jesus specifically commanded his followers to carry on after his death, according to the Protestant reading of the New Testament. The age for baptism varies; many Protestants baptize babies, but not all do. Immersion, pouring, and sprinkling each have their advocates within the Protestant community. Likewise, the exact understanding of the Lord's Supper varies, but Protestants are united in their denial of its sacrificial character. Architecturally, its context is that of a table that echoes the one around which Jesus and the disciples are said to have gathered, rather than the altar of sacrifice. Some congregations pass the elements through the pews, and others come to the front of the church. The roles played by the minister and lay people vary somewhat. All use bread, leavened or unleavened; some use wine, and some use unfermented grape juice.

Here again, we can note both Protestantism's uniformity and its diversity. On the one hand, the Episcopal Church celebrates all seven of the traditional sacramental rituals. On the other, Baptists, although they observe the Lord's Supper and baptize believers, do not consider these acts to be sacraments. They are ordinances, important rites of the church with no sacramental character.

The second thing that stands out is the *importance of preaching*. The pulpit occupies a prominent place in Protestant churches, and the sermon is considered the focal point of worship. Ministers usually receive extensive training in biblical preaching, and a potential minister's skill as a preacher plays a large role in the selection process when it is time to call a new pastor. Because of the centrality of the Word made flesh, words become very significant in Protestantism.

Organization

Finally, what can we say about Protestant *organization* or structure, its institutional arrangement? First of all, there is no central authority or world wide organization. Each Protestant denomination is self-governing. Individual denominations have various organizational patterns. All, in one way or another, allow for and encourage active participation of the laity in the life of the church.

Another institutional feature is that most ministers are married rather than celibate. The rejection of monasticism goes together with a rejection of celibacy as the proper lifestyle for ministers. Some denominations, although not all, ordain women as well as men to the ministry.

MAINLINE PROTESTANTISM

Mainline or denominational Protestantism continues to reflect the religious sensibilities of many people in our culture. It has been an important aspect of American religion for a long time. Mainline Protestants are those churches that historically have tried to relate religion to the larger culture in positive ways.

Denominations recognize themselves as one religion among many. They appreciate their own distinctiveness but maintain friendly or at least tolerant relationships with other religions and with secular groups as well. They also understand religion as a part of the culture and one among many aspects of life with a legitimate claim on people's time and attention. They rely on birth more than evangelism to increase membership. Their outreach focuses on those without any church affiliation rather than on those who are members of another

---

Box 4-1

DISTINCTIVE PROTESTANT BELIEFS AND PRACTICES

Beliefs
1. The centrality and sole authority of the Bible in matters of religious truth
2. Salvation by grace through faith
3. The church as the gathering of believers
4. The priesthood of all believers

Lifestyle
1. For most, religion lived out in the midst of world
2. For some, separation from the world
3. Morality is of central importance

Ritual
1. Two sacraments: Baptism and the Lord's Supper/Holy Communion
2. Preaching is an important aspect of worship

Organization
1. No central authority
2. Clergy usually marry; women ordained in some denominations
3. Variety of organizational styles

---

group. They accept changes in teaching and practice as circumstances change and value diversity of interpretation within the denomination. In general, mainline Protestants accept a wide range of views on issues of personal morality, with most tending toward liberal views on matters such as abortion rights, human sexuality, and divorce. Worship is relatively routinized and is led by educated, professional clergy.[3]

Sociologists often describe denominations as forms of religious organization that are a stage between a sect and a church. Historically, this has been the case. However, denominations in the United States are a permanent form of religious organization, indeed the dominant form. This is a hallmark of the position they occupy in the social structure of religion in the United States.[4]

The mainline emphasizes cooperation, accommodation, and merger and tends to minimize distinctiveness. Large ecumenical organizations often provide a forum and a method for working together to achieve commonly shared goals. *The National Council of Churches of Christ in the United States* came into being in 1950 when a group of churches agreed to demonstrate in their organization the unity they believed the Christian church should have. It was the successor to the Federal Council of Churches, which had begun in 1908. It has become known as an organization of liberal Protestant denominations which includes many Eastern Orthodox and other Christian churches as well. Its position statements characteristically have affirmed social action and justice while downplaying evangelism and doctrinal precision. They have also taken positions that favor individual freedom over legal control in matters of personal morality. The magazine *Christian Century* is an important national voice for this perspective. It sums up its contents with the phrase, "faithful living, critical thinking."

Since the early 1960s, an ecumenical organization called the Consultation on Church Union (COCU) had worked to further ecumenical dialogue and participation among mainline Protestants. That organization disbanded in 2002 in order to form a new organization, *Churches Uniting in Christ (CUIC)*. Individual denominations in CUIC maintain their own identity and governance structures. They pledge to share the Lord's Supper together regularly and undertake shared mission efforts, which focus on combating racism.

> Churches Uniting in Christ is not a new structure. It is an officially recognized invitation to live with one another differently. Christians in the pews know that we belong together because we all belong to the same Lord. Churches Uniting in Christ is a framework for showing to the world what we truly are—the one Body of Jesus Christ.[5]

---

[3]Ronald L. Johnstone, *Religion in Society: A Sociology of Religion*, 8th ed. (Upper Saddle River, NJ: Prentice Hall, 2007), p. 64.

[4]Ibid., p. 344.

[5]What Is UIC? www.eden.edu/cuic/whatiscuic/whatiscuic.htm

Figure 4-3   The influence of mainline churches such as this one in Washington, D.C., has waned over the last decade. *(Photo by the author.)*

After we describe the major denominations that historically comprised the mainline, we will turn our attention to a more recent development within American Protestantism, the rise of evangelicalism.

DENOMINATIONAL DISTINCTIVENESS

Denominational differences play a much smaller role in religion in the United States than they did a few decades ago. At least in that sense, we are a postdenominational religious culture. Nonetheless, there remain distinguishing features of denominations that are important to those who are a part of them. It is to those that we now turn.

About 60 percent of adults in the United States are Protestants. About one-third of these are Baptists. Methodists account for between 10 and 15 percent and Lutherans for about 8 percent. About 4 percent are Presbyterians, and another 4 percent are Episcopalians. The last three groups described in this section each account for less than 1 percent of all Protestants.[6]

[6]http://www.thearda.com/quickstats/qs_29.asp

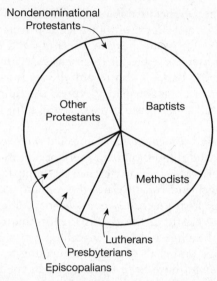

Figure 4-4   About 60 percent of adults in the United States are Protestants. About one-third of these are Baptists. Methodists account for between 10 and 15 percent and Lutherans for about 8 percent. About 4 percent are Presbyterians, and another 4 percent are Episcopalians. *(Data from the 2007 Pew Forum U.S. Religious Landscape Survey.)*

Baptists[7]

About three-fourths of Baptists in the United States are members of either the Southern Baptist Convention or the American Baptist Convention. The rest are part of one of many smaller Baptist groups or are independent Baptists. Baptists are the largest Protestant denominational family in the United States and second only to the Roman Catholic population in size.

Baptists first came to the colonies that would become the United States as part of an influx of Puritans fleeing from persecution in England during the reign of King Charles I (1625–1649). The accounts of early Baptist history are not in complete agreement, but the best-supported view is that the first Baptist church in America was founded by Roger Williams in 1639 at Providence, Rhode Island. Though not a Baptist for very long, Roger Williams had a profound influence on Baptist thought in America. He was an ardent defender of freedom of conscience and full religious liberty.

These views were unpopular and illegal in England, and those who held them faced threats of punishment and death, leading those who could to flee. The adoption of the Constitution of the United States and especially the Bill of Rights provided a climate in which Baptists as well as other groups could flourish. Substantial growth occurred and by the 1800s, the Baptists were the largest denomination in the young nation.

[7]American Baptist Churches: www.abc-usa.org; Southern Baptist Convention: http://www.sbc.net/

A sermon on the Cooperative Baptist Fellowship Web site expresses the essence of Baptist faith in the form of four related affirmations.[8] *Bible freedom* is central for Baptists. Christians have the freedom and the responsibility to read, study, and interpret the Bible for themselves. Neither creeds nor leaders can demand conformity. Baptists also regard all creeds as inadequate because they believe that no creed can adequately express the fullness of the Christian gospel and that the full significance of vital, living faith cannot be bound by any statement.

Baptists also affirm *soul freedom*. Also called *soul competency*, this means "the inalienable right and responsibility of every person to deal with God without the imposition of creed, the interference of clergy, or the intervention of civil government." Each individual relates to God and to Christ directly, personally. This is why Baptists practice *believer's baptism*, often regarded as a main distinguishing characteristic of the Baptist denominational family. Baptists believe baptism must be a free and knowledgeable act of the one participating in it, not something done on behalf of a child too young to understand. Church members are people who have been baptized upon their profession of faith in Jesus Christ as Lord and Savior. Many Baptists say that people are not Baptist by birth, but by rebirth.

For Baptists, *church freedom* means that each local congregation is self-governing, free to order its own internal life as it sees fit. Although Baptists cherish their congregational independence, they are interdependent, and these larger denominational organizations (frequently called *conventions*) are important for the whole fellowship of Baptists. The conventions also perform activities that cannot be maintained efficiently by local congregations alone, such as higher education, missionary, and social service work and retirement programs for church employees. Some local congregations, however, do refuse to join any larger group, maintaining their independence.

Also strongly related to the dominant themes of freedom and choice, *religious freedom* means freedom of, for, and from religion. Baptists are passionate supporters of religious liberty. Freedom of religion is an inherent right of the human soul, say the Baptists, because human beings are created to be both free and responsible. For freedom of religion to be a reality, religion and the civil government must be kept strictly apart. Baptists certainly are not alone in their support of religious liberty and the official separation of church and state. However, these concepts play an especially significant role in both Baptist history and present-day concern.

Baptists are the most likely of any of the Protestants to be fundamentalist in their religious outlook. Some, particularly in the South, in rural areas of the country, and in smaller, more conservative Baptist groups, also advocate a stricter personal morality than is the prevailing custom in the culture. Some of these groups also advocate a close alliance of church and state that is different from historic Baptist teaching.

[8]David W. Hull, "What Is a Baptist?" (http://www.thefellowship.info/About-Us/Who-We-Are), July, 2003. All quotations are from this sermon.

In worship, many Baptists emphasize openness to the leading of the Holy Spirit over the use of set format and ceremony. Their worship tends to be somewhere more emotional and evangelistic than that of the other denominational Protestants, although this is not always the case. The Lord's Supper is celebrated as a remembrance of Jesus's last supper with the disciples and as a memorial of his sacrificial death. Baptists do not believe that Jesus is present spiritually or symbolically in the elements.

Many denominations in the Baptist family of churches joined together in 1936 to sponsor the Baptist Joint Committee on Public Affairs in Washington. This committee reflects the Baptists' commitment to religious liberty. It is the only church office of any faith that works full time on religious liberty and church-state issues.

The Southern Baptists are distinguished by being considerably more conservative theologically than their American Baptist counterparts. For example, they affirm the importance of converting Jews to Christianity and of traditional roles for women and men. Beginning prior to 1980, fundamentalist leadership came to the foreground of the Southern Baptist Convention. The denominational agenda came to be focused on the necessity to read the Bible literally and to stand against abortion rights and gay rights, as well as against the ordination of women. Over time, this led to a rift in the Southern Baptist Convention. The Cooperative Baptist Fellowship is the largest of several groups that came about as those who felt disenfranchised after the fundamentalist ascendancy organized their dissent.[9]

More recently, the New Baptist Covenant group has formed. The New Baptist Covenant is "an informal alliance of more than 30 racially, geographically, and theologically diverse Baptist organizations from throughout North America that have come together to demonstrate a common commitment to the Gospel of Jesus Christ in word and deed."[10] Former Presidents Bill Clinton and Jimmy Carter, both Southern Baptists by upbringing, are among the founders of the new group. The group, convening its first national convention in 2008, seeks to direct the Baptist agenda away from its focus on abortion rights and gay rights. Instead, the group wants to emphasize social issues such as poverty, the need for health care, racial conflict, global religious conflict, and ecological degradation.[11]

Methodists[12]

The denominational family that we know today as the Methodists came to America from England. It began with John Wesley (1703–1791), a devout priest of the Church of England. Wesley was influenced by late seventeenth-century Pietism, a movement whose followers emphasized religious experience

[9]www.thefellowship.info/About-Us
[10]"New Baptist Covenant Talking Points," www.newbaptistcelebration.org
[11]Special thanks go to Chaplain Emeritus Robert Burton, Ball Memorial Hospital, for assistance with the New Baptist Covenant section.
[12]United Methodist Church, www.umc.org

and expression. Wesley organized small groups within the church. The group members were to pray and study the Bible together, watch over each other, and encourage one another to live the best Christian life of which they were capable. The name "Methodist" began as a term of contempt with which those who disagreed labeled this methodical approach to religious life. The movement was given additional strength by John Wesley's brother Charles, a prolific hymn writer who wrote over 6,000 hymns, many of which are still sung in Protestant and some Catholic churches today.

The Wesleys came to the colonies the first time in 1736. Methodism later spread rapidly because of the circuit-riding itinerant preachers for which the denomination was known for decades. The circuit riders went from place to place, taking their message to far more people than would have been possible had they stayed in one place. Eventually, Methodists outnumbered Anglicans (Church of England), Presbyterians, and even Baptists. Philip Embury organized the first Methodist society in the United States in about 1766, and the first official conference was held in 1773. The well-known Christmas Conference in 1784 organized the church as a fully functioning denomination.

In their beliefs, Methodists are distinguished by latitude and variety in what is acceptable. They affirm the central beliefs of Protestant Christianity while continuing Wesley's emphasis on experience over the details of doctrine. Their focus has always been more on how life is lived than on what is believed. Wesley taught that religion should be *of the heart* and that believers should trust in God's love and accept Christ's redemption in faith. It should be *of the will*, manifested in personal piety and devotion and steadfast love and concern for one's neighbor. Belief in the inner experience of religion and its social application in love and charity toward other people are still hallmarks of Methodism. Methodists summarize their interpretation of Christianity this way:

> John Wesley and the early Methodists were particularly concerned about inviting people to experience God's grace and to grow in their knowledge and love of God through disciplined Christian living. They placed primary emphasis on Christian living, on putting faith and love into action. This emphasis on what Wesley referred to as "practical divinity" has continued to be a hallmark of United Methodism today.[13]

Methodists cite four sources of religious truth. It is unique in its spelling out of these four, although other denominations use similar sources.

- The first and most important source is the *Bible*, primarily—but not exclusively—the New Testament.
- Methodists recognize their roots in the *tradition* of the theology and worship of the church.
- Methodists take *experience* into account—what has been found to work for people in particular circumstances.
- Faith must be in accord with what the mind says is rational and true.

[13]"Beliefs," www.umc.org

Methodists teach a threefold order of salvation that is based very closely on Wesley's teaching. *Justification* is the individual's acceptance of salvation as the free gift of God's grace. *Conversion* is regeneration and cleansing through the action of God. Finally, *sanctification* is the ongoing and increasing expression of holiness through a life of prayer and works that attempts to do something positive in the face of the ethical and social problems that prevail in one's time and place.

Although there are doctrinal standards set out by the denomination as a whole, each congregation and each individual is free to use them as they see fit. There is thus no precise answer to the question: What do Methodists believe? Their use of the four guidelines and the threefold order of salvation to interpret the basic Christian teachings, with the accent on the love and mercy of God, are emphases that began with John Wesley himself.

Methodists have also highlighted the social dimension of the Christian life. As with most Methodist teachings, this is a particular emphasis on a theme widely shared among Christians, as well as among many non-Christians. "We insist that personal salvation always involves Christian mission and service to the world. By joining heart and hand, we assert that personal religion, evangelical witness, and Christian social action are reciprocal and mutually reinforcing."[14]

John Wesley formulated three guidelines for members of his religious societies:

- Do no harm and avoid evil of all sorts.
- Do good of every possible sort and insofar as possible to all people.
- Observe the ordinances of God, including public worship, the ministry of the Word both read from Scripture and explained in preaching, participation in the Lord's Supper, family and private prayer and Bible reading, and fasting and abstinence.

With the exception of fasting and, in some instances, abstinence from alcohol, many Methodists' lives today can be described in the same way.

Like their beliefs, Methodists' patterns of worship vary widely. There is no required form of worship, although the *Book of Worship* gives suggested forms for Sunday services as well as for several special services, including those for the special occasions of the church year, the significant passages of human life, and a service of healing. Local congregations make use of it and modify it as they adapt it to their particular needs.

Methodists baptize people of all ages. Water is usually sprinkled on the head of the person being baptized. It is a rite of incorporation into the community of faith. Most Methodists believe that Christ is symbolically present to the faithful in the elements of bread and grape juice in the communion service in a "heavenly and spiritual manner." It is a solemn yet joyful service, taken with great seriousness by most members of this diverse group of Protestants.

[14]"Doctrinal Standards and Our Theological Task," The United Methodist Church Web site www.umc.org. The United Methodist Social Creed can be found on this site.

Like the Baptists, though to a somewhat lesser extent, Methodist organization is marked by its being a large family of related church groups. There are more than 20 separate religious bodies that claim the Methodist heritage. The United Methodist Church came into being in 1968 with the merger of the Methodist Church and the Evangelical United Brethren, both of which were themselves products of earlier mergers. The United Methodist Church includes approximately 80 percent of the Methodist population.

Besides the United Methodist Church, there are three large, predominantly black churches in the Methodist group: the African Methodist Episcopal Church, the African Methodist Episcopal Zion Church, and the Christian Methodist Episcopal Church. In addition, there are several smaller groups, the names of which often point to either their geographic region or a particular point of view, such as the Free Methodist Church of North America, the Southern Methodist Church, and the Evangelical Methodist Church. Others use the name *Wesleyan* to refer to their link with John Wesley and his teachings.

Lutherans[15]

A group of Lutherans—followers of Martin Luther's reforming movement in Germany—arrived in the Hudson's Bay area in 1619. They tried without success to found a colony. The first permanent settlement of Lutherans in what would become the United States began in 1638 when a group of Swedish colonists built a church on the shore of Delaware Bay. Later, in 1649, Dutch Lutherans organized New Amsterdam, New York. Lutheran growth in the colonies was hampered because each European group clung tightly to its national identity, but growth did occur. Henry M. Muhlenberg arrived in 1742 and in 1748 founded the first regional organization of Lutheran churches. He also led the writing of a constitution for American Lutheranism in 1792. Immigrants from central Europe and later Scandinavia enlarged the Lutheran population in the 1800s.

The Lutheran family of churches, including the large Evangelical Lutheran Church in American (ELCA) and the more conservative Lutheran Church-Missouri Synod, embrace the basic teachings and practices of Protestant Christianity as interpreted by the founder, Martin Luther, the German "Father of the Protestant Reformation." Some of the things that help to distinguish Lutherans from other Protestants is an emphasis on doctrine and liturgy:

> You don't hear Lutherans say, "It doesn't matter what you believe, just so you live right." Lutherans think that a way of living is a by-product of a way of believing. Since Lutheranism developed from Luther's intense experience of salvation through faith, it has been marked by a concern for faith as the essential part of religion. So Lutherans, more than most other Protestants, emphasize doctrine. They insist on unusually thorough education of their pastors and

---

[15]Evangelical Lutheran Church in America, www.elca.org; Missouri Synod Lutheran Church, www.lcms.org/

require young people to engage in a long period of study of Lutheran Catechism before being admitted to full church membership . . .

Lutherans observe the festival and seasons of the historic church year. In their churches, they have the altar, cross, candles, vestments, and other equipment of worship that most other Protestants discarded as "too Catholic." Lutherans believe that these forms of liturgy . . . are valuable because of their beauty and because, through them, we share in the experiences of the family of Christian worshippers of all ages.[16]

Unlike Baptists and Methodist Christians, Lutherans are a creedal denomination. For Lutherans, the Bible is the inspired Word of God, containing God's full revelation to humankind. It is the only source of true Christian teaching and the only rule and norm of Christian faith and life. The creeds have no authority in themselves but are of value only as they reveal the true Word of God. The three *ecumenical creeds* of the whole church are among them: the Apostles', Nicene, and Athanasian creeds. The *Augsburg Confession*, written in 1530, is a central statement of Lutheran essentials. Many of the important creeds of Lutheranism are drawn together in the *Book of Concord*, first published in 1580.

Lutherans teach that both the law and the gospel are necessary. The law is necessary to awaken sinners to their sinful condition and to arouse them to repentance and a longing for redemption. The gospel assures the repentant sinner of God's forgiveness in Christ. Thus, both must be held together. Like so much in Lutheranism, this belief follows Luther's own teaching closely.

One of the more conservative branches of the Lutheran family, the Missouri Synod Lutheran Church, sponsors a church-related school system in the United States that is second in size only to the Catholic school system. Like the Baptists, who are involved in the Christian school movement, these Lutherans want the education their children receive at school to reinforce and complement that which they receive at home and at church.

Lutheran worship follows a precise liturgical format that uses an adaptation of the worship of the early church as interpreted through Luther's modifications. Many hymns are used. Prominence is given to hymns written by Luther, who is often regarded as one of the greatest hymn writers the Christian church has ever known. He is probably best known for "A Mighty Fortress is Our God," which became a key hymn of the Reformation.

Preaching and the sacrament of Communion are both very important elements in Lutheran worship. The altar, a symbol of Christ's presence in the sacrament, and the pulpit, symbolizing God's presence through the Word, are equally important in their church architecture. This contrasts with many Protestant churches, in which the pulpit (perhaps along with a lectern from which the Bible is read) vastly overshadows the altar, which is frequently a simple table.

---

[16]G. Elson Ruff, "What is a Lutheran?" in *Religions of America: Ferment and Faith in an Age of Crisis*, ed. Leo Rosten (New York: Simon and Schuster, 1975), p. 159. This older statement is still accurate.

Lutheran congregations are encouraged to include Communion as a part of each Sunday's worship. The distinctive Lutheran view holds that the risen Christ is truly present in the bread and wine. The bread and wine continue to exist as bread and wine, but along with this, Christ is actually present. This teaching is sometimes referred to as the *Real Presence*. Lutherans believe this is what Christ promised at the Last Supper.

The Evangelical Lutheran Church in America, the largest Lutheran body, is firmly within the sphere of mainline Protestantism. As the religious consensus in the United States has become more conservative, religious groups that would have been outside the consensus a decade or two ago are now within it. The Missouri Synod Lutheran Church is one of two major evangelical and conservative Protestant groups in the United States that is now a part of the broad consensus, along with the Southern Baptist Convention. Neither completely fits the description of mainline Protestant churches. For example, both have remained outside the National Council of Churches. However, their size and the increased conservatism of the consensus warrant their mention here.

Presbyterians[17]

What is now the Presbyterian Church began in Scotland, founded by John Knox, who followed the theology and church organizational structure taught by the reformer John Calvin. The Reverend Francis Makemie, known as the "father of American Presbyterianism," came to the colonies in the late 1600s. Makemie founded the first American Presbytery (regional governing body) around 1705 in Philadelphia (historians do not fully agree on the date, but 1705 is widely supported).

These early Presbyterians, most of whom were highly educated for their time and well cultured soon assumed positions of considerable influence, so that their importance came to outweigh their numbers. They were the most influential religious group in the rebellion of the colonies, which led the English House of Commons to ruefully dub the uprising the "Presbyterian rebellion." At least 14 signers of the Declaration of Independence were Presbyterians.

Presbyterian churches are distinguished by their theology, which usually called "reformed," and their form of church government, which is strongly connectional, so much so that this type of church organization is sometimes called *presbyterian* (lowercase *p* to distinguish it from the denomination). The Presbyterian Church (U.S.A.) is the largest embodiment of reformed theology among churches in the United States. Another denomination in the reformed theological tradition is the United Church of Christ, described later in this chapter.

---

[17]Presbyterian Church in the U.S.A., www.pcusa.org

A recent statement about the uniqueness of the Presbyterian Church describes its theology and organization:

> Presbyterians are distinctive in two major ways: they adhere to a pattern of religious thought known as Reformed theology and a form of government that stresses the active, representational leadership of both ministers and church members . . . Reformed theology . . . emphasizes God's supremacy over everything and humanity's chief purpose as being to glorify and enjoy God forever.[18]

Like Lutheranism, Presbyterianism is a creedal faith. A group of religious leaders gathered at Westminster Abbey from 1643 to 1648 to write the Westminster Confession of Faith, as well as the Larger and Shorter Catechisms that are based on it. A later *Book of Confessions* (1967) contains these creeds and confessions. Following a merger in 1983, a new statement of faith was written for the newly formed Presbyterian Church (U.S.A.). It is not intended to stand apart from the other confessions of faith included in the *Book of Confessions* but to continue them.

Biblical and theological interpretation among Presbyterians ranges from fairly conservative and literal to more liberal and figurative. The larger denominations within the Presbyterian family of denominations tend toward the liberal, while the smaller ones, many of which grew out of doctrinal disputes, tend to be more conservative.

Presbyterian worship is usually carried out with great dignity and order. It is stately, befitting the worship of a sovereign God. Presbyterian worship is usually more intellectual than emotional and gives the worshiper an experience of logical thoughts, ordered behavior, and a restrained atmosphere. Presbyterians believe that worship is not something done for God, who does not need to be worshipped, nor is it something done for the people themselves. It is pre-eminently a part of God's work in the world, one of the means whereby God interacts with the created order. It is centered on the sermon, including the exposition of the Scriptures and the ordered presentation of the great truths of the Christian faith as Presbyterians understand them. The sermon has mainly a teaching function. Presbyterian ministers are formally called *teaching elders* to distinguish them from the *ruling elders*, whose function is church governance.

Presbyterians believe very strongly that children, along with their parents, are members of the "household of faith," and they baptize people of all ages. While baptism is not thought to be necessary for salvation, it is considered a sacrament and is important as the rite of incorporation into the church. It is usually performed by sprinkling.

Presbyterians do not accept either the real presence of Christ in the elements of Communion or the view that Communion is only a memorial. In the elements of bread and (usually) unfermented grape juice, Christ is spiritually present and is known by faith. Being in a proper frame of mind and spirit to receive Communion is important to Presbyterians, for whom this is a very solemn service of worship.

---

[18]Presbyterian Church (U.S.A.), www.pcusa.org/101/101-distinct.htm

The Presbyterian Church (U.S.A.) was formed in 1983 by a merger of the Presbyterian Church in the United States (the southern branch) and the United Presbyterian Church in the U.S.A. (the northern branch). In addition, there are several smaller groups that are part of this denominational family, such as the Cumberland Presbyterian Church, the Orthodox Presbyterian Church, and the Reformed Presbyterian Church. Most of these smaller branches are more conservative to fundamentalist in their thinking and are not regarded as part of the mainline.

Episcopalians[19]

The first Episcopal worship in the New World probably took place in 1578, when the Reverend Francis Fletcher, who had sailed with Sir Francis Drake, raised a cross and read a prayer of thanksgiving on the shore of what is now California. The Church of England came to the colonies with some of the very first explorers. The first settlement was at Jamestown, Virginia, in 1607. Soon, several of the southeastern coastal colonies, such as Georgia, the Carolinas, and Virginia, were predominantly Anglican (another name for the Church of England). Anglicanism frequently had official government support in the Southeast. The church in the colonies remained firmly attached to the church in England for sometime.

The church suffered greatly and was nearly destroyed by the Revolutionary War. Although most of its members and clergy alike supported the Revolution, or at least did not support the Loyalists, it was branded the Tory Church, and many clergy fled to England and Canada. A reorganized church came out of the chaos. At its General Conference in 1783, it took the name *Protestant Episcopal Church* to indicate its separation from the English monarchy. A constitution for the new American church was adopted in 1789, and the *Book of Common Prayer* was revised for American use. The Protestant Episcopal Church was now fully independent and self-governing.

The Episcopal Church is regarded as a bridge between Protestantism and Catholicism and is sometimes said to be *Protestant in belief* while being *Catholic in worship*. Some interpreters describe it as "a different way of being Christian than Protestantism, Roman Catholicism, or Eastern Orthodoxy."[20] It accepts the Apostles' and Nicene creeds as accurate reflections of the teachings of the Bible. *The Thirty-Nine Articles of Religion* is a distinctive statement of Episcopal belief in the United States. The Episcopal Church accepts a wide range of opinion in matters of theology and doctrine. It stresses the importance of "loyalty in essentials and liberty in nonessentials," and the smaller points of theological difference fall into the nonessential category.

The *Book of Common Prayer* is the product of the service books used in the church throughout the centuries and contains orders for Sunday worship and

---

[19]Episcopal Church, www.episcopalchurch.org/
[20]David L. Holmes, "The Anglican Tradition and the Episcopal Church," in *Encyclopedia of the American Religious Experience*, vol. 1, ed. Lippy and Williams, p. 392.

for many other services of worship. A contemporary American revision that was approved in 1980 was the first major revision since 1928. The use of the *Book of Common Prayer* for worship is generally regarded as more important in defining Episcopalianism is than is doctrine.[21]

Most Episcopal priests are married and whether to marry or not is left up to the individual. Women can be ordained priests. The Episcopal Church does have a few groups of nuns and monks who take the traditional three vows of poverty, chastity, and obedience.

The sacraments are at the center of Episcopal worship. Episcopalians believe that the sacraments are "visible signs and effectual means," having power in and of themselves to convey God's grace, and that belief sets Episcopalians apart from other Protestants.

The principal act of Christian worship on Sundays and on other significant church festivals is the Holy Eucharist, which is similar to the Catholic Mass. The Eucharistic service is frequently called a mass. *The Eucharist* is the most frequently used term for Holy Communion among Episcopalians. *They believe that Christ is actually present within the elements of bread and wine*, although they refrain from trying to express or explain what they consider to be a holy mystery.

Infants, as well as children and adults, are baptized, usually by sprinkling. Baptism is believed to cleanse from sin, unite the person with Christ in Christ's death and resurrection, bring about rebirth by the action of the Holy Spirit, and make people adopted children of God, the Divine Parent. These two sacraments are understood to have been instituted by Jesus as the chief sacraments of the church.

Episcopalians also believe that other traditionally important rites, including confirmation, reconciliation of a penitent (also called confession and forgiveness), marriage, ordination to the priesthood, and the anointing of the sick, have sacramental significance. The importance placed on the seven traditional sacraments is distinctive for this group of Protestant Christians.

The word *Episcopal* in the name of the church refers to the importance of bishops in its governing structure. Bishops' authority is believed to have been handed down across the centuries in an unbroken line of succession. They trace this back to an account in Matthew 16, in which Jesus is said to have given Saint Peter the keys to the kingdom of heaven. Usually, the clergy person is called a priest. In recent years, the Episcopal Church has involved lay people more at all levels. Each congregation elects a *vestry* to govern the local church. The spiritual head of the Episcopal Church worldwide is the Archbishop of Canterbury, England. Although the American church is self-governing, its members honor him as the head of the whole Church of England.

In the 1970s, the Episcopal Church voted to ordain women to the priesthood and also revised the *Book of Common Prayer.* These two actions gave rise to the Anglican Church of North America (or Anglican Catholic Church; both names are used), dedicated to upholding traditional Episcopalianism. There are also several other small Episcopal denominations.

---

[21]An online copy of the *Book of Common Prayer* can be found at www.bookofcommonprayer.net/

The Episcopal Church is the Church of England in the United States. Although it has spiritual ties to England, it is independent. Its churches combine wide latitude and tolerance in matters of belief, with uniformity in dramatic, liturgical worship that is centered on the seven sacraments.

Other Mainline Protestants

We now turn to a consideration of three more Protestant denominations that are not as large as the major five but which clearly fit into the category of mainline Protestantism. These include the United Church of Christ, the Christian Church (Disciples of Christ), and the Friends Yearly Meeting, also known as the Quakers.

The United Church of Christ[22]   The beliefs and practices of the United Church of Christ are very similar to those of other mainline Protestants. A statement of faith adopted in 1959 loosely follows the format of the Apostles' Creed, with sections on God the Father, Jesus Christ the Son, and the Holy Spirit. Concluding paragraphs discuss the nature of the church and the role of Christians and affirm the two Protestant sacraments and eternal life in the Kingdom of God. The statement of faith is not binding on any local congregation nor is it used as a test of faith for individual members. It is regarded as a *testimony* of faith, never as a *test* of faith.[23]

This denomination is a strong supporter of ecumenism, and, with other consensus Protestants, is a member of both the World and National Councils of Churches. The United Church of Christ is one of the most socially liberal and activist churches in the United States.

The Christian Church (Disciples of Christ)[24]   The Christian Church (Disciples of Christ) is one of the communities of faith that grew out of what we now call the *Restoration Movement* in American Christianity. It is the only one of the denominations in this chapter that began in America.

Prior to the Civil War, religious thinkers in many parts of the country were dismayed over the divisions within the Christian churches. They believed that the Bible taught that there was to be but one Christianity, yet there were many churches. Often, the relationships between these churches were not friendly, marred by arguments over creeds and church structures. The Restoration Movement sought to end these divisions.

A passionate desire for Christian unity lay behind the Restoration Movement. Everyone in the movement believed that the multitude of divisions in the Christian Church was offensive to Jesus's intentions for his followers. They believed that the unity that they sought could be achieved by a return to the New Testament as the only guide to faith and practice, down to the smallest detail of church government. An early slogan, "No creed but Christ," highlights their belief in the importance of avoiding humanly invented creeds.

[22]United Church of Christ, www.ucc.org
[23]This statement can be read at www.ucc.org/faith/faith.htm
[24]Disciples of Christ, www.disciples.org

Congregational worship is dignified and rather formal, with both instrumental and vocal music. Disciples emphasize both Baptism and the Lord's Supper:

> Two really important things to Disciples are communion and baptism. We celebrate communion, or the Lord's Supper, each time we get together to praise God. We like it when there are a lot of different people at communion. We believe that Christ heals the pain of human separation around the communion table.

> People who become Christians in a Disciples congregation do a couple of things. First, they say "I believe that Jesus is the Christ, the Son of the Living God, and I accept him as my personal Savior." Then, usually on another day, they are baptized—that is, they are dunked fully under water in a small pool right there in the church. When they come up they are new people in Christ and their congregation pledges to support them and help them grow into a deeper relationship with God through Jesus Christ. People who have been baptized in another way in another Christian tradition are welcome.[25]

The Restorationists believed that each local congregation should be autonomous or self-governing. They held that each local gathering of believers was, in fact, the church. A strong national structure has been developed, beginning in 1968, but the local congregation remains the basic unit.

***The Friends*[26]**   The Religious Society of Friends, also known as the *Quakers*, is the last community of faith we will consider in this chapter. The name "Friends" comes from John 15:15 in the Christian New Testament, in which Jesus says to his followers, "I have called you friends." The Friends began in England in the 1600s.

The Quakers or Society of Friends are distinctive in a number of ways.[27] They do not regard the Bible as the final, complete revelation of God. Revelation continues as the Holy Spirit speaks to persons and groups through the words of scripture. Each individual is endowed with the *Inner Light*, a measure of Christ's own light and truth. For this reason, individual conscience is inviolable. People receive guidance and direction from God by listening for God's voice within in contemplative silence. Everyone—both genders, all races, nationalities, sexual orientations, economic classes, ages—is equal before God and thus ought to be dealt with as equals by human beings as well. All of life is sacramental; outward sacraments are not necessary and are not observed in Quaker meetings for worship. The distinctively Quaker way of worship is the unprogrammed format, in which worshippers sit in silence and anyone may speak as led by the Spirit to do so. Friends also follow the practice of waiting in silence when making decisions in meetings, seeking the "sense of the meeting." This is not just a search for consensus; rather, it is seeking for God's will to be expressed through the meeting. Other meetings of Friends worship in ways that resemble other Protestant services.

---

[25]Christian Church (Disciples of Christ), www.disciples.org/general/whoare.htm
[26]Based on information found on the Web sites of the Friends General Conference (www.fgcquaker.org) and the Friends United Meeting (www.fum.org).
[27]Friends General Conference, www.fgcquaker.org; Friends United Meeting, www.fum.org

One of the most distinctive emphases of the Friends is their *peace testimony*, their opposition to all war, and their commitment to nonviolence in every aspect of life. A late colleague of mine, for example, whose outlook was strongly influenced by Quaker teachings, helped make us all more aware of the violence implied in certain expressions that are very common in our language, such as "I could have killed him!" or even "That was a killer exam!" The Friends' commitment to the sanctity of individual conscience, however, leaves room for participation in the military for those to whom it seems right, and there are Quaker chaplains in military service.

Although the "thee" and "thou" of Quaker plain speech and the simplicity of traditional Quaker dress have largely disappeared, the Friends remain distinctive in their emphasis on the Inner Light and their witness to peace, as well as their unprogrammed style of worship.

EVANGELICALS: THE NEW CENTER IN AMERICAN PROTESTANTISM

As noted above, denominational differences play a much smaller role in religion in the United States than they did a few decades ago. American religion has been "restructured" along a different set of lines. As sociologist Robert Wuthnow points out, the "symbolic boundaries have changed."[28] Evangelicalism has emerged over the last several decades as the new predominant style of being Protestant Christian in the United States. Notable historian of religion Dr. Martin Marty announced to the Association of Evangelicals in the spring of 2003, "You've won. You, the evangelicals, have won." It was an acknowledgement from a scholar more frequently associated with the traditional mainline that evangelicals had become the new center.[29] It is now one of the most prominent, if not the most prominent, expression of Protestant Christianity in the United States.

Evangelical Protestantism

Descriptions of evangelical Christianity vary somewhat, but nearly every list would include these characteristics.

- Evangelicals take the Bible as the objective, authoritative word of God. It is inerrant, although not all of it is to be taken literally. There is metaphor and poetry in the Bible, but the truth contained in it is without error.
- The only way to salvation is through faith in Jesus Christ. Jesus is the only way, not one among other ways.
- Along with this, evangelicals tend to emphasize the death and resurrection of Jesus for the forgiveness of human sin more than the moral example of Jesus's life.
- Evangelicals emphasize the necessity of conversion, of a turning of one's life toward Jesus. Although it may be recognized only in retrospect, this specific turn is usually regarded as a necessary element of religious life. Being born again and asking Jesus

---

[28]Robert Wuthnow, *The Restructuring of American Religion: Society and Faith Since World War II* (Princeton, NJ: Princeton University Press, 1988), p. 10.

[29]Cited in an interview with Richard Cizik of the National Association of Evangelicals, www.pbs.org/wgbh/pages/frontline/shows/jesus/interviews/cizik.huml (2003).

Figure 4-5   Evangelical Christians now comprise the majority of Christians in the United States. *(Mark Richards Photo Edit Inc.)*

to come into their lives establishes a warmly personal relationship with God that far exceeds anything they might have experienced prior to their conversion. Even those who had been active church members say that they became a Christian at that point in time. They distinguish sharply between being a member of a church and being a Christian. Usually, it is understood that virtually all Christians are church members, but not all church members are Christians. The emphasis on an identifiable conversion experience goes back to Puritanism. The Puritans required testimony of such an experience as a condition of full church membership. Among all Christians, about half can identify such an experience in their religious lives.

- The word *evangelical* comes from a Greek word that means good news, and evangelicals place great importance on sharing this good news with other people. Witnessing, sharing their faith, or evangelizing is felt to be a mandate from God.
- Finally, evangelicals tend toward conservative moral positions, especially on issues of personal morality such as abortion rights, gay rights, marriage and divorce, and school prayer. They uphold what they interpret as traditional family and social values.

These concerns are echoed in the first of a list of values statements affirmed by the National Association of Evangelicals, the largest and most prominent organization linking evangelical churches, organizations, and individuals in the United States.

"We believe in a biblical faith demonstrated by loyalty to the Word of God and commitment to proclaiming its message worldwide . . . Together we stand on God's revelation in Scripture of redemption alone in Jesus Christ the son of God, by grace through faith.[30]

[30]www.nae.net/

Evangelicalism is not new in the United States. It has been a part of the religious landscape at least since revivals that began in the eighteenth century. In the mid-1700s, the northeastern and the mid-Atlantic colonies were the site of the first of a number of religious revivals that swept through America. Scholars have named this first outpouring of revival enthusiasm the Great Awakening.

The revivalist's messages were simple and straightforward. They concentrated on the outlines of the Christian message as Puritans interpreted it: People are lost, trapped in sin, without any hope of saving themselves. God's free offer of salvation through grace and faith in Jesus must be accepted, because there is no other hope. Acceptance of God's gracious offer brings release from the terrible anxiety of the sin-stricken soul. The preaching style of Jonathan Edwards, George Whitefield, and other Great Awakening preachers assured that their hearers would be moved both intellectually and emotionally. Intense, abrupt experiences that people interpreted as conversion from their old lives to new lives in grace became the standard by which people's response was judged.

The Second Awakening occurred on the frontier in the 1800s. The basic theology and the simplicity of the message remained the same. The frontier population, however, was less educated and much less stable geographically; these factors brought about a change in revival preaching. The Second Awakening revivalists developed a style that was more emotional and less intellectual than that of their predecessors. A strong appeal to people's emotions and equally emotional responses were very common. Preachers pressed their hearers for immediate conversion, because many in the audience might well move on in a matter of hours.

The simple message and the emotional style of the Awakenings continue in modern-day revivals. Testifying to one's faith and the centrality of the conversion experience are still important aspects of the evangelical way of being religious.

Billy Graham (b. 1918) is the foremost contemporary exemplar of the evangelical and revivalist tradition in American religion and is the most public symbol of the style of evangelicalism that began in the 1950s and continues today. His radio program, *The Hour of Decision*, began in 1950, and he was soon familiar to television viewers as well. The core of Graham's message is traditional: Repent and surrender to Jesus as Lord and Savior. However, his preaching also addresses social problems and national sins. He has spoken out strongly against racism and classism in the United States and supports nuclear disarmament. His style of presentation is restrained and theologically informed. He established a close working relationship with the White House in the 1950s during the Eisenhower administration, a relationship that has continued with Eisenhower's successors. Graham has since passed the responsibility for his ministry to his son, Franklin Graham.

Evangelicals usually distinguish themselves from fundamentalists, who are their closest ideological neighbors. Most evangelicals regard fundamentalists as too militant, too exclusive, and as having too low an opinion of modern scholarship. Evangelicals, although certainly conservative in both theology and ethics, do accept some compromise. The new style of evangelicalism is characterized by a cautious acceptance of some of the insights of biblical scholarship, while maintaining that the Bible is inspired by God. Evangelicals affirm the generally agreed-upon doctrines of Christianity in their traditional forms. Historically, evangelicals have emphasized personal morality, and this emphasis remains. There is a new spirit of sociopolitical involvement, too, that replaces the tendency of earlier evangelicals to remain outside the rough-and-tumble of political action.

Loci of Protestant Evangelicalism

There are now three principal loci of evangelicalism within American Protestantism: The last several decades have seen a dramatic growth in evangelical churches, many of them independent of denominational structures. There are also predominantly evangelical congregations within traditionally mainline denominations. Third, virtually every mainline congregation has within it at least a substantial minority, if not a majority, of evangelical individuals. Evangelical churches are not a recent development. What has transformed the shape of American Protestantism is the substantial presence of evangelical Christians in the traditionally mainline churches.

The Growth of Evangelicalism

There are several reasons usually cited to explain the growth of evangelical Christianity, in the form of both evangelical churches and evangelicals within the mainline. Some of these are social and demographic factors; others have to do with the nature of both evangelical religion and that of the traditional mainline. First, those that are sociological and demographic in nature: From its early beginnings in the rural South, evangelicalism moved northward and became more urban. With that geographic shift came higher education and greater affluence, which eventually drew evangelicals into mainstream culture. Demographically, traditional mainline congregations have shrunk in size. Birth rates have not replaced members lost to death. Meanwhile, birth rates among evangelicals have continued to climb. It has proven difficult for the mainline denominations to hold on to their adult members, as well. Some have become evangelicals, while others have embraced some other form of spirituality or become religiously unaffiliated. Yet another factor is the growth of more generalized social conservatism in the United States. As noted above, evangelical Christianity typically teaches conservative views on personal moral issues such as human sexuality and what are perceived as traditional family values. Religiously, it is a good match for the growth of social conservatism, which it has both benefited from and helped foster.

The increase of social conservatism among the voting public in the United States was in part what led to the election of George W. Bush to the Presidency in 2000. Most if not all U.S. presidents have used religious rhetoric in their official speeches; this is part of what constitutes American civil religion, described in Chapter 2. George Bush was a president whose use of religious rhetoric and symbolism is much more explicitly evangelical than any president who had preceded him. As one political analyst notes, "President Bush is well known for the religious references in his off-the-cuff remarks as well as in his prepared speeches. A lot of this comes from Bush himself. He really does understand his life in religious terms, and often talks about his faith quite personally." He goes on to say that Bush is distinctive in that he "connects his personal faith and his personal experience much more directly than many other presidents do . . . Most American presidents simply invoke religious symbols; President Bush advocates on behalf of religious symbols."[31] Bush also exemplifies the presence of evangelical Christians in mainline denominations. He is a United Methodist by affiliation; he also talks freely about having had a born again experience that remains an important milestone in his life. The eight years of his presidency were a heartening example for evangelicals as a whole.

Another feature of the George W. Bush presidency is worth noting in this regard. Franklin Graham, son of well-known and respected evangelical leader Billy Graham and heir to his ministry, gave the invocation at the 2000 inaugural. A religious leader usually does so. What made this invocation distinctive was that Franklin Graham used the name of Jesus, the first time that had been done in an inaugural invocation, in what concluded as a distinctively Christian prayer:

> May this be the beginning of a new dawn for America as we humble ourselves before you and acknowledge you alone as our Lord, our Saviour and our Redeemer. We pray this in the name of the father, and of the son, the Lord Jesus Christ, and of the Holy Spirit. Amen.[32]

In a culture in which religious affiliation is wholly voluntary, religions that offer a more compelling vision often do better than those whose identity is less clearly defined. Typically, evangelicals have been much clearer about who they are and precisely what they believe than the mainline has been. This is not a matter of who's right and who's wrong, theologically speaking, but of who's clearer in how they present it. As the mainline has become less theologically distinct, evangelicalism has become more so. As a recent blog by a self-identified liberal graduate student in religious studies put it, "If you have a preference for religion, and for strong religion in particular, the evangelical product is probably more attractive. Evangelicalism offers strong and compelling explanations, strong and meaningful interpersonal connections, exclusive benefits, and so on.[33] Evangelical Christianity offers its adherents a clearly defined vision, with the added assurance that it is God's own way in this world and the path to eternal life with God after death. This point is emphasized in a similar way by well-known analyst of religion and politics John Green, who

---

[31]Interview with John Green, www.pbs.org/wgbh/pages/frontline/shows/jesus/interviews/green.html
[32]http://www.saintsalive.com/newsletters/jan2001.html
[33]Stephen Merino, http://reasonandreverence.blogspot.com/2007/07/decline-of-mainline-protestantism-what.html

notes that stronger religious communities find it easier to maintain themselves, to educate their youngsters, to keep those youngsters committed as they mature, and to attract new members.[34]

Most evangelical churches are not members of the National Council of Churches, because they believe that the strong desire for cooperation that led to the formation of the National Council also led to a compromise of biblical faith. Many, however, are members of the National Association of Evangelicals. *Christianity Today* magazine articulates this point of view. It describes itself as "a magazine of evangelical conviction."

The traditional Protestant mainline rose to its position of religious hegemony prior to the 1960s. Over the next several decades, it declined. There is some evidence that this decline may have stabilized, with the mainline now occupying a marginal but stable position in the culture. As Randall Balmer, an astute observer of the interplay between the mainline and evangelicalism in American culture, observes, this marginalization may not be a bad thing for the Protestant mainline. The mainline emerged in the 1960s and 1970s as a prophetic voice on social issues such as "civil rights, the war in Vietnam, and women's equality." It spoke, however, "from the safety of the establishment," confident in its cultural status, denominational connections, and funding. Now, its position in the culture both forces and allows it to "speak truly from the margin."

> Speaking from the periphery of American religious life affords the opportunity to be truly prophetic on such issues as race, gender, and sexual identity. But it also means that mainline Protestants must resign themselves to minority status and thereby surrender any aspirations they have to the cultural power they enjoyed in the 1950s.[35]

Evangelicals in Mainline Churches

The rising evangelical presence within mainline churches is reflected in the formation of evangelical organizations within these churches and of a larger organization that links them together. Members of these organizations are committed to remaining in their churches rather than leaving, working for a return to more traditional teaching and practice. The Association for Church Renewal links them together. It focuses "on common concerns and issues" that unite the evangelicals within the mainline, such as "orthodox faith, holy living, moral relativism, marriage and family, human sexuality, neo-pagan worship, God-language, the free exercise of religion at home and abroad, the sanctity of life, and world mission and evangelism." It also seeks to "promote orthodox leadership" within the mainline churches.[36]

---

[34]Interview with John Green, www.pbs.org/wgbh/pages/frontline/shows jesus/interviews/green.thm., 2003, retrieved 10/25/2007.
[35]Randall Balmer, "Trading Places: Evangelical and Mainline Protestantism at the Turn of the Twenty-first Century," *Word and World*, vol. XIX, No. 1 (Winter, 1998), p. 9.
[36]www.ird-renew.org

Most of the evangelical organizations within individual denominations publish magazines for their constituents and maintain Web sites as well. A survey of these sites indicates the range of their concerns.

- Anglicans United (Episcopalian) states its purpose as "to grow a faithful church for the promulgation of the Gospel while forming Christian disciples in the evangelical, catholic, and reformed Anglican Way."[37]
- American Baptist Evangelicals (American Baptist) includes among key spiritual values biblical authority and literacy, Jesus as the only way to salvation, and a focus on winning people to Christ.[38]
- The Biblical Witness Fellowship (United Church of Christ) "formed in alarmed response to decades of continual denominational decline that has resulted from the UCC's theological surrender to the moral and spiritual confusion of contemporary culture."[39]
- The Disciple Heritage Fellowship (Disciples of Christ) affirms Jesus as the only way to salvation, the unique authority of the Bible, and evangelism of the world as the primary goal of the church.[40]
- The Evangelical Lutheran Confessing Fellowship (Evangelical Lutheran Church in America) states its purpose this way: "In recent years, traditional Christian churches have seen an unprecedented erosion of the commonly held beliefs of the one true Faith in Jesus Christ. . . . The ELCF was created to stand against these false teachings."[41]
- Good News (United Methodist Church) has among its stated goals encouraging evangelical witness within the United Methodist Church, "to proclaim biblical truth," and to "sound the alarm about unbiblical philosophies."[42]
- The Presbyterian Layman (Presbyterian Church U.S.A.): An article on their Web site charges that the church has a "decapitated Christology [teaching about Christ], a theology that has caved in to a culture of hopeless relativisms" in which truth "has been reduced to mere opinions and morality adds up to nothing more than your own particular set of preferences."[43]

As these brief statements from evangelical organization within the mainline demonstrate, evangelicals disagree with most of what the mainline stands for. Some have elected to leave. Others have chosen to remain and work for change within the mainline itself.

WOMEN IN PROTESTANTISM

Before you read this section, take a moment to reflect on your own experience. Have you thought about the role and status of women in religious organizations? What is your impression? If you attend or have attended worship services,

[37]www.anglicansunited.com
[38]www.abeonline.org
[39]www.biblicalwitness.org
[40]www.disciple-heritage.org
[41]www.elcf.org
[42]www.goodnewsmag.org
[43]Kibler, Craig M., "Churches Staying in the PCUSA are about Changing the World," October 31, 2007, www.layman.org

what roles did women play? Have you heard a female minister or pastor preach? If so, how did you feel about that? If you had a personal problem that you wanted to discuss with a religious counselor, would it matter to you if that person were a woman or a man? Why or why not? How much do you think your answers to these questions are influenced by your own gender?

Tradition and Change

A lot of attention has been paid to the role of status of women in American religious organizations. Religion has often limited women to traditional female roles. It has often supported and encouraged the belief that women's proper roles were those of wives and mothers. The home was often believed to be women's only proper sphere of action. Until the last half of the twentieth century, women usually were unable to be ordained as ministers, pastors, rabbis, or priests in most of America's communities of faith. Nor have they been able to be deacons, elders, or other lay officers of their congregations. Religion has also offered encouragement and comfort to those women who themselves support traditional female roles in the face of cultural demands for change.

But this is only one side of the story, because religion has also been a catalyst for change. Women have found encouragement in the scriptures of both Judaism and Christianity to work toward full equality and rights. Churches and synagogues have supported movements for women's rights. Although many communities of faith denied official roles to women, in others, men and women functioned as equals. It is very important to evaluate the role that religion has played in the context of its own time. Feminist theologian Rosemary Radford Ruether cautions us that if we approach history from the viewpoint of our own time, religion's tendency to support traditional roles will loom larger than it actually was, and we will be in danger of missing the extent to which religion has encouraged change.[44]

Women's Responses

Women, and men who share their concerns about continuing male predominance in Protestantism, respond in a number of ways. The tradition-supporting response remains common, whether in an active or passive mode. People remain in their religious institutions and do not challenge practices and policies. For example, women continue to worship in services that use gender-exclusive language, either actively affirming that tradition or simply not challenging it.

Others remain in their religious traditions and work actively for change. One approach entails renewed examination of the scriptures and traditions of a group from the standpoint of women's experience to reconstruct beliefs, rituals, and history that have been obscured and neglected by male history and interpretation having been taken as universal. For example, while parts of the

---

[44]Rosemary Radford Ruether and Rosemary Skinner Keller, eds., *Women and Religion in America, volume I: The Nineteenth Century* (San Francisco: Harper and Row Publishers, 1989), p. x.

Christian New Testament have been used to justify "keeping women in their place," other passages can be shown to challenge that view in favor of greater equality. Other men and women in those groups that do not ordain women to the clergy work actively to change that policy. Still others remain active in their community of faith but supplement that involvement with participation in a variety of distinctively women's spirituality groups in which clearly feminist ideas and rituals are embraced. For most people within a community of faith, its scriptures and history have to be taken into account. They may have to be reinterpreted, parts may simply have to be discarded but scripture and history set the boundaries and must be dealt with.

It is especially important to note that *most* of the women (and men) who feel alienated from their communities of faith are not leaving but are "defecting in place," choosing the path of working actively for change within their local, regional, and national organizations.[45]

However, there are those for whom their traditions seem so alienating and bankrupt that they do make the equally difficult decision to abandon them altogether. Some become secular persons, without religious affiliation or participation. Others develop their own spirituality essentially in solitude, working out values, ideas, and sometimes rituals that provide spiritual sustenance without a group context. Still others find their way to, or form, women's spirituality groups that focus on goddess worship or espouse a nongendered view of the sacred.

Continuing Issues

While great strides have been made to redress the grievances that feminists have with their communities of faith and the institutions that undergird them, many feminists beleive, a lot more needs to be done. For many consensus Protestants, women's ordination and participation in the higher ranks of church leadership are a limited reality. Men more than women shape the church's theology and its ministry. Their professional identity is in closer proximity to the centers of ecclesiastical power, and they govern the life of larger churches.[46]

Mainline Protestantism usually has been receptive to the cultural and social changes that have brought about new opportunities for women. Most mainline churches ordain women to the ministry. Examples include many Baptist congregations, the United Methodists, the Presbyterian Church (U.S.A.), many of the Lutheran churches, the Episcopal Church, the United Church of Christ, the Disciples, and the Friends. Women are entering the ministry in increasing numbers. By and large, the opportunities have never been better for women who want to enter the professional ministry, although a disproportionate number are still employed in smaller churches that pay less than their larger counterparts. Most of the churches that have called a

[45]Miriam Therese Winter, Adair Lummis, and Allison Stokes, *Defecting in Place: Women Claiming Responsibility for Their Own Spiritual Lives* (New York: Crossroad, 1994).
[46]Frederick W. Schmidt, Jr., *A Still, Small Voice: Women, Ordination, and the Church* (Syracuse, NY: Syracuse University Press, 1996), pp. 169–170.

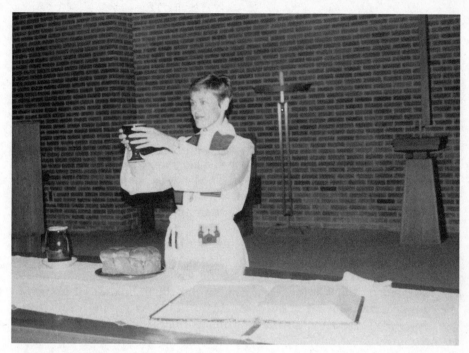

Figure 4-6   Prebyterians, like most consensus Protestants, ordain women to the ministry. *(Courtesy of Pastor Jean Holmes, Nauraushaun Presbyterian Church, Pearl River, NY.)*

woman as a minister or pastor are well satisfied with that choice. Women have also moved into the ranks of church officials in larger numbers than before.[47]

Lay positions that historically had been closed to women, such as usher, communion server, and membership on the board of trustees or board of elders, are usually open to both sexes equally. Some local churches have made it a policy to have equal numbers of women and men in such capacities.

Mainline Protestants usually use gender-inclusive language in worship and in publications. They have supported publication of revisions of the biblical books of Psalms, the Gospels, and the Pauline Letters in which inclusive language is used. They have also supported publication of inclusive language lectionaries.[48]

The following examples are representative of the ways in which these churches address the need for gender-inclusive language. In the United Church of Christ publications, it is no longer permissible to use language that refers to

[47]Edward C. Lehman, Jr., *Women Clergy: Breaking through Gender Barriers* (New Brunswick, NJ: Transaction Books, 1985).
[48]A *lectionary* is a book of biblical readings arranged for use in worship.

God as "Father, Son, and Holy Spirit." An acceptable alternative is God as "Creator, Redeemer, and Sanctifier." A *Book of Worship* endorsed by the United Methodist General Conference includes prayers addressed to God as "Mother and Father." The United Church of Christ revised its statement of faith to eliminate gender-specific language. The language of the new Presbyterian statement is inclusive as well.

Mainline Protestant churches have been instrumental in supporting women's rights in general. Most have national boards that focus on women's issues, both within and outside the church. For example, most of them do not discourage women who work outside the home or who choose to remain single. Many also help sponsor day-care centers. The National Council of Churches of Christ in the U.S.A. formally supported the passage of the Equal Rights Amendment to the U.S. Constitution, unanimously upholding a resolution urging its passage.

Evangelical Protestants typically maintain a more conservative stance that do their mainline counterparts on the proper roles of women, although there is more flexibility here than in the fundamentalist Christian tradition (see Chapter 5). Not all evangelicals approve of the ordination of women to the ministry, and not all permit women to hold key lay positions in the church. There is greater emphasis on women's roles in the home, as the heart of the home and as wife and mother. There is frequently less acceptance of divorce.

QUESTIONS AND ACTIVITIES FOR REVIEW, DISCUSSION, AND WRITING

1. Describe what is distinctive about Christian faith and practice.
2. Do the same for Protestant faith and practice.
3. Describe mainline religion in your own words. How is it related to religious pluralism and diversity?
4. What is the National Council of Churches?
5. Compare and contrast the Protestant mainline with evangelical Protestantism.
6. Describe the variety of response to male predominance in religion.
7. What roles do you think women should be able to play in their communities of faith? Why do you feel as you do? You might want to organize a discussion of this issue as a class project.
8. If you had a problem that you wanted to discuss with a pastor, minister, priest, or rabbi, would it make a difference to you if this person were female or male? Why?
9. With your professor, invite a female minister, priest, or rabbi to discuss with your class how she perceives the situation of women in mainline religion. Or organize a panel discussion on this topic.
10. Why are denominational differences less important in American religion than they were formerly?
11. What is unique and distinctive about each of the Protestant denominations described in this chapter?
12. Visit the Web site of the National Council of Churches and write a paragraph in which you described what is self-understanding is appears to be.
13. Do the same for the National Association of Evangelicals.

FOR FURTHER READING

BALMER, RANDALL, AND LAUREN F. WINNER, *Protestantism in America.* New York: Columbia University Press, 2005. A cogent exploration of how key issues such as feminism, homosexuality, and social justice affect both liberal and conservative Protestantism. This is a nicely done analysis which highlights the complexity of Protestantism in the United States.

BUTLER BASS, DIANA, *Christianity for the Rest of Us: How the Neighborhood Church is Transforming the Faith.* New York City: HarperCollins, 2007. The author describes 10 mainline churches that continue to flourish despite the reality of mainline decline. She identifies 10 practices that are characteristic of these thriving churches, which may be "signposts of renewal" for the mainline as a whole.

WUTHNOW, ROBERT, *After the Baby Boomers: How Twenty-and Thirty-Somethings are Shaping the Future of American Religion.* Princeton, NJ: Princeton University Press, 2007. A noted scholar of religion in the United States, the author presents a careful analysis of the religious views and participation of adults between 21 and 45.

RELEVANT WORLD WIDE WEB SITES

National Council of Churches: www.ncccusa.org
National Association of Evangelicals: www.nae.net

CHAPTER 5

Christianity in American Culture: Diverse Themes

My dad was very "God and rule," and my mom sort of took it all with a grain of salt. But they were very strict about everything. They kept the Sabbath on Sunday. You couldn't watch any TV or listen to the radio, or even just read a book that wasn't a religious book or listen to music that wasn't religious.[1]

After one year of disappointing results Demos [Demos Shakarian, founder of Full Gospel Businessmen's Fellowship International] decided to give up the Fellowship. While pouring out his heart in prayer the Friday night before the final meeting, he was lifted by the Spirit high into the air. In this vision, as the earth revolved each continent came into view.

"I could see people around the world—their race and color of skin," he said. "As a zoom camera can show minute details from a distance, I could see people close together but no real contact between them. Every face rigid, wretched, locked in his own private death." Billions of lost souls from every nation. Demos cried out, "Lord, help them!" Suddenly God showed him these same men, faces radiant, their hands raised to heaven, praising the Lord. At that moment, Demos' wife, Rose, gave the prophetic utterance, "My son, the very thing you see before you will soon come to pass."[2]

This chapter brings together a number of movements that are not confined to one denomination within Christianity. Neither are they specific groups, by and large, but themes and sensibilities that cut across groups. Most occur largely or exclusively within Protestantism. Some, such as the charismatic renewal movement, have affected Catholic Christianity as well. We first describe several manifestations of evangelical Christianity that have become very much a part of American culture in the twenty-first century. We then conclude the chapter with three movements which tend to set their adherents apart from the larger culture.

---

[1]Penny Edgell Becker and Nancy L. Eiesland, *Contemporary America Religion: An Ethnographic Reader* (Walnut Creek, CA: AltaMira Press, 1997), pp. 106–107.
[2]Full Gospel Businessmen's Fellowship International (www.fgbmfi.org).

CHRISTIANITY IN AMERICAN CULTURE: DIVERSE THEMES   95

Evangelical Christianity in American Culture: Three Cases

One contemporary manifestation of the evangelical spirit is *Promise Keepers*, a men's organization founded in 1990 by Bill McCartney, former University of Colorado football coach. Unlike women, who have historically come together for spiritual support, men have lacked such groups. Promise Keepers was founded in order to provide such fellowship and to provide specific structure for men seeking to live an evangelical Christian life. Their motto, "Men Transformed Worldwide," echoes the evangelical emphasis on conversion. Their statement of faith outlines many traditional evangelical beliefs including

- The inerrancy and authority of the Bible,
- The reality and pervasiveness of human sinfulness,
- The atoning death of Jesus and salvation by grace through faith,
- Their "primary calling" to "communicate the Gospel to everyone in our generation."

Promise Keepers commit themselves to keeping seven promises and to helping other members keep them as well. Among others, these promises include maintaining "spiritual, moral, ethical and sexual purity" and "building strong marriages and families," both core evangelical concerns.[3]

A second measure of evangelical interest in the United States is the phenomenal publishing success of the *Left Behind* series of novels. The novels, authored by Timothy LaHaye and Jerry Jenkins and published by evangelical Christian publisher Tyndale House,[4] are a series of sixteen books. There are a dozen in the *Left Behind* series itself, plus three prequels and a sequel. The final volume, the sequel, was published in 2007.

The novels are loosely based on the book of the Revelation of John in the Christian New Testament. The basic plotline is a particular interpretation of the return of Christ to earth called "premillennial dispensationalism." The series focuses on the lives of people who have been "left behind" when the rapture occurs and the faithful are taken up into heaven. This rescue of those of true faith is followed by the tribulation, a period of wars, famines, and upheaval during which the Antichrist rules the world. This period ends with the battle of Armageddon, in which Christ conquers Satan and the millennial rule of Christ begins.

The sales record for the series is mind-boggling. Together, the books have added up to over 65 million copies sold since the first one was published in 1995. The nearly two million initial print run of the twelfth book in the series sold out before it went on sale. Every one has been on best-seller lists such as those in the *New York Times*, the *Wall Street Journal*, *USA Today*, and *Publishers Weekly*. One *(Desecration)* was the top selling hardcover novel for 2001. Some have been made into movies for the theater and on DVD. A video game, *Left Behind: Eternal Forces* came out in 2006. The official Web site,[5] along with

---

[3]www.promisekeepers.org
[4]Tyndale House Publishers, Inc., Carol Stream, IL.
[5]www.leftbehind.com

book-related information and discussions, has free downloads of desktop wall-papers, myspace skins, screen savers, e-cards, and daily devotionals. What distinguishes this series from earlier books, such as Frank Peretti's spiritual warfare novels and Janette Oakes' Christian romances, is their robust sales outside the evangelical Christian community.

Christian television is yet another way in which the evangelical perspective makes its way into contemporary culture. The religious message that is broadcast on Christian television is not new. Nor is religious broadcasting itself new. It began with radio and continued with commercial television. What *is* new is the medium. Communications technologies such as cable television and communications satellites have revolutionized the religious broadcasting industry. Christian networks, satellite connections, super high-tech studios, and computers have transformed Christian broadcasting from a small segment of broadcasting over all to a major component in the field. Major Christian networks such as the FamilyNet, Trinity Broadcasting Network, and the Christian Television Network provide most of the programs that make up Christian television today.

The electronic church, as it is often called, has been hailed by those favorable to it as the greatest tool the church has ever had for telling "the greatest story ever told." It has also been the most harshly criticized method of outreach the church has ever used. Whatever one's opinion of religious television, it now has a firm place in the overall landscape of the American love affair with both television and religion.

This particular form of religious broadcasting has often been referred to as *televangelism*. That word is somewhat inaccurate, because its main audience is composed of those who already share its point of view and religious beliefs. *Christian television* is a more accurate term. It is an outgrowth and an integral part of the conservative/evangelical/fundamentalist point of view in American Christianity. It provides alternative television for those who find it difficult to locate acceptable programs on the commercial channels. For the largely convinced viewing audience, what they see and hear models the behavior and beliefs they themselves are trying to live. It reinforces and supports and many come away from its programs with renewed conviction and determination.

This designation also helps us to understand the importance of the resurgence in evangelical and fundamentalist Christianity in the United States for Christian television. There is now a group of consumers available who have clearly defined tastes in entertainment. It is this group of consumers that makes up the viewing audience for Christian television. It is also important to note that persons who do not identify themselves as conservative evangelical Christians are also part of the viewing audience.

Who watches Christian television? Several studies have been done in an attempt to answer this question, and they all agree on the main points. Holding evangelical and fundamentalist or very conservative religious beliefs is the factor most strongly correlated with watching Christian television. Most viewers live in the South and the Midwest, with a disproportionate number in the South. The majority of viewers are female, and viewers are older than the general population.

Between two-thirds and three-fourths are age fifty or over. Another important fact that emerges from these studies is that watching religion on television does not substitute for church attendance and participation. Most viewers are regular churchgoers and contribute to the financial support of their local congregation as well. The early predictions that Christian television would be the downfall of many a local congregation have not proven accurate. Christian television is used as a substitute for attendance by only one category of people—those who, for whatever reason, find it difficult to get out to attend church. Ratings indicate, finally, that there are fewer viewers by far than the massive audiences claimed by the broadcasters themselves. There are, especially, fewer regular viewers.

We can best think of Christian television as viewer-supported alternative television. A significant number of people cannot find many programs on commercial television that do not run afoul of their values and tastes in entertainment. They want something more from television. One segment of the population turns to public television for what they want. A larger segment turns to Christian television. It is, in other words, a response to a need for viewing options other than those provided by commercial networks, most cable and satellite channels, and public television. As the percentage of conservative, fundamentalist, and evangelical Christians in the population has increased, so has the need for and the popularity of Christian television. The increasing conservatism and evangelicalism of American Christianity indicates that Christian television will continue to be an important element in the entertainment industry and in religion.

Religious television is not limited to Christian television, although that is clearly its largest component. The Interfaith Broadcasting Commission is a cooperative organization that includes the National Council of Churches, the United States Conference of Catholic Bishops, the Islamic Society of North America, and a coalition of Jewish organizations. It seeks to draw media attention to monotheistic values and "to demonstrate through programming a variety of ways in which faith is expressed in the lives of individuals."[6] Among other things, they provide documentary programming to major networks, including ABC, CBS, and NBC.

Faith and Values Media works "to use the electronic media to enrich spiritual life and to build bridges of understanding among people of faith."[7] Listings in their catalog of videos that can be viewed online include a program titled "Listening to Islam," an exploration of contemporary Jewish worship, a program on miracles, angels, and the afterlife, and a program on the life of Saint Francis.

Evangelicalism is very public in America in other ways as well. On college campuses, evangelical groups like Navigators, Campus Crusade for Christ, and Intervarsity Christian Fellowship draw many students, many of whom have participated in Young Life in high school. Members of these groups often witness to other students in the library or student center. There are evangelical groups within professional fields, such as Christian Nurses and the Society of Christian

[6]www.interfaithbroadcasting.com
[7]www.faithandvaluesmedia.org

Philosophers. Christian bookstores can be found in most cities. They offer a wide selection of books, music, videotapes, and jewelry that reflects the evangelical viewpoint. Christian music has become the music of choice for many listeners, and hymns such as "Amazing Grace" and "Morning Has Broken" have become easy-listening standards. Christian music has its own awards program, the Dove Awards.

MEGACHURCHES

The growth and expansion of megachurches since the 1970s is one of the most notable phenomena in American religion in the past three or four decades.

Megachurches are Protestant churches with a consistent weekly attendance of 2,000 or more at Sunday worship services. The largest, Lakewood Church in Houston, Texas, averages over 35,000. There are now over 1,200 such churches in the United States. They share several characteristics. The vast majority are conservative and/or evangelical in their theology. Thirty-four percent are nondenominational, 16 percent are Southern Baptist, and the rest are divided among a variety of denominations. Almost two-thirds are located in the southern Sunbelt region, with the highest concentrations found in California, Texas, Georgia, and

Figure 5-1 "Megachurches" with very large attendance and diverse programming have developed in the United States in the last two decades. (*Jessica Kourkounis/AP Wide World Photos.*)

Florida. They are almost always suburban churches. There are Catholic churches whose attendance would put them in the megachurch category. However, research indicates that they do not share the other characteristics that describe megachurches.[8]

In addition to the size of their congregations, the diversity of their physical plants makes them distinctive. They may have "gymnasiums, ball fields, lounges and dining facilities seating hundreds, nursery schools, exercise facilities, classrooms and meeting rooms by the score, Starbucks coffee lounges, McDonald's restaurants, credit unions, and electronic media installations that rival commercial television studios,"[9] among other facilities.

They emphasize programming. Their large size makes it both possible and necessary to support a range of programs that offers something—many things, in fact—for everyone. Programming is typically anchored by worship services that are productions whose quality and approach rival the secular productions the congregants are used to. They are well produced and not at all amateur. Like programming in general, several worship services throughout the week offer different approaches. Although commonly focused on preaching, they usually make use of the arts, too, including choral and instrumental music, dance, and drama.

Megachurches also offer a very wide range of ministries and groups within the congregation. These may be focused on religious and spiritual issues (e.g., Bible study groups for all ages and interests), strengthening ties and ministering to specific needs of persons in the congregation (new members groups, discipleship groups, singles groups, parents' groups, or grief groups, for example), and groups to train the large numbers of volunteers their programs require. Many support elementary and secondary schools. Many offer literally hundreds of social and religious activities from which congregants may choose. Intense involvement is strongly encouraged and supported by how congregational life is structured. However, their large size allows for anonymity for those who seek it.

Their preachers, most usually the founders of the congregations, are in effect religious stars or C.E.O.s, whose churches reflect their charisma and personality. Although the organization and size of megachurches calls for a large cadre of subordinate staff, they frequently are *quite* subordinate to the guiding vision of the founding minister/executive.

Megachurches typically attract people with identifiable characteristics: They are mainly young, with a median age of 38 or less. They are predominantly female, white, and married with children. They are both mobile and transient. Interestingly, most come to megachurches from other Christian churches rather than from the ranks of the unchurched. Although these are the generalizations, there is considerable diversity in some megachurches, and some emphasize their diversity as a selling point. Although the majority of members are upper-middle class, membership includes all socioeconomic levels. Members tend to be highly involved in church activities, a trait which these congregations

[8]Information compiled from "Megachurch Definition," http://hirr.hartsem.edu/megachurch/definition.html.
[9]Ronald L. Johnstone, *Religion in Society: A Sociology of Religion*, 8th ed. (Upper Saddle River, NJ: Prentice Hall, 2007), p. 373.

carefully nurture. But in addition, one of the emphases of the megachurches is usually that religion has to be lived 24/7.

Megachurches rely heavily on modern communications technology to stay in touch with their vast and scattered congregations. Web sites are the norm, and written, audiotape, and video communication is also commonly used. Their large staffs make extensive use of modern electronic communication tools such as e-mail, pagers, and cell phones to be always and instantly accessible.

Although the large megachurch itself stands out, they frequently draw a constellation of smaller, loosely associated churches into their sphere of influence. This structure of constellations of smaller churches around the larger one is itself an innovation in American religious organization. These affiliations tend to be looser than denominations and the member churches choose to belong.

American culture at the beginning of the twenty-first century provides a cultural context for megachurches. Many of us deal with mega-institutions on a daily basis. Many of you attend universities and colleges that might be described this way, and some of you work in such institutions or are preparing for such a career, if not both. We are accustomed to going to malls and selecting from a truly amazing array of options. We are at home in such settings, and we've come to expect and value the range of choices such settings provide. We are consumers, whether of raisins or religion.

The centrality and the "star" status of the founding pastors of most megachurches has raised questions about their ability to survive the retirement or death of their founder. Few of these churches are old enough to have experienced this transition. The evidence suggests, however, that they will be able to do so. "Although some researchers argue the era of megachurch proliferation is drawing to a close, the total number has increased from 350 in 1990 to over 600 in 2000 and there are now over 1200 megachurches in the US. It seems clear that reports of the demise of the megachurch are greatly exaggerated."[10]

THE RELIGIOUS-POLITICAL RIGHT

Evangelical religion was a strong force in American politics until the second decade of the 1900s. During the period between the end of World War I and the early 1970s, its influence on American government lessened dramatically. The early 1970s saw a renewal of evangelical and fundamentalist involvement in the political life of the nation, a trend that continued into the new century.

The *religious-political right* is a loose coalition of groups and individuals who are united by their conviction that the United States is in the midst of a severe spiritual and moral decline, a decline that could well snowball into a landslide that would lead to downfall of the United States and the defeat of democracy in the world. They believe that a *return to the traditional values of American life*, best safeguarded by fundamentalist Christianity, will prevent this landslide and again make America the strong and righteous nation that they

[10]"Megachurch Definition," www.hartsem.edu/megachurch

believe existed in an earlier time. They are also united in their desire to *use the legislative process to make their goals into the law of the land.*

There are several groups whose alignment with the goals and concerns of the religious-political right is fairly constant. The most reliable support, in terms of both programs and finances, comes from *those whose religious outlook is very conservative or fundamentalist,* some of whom are evangelicals and some of whom are not. Some are Pentecostals, while some are not.

Protestants are clearly the backbone of this group. On certain issues, such as the movement to limit legal abortions, support also comes from Catholics, Eastern Orthodox Christians, and even some Orthodox Jews. On others, such as the campaign against ratification of the Equal Rights Amendment (ERA), the coalition has included support from the *Latter-day Saints,* who value traditional male and female social roles. *A second major segment of support comes from political conservatives.* They desire to see the balance of government power shifted from the federal to the state government and hope to return the responsibility for welfare programs to the private sector of American life. This leads them to support the religious right on these types of issues. A third group is related to the second. *Social and economic conservatives* share many of the same concerns that motivate the political conservatives' involvement with the religious-political right. Economic conservatives especially favor the modifications in the welfare program it encourages, as well as its support for private business interests. We can also cite a fourth group—those who, without any clearly defined religious motivation, subscribe to the *belief that America has a special role to play in the history of the world.* They describe this role using the biblical metaphors of a light to the nations and a city set on a hill. A final group is more difficult to define but just as important. We can call them the *social traditionalists*—those whose motivations are not clearly religious, political, or economic but who believe that a return to older values would be a beneficial course for America to follow. They comprise a loose back-to-the-basics interest.

The goals of the religious-political right are stated in various ways. However they are described, they revolve around the *intention to bring about major changes in American government and American life.* They seek to make the United States a moral and righteous nation, defining morality and righteousness in terms of the authority of the Christian Bible as the only legitimate guide.

The religious-political right also describes its goals as an all-out war on an enemy that they have identified as being at the root of America's moral problems: secular humanism (see Chapter 11 for a discussion of humanism). Secular humanism stands for nearly everything that the new right believes is wrong. Most supporters subscribe to an interpretation of recent history that holds that secular humanists in high government positions are conspiring to make secular humanism the official religion of the land. A significant part of this conspiracy centers on what is being taught and what is permissible in the public schools.

Not all the groups involved in this coalition fully agree about what its specific agenda should be. Nor do they agree on the relative importance of the various items. There are, however, certain planks that can be found in nearly all statements of their platform.

The religious-political right regards the family as the mainstay of American culture. They approve of only one form of family structure, which they identify as the *traditional form of family organization* in the United States. The traditional family is the family that consists of a man and a woman, married for life, with children. Premarital chastity and marital monogamy are the only acceptable forms of sexuality. Both the Old and New Testaments of the Christian scriptures are cited in support of the position that homosexuality is a heinous sin and a prime contributor to America's spiritual degeneracy. Sex education should be taught only by Christians to ensure that proper values will be taught along with factual information. The ERA and the "feminist revolution" appear in every list of national errors that are said to threaten America. Opposition to abortion, especially government support for abortion in the form of Medicaid payments and federal funding for abortion clinics, is another important part of their family policy.

They also support a thorough cleanup of commercial television, not only to eliminate violence and the use of sexually suggestive advertising but also to eliminate the portrayal of alternative lifestyles. They oppose pornography in all its forms and want to have laws enacted that would mandate stiff penalties for those who create and distribute pornographic literature, films, videotapes, and so forth. Another priority is support for programs that will help to solve the problem of illegal drug use.

These concerns are shared by people who do not identify with the religious-political right explicitly. Survey data indicate that approximately 90 percent of Americans believe that extramarital sex is always or nearly always wrong. About 80 percent feel that way about active homosexuality. Over half support at least some restrictions on the availability of legal abortion. Over half the population favors laws prohibiting the sale of pornography to people under the age of 18, and almost half oppose the sale of pornography to anyone, regardless of age. Many Americans are concerned about illegal drugs, as they are about sex and violence (and the frequent close association of the two) on commercial television.

The large role the federal government has assumed in administering welfare programs is another concern. The religious-political right does recognize that there will always be people who cannot care for themselves because of age or physical or mental infirmity. They want to shift the responsibility for the care of such people from the government to the private sector, including churches, businesses, and, above all, the families of the people themselves. For example, they support tax credits for those families who have a dependent elderly parent living with them.

Government regulation of business and industry is yet another concern. Free enterprise, ambitious management, and competition unfettered by government regulation are held to be biblical values that are a part of God's plan for humanity.

The religious-political right wants the nation to return to the values of an earlier, much less complicated period in history, when the population was much smaller. The members of this movement believe that the values that worked in that setting are what America needs now. Although not all Americans agree with them, their vision of a renewed America based on traditional values has captured the hearts and minds of a significant number of people. The religious-political right is one of the most significant religious and political movements of recent history.

The religious-political right believes the schools, both public and private, bear the responsibility, alongside the family and the churches, for rearing children who have a strong sense of and commitment to these values. Their approach to education has two main facets. The first is what they want to see happen within the public school system. The second is their goals concerning the establishment of a system of private Christian schools and support for home schooling to supplement the public schools.

The *public schools, according to this analysis, have been taken over by secular humanists* and are being used as the main tool for indoctrinating youngsters with the values held dear by humanists. The U.S. Supreme Court decision that made mandated prayer and other school-sponsored devotional exercises in the public schools illegal is of particular concern. They want voluntary prayer and other devotional exercises returned to the public school classroom. They also want any academic study of religion eliminated, because it maintains a position of neutrality concerning the truth of specific religions. This conflicts sharply with their belief that Christianity is the one true faith. To help accomplish these goals, they have increasingly focused on getting supporters elected to local school boards.

A related concern is that the public schools do not teach one absolute truth in any area. For example, in dealing with families in a high-school sociology class, a classroom discussion of many styles of relationships between adults and many approaches to parenting takes the place of the promotion of the traditional family as the only acceptable family. Rather than advocating that women remain at home as wives, mothers, and homemakers, the public schools attempt to prepare their students to assess the strengths and weaknesses of various arrangements. Rather than teaching the immorality of premarital sex, health teachers encourage their students to explore their own values and attitudes and introduce the cautions deemed necessary in the face of disease and the possibility of unwanted pregnancy. Government classes, instead of promoting democracy and condemning other forms of government, have students evaluate various forms of government.

You might want to pause a moment here and think back over the textbooks from which you learned as a child. How was religion portrayed, if at all? What messages were being presented in the pictures of boys and girls, men and women? When you took the required (in most school systems, at any rate) government or civics course, were different types of government portrayed equally, or was democracy held up as an ideal?

The teaching of evolution is another focal point for the critique of public school education. Some want the theory of evolution dropped from the curriculum completely in favor of teaching an account of the beginning of the world and humankind that is compatible with the creation stories in Genesis. Others want to see evolution and creationism or creation science taught alongside each other as theories. Again, think back to your high-school (perhaps junior-high or middle-school) biology, botany, or life-science classes. Were you taught about evolution? Were you taught the creation stories in Genesis? Was the entire subject ignored? Some textbook publishers and some schools have taken this last approach to avoid a confrontation over this explosive issue.

A final point of contention with the public schools has to do with the teaching of sex education. In the first place, many supporters of the religious-political right want all sex education removed from the schools and left in the hands of parents and the churches. If sex education is to be taught in the public schools at all, the values of premarital chastity, marital fidelity, and lifelong monogamy should be the only things taught. Sex education cannot be separated from family life education, and the traditional family style must be upheld in the public schools.

An editorial reflection is in order here. The values of traditional Christianity have been a major influence in American life for many centuries. The Genesis accounts of how the world began have guided the thinking of uncounted millions of people and continue to do so. Sexual morality based on the teachings of the Christian Bible is the framework that has made family life meaningful and good for generations of Americans. These values deserve a place in public school education because they are a significant part of the story of humanity and of the history and present culture of the United States. However, in a pluralistic culture, they must be presented as one set of values alongside others from which people have chosen. They must not be taught as the only right values, to the exclusion of others. A similar point can be made concerning the omission of religion in descriptions of the history and present culture of the United States. Religion has been and continues to be an important factor in American life. To omit it is to present an inaccurate picture of both past and present. The distinction between teaching religion and teaching about religion must be scrupulously maintained, however, and the approach must always be descriptive rather than normative.

Every bit as important in the religious-political right's approach to public education is its *support for a network of private Christian schools*. When we discuss Catholicism in Chapter 6, you will learn that the Catholic Church sponsors the largest private school system in the United States. It is usually called the parochial school system. Among Protestants, the Lutherans sponsor a number of schools. The network of Christian schools has grown steadily in the United States. Those who support Christian schools do so largely because they believe that home, church, and school should reinforce each other by presenting the same values and truths. Supporters of Christian schools want to see the development of a system that exists apart from the teacher training and licensing requirements enforced by the states. They do not want to be subject to the same curriculum requirements that guide the public schools.

There is more at stake, according to the supporters of private Christian schools, than simply being able to begin and end the school day with prayer and Bible reading or to say grace before lunch. Christian school advocates are asking for the right to control their children's education with minimal interference from the government. Government regulation is looked upon as harassment and as infringement on freedom of religion. For those whose values and home life are guided by the views and principles of fundamentalist Christianity, public school attendance is a very real threat to their children's spiritual welfare. It threatens both their earthly happiness and their eternal life. As we noted earlier, home schooling allows for even more parental control than do private schools.

Catholics earlier had pressed for and won the right to their own schools because they believed that there was a clear Protestant bias in the public schools. Fundamentalist Christians believe there is a clear humanistic bias in the public schools. They seek the right to take decisive action to protect their youngsters. It is for this reason that education has become such a pressing issue.

The *military strength of the United States* and its position in relation to the other nations of the world are also important to the religious-political right. They believe that the United States must always be the first and foremost world military and economic power. They believe this is necessary mainly to protect the values of democracy and capitalism both in the United States itself and in the world. They believe the strongest possible national defense is not only a political necessity but a religious obligation. The United States has been chosen by God for a special destiny in the history of God's interaction with the world and defending that destiny militarily is part of carrying out the divine plan.

The religious-political right works through *direct political action* as well as through its efforts to educate people and persuade them to support their point of view. It seeks to elect public officials who are sympathetic to its programs and views. Those who think along these lines describe government as the provision of "godly leadership."

Followers of this perspective believe that only by governing according to the Bible can a leader govern rightly. A direct practical implementation of this point of view came from the Christian Voice organization when it developed the Congressional Score Card to track the way that members of Congress voted on certain critical moral issues such as abortion support and the ERA. Voter registration drives have been another important focus, and voter registration has been done after Sunday morning worship in some fundamentalist churches.

The Christian Coalition

The Christian Coalition exemplifies the organizational embodiment of the religious-political right. It describes itself as "largest and most active conservative grassroots political organization in America." The Christian Coalition of America offers people of faith the vehicle to be actively involved in shaping their government—from the county courthouse to the halls of Congress.[11]

The Coalition employs methods that have a long history in political activism both secular and religious, such as conferences and training seminars for activists, federal and state lobbying, telephone and e-mail alerts for members on important issues and upcoming votes, and attempts to get out the vote on issues of concern.

---

[11]The Christian Coalition, www.cc.org

Separatist Fundamental Christians

The word *fundamentalism* derives from a series of pamphlets called "The Fundamentals," written in the early 1900s as a reference point for conservative Protestants. As you learned in Chapter 4, evangelical Christians are very much a part of the mainstream. The increase in religious conservatism in the last several decades has brought some fundamentalists into the mainstream as well. The type of fundamentalism with which this chapter deals is different. It is characterized by a strong desire to remain separate from other groups and individuals who do not believe as they do. Many of these churches are members of the *American Council of Christian Churches*, founded in 1941 by Dr. Carl McIntire.

The Preamble to the Constitution of the Council clearly describes the concern that motivates separatist fundamentalists:

> WHEREAS, It is the duty of all true churches of the Lord Jesus Christ to make a clear testimony to their faith in Him, especially in these darkening days of apostasy in many professing churches, by which apostasy whole denominations in their official capacity, as well as individual churches, have been swept into a paganizing stream of modernism under various names and in varying degree; and. . . .
>
> WHEREAS, The commands of God to His people to be separate from all unbelief and corruption are clear and positive; and
>
> WHEREAS, We believe the times demand the formation of an agency, for fellowship and cooperation on the part of Bible-believing churches for the maintenance of a testimony pure and steadfast to the great fundamental truths of the Word of God as held by the historic Christian Church through the centuries, for the accomplishment of tasks which can better be done in cooperation than separately, and to facilitate the discharge of the obligations which inhere in the Commission of Christ to His Church.[12]

Separatist fundamentalists firmly believe that biblical Christianity is completely incompatible with Christian modernism or liberalism, as well as with anything secular. They try to keep the boundaries between themselves and the secular world drawn sharply. Nonfundamentalist Christians are regarded as part of the unsaved world, so fundamentalists remain separate from them as well as from the secular world.

Fundamentalism is not only a matter of religious belief in certain doctrines regarded as absolutely true and fundamental to faith and salvation. Scholar Karen Armstrong notes that separatist fundamentalists believe that religion is under attack in contemporary culture and experience a "profound fear of annihilation":

> It is a defensive, embattled religiosity that is fighting for its life. . . . Most [fundamentalists] are simply trying to live what they regard as a true religious life in a world that seems increasingly hostile to faith, and all have developed in symbiotic relationship with a secularism that is felt as invasive and destructive.

[12]The American Council of Christian Churches, www.amcouncilcc.org

Every single fundamentalist movement that I have studied is convinced that modern secular society is trying to wipe out religion. And besides religious fundamentalists, there are secular fundamentalists who often have as bigoted and inaccurate an idea of religion as fundamentalists have of secularism.[13]

Fundamentalism reflects the reality that a substantial and significant part of the population of the United States perceives themselves as cultural "outsiders" in contemporary American culture. Secularization, the privatization of religion, and the dramatic changes in moral standards that followed the turbulent decade of the 1960s helped to create a culture in which some people could not feel at home. "Fundamentalists would not be fundamentalists without deep-seated feelings of dispossession, resentment, and alienation, and it is important to understand . . . these emotions."[14]

Relatively more women than men are fundamentalists, by a ratio of about four to three. Fundamentalism as an outlook reflects the kind of passivity that our culture has traditionally associated with women. The fundamentalist emphasis on God rather than on human potential encourages that passivity and gives it divine support. Fundamentalism often encourages women to be submissive to their husbands, remain at home, and accept a limited and traditional (although significant) role in the life of their church. While this seems restrictive to some women, for others, it means the security of clearly defined roles that relieve the murkiness that cultural change has brought to women's lives in the last several decades.

Separatist fundamentalists have also been among the strongest supporters of the private *Christian school movement*, as well as of the home-schooling movement. Private Christian schools provide a way for parents to shield their children from the secular and humanistic influence of the public school system. They also offer greater control over the curriculum. In most private Christian schools, children do not learn the Darwinian theory of evolution nor do they study sex education and other subjects deemed inappropriate by fundamentalists. Their textbooks support traditional values and attitudes. More important, all subjects are taught from a Christian perspective. The school day begins with worship. The teachers are committed Christians, most of whom understand their work as a religious calling.

Perhaps most important in understanding why fundamentalist Christians view the Christian school movement as so important, Christian schools are a primary element in the advancement of fundamentalism's sociocultural goals. "By reuniting the three major socializing institutions of family, church, and school, [fundamentalists] hope to achieve a greater coherence in their own lives, bring their children up in the faith, and bring morality back to the United States."[15]

---

[13]Andrew Cooper, "The Freelance Monotheist: An Interview with Karen Armstrong," *Tricycle: The Buddhist Review*, XII/4 (Summer, 2003), p. 110.

[14]Joel A. Carpenter, *Revive Us Again: The Reawakening of American Fundamentalism* (New York: Oxford University Press, 1997), p. 242.

[15]Susan D. Rose, "Gender, Education, and the New Christian Right," in *In Gods We Trust*, eds Thomas Robbins and Dick Anthony (New Brunswick, NJ: Transaction Books, 1981), p. 100.

The private Christian school movement continues to grow, but not as rapidly as the home-schooling movement. *Home schooling* means that parents teach their children at home, often using materials provided by Christian organizations. Individual parents have even more control with home schooling than with private schools. Both methods help to guarantee that children during their younger, most formative years will be socialized into the values that are central to fundamentalist Christians and into those values only.

Fundamentalist Christians also support a number of colleges in which higher education is carried out within the framework of their values and concerns. Among the best known of these schools is *Liberty University in Lynchburg, Virginia*. It is arguably the flagship school of Christian fundamentalism. Liberty University was founded in 1971 by Jerry Falwell, who is perhaps better known for having founded the Moral Majority. It now offers over 40 regionally and nationally accredited undergraduate and 30 graduate programs and participates in NCAA athletics. The following are among a list of "LU Distinctives" written by the founder. They give a good idea of how Liberty reflects the values of Christian fundamentalism.

- Academic excellence in a Christ-centered environment.
- A commitment to training visionary champions for Christ.
- An uncompromising doctrinal statement, based upon an inerrant Bible, a Christian worldview beginning with belief in biblical Creationism, an eschatological belief in the premillennial, pretribulational coming of Christ for all of His Church, dedication to world evangelization, an absolute repudiation of "political correctness," a strong commitment to political conservatism, total rejection of socialism, and firm support for America's economic system of free enterprise.
- Behavioral standards which include the prohibition of drug, alcohol and tobacco use, coed dorms, and sexual promiscuity.
- A modest dress code, reasonable curfews, and respect for authority.[16]

Many separatist fundamentalist churches are independent, with no ties outside the local congregation. They believe that this most closely resembles the way in which the church was organized in New Testament times. It also affords each congregation the greatest opportunity to set its own standards of correct belief. Two groups of churches, however, do fit in here. In Chapter 4, you read about the Restoration Movement and the Christian Church/Disciples of Christ that is a part of it. Two other churches whose roots go back to the Restoration Movement reflect the separatist fundamental approach to Christianity.

The *Christian Churches/Churches of Christ* have no organization beyond the local congregation. There is less variation in belief among members of these independent churches than among the Disciples. Most are strongly conservative to fundamentalist. As in the other Restoration churches, the Lord's Supper is served weekly. Like that of the Disciples, their worship includes instrumental

[16]Liberty University, www.liberty.edu

music as well as the singing of hymns. The Christian Churches do not participate in ecumenical discussions or organizations, and the network of schools,
colleges, and benevolent organizations they sponsor is supported entirely by
local churches. They are located primarily in the lower Midwest and in
Kentucky.

The *Churches of Christ* is the largest group within the Restoration
churches. They are centered in the South and Southwest, although there are
congregations throughout the United States. Like the Christian Churches,
there is no organizational structure beyond the local church and no participation in ecumenical boards or groups. These churches seek "to speak where the
Bible speaks and to be silent where the Bible is silent" in matters of faith and
morality. They believe that this is the biblical pathway to Christian unity. As in
the other Restoration congregations, the Lord's Supper is a weekly celebration
and believers are baptized by full immersion. Unlike the Disciples and the
Christian Churches, the Churches of Christ use no instrumental music in their
worship. Instrumental music, these Christians believe, is not biblical but is
instead one of the ways the church accommodated itself to the demands of
more wealthy members.

HOLINESS CHRISTIANS

Holiness is a movement that involves several groups of Christian believers,
rather than being a group in and of itself. It is rooted in Jesus admonition that
his followers be perfect, even as God is perfect (Matthew 5:48). To follow this
directive means to work toward ever-increasing holiness and perfection of life
in this world. Sin and the evidences of sin are to be progressively rooted out.
The search for perfection usually has been accompanied by a sense of separation from those who are not engaged in a similar search. Holiness is a matter of
both belief and lifestyle. Its adherents believe in the possibility and the necessity of sanctification, understood as a work of the Holy Spirit distinct from justification. By *justification*, a person is forgiven for past sin and placed in a new
relationship with God. By *sanctification*, that new relationship becomes more
and more evident in the person's life as the Holy Spirit continues to bring
about growth in grace. Other people are likely to be made aware of someone's
membership in a holiness church by their lifestyle, which reflects, in ways that
vary somewhat from church to church, their understanding of how a sanctified
life is to be lived.

When it began, the *holiness movement* in the United States took many of
its cues from John Wesley's teaching about Christian perfection. Wesley, you
remember, was the founder of Methodism in England. When Methodism came
to the United States, it brought Wesley's emphasis on sanctification and perfection with it. Originally, Methodists had many of the characteristics that have
come to be associated with the holiness movement. As Methodism grew in
numbers and wealth and became more a religion of the middle class, outward
holiness was downplayed. Groups that disagreed with this lessening of outward

holiness broke away. They often referred to themselves as Wesleyans, in order to distinguish themselves from the Methodists and to express their loyalty to the original intention of John Wesley.

The rejection of that which is "of the world" in order to attain holiness brought with it disagreements over precisely what was to be rejected. Over time, these disagreements led to the existence of many divisions within the movement. There are now several holiness groups made up of many churches as well as many independent communities of believers without ties outside their own group.

What, then, are some of the things that holiness Christians reject as being too much of the world? The use of alcohol, tobacco, and illicit drugs are universally banned among such groups. They are very careful in their language, avoiding not only obvious swearing and blasphemy but much of the common slang used in our culture. Gambling, too, is universally forbidden. Attending movie theaters and sometimes watching television are not permitted. Dancing is avoided by most. Swimming, or swimming in mixed groups of males and females, is sometimes disallowed. Children often do not participate in physical education classes that violate their standards, such as those involving folk dancing or those that require girls to wear slacks or shorts. Some holiness students also ask to be excused from participating in regular classroom work that conflicts with their beliefs. Examples include the teaching of evolution in biology or botany classes, sex education in health classes, or when movies are shown in class.

It is especially important, according to holiness teaching, that women follow a virtuous lifestyle. Women's role in the home and in the rearing of children makes them the primary transmitters of holiness. Frequently, women are discouraged from cutting their hair or at least from wearing it shorter than shoulder length. The use of cosmetics and the wearing of much jewelry are frowned upon. A simple wristwatch and a wedding band are often the only permissible jewelry. High-cut necklines and at least elbow-length sleeves are the norm, and women wear dresses or skirts rather than slacks or shorts.

Those in search of holiness tend to socialize with like-minded people who reinforce their values and way of life and who support them in their difference from the world. Marriages usually take place within the group, and children are encouraged to find their playmates among church members' children. Families are often large, and divorce is strongly discouraged if not forbidden. This pattern of socialization has the twofold effect of reinforcing the sense of community within the group and maintaining the separation between those who are "of the world" and those who are not.

There are many independent churches within this movement. There are also some groupings of churches. Some of the better-known groups include several in the Church of God family, the Churches of Christ in Christian Union, and some conservative Mennonite groups. Two of the largest are the Church of the Nazarene and the Wesleyan Church, both of which are especially strong in the Midwest. Lifestyle requirements for full members of Wesleyan churches include the following, and failing to follow them can subject the member to church disciplinary action. These two sections provide a good example of the central concerns of a holiness lifestyle. Members should

> demonstrate a positive social witness by abstaining from all forms of gambling and by abstaining from using or trafficking (production, sale or purchase) in any substances destructive to their physical, mental and spiritual health, such as alcoholic beverages, tobacco and drugs (other than proper medical purposes of drugs); and by refraining from membership in secret societies and lodges which are oath bound, believing that the quasi-religious nature of such organizations divides the Christian's loyalty, their secret nature contravenes the Christian's open witness and the secret nature of their oaths is repugnant to the Christian conscience.[17]

Another section outlines the church's views on marriage and divorce. Members should

> follow the teachings of the Scriptures regarding marriage and divorce. We affirm that sexual relationships outside of marriage and sexual relationships between persons of the same sex are immoral and sinful. We further affirm that heterosexual monogamy is God's plan for marriage, and we regard sexual sin of the spouse, such as adultery, homosexual behavior, bestiality or incest, as the only biblical grounds for considering divorce, and then only when appropriate counseling has failed to restore the relationship.[18]

Perhaps the best known of all the holiness organizations, because it maintains the highest public profile, is the *Salvation Army*. While most people probably associate the Salvation Army with thrift shops and Christmas bell ringers, it is also a fully functioning church. In addition to the social programs for which it is best known, Army citadels hold Sunday and midweek services for a membership of over 500,000. Their wholehearted identification with the poorest of the poor and the outcasts of society make them able to reach out to people who are likely to be overlooked by other churches. They also engage in far-reaching disaster relief work in the United States and around the world, numerous other outreach ministries, and maintaining an extensive Web site.

Some of you may feel that the restrictions that holiness imposes amount to a program for avoiding life in the real world. It certainly is true that there are fewer worldly temptations for people who conscientiously follow this path. Consider, however, the burden of difference that these people take upon themselves for the sake of the higher goals they seek. Students who are not a part of the ordinary round of school activities, and whose dress and behavior set them apart from other students, may be ridiculed, or at least misunderstood and socially isolated. Acceptance by others comes slowly or not at all under these circumstances. Those of all ages voluntarily limit social contacts and activities taken for granted by the majority culture. It is a life of difficult choices, the final validation of which must of necessity wait until an unspecified time in the future.

[17]The Wesleyan Church, www.wesleyan.org
[18]Ibid.

Pentecostal Christianity

Part of the variety in American religion stems from variations in the way that different communities of faith balance out their appeal to the intellect, the will, and the emotions. Some services of worship are calm and dignified and offer stimulation primarily to the intellect. Those that emphasize ethical behavior and social service appeal to the will. Some offer more in terms of emotional appeal. Pentecostal Christianity is one of these, perhaps the foremost among them.

The experience of highly emotional worship and religious ecstasy is the foundation of Pentecostalism. It has been a part of American religion for many years in the form of traditional Pentecostalism and has continued into the present time in that form and others. Pentecostalism is also one of the fastest-growing forms of Christianity, both in the United States and around the world. Two of the American denominations showing the most rapid recent growth—the mostly white Assemblies of God and the mostly black Church of God in Christ—are pentecostal. Some holiness churches are also pentecostal, while others are not.

The word *Pentecostalism* refers to an event recorded in the Christian New Testament, in the Book of Acts. Following His death, Jesus had appeared to the disciples a number of times. He spoke with them about the Kingdom of God and promised them they would be baptized with the Holy Spirit. As the biblical account goes, the Holy Spirit came to the disciples in a new and powerful way, described as tongues like flames of fire touching each one. They began to speak in languages other than those they usually used, and all present heard in their

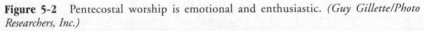

Figure 5-2   Pentecostal worship is emotional and enthusiastic. *(Guy Gillette/Photo Researchers, Inc.)*

own languages (Acts 1:3–5 and 2:3–4, New Revised Standard Version). In the confusion that followed, Peter is said to have spoken, quoting the Hebrew prophet Joel whose prophecy had foretold such an event (Joel 2:28). Most Christian churches celebrate this event annually in the spring, on Pentecost Sunday, as the anniversary of the founding of the church. For some Christians, however, it has meant much more. Pentecostal Christians believe that what God did at Pentecost continues to happen today. People can receive the Holy Spirit in the same way as did the disciples, according to the Book of Acts.

Pentecostals believe that certain phenomena accompany and give evidence of the work of the Holy Spirit. The principal evidence of this gift is usually said to be the ability to *speak in tongues*. This phenomenon is also called *glossolalia*. Speaking in tongues takes two forms. People may speak in a recognizable human language. On the other hand, some Pentecostals say that their tongues are not recognizable human languages, but a private language given by God. Linguists who have studied this type of glossolalia have found that, although it is not a known human language, it has the characteristics that identify it as distinctly human speech. Pentecostal Christians are urged to expect and actively seek this gift. An Assemblies of God statement expresses this core belief this way: "All believers are entitled to and should ardently expect and earnestly seek the promise of the Father, the baptism in the Holy Ghost and fire, according to the command of our Lord Jesus Christ. This was the normal experience of all in the early Christian Church. With it comes the enduement of power for life and service, the bestowment of the gifts and their uses in the work of the ministry."[19]

Pentecostals make another distinction as well. For some, tongues are a prayer language between the individual and God and do not call for interpretation. Others believe that tongues are a way that God uses to communicate with an entire congregation. In these instances, an interpreter is required to translate the message. Interpretation is also thought to be a gift of the Spirit. Usually, the speaker and the interpreter are two different people.

Speaking in tongues is regarded as the primary manifestation of the action of the Holy Spirit. The United Pentecostal Church International considers it "the initial, outward evidence" of the Holy Ghost's indwelling, available to everyone.[20] Other gifts of the Spirit are mentioned in the New Testament. Examples of such lists can be found in 1 Corinthians 12:8–10, 28, and 29–30. The healing of physical and psychological illnesses is considered second only to tongues by most Pentecostals. Prophecy and the interpretation of tongues receive considerable attention. Preaching and administration in the church are considered gifts. Exorcism, or the removal of unclean spirits, is practiced by some. Wisdom and knowledge are gifts, as is the ability to distinguish good from evil spirits. A very few Pentecostals handle venomous snakes and drink poison in response to a statement attributed to Jesus in the Gospel of Mark, which says that believers can do these things without harm (Mark 16:17–18).

---

[19]Assemblies of God, www.ag.org
[20]The United Pentecostal Church International, www.upci.org/doctrine/holyGhost.asp

Some of the divisions that occurred within the holiness-pentecostal movement came about as churches began to differ about the role of glossolalia. The Wesleyan Church's statement on this topic illustrates the position that some churches take:

> The Wesleyan Church believes in the miraculous use of languages and the interpretation of languages in its biblical and historical setting. But it is contrary to the Word of God to teach that speaking in an unknown tongue or the gift of tongues is the evidence of the baptism of the Holy Spirit or of that entire sanctification which the baptism accomplishes; therefore, only a language readily understood by the congregation is to be used in public worship.[21]

We can explore the history of Pentecostalism in terms of three "waves." The first, traditional Pentecostalism, began in America in the late nineteenth and early twentieth centuries at Bethel Bible College in Topeka, Kansas, and most decisively at the Azuza Street Mission in Los Angeles. It was an outgrowth of the holiness movement. Like holiness, traditional Pentecostalism usually emphasizes the necessity of outward holiness. More important, Pentecostals focus on what they call the baptism of the Holy Spirit (often referred to in these churches as the Holy Ghost). This is said to be an encounter with God that can precede or follow water baptism. The specific religious experiences believed to be associated with the gift of the Holy Ghost became more important than the lifestyle associated with the holiness movement.

The key person behind the development of Pentecostalism as a movement, however, was William Joseph Seymour, a former slave. After receiving the gift of tongues himself in 1906, Seymour rented a run-down building on Azuza Street in Los Angeles, which became the site of the well-known Azuza Street Mission. Seymour held very enthusiastic religious revivals at Azuza Street, and many people received the various spiritual gifts under his leadership. The mission was eventually renamed the Apostolic Faith Gospel Mission, developed a missionary program both at home and overseas, and published a monthly newsletter plus several other publications. A movement had been born.

Several of the early pentecostal churches still exist in the United States, including the Assemblies of God (the largest), the Church of God (Cleveland, Tennessee), the Church of God in Christ, the Pentecostal Holiness Church, the Foursquare Gospel Church, and the United Pentecostal Church International. Many still retain at least some emphasis on holiness, as well. There are also numerous independent churches in the pentecostal category, which are more likely to require a holiness lifestyle in addition to clear-cut evidence of the spiritual gifts. Their membership tends to come from the lower socioeconomic classes. Many congregations, although certainly not all, are predominantly black. Although they are not limited to any one geographical area, their greatest strength is in the Midwest, the lower Midwest, and the South.

[21]Wesleyan Church, www.wesleyan.org

The second wave is sometimes referred to as the new charismatic or neocharismatic movement. It began in the 1960s. Unlike the first wave, this movement crossed Protestant denominational lines rather than forming new denominations. It also became a part of the Catholic Church. Like the earlier movement, it too emphasized the "gifts of the Spirit," most notably speaking in tongues. Prior to the 1960s, most of the mainline churches either ignored the Pentecostals or criticized their worship as undignified and excessively emotional. This new charismatic movement brought Pentecostal experiences to Christians who had not previously had them and who were not members of traditional pentecostal churches. It began in the United States, as far as we know, when the Reverend Dennis Bennett of Saint Mark's Episcopal Church in Van Nuys, California, his wife, and about seventy other members of his congregation received the gift of tongues during a prayer meeting. The phenomenon spread very rapidly and soon had appeared in every major Protestant denomination as well as in the Roman Catholic Church.

There are several characteristics of this second wave that set it apart from traditional Pentecostalism. For the most part, there has been no large-scale exodus of charismatics from noncharismatic churches. Usually they meet together in small prayer groups in addition to remaining involved in other church activities. In addition, however, the movement has given rise to charismatic groups that include charismatics from all sorts of church backgrounds. The movement emphasizes experience rather than doctrine and has become thoroughly ecumenical, with people of different backgrounds and theologies united in a common bond of experience.

The largest of these ecumenical organizations is the *Full Gospel Businessmen's Fellowship, International*,[22] founded in 1951. The organization has grown rapidly and now has male and female members from all walks of life, a women's group (Women's Aglow Fellowship), and teen and youth groups. The Fellowship is both pentecostal and holiness. There are also groups of charismatic students who meet regularly on most college campuses in the United States.

In contrast to the highly emotional outpourings of early Pentecostalism, this phase of the movement was quieter and its adherents remain so today. This toning down clearly reflects the middle-class and upper-middle-class nature of the movement, another feature in which it differs from traditional Pentecostalism. Most charismatics say that they receive the Holy Spirit in quiet prayer with a small group of other Christians. Those who have already had such experiences gather around people who are seeking the experience, pray with them, and place their hands on the seekers' heads. The initial experience of tongues is usually followed by continuing to speak in tongues and receiving other spiritual gifts. Because it is ecumenical and experiential, it is theologically diverse as well, with very little commonly held theology. Those who have had these experiences are bound together by their experience and by their belief in that experience.

[22]http://www.fgbmfi.org/

The third and current manifestation of this style of Christianity is referred to as the "third wave" or the "signs and wonders" movement. It began in the early 1980s at the Vineyard Church in California. Those who are a part of this wave emphasize demonstrating the truth of the Christian gospel by "signs and wonders." "Power evangelism" reinforces the presentation of the Christian message about human sin and salvation with demonstrations of spiritual gifts in order to reinforce the authenticity and power of the message. Although they downplay speaking in tongues, they emphasize modern day prophecy and the gift of healing.

All three waves of this movement offer people who participate in them the assurance that their God is present with them. Belief is superseded by experiential evidence. Those outside the movement often wonder how those inside it can be sure that what they experience is in fact the work of the Holy Spirit. Nonparticipants often believe that phenomena such as speaking in tongues are the result of self-induced hysteria. There is a middle ground between the uncritical acceptance of the believer and the skepticism of the nonbeliever. When viewed from the empathic perspective of the academic study of religion, the heart of pentecostal religion, old or new, is seen to be both the experience itself and the meaning that it has for those who are a part of it. Whatever the explanation for the experience, it is clear that its meaning to those who are the recipients of it is religious and provides the certainty that they seek.

QUESTIONS AND ACTIVITIES FOR REVIEW, DISCUSSION, AND WRITING

1. Describe briefly how Promise Keepers, the *Left Behind* book series, and Christian television programming reflect the role of evangelical Christianity in American culture.
2. Has anyone ever witnessed to you? How did you feel, and why? If you yourself witness to other people, reflect on what doing so means to you.
3. Write a brief essay in which you describe and then respond to the megachurch phenomenon as a distinctive expression of American culture.
4. What is your response to the views of the religious-political right? Be sure that you can state the reasons for your response.
5. What might be the advantages and disadvantages of separatist fundamentalism for its adherents?
6. If you are not a holiness Christian yourself, how would your life be different if you were? Try to see both positive and negative possibilities. If you are, reflect on what being a holiness Christian means to you.
7. If you are not a pentecostal or charismatic Christian yourself, discuss with friends or classmates who are what that experience means to them. If you are, reflect on what it means to you.
8. If possible, attend a pentecostal or charismatic worship service and write an essay in which you reflect on what you observed and experienced. Women: If you attend a traditional pentecostal service, remember that many of these churches do have a dress code for women. You may want to call first and inquire.

FOR FURTHER READING

COWAN, DOUGLAS E., *The Remnant Spirit: Conservative Reform in Mainline Protestantism.* Westport, CT: Praeger Publishers, 2003. Cowan describes and analyzes the growth of conservative sentiment within mainline Protestantism, especially in response to denominational involvement with controversial social and moral issues.

LOVELAND, ANNE C. AND OTIS B. WHEELER, *From Meetinghouse to Megachurch: A Material and Cultural History.* Columbia, MO: University of Missouri Press, 2003. This is an excellent historical study that clearly documents how megachurches have arisen out of a complex matrix of historical and sociocultural factors.

PATTERSON, ERIC AND PATTERSON, ERIC EDMUND RYBARCZYK, eds. *The Future of Pentecostalism in the United States.* Lanham, MD: Lexington Books, 2007. This is an edited collection of essays from a wide range of disciplinary perspectives.

RELEVANT WORLD WIDE WEB SITES

Promise Keepers: www.promisekeepers.org
National Association of Evangelicals: www.nae.net
Hartford Institute for Religion Research: http://hirr.hartsem.edu/
Christian Coalition: www.cc.org
American Council of Christian Churches: www.amcouncilcc.org

CHAPTER 6

Catholic Christianity:
Sacramental Community

If you are not a Catholic Christian, ask yourself what your attitudes and feelings about Catholic people are. If you are a Catholic, are you aware of any anti-Catholic prejudice? You might want to discuss these questions with friends who are and are not Catholic.

Catholics make up approximately one-fourth of the population of the United States, making this group the largest single community of faith in the nation. It is these people's story, or rather, stories, to which we now turn in our exploration of the Christian majority in the United States. In Chapter 4, we looked at the distinctiveness of Christianity and then of Protestant Christianity. Now we turn to Catholicism, its similarities to Protestantism and its distinctiveness.

Catholics were likely the first Europeans to set foot on the shores of what would become the United States. The first Catholic Mass[1] was probably celebrated by a missionary Spanish Catholic priest. Spanish Catholic missionaries were active in the Southwest and in Florida, while French Catholic missionaries traveled throughout what we know as New York, Maine, Pennsylvania, Wisconsin, Michigan and Illinois, as well as down the Mississippi River to Alabama and Louisiana. These Spanish and French explorer-missionaries came to the New World with the two goals of gaining territory and evangelizing the native peoples.

English Catholics came as settlers rather than as missionaries in search of territory and converts. They arrived in the eastern seaboard area after the persecution of Catholics in England launched by King Henry VIII forced them to flee for their lives. They did not get on well with their Spanish and French predecessors, bringing Old World hostilities with them into the New World.

Throughout the colonial period, as before, the number of Catholics remained small, less than one percent of the population. This changed as more European immigrants, including those from Ireland, swelled their ranks. Perhaps more than any other American church, the Catholic Church still

---

[1]The Mass is the central act of Catholic worship.

Figure 6-1   The Mission of San Diego de Alcala founded by Father Junipero Serra was the first Catholic Church in California. *(Photo by the author.)*

remains distinctive for its proportion of immigrant members, who bring with them varying styles of Catholicism.

The decade of the 1960s had a tremendous effect on Catholicism in the United States. Three events are particularly noteworthy:

- John F. Kennedy became the first (and so far, only) Catholic President. His popularity, charisma, and the integrity with which he was both American and Catholic reassured non-Catholic Americans that Catholics could be trusted.
- Pope John XXIII, who had been elected to his office two years earlier, became one of the most popular Popes in history and reached out in friendship to both non-Catholic Christians and non-Christians.
- The Second Vatican Council (1962–1965) brought about substantial innovations in the Catholic Church, many of which made Catholicism seem less foreign to non-Catholics.

Most people in the United States today regard Catholicism as a part of the religious mainstream. This has not always been the case. The history of Catholics in America has in part been a history of prejudice and discrimination. In some of the original thirteen colonies, being Catholic was illegal. In all the colonies, there were times when Catholic people could neither vote nor hold public office.

Unorganized and informal anti-Catholic sentiment has existed as long as Catholics have been here. An attitude of "America for Americans" has far too often meant America for white Protestant Americans. This same attitude, it should be noted, has affected and sometimes continues to affect Jews, Muslims, Asian Americans, and African Americans, among others. Non-Catholic Americans have feared that if Catholicism were to become dominant, religious liberty would be lost. This fear overlooks the constant and outspoken support America's Catholic people have given to the separation of church and state. Some people have also thought of Catholics as subjects of a foreign ruler, the Pope, and hence less than fully loyal to the United States. This, too, overlooks the historical record. Especially prior to Vatican II, Protestant Americans reacted with puzzlement, misinterpretation, and disdain to Catholicism's ritually ornate style of worship and have sometimes referred to it as "superstitious mumbo-jumbo." Occasionally, Catholics, both laity and leaders, have responded in kind with anti-Protestant sentiment.

This informal prejudice became organized into specific groups at various times in history. The American Party, also known as the Know-Nothing Party, actively opposed Catholics in the 1800s. The American protective Association was formed in 1887. Although its stated goals were political rather than religious, its aim was said to be to change the minds and hearts of those who were in "the shackles and chains of blind obedience to the Roman Catholic Church." There was another outburst of organized prejudice in the first half of the 1900s. A resurgent Ku Klux Klan directed its energies as much against Catholics as against blacks and Jews.

THE DISTINCTIVENESS OF CATHOLIC CHRISTIANITY

Before examining the distinctiveness of Catholicism, it is important to locate Catholicism within the larger environment of which it is one aspect. American Catholic theologian Richard P. McBrien helps us to do that: "Catholicism is not a reality that stands by itself. The word *Catholic* is not only a noun but an adjective. As an adjective it is a qualification of *Christian*, just as Christian is a qualification of *religious*, and religious is a qualification of *human*."[2] To be a Catholic, then, is to be a religious human being whose faith and life are guided by the Catholic interpretation of Christianity.

Catholicism shares most characteristics with the whole Christian family of faiths. There are, however, characteristics that distinguish Catholicism, "a particular *configuration* of characteristics within Catholicism that is not duplicated anywhere else in the community of Christian churches."[3] These characteristics are sacramentality, mediation, and communion.[4] In a finely nuanced explanation, McBrien highlights the distinctiveness of Catholicism that shows how Catholicism and Protestantism *together* describe a balanced approach to Christian faith.

---

[2]Richard P. McBrien, *Catholicism*, 3rd ed. (San Francisco: HarperSanFrancisco, 1994), p. 6. Italics in the original.
[3]Ibid., p. 9.
[4]Ibid., pp. 11–14.

Sacramentality points to the understanding that all of reality is sacred. God can be seen in all things. As God became human and very visible, in Jesus, whom Christians call the Christ, so too that which is visible, tangible, finite, and historical reveals the God who is invisible, intangible, infinite, and eternal. The transcendent God is also the indwelling God. There is, for Catholics, no sharp dichotomy between nature and grace because the two interpenetrate each other. The Catholic experience of God in and through the entire created order complements the Protestant experience of God's transcendence that reaches beyond creation.

Mediation further develops the principle of sacramentality. Protestants believe that the sacraments signify or represent sacred realities. Catholics experience the sacraments as actually bringing about what they signify. They are not just signs, but effective signs. They make the spirit of God truly present for the faithful. This is quite similar to how Episcopalians understand sacraments as well.

Communion highlights the importance of the community of faith in the Catholic tradition. Even in its most individualistic aspects, people's relationship with God is mediated through a community of faithful persons. The fellowship of the Church, clergy, and sacraments of the Church are the mediators, the primary means by which people experience God. This, according to McBrien, is the heart of Catholic distinctiveness, because in the Church, the three principles of sacramentality, mediation, and communion converge. The Catholic emphasis on the importance of the community of faith balances the Protestant emphasis on the importance of the individual's relationship with Jesus and God.

Additionally, McBrien points out the importance of the Church's self-understanding:

> Catholicism is distinctive among American denominational forms of Christianity, as well, in that it considers itself the only complete instance of the Church as the Body of Christ on Earth. In particular, the Catholic understanding of the Eucharist and tracing the papacy back to Peter [see Additional Distinctive Catholic Beliefs] demarcate its self-understanding as the true Church. As much as the Second Vatican Council opened the Church to ecumenical[5] understandings and endeavors, it did not change this basic teaching.

ADDITIONAL DISTINCTIVE CATHOLIC BELIEFS

Catholics share with Protestants the belief that *salvation comes to people by the grace of God. However, a great deal more emphasis is placed on the role of the Church as the official agent and mediator of God's grace.* The Church mediates by its official teaching and interpretation of the Bible, and it mediates through its administration of the sacraments. The sacraments as administered by the Church are believed to be channels through which the grace of God flows to people.

Catholics, although they regard the Bible as the original revelation, also teach that the tradition of the Church is equal with the Bible in authority. They

---

[5]*Ecumenical* refers to dialogue and cooperation among various Christian churches and organizations.

believe that the Church is the official interpreter of the Bible. Tradition and Scripture together are accorded the same respect and veneration. The writings of the Church Fathers, the decisions of Church councils, and the pronouncements of the Popes from Peter onward are all regarded as genuine sources of religious truth and as a part of the whole revelation of God to the Church. The Second Vatican Council placed greater emphasis on the Bible. For example, it said that the Liturgy of the Word, in which the Bible is read, is not just preparation for the Liturgy of the Eucharist in the Mass but is an integral part of a single act of worship. It also urged people to seek renewed spiritual vitality through increasing attention to the word of God in the Bible, as well as through continued participation in the Eucharist. The sharing of authority between the Bible and the Church and the Church's role as the official interpreter of the Bible are distinctive Catholic beliefs.

The doctrine of papal infallibility is unique to the Catholic Church. Many non-Catholic people misunderstand this teaching of the Church. It does not mean that the Pope never makes a mistake or never sins. In reality, this doctrine applies in only a very few circumstances. When the Pope speaks officially on matters of faith and morals that are absolutely central to the life of the Church, it is believed that God prevents him from making errors. The current *Catechism of the Catholic Church* describes infallibility in a way that relates it to the whole Church and its founding:

> In order to preserve the Church in the purity of the faith handed on by the apostles, Christ who is the Truth willed to confer on her a share in his own infallibility. . . . The Roman Pontiff, head of the college of bishops, enjoys this infallibility in virtue of his office, when, as supreme pastor and teacher of all the faithful—who confirms his brethren in the faith—he proclaims by a definitive act a doctrine pertaining to faith or morals. . . . The infallibility promised to the Church is also present in the body of bishops when, together with Peter's successor [the Pope], they exercise the supreme Magisterium [authority].[6]

Catholics also believe that authority in the Church has come down in a direct line from Peter and hence from Christ himself. This view is called *apostolic succession*. This doctrine, operative through the sacrament of Holy Orders by which men are ordained to the priesthood, is the temporal foundation of the Church. The principal biblical support for apostolic succession comes from a passage in the Gospel of Saint Matthew. In these verses, Jesus is speaking to one of the apostles: "You are Peter, and on this rock I will build my church, and the powers of death shall not prevail against it. I will give you the keys of the kingdom of Heaven; and whatever you bind on earth shall be bound in heaven, and whatever you loose on earth shall be loosed in heaven" (Matthew 16:17–19). "The Lord made Saint Peter the visible foundation of his Church. He entrusted the keys of the Church to him. The bishop of the Church of Rome [the Pope], successor to

---

[6]*Catechism of the Catholic Church*, 889 and 891. This document itself is an excellent example of the official nature of the Magisterium of the Church, in that it is the English version of the official teaching of the Church.

Saint Peter, is head of the college of bishops, the Vicar of Christ and Pastor of the universal Church on Earth."[7]

There are other mediators as well. Any discussion of Catholic belief and practice would be incomplete if the Catholic *devotion to Mary*, the mother of Jesus, *and to the other saints* were not mentioned. Unlike Jesus, who, most Christians believe, was both divine and human, the saints and Mary were fully human and no more while alive on Earth. A good deal of Catholic private devotion centers on these figures, who are in a sense "closer" to the believer because of having shared their human condition without benefit of simultaneous divinity. Catholics teach that Mary and the other saints pray to God on the believers' behalf and watch over the needs and concerns of the faithful. As the author of a study of Catholic women states,

> For Catholics . . . Mary the mother of Jesus has been the feminine face of God. To be sure, Mary is not God, according to orthodox Christian theology. . . . Nevertheless, people pray to Mary. She may not be God in their spoken creed, but in the language of the heart, she functions as God.[8]

The unique Catholic doctrine of *purgatory* illustrates the mediating role of the Church, as well. Catholics believe with other Christians that the faithful will have life after physical death. Purgatory is believed to be *a place or condition of further purification after death in which some must exist before they attain the beatific vision of God*. Upon death, individuals without any taint of sin may enter heaven directly. However, few people are this pure. In purgatory, people make amends for less serious sins that were not forgiven or for more serious sins that had been forgiven prior to death. Freed from guilt and punishment, the soul can enter into heaven, not only beholding God directly but being of the same mind and heart with God. The justice of God that requires that sin be punished and the mercy of God that seeks the salvation of all are thus reconciled. The doctrine of purgatory also provides a means by which the living may assist the souls of the dead through prayers and good works, because it is taught that such prayers and works may shorten the length of time a soul spends in purgatory. In this way, the belief in purgatory can help those who grieve for a loved one to work out their grief. It is important to note here that Catholics believe that God is an infinitely loving parent who will not reject anyone who does not reject God. God creates people with free will and the freedom to sin or to obey, and God goes to great lengths to see to it that disobedience does not result in condemnation unless there are no other alternatives.

CATHOLIC WORSHIP: WORD AND SACRAMENT

The central act of Catholic worship is called the *Mass*. The Mass is an integrated experience of worship that is made up of two parts that work together. The *Liturgy of the Word* includes those parts of the Mass that focus on verbal

[7]Ibid., 936.
[8]Jane Redmont, *Generous Lives: American Catholic Women Today* (Liguori, MO: Triumph Books, 1992), p. 102.

communication, such as Bible readings, prayers, responsive readings, and a sermon, often called a *homily* by Catholics. The Bible readings always include a reading from one of the four Gospels and another reading from either the New Testament or the Old Testament. The *Liturgy of the Eucharist* reenacts, in words and actions, Jesus's sharing bread and wine with the disciples at the Last Supper. Catholic worship is highly liturgical, with ornate symbolism; the use of incense and chanting, symbolic colors, and vestments worn by the priest; and an air of high solemnity. Since the Second Vatican Council, many Catholic Churches have experimented with more casual masses that often include folk songs and liturgical dance, but the twin elements of the Liturgy of the Word and the Liturgy of the Eucharist are always present.

Catholics believe that in the *sacrament of the Eucharist*, the bread and wine actually become the body and blood of Jesus Christ when the priest speaks the words of consecration ("This is my body. . . . This is my blood"— words that the Gospel records as Jesus saying to his disciples at the Last Supper). This belief in *transubstantiation* is based on a philosophical distinction between what something actually is (its substance) and what it appears to be. In transubstantiation, the substance of the bread and wine become the body and blood of Christ, who is fully present under the appearances of bread and wine. This sacrament, received often throughout a Catholic's life, is ordinarily received at Mass, but it may also be received privately when circumstances such as illness call for doing so.

> The Eucharist is the heart and summit of the Church's life, for in it Christ associates his Church and all her members with his sacrifice of praise and thanksgiving offered once for all on the cross to his Father; by this sacrifice he pours out the graces of salvation on his Body which is the Church.

> As sacrifice, the Eucharist is also offered in reparation for the sins of the living and the dead and to obtain spiritual or temporal benefits from God.[9]

Other Sacraments

The first sacrament in which Catholics participate is *baptism*. "Baptism is birth into the new life in Christ. In accordance with the Lord's will, it is necessary for salvation, as is the Church herself, which we enter by baptism."[10] Catholics believe that baptism is necessary for the removal of the inborn sin that is a part of all persons simply because they are human. Most Catholics are baptized when they are babies. When the sacrament is performed for an adult, it is often called the *Rite of Christian Initiation*, a name that points to its other function as the ritual of incorporation into the Church.

The sacrament of *confirmation* completes what is begun in baptism. It signifies that the person has become an adult in the eyes of the Church and

---

[9]*Catechism of the Catholic Church*, 1407 and 1414.
[10]Ibid., 1277.

confirms the promises made by others at baptism. The one who is being confirmed is anointed on the forehead with oil that has been blessed to signify the seal of the Holy Spirit. This sacrament is believed to give the grace necessary to live a mature Christian life in the Church:

> Confirmation perfects Baptismal grace; it is the sacrament which gives the Holy Spirit in order to root us more deeply in the divine filiation, incorporate us more firmly into Christ, strengthen our bond with the Church, associate us more closely with her mission, and help us bear witness to the Christian faith in words accompanied by deeds.[11]

The sacrament of *reconciliation*, or *confession*, nourishes and supports Catholics throughout their lives. Penitents confess their sins to God through the priest, who, in the name of God and with the authority of the Church, pronounces forgiveness. Special prayers or other activities (sometimes called *penance*) may be assigned to assist people in recovering from the effects of their sins. Catholics are expected to confess through a priest at least annually, but many find that the practice helps them be aware of God's forgiving grace and confess more frequently. Non-Catholics often stereotype Catholics by saying that Catholics can confess to a priest and then go out and sin all over again. Catholic Christians, however, believe that the rite of reconciliation must be accompanied by genuine sorrow for having sinned and by a clear intention to avoid it in the future.

The Second Vatican Council revised the Church's understanding of this sacrament somewhat, lessening the emphasis given to the penance performed and emphasizing the rite as one of reconciliation, which is the spiritual reuniting of the penitent with God, other persons, and the Church.

A fifth sacrament is now commonly known as the sacrament of *anointing the sick*; formerly, it was called extreme function or, simply, the last rites. This sacrament, in which a priest uses oil to anoint a person who is ill or in danger of dying from accident or old age, is a way of mediating the concern of Christ and the Church for the suffering person. Catholics believe that the sacrament gives grace for healing, if that is God's will, or to assist a person in the passage from life to death and beyond, if that is to be the final outcome. The understanding of this rite was broadened by Vatican II to include its use for those who are seriously ill but not in immediate danger of death.

The sacrament of *marriage* is one to which most Catholics look forward. The majority of Catholics, like the majority of all Americans, marry at some time in their lives. Although the stereotype of Catholics having larger-than-average families no longer holds true, marriage and family continue to be very important, because marriage is a sacrament. Blessed by a priest, authorized by the Church, and entered into only after a period of required counseling, Catholics believe that the sacrament of marriage gives the couple the special grace necessary to carry out the promises they make to each other. Because marriage is a sacrament in

[11]Ibid., 1316.

which two people are believed to be joined by God, the Catholic Church teaches that it is a lifelong commitment:

> The sacrament of Matrimony signifies the union of Christ and the Church. It gives spouses the grace to love each other with the love with which Christ has loved his Church; the grace of the sacrament thus perfects the human love of the spouses, strengthens their indissoluble unity, and sanctifies them on the way to eternal life.[12]

The Church does not recognize divorce and teaches that persons who divorce and remarry are held to be living in sin and are barred from receiving the sacraments. There is a process through which a couple can obtain an *annulment* of their marriage. If an annulment is granted, it is as if the marriage had never happened. People whose marriages have been annulled can remarry in the Church. Because the marriage bond is sacred, however, such annulments are difficult to obtain. Statistical data indicate that, in actual practice, American Catholics divorce and remarry in about the same proportions as do non-Catholics. In this matter, American Catholics are influenced more by the culture of which they are a part than they are by the teachings of their Church.

The sacrament of *orders*, or *ordination to the priesthood*, sets a man apart for the official sacramental ministry of the Church. Catholics believe that it gives the priest the grace required to carry out the demands of his priesthood. Only men are ordained to the Catholic priesthood.

> Holy Orders is the sacrament through which the mission entrusted by Christ to his apostles continues to be exercised in the Church until the end of time; thus it is the sacrament of apostolic ministry.

> Through the ordained ministry, especially that of bishops and priests, the presence of Christ as head of the Church is made visible in the midst of the community of believers.[13]

CATHOLIC LIFESTYLES IN THE UNITED STATES

In the main, the moral views of Catholic people in the United States differ little from those of their non-Catholic counterparts. This is true even in those areas in which the Church speaks the most forcefully: artificial conception control, abortion, premarital sexual activity, and homosexuality. For example, recent survey data show Catholic teens are more likely, and in some cases far more likely, than their Protestant counterparts to approve of marriage between homosexual persons, as well as to approve of premarital sex and premarital cohabitation. These views closely reflect those of Catholic adults. Neither group, however, condones extramarital affairs.[14]

[12]Ibid., 1661.
[13]Ibid., 1536 and 1549.
[14]The Gallup Organization, "Gallup Tuesday Briefing," April 9, 2002, p. 5.

The context in which these issues are set for Catholics is distinctive, however. The Church's opposition to abortion is a useful case in point. In Protestant fundamentalism, opposition to abortion is usually linked with support for capital punishment, welfare conservatism, support for nuclear arms, and for defense spending. In the Catholic Church's *consistent life ethic*, opposition to abortion is linked with support for both private and government-funded services for pregnant women and for the children of single mothers and with opposition to capital punishment, nuclear weapons, and excessive funding for the military. Except for questions of personal sexual morality, the positions that U.S. bishops take are usually to the liberal end of the continuum of American views, particularly on economic and defense issues.

Another example is the noteworthy range of things covered under the discussion of the fifth commandment ("you shall not kill") in the contemporary *Catechism*: The core point is that no one can claim the right to end a life because God alone is Lord of life from beginning to end. Killing when necessary in self-defense or in defense of another is upheld. The death penalty is held not to violate the commandment "in cases of extreme gravity" to protect society, but "if bloodless means are sufficient" then "public authority should limit itself to such means." Refusing assistance to people in danger violates the commandment. Societal acceptance of widespread famine is given as an example. Direct abortion is of course included among violations, as is direct euthanasia. Discontinuing heroic medical measures and the use of painkillers to alleviate suffering even when such use may shorten life is, however, acceptable. Suicide also goes against the commandment. Society is charged with the responsibility to help all of its citizens to attain "living conditions that allow them to grow and reach maturity: food and clothing, housing, health care, basic education, and social assistance." Temperance and the avoidance of excess is mentioned, and it is noted that people "who, by drunkenness or a love of speed, endanger their own and others' safety on the road, at sea, or in the air" are said to "incur grave guilt." Kidnapping, hostage taking, and other terrorist acts are forbidden by the commandment, as are any but therapeutic amputations, mutilations, and sterilizations performed on innocent people. Autopsy and organ donation are acceptable. Safeguarding peace and avoiding war is encouraged. In conjunction with this, acts of war that destroy entire cities or vast areas and the people in them are condemned, and the specific danger of weapons of mass destruction is addressed.[15]

A key feature of life for a minority of Catholic youngsters is that they attend parochial schools sponsored by their Church. Parochial schools provide education within the context of Catholic values. Education about their faith and regular participation in Mass are included in their school experience. So is learning about religions other than Catholicism. They may be taught by nuns or brothers or by lay teachers. A flourishing parochial school is a focal point of the parish and a center for its social life as well as an educational institution.

Fewer Catholic youngsters attend parochial schools now than in the past, a part of the loss of distinctiveness of Catholic life in the United States. Slightly over

[15]*Catechism of the Catholic Church*, 2258 through 2317.

one-fourth of Catholic elementary- and middle-school children and under one-fifth of Catholic high-school students attend parochial schools. Among Catholic college students, only 10 percent attend colleges sponsored by the Church.[16]

Catholic education is not limited to parochial schools. About 600,000 students are enrolled in 236 Catholic institutions of higher education. These include one of the historically black universities and 49 women's colleges, which account for half of the women's colleges in the country.[17] Although the question of what exactly is *Catholic* about education in these institutions is difficult to answer, their place in the overall picture of American higher education remains very important.

In addition, the Catholic Church maintains an active ministry to Catholic students on both Catholic and non-Catholic campuses. In the late 1800s, a society where Catholic students could meet regularly for fellowship and support was organized. Cardinal Newman was a well-known name in Catholic circles and was associated with university education, having been involved in the founding of the Catholic University of Ireland in Dublin, and his name was picked for the organization. By 1920, there were "Newman Clubs" on many campuses. Following the Second Vatican Council, the name was changed to the *Catholic Student Ministry*; many local groups still retain a reference to Cardinal Newman in their name.[18]

THE CHURCH AS A SOCIAL INSTITUTION

As you learned in Chapter 4, the Protestant way of being Christian strongly emphasizes the individual's relationship with God, mediated through Jesus who is believed to be God incarnate. Catholics experience this relationship somewhat differently, although the difference is one of degree rather than of kind. As Catholics experience it,

> We relate more fully to God with the help of others than when we try to do it by ourselves. . . . Hence the Catholic community, organized however imperfectly by the Church institution, is a sacrament of God, especially in the experience of the local parish community.[19]

The Catholic Church is hierarchical in its formal organization. The *Pope* is the worldwide leader and is revered by Catholics as the *Vicar*[20] *of Christ on Earth* (Figure 6-2). He is also *Bishop of Rome*. The Pope is assisted by the College of Cardinals and by the Roman Curia. The College of Cardinals advises the

---

[16]Dean R. Hoge, "Catholics in the U.S.: The Next Generation," in *The Public Perspective: A Roper Center Review of Public Opinion and Polling*, vol. 2, no.1 (November/December 1990), p. 11.

[17]David J. O'Brien, *From the Heart of the American Church: Catholic Higher Education and American Culture* (Maryknoll, NY: Orbis Books, 1994), p. 70.

[18]Thanks to the late Rev. James R. Bates, former Director of Ball State University's Newman Center, for information on the Catholic Student Ministry.

[19]Andrew M. Greeley, "The Catholics in the World and in America," in *World Religions in America*, 3rd ed. Jacob Neusner (Upper Saddle River, NJ: Prentice Hall, 2003), p. 74

[20]*Vicar* means "official representative."

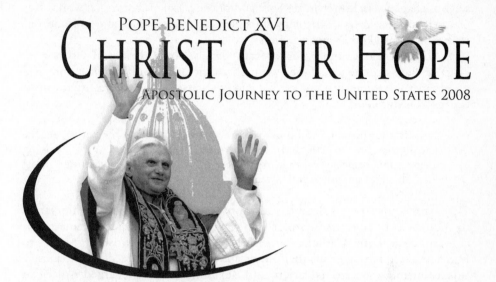

POPE BENEDICT XVI
CHRIST OUR HOPE
APOSTOLIC JOURNEY TO THE UNITED STATES 2008

Figure 6-2   Pope Benedict XVI made an official apostolic visit to the United States in 2008. *(United States Conference of Catholic Bishops/Dorling Kindersley.)*

Pope and is responsible for electing a new Pope upon the death of the previous one. The Curia has a more administrative function. Archbishops and bishops are appointed by the Pope, taking into account the recommendations of local leaders. Archbishops are in charge of large geographical or population units, and bishops have authority over smaller areas. Local priests have jurisdiction to the extent that it is delegated to them by their bishops. In the Catholic Church in America, local councils of priests and bishops meet in an advisory capacity, and lay parish councils in the local church advise the priest and serve as a link between the ordained leadership and the lay people who make up the broad base of the organizational pyramid.

The Catholic Church has many male monastic orders and many orders of nuns for women. Nuns and monks serve as full-time religious workers in parochial schools, in Church-sponsored hospitals and other agencies, as teachers in Catholic colleges and universities, and in a variety of other tasks. Much of the outreach work of the Church is done by these dedicated men and women who, while not priests, have a ministry that is of equal importance in the life of the Church. The requirement that priests remain unmarried is an important part of Catholic practice. Although this practice has not always been a part of the Church's teaching, and its historical development is somewhat confusing, its present-day practice seems to have two main functions: The priest is understood to be in the likeness of Christ, and, as far as we can know from the biblical accounts, Jesus never married. Not having the responsibility for a family also frees the priest to devote his full attention to his priesthood.

There are many laymen and laywomen who work professionally in Catholic churches, as well. They often have seminary training, as do the ordained. They serve as chaplains in hospitals, schools, and prisons; as parish outreach workers; as counselors; as teachers of theology in colleges and seminaries; and as leaders of retreat centers and other organizations.

For American Catholics, as for Catholics elsewhere, their local parish is the heart of their experience of their Church. Although the official structure and governance are somewhat monolithic and centralized, the lived reality for most Catholics is different:

> In fact, from the empirical point of view of most Catholics, the parish and the parish priest *are* the Church. If they like their parish priest and think he's doing a good job (especially in liturgy—that is, worship and preaching), most Catholics are content with their church.[21]

This leads to considerable variation in actual practice from one parish to another as the rules are interpreted in ways that take local circumstances into account. As a result, Catholics sometimes "shop" among parishes in order to find a local church that suits their needs and preferences. Indeed, it "is precisely this astonishing grassroots variety and flexibility that has enabled American Catholics to remain Catholic on their own terms during the troubling last thirty years of Catholic history."[22] This flexibility will in all likelihood remain an important aspect of Catholicism in the United States, displeasing to conservatives within the Church and equally pleasing to those who are more liberal.

THE SECOND VATICAN COUNCIL, 1962–1965

Prior to Vatican II, the boundaries that marked Catholicism off from other Christian communities of faith were drawn quite clearly or at least so it seemed. Those boundaries became much less distinctive after Vatican II. There is continuity between the pre-Vatican II church and the post-Vatican II church, but they are also quite different, and the differences make the post-conciliar church less distinctive as a way of being Christian in the United States.

The council "solved some of the lingering problems of being a Catholic in the United States." Catholics no longer felt as "different" nor did their non-Catholic neighbors regard them as such:

> Most important, the Council reversed earlier Catholic teaching by affirming the separation of church and state and religious liberty for all. In one stroke a major sore point for American Catholics was removed. Also, the Council redefined the Church as the "People of God" and advocated increased democratization of church structures, a more participative liturgy [worship], use of the vernacular in worship, reduction of rules of abstinence [here, from meat], ecumenical goodwill with other Christians, an open door to biblical scholarship, and greater self-determination for

---

[21]Andrew M. Greeley, "The Catholics in the World and in America," in *World Religions in America*, 3rd ed. Jacob Neusner (Upper Saddle River, NJ: Prentice Hall, 2003), p. 69
[22]Ibid., p. 71.

men's and women's orders. . . . The siege mentality of the early twentieth century was gone. Ever since, the dominant mood of Catholics has been to embrace American society with little reservation . . . and to feel like full participants in American life.[23]

WHO ARE AMERICAN CATHOLICS?

There is very wide diversity within Catholicism in the United States, as there is within most Christian denominations and other religions as well. One source of this diversity is the presence of three distinctively different generations of Catholic laity and clergy, each of which had a distinctive religious upbringing:

- Pre-Vatican II Catholics who matured before the council tend to prefer the older model of the Church with which they are familiar, hierarchical, and traditional in its ways of doing things and having a great deal of authority in the lives of believers. Being Catholic and being Christian are believed to be the same thing, and God's law and the Church's law are experienced as one. They tend to take their Church's teachings "whole," without distinguishing among them. This group of American Catholics is shrinking due to death, although some younger Catholics fit this description as well.
- Vatican II Catholics, those who came of age during the council, have one foot in each Church, so to speak, and their views tend to lie between those of the younger and the older generations.
- Post-Vatican II Catholics have experienced only the post-conciliar Church, prefer the more democratic and less institutional Church of their formative years, and are much more individualistic in their interpretation of what it means to be Catholic. They distinguish between being Catholic and being Christian and between God's law and the laws of the Church.[24]

Another source of diversity, somewhat related to the first, is the variety of styles of being Catholic practiced by individual Catholics. One Catholic sociologist identifies five categories.[25] Although Gillis describes Catholics, these types can be found throughout the religious world. (See especially Chapter 5 for how these distinctions play out in Protestantism.) Although they do not occur in precisely the same ways, they are also evident among followers of Judaism, Islam, and of Asian religions in the United States (see Chapters 9, 10, and 12).

- Some Catholics fit the profile of what would traditionally have been described as "good Catholics." They attend Mass at least weekly, obey the Church's teachings in matters of faith and morals, and in general look to their Church as their primary guide through life.
- Another group identifies with the Church and participates in its worship and programs regularly but disagree with the Church on certain points. They might,

[23]William V., James D. Davidson, Dean R. Hoge, and Ruth A. Wallace, D'Antonio et al., *Laity American and Catholic: Transforming the Church* (Kansas City: Sheed and Ward, 1966), pp. 9–10.
[24]D'Antonio et al., *Laity American and Catholic*, Chapters 4 and 5.
[25]Chester Gillis, *Roman Catholicism in America* (New York: Columbia University Press, 1999), Chapter 1.

for example, practice artificial birth control or believe that premarital sex is acceptable under certain circumstances.

- Others go to Mass irregularly and pick and choose which teachings and practices they will follow. In making these decisions, their own point of view and conscience clearly take precedence over official Church teaching and practice. They are within the Church yet operate to a large extent independently of it.
- Others whose ties to the Church are less central in their lives claim Catholicism as their faith but have little contact with the Church except at times of crisis and major Christian festivals such as Christmas and Easter.
- There are also those who were baptized into the Catholic Church but this is their only connection with it. They do not participate and do not look to the Church for guidance and support. They may still, however, wish to marry in the Church, have their children baptized, and be buried with its blessing.

The relationship between official Catholicism—its doctrines, *Catechism*, dogmas, conciliar documents, papal encyclicals and bishops' pastoral letters, and official ritual life—and Catholicism as it is interpreted and lived out by the diverse American Catholic population is thus a complex one. Jay P. Dolan, an emeritus professor of history at Notre Dame University, a prominent Catholic university, writes, "I believe American and Catholic represent two souls, two strivings. . . . These two fundamental strivings, to be both Catholic and American, have animated me throughout my life, and they are not unreconcilable."[26]

Although the major Protestant denominations were also imported into the United States, they had been shaped from birth by the democratizing tendencies of the Protestant Reformation itself, which was in part a struggle to make religion of the people and for the people, to shift its focus away from the institutional church. Catholicism did not have that prior democratizing influence. In coming to the United States, the Catholic Church came to a country whose ways of doing things challenged it and invited, sometimes necessitated, adaptation. That process continues to this day.

Dolan identifies five themes or issues in the challenge of being both Catholic and American.

- The first is the democratization of local parish life. How much say should lay people have in how their local churches are run? How much authority should the hierarchy exercise over local church affairs? Increasing involvement of lay people has meant correspondingly less control in the hands of their priests. American Catholics have faced a dilemma brought about by the interface of America's long heritage of democracy with the structure of their church, which has not been at all democratic.[27]
- Immigrant American Catholics, coming as they did from various parts of Europe, brought with them styles of devotional Catholicism that were part of their home cultures. The liturgy, although standardized in structure, was nevertheless strongly

---

[26]Jay P. Dolan, *In Search of an American Catholicism: A History of Religion and Culture in Tension* (New York: Oxford University Press, 2002), pp. 3–4.

[27]Ibid., p. 84. This discussion draws on Chapter 3 of Dolan's excellent study.

influenced by the piety of national origins, as were the styles of private devotion. As time went on, immigrant Catholics, and especially their descendants, became less identified with their countries of origin and became more American. Change and adaptation occurred as they sought to develop a style of worship and devotion that was more suited to their new environment. Two very visible results were a decline in the observance of pietistic devotions such as praying the rosary, and the presence of fewer religious artifacts such as statues and crucifixes, in Catholic homes.

- The question of national identity itself became a source of debate. The Catholic Church encompassed a great deal of diversity in national and ethnic parishes in which people could continue not only their familiar style of Catholicism but their larger cultural identity as well. As American nativism burgeoned in the final decades of the nineteenth century, Catholics came under attack. Prejudice flared against the persistent national identities of immigrant Catholics. In addition, Protestant America interpreted Catholics' loyalty to Rome as a threat. Could the Catholic Church become a truly American church?[28]

- A fourth debate was over the development of a distinctive American Catholic doctrine. How distinctive should the American Church be? How different from the "faith of the fathers" in Rome? And if it were to develop distinctively, then what of its relation to the worldwide Church? The forces that tended toward "Americanization" and the proponents of American Catholic distinctiveness called for change in a church in which unity and tradition were paramount.

- Finally, changes in the roles of women in the United States challenged Catholics' thinking about the roles of women in society and in the Church itself. The traditional idea of women primarily as mothers was embraced by most Americans, Catholic or not. Tensions developed as women sought to redefine women's roles and place in society. These tensions affected Catholic women acutely. Catholic women felt and continue to feel that they receive mixed messages about women's proper roles from their Church.[29]

The tension between religion and nationality continues today, stimulated by the steady arrival of Catholic immigrants. As you are probably aware, there are many immigrants coming to America's shores. These newly arrived Catholics come from many places, including the Philippines, Korea, Vietnam, India, and Africa. They also come from Puerto Rico, Cuba, the Dominican Republic, El Salvador, and Guatemala, as war, political and social unrest, and economic problems have shaken those nations. The greatest proportion are Hispanics, who now account for about 40 percent of Catholics in this country. By 2020, it is estimated that over half of all Catholics in the United States will be Hispanics.[30] This high proportion of immigrant members is one thing that makes the Catholic Church in the United States different than the Catholic Church elsewhere in the world.

Hispanic Catholics bring unique traditions and practices with them. Two notable ones include their devotion to the Virgin of Guadalupe and the posadas. The Virgin of Guadalupe, understood as an appearance of the Virgin

[28]Ibid., pp. 92–93.
[29]Ibid., p. 124.
[30]"The Church in Transition: Immigration Brings New Hope," *The Catholic Spirit: On Line Edition*, www.catholicspirit.com/stories/2007/may/10immigration.html

Mary to a poor Mexican Indian named Juan Diego, symbolizes "empowerment and vindication for the oppressed native inhabitants of these lands, and in general for all the poor and the downtrodden.[31] Posadas means "lodgings." For nine days preceding Christmas Eve, people reenact Mary and Joseph's quest for lodging before the birth of Jesus. Catholic scholar Justo Gonzales writes that the posadas are "lots of fun."

But more than that, they have become very important for people who have had to move repeatedly looking for work, many of whom do not have legal papers for residence in the United States, while others, even those who are citizens by birth, are often told in many different ways that they are foreigners. In such a situation, it is comforting and strengthening to remember that Jesus too had difficulty finding a place, that he was born away from home, and that thereafter he was an exile in Egypt.[32]

The situation in which the American Church found itself—pluralism, disestablishment, and freedom of religion in a democratic state—differed greatly from that which has prevailed throughout most of its worldwide history. This led directly to the questions of adaptation or inculturation described earlier. Inculturation, according to one Catholic author, is "the process of deep, sympathetic adaptation and appropriation of a local cultural setting in which the Church finds itself in a way that does not compromise its basic faith in Christ."[33] Inculturation, then, is something the Catholic Church has done worldwide. In the United States, it has taken place almost from the beginning of the Church's presence here. However, the pace of change in the United States, especially since the 1960s, and the wide divergence between American and traditional ideas and ideals, has made these issues particularly intense here.

These issues have also led to liberal and conservative disagreement within the Church. While most American Catholics find themselves somewhere in the middle between these two extremes, there are vocal proponents of both extremes. The heart of the divide seems to be the question of authority: To what extent must Catholics accept their Church's authority over their lives and to what extent may they rely on their individual conscience in making religious and moral decisions? Additional issues include the democratization of the Church and appropriate roles for laypeople, differences related to ordination, and disagreements on specific moral issues.

Typically, for example, *Catholic conservatives*

- believe Catholics are duty-bound to follow the directives of the Church on all matters of faith and morals and believe that obedience to the Church is obedience to God
- support papal infallibility
- believe that the values of the secular world are unalterably opposed to those of the Church

---

[31]Justo L. Gonzales, "The Religious World of Hispanic Americans," in *World Religions in America: An Introduction*, 3rd ed., ed. Jacob Neusner, p. 87.

[32]Ibid.

[33]William Reiser, "Inculturation and Doctrinal Development," *Heythrop Journal*, No. 22 (1981), p. 135.

- believe the government of the Church must remain in the hands of the hierarchy
- accept the decisions of the Second Vatican Council, but cautiously, and believe their implementation by the Church in the United States has been too extreme
- are concerned that changes in the liturgy of the Mass imperil its holiness or erode the sense of mystery and divinity it should have
- support the Church's ban on artificial birth control, homosexual activity, pre-marital sex, abortion, the ordination of women, and the marriage of priests.

On the other hand, *liberal or progressive Catholics* more often

- believe Catholics may follow their individual conscience on matters of faith and morals and distinguish between obedience to the Church and obedience to God
- have reservations about the doctrine of papal infallibility
- believe that the values of the secular world are not inherently dangerous and that some may be incorporated into the life of the Church, using appropriate caution
- support the democratization of Church government at all levels
- affirm the decisions of the Second Vatican Council and encourage their full implementation
- believe that changes in the liturgy of the mass make it more alive and accessible to lay people
- challenge the Church's ban on artificial birth control, homosexual activity, pre-marital sex, abortion, the ordination of women, and the marriage of priests.

WOMEN IN THE CATHOLIC CHURCH

The Catholic Church's attitude toward women has always been complex. Mary, as the mother of Jesus, has been given great respect and honor and is looked upon as the first among women. Her status comes from her mother-hood. She fulfilled in a very special way the role traditionally held up as the most important one for women. Traditional Catholic teaching also empha-sizes Eve, the temptress, as the key figure in the drama of original sin and the human fall from grace, partially offsetting the effect of the veneration of Mary.

Catholic orders of nuns are another example of this complexity. These orders were the first institutional opportunity for the involvement of women in religion in America. They provided a setting in which women could carry out specific duties within the context of a close-knit community of women. Especially for those who did not have the desire or the opportunity to marry, these orders were a means to security and respectability. Negatively, the female orders were closely governed by male superiors in the Church and had little, if any, autonomy in their early years.

In the nineteenth century, many nuns taught in public and private schools, as well as in parochial schools. Others worked as nurses in hospitals and other institutions and in private homes. They served heroically as nurses during the Civil and Spanish-American Wars. They played a major role in overcoming

American suspicion and hostility toward Catholicism and Catholic people because of their dedicated work in these areas.[34]

During the nineteenth century, nuns in America sought ways to adapt to democracy. They often broke with their European motherhouses (the American nuns were branches of European orders and responsible to them) in order to adopt regulations that were better suited to their new environment.[35] They also founded American orders. *Mother Elizabeth Bayley Seton* was the first American to be officially declared a saint by the Catholic Church. Seton established the *Sisters of Charity*, the first religious order founded in the United States, in 1809. She is also remembered as the founder of the American Catholic parochial school system.

In the twentieth century, nuns have demonstrated continued commitment and service in the areas of nursing, education, and social work. They have also broadened their participation in the cause of international peace and in addressing the plight of the Third World nations. They are in the forefront of a more general Catholic concern for personal spiritual formation, developing and practicing new ways of personal and community devotion that are compatible with life in the modern era.

The Second Vatican Council brought about new opportunities for nuns. It permitted greater self-government in religious orders. It allowed nuns to increase their contact with the world outside their convents. They no longer had to live in communities with groups of nuns but could live much more on their own in the society. They could find employment in agencies that were not related to the Church. Nuns began attending graduate schools in significant numbers and went on to teach in colleges, universities, and seminaries. In many orders, being a nun no longer meant wearing the distinctive clothing that set them apart from other women in the population.

A cluster of reproductive issues has been at the forefront of much of the discussion about the Catholic Church's attitude toward women. The U.S. Catholic Conference (USCC), the official Washington lobby of U.S. Catholic bishops, has consistently worked to have *abortion* and abortion funding banned. It has voted to work to eliminate clinics that make contraceptive information available in public high schools. The Church continues to restate its well-known teaching that the use of *artificial birth control* is sinful. The Church teaches that the natural result of sexual intercourse is the procreation of children and that any method of contraception that interferes with this end is against the laws of God and the Church. The Church also teaches that the fetus has a soul and is a human being from the moment of conception. Therefore, abortion is murder. Feminists see the Church's position on all these issues as a violation of women's rights to control over their own bodies.

Many women view traditional Catholic teaching about marriage and divorce as yet another unwarranted intrusion of the Church into areas that are best left up

[34]Mary Ewens, "The Leadership of Nuns in Immigrant Catholicism," in *Women and Religion in America, volume I: The Nineteenth Century*, eds. Rosemary Radford Ruether and Rosemary Skinner Keller (San Francisco: Harper & Row, Publishers, 1981), pp. 101–102.
[35]Ibid., p. 105.

to individual morality. The Church's teachings limit women's (and men's) options to lifelong marriage or celibacy. The presence and at least partial acceptance of other options in the larger culture has caused many Catholics to question and sometimes openly challenge their Church's official teachings.

Ordination to the priesthood is a particularly troublesome issue. As it is now, only men can be ordained priests. The Church's teaching on the ordination of women to the priesthood, repeatedly restated throughout Pope John Paul II's papacy (1978–2005), is unequivocal: Jesus chose men to be his apostles, and they did likewise when they chose their successors. The sacrament of ordination links the priests with the twelve apostles, making the apostles, in effect, present today. "For this reason, the ordination of women is not possible."[36]

Many women are particularly distressed that full priesthood is denied to them. The Second Vatican Council allowed women to serve in many important lay ministries such as assisting with the Eucharist and reading the Bible during Mass. As a result, many, if not most, Catholic churches in the United States permit this. Girls as well as boys can now be altar servers. In most instances, any lay position available to men is now also available to women. Progress? Yes, say the women who want full ordination as priests in the Church—but not enough. For many, the only way for their Church to make good on its pronouncements about the equality and full personhood of all people is to grant women full ordination to the priesthood and accept women as equals for ordination to the higher ranks of bishop, arch-bishop, and cardinal. According to these women, the necessary changes will not have been made until it is possible for a woman to be named Pope.

Many Catholic women also think that the ordination of women would help to solve the severe shortage of priests that the Church faces. Fewer and fewer men have entered the priesthood in recent years, leading to shortages that are nearing crisis proportions. These women claim that the Church can ill afford not to use the additional resource that their ordination would make available. Often, people who urge the ordination of women also urge that priests be allowed to marry, another move that many feel would help to increase the number of candidates for ordination.

One current manifestation of women's desire for ordination concerns ordination to the diaconate. Deacons (male) are ordained to service ministries as well as it being a transitional ordination on the way to priesthood. Many Catholics in the United States feel that, because women serve in recognizably diaconal ministries already (in hospitals, prisons, and religious education, for example), they should be able to be ordained as permanent deacons (deacons for whom diaconal ordination is not a stepping stone to ordination to the priesthood). It is unclear at this point what the final outcome of this discussion will be.

For some Catholic women, the quest for ordination has transformed into a quest for an entirely new approach to worship and liturgy, one that does away with the need for priests altogether. The *Woman-Church* movement understands all Christians to be engaged in equal ministry to each other, with no hierarchy. While it is difficult to say exactly how many women are involved,

[36]*Catechism of the Catholic Church*, 1577.

such communities are being formed nationwide, and national Woman-Church conferences draw thousands of attendees.[37]

All this having been said, two things bear noting. While some Catholic women are dissatisfied with how their Church deals with their specific concerns as women, most are not talking about leaving the Church. Second, the conservative/traditionalist movement, discussed earlier, includes women among its strong supporters. Specifically, Women for Faith and Family organized in 1984 as a voice for such women. One point in their "Affirmation for Catholic Women" document reads, "We affirm and accept the teaching of the Catholic Church on all matters dealing with human reproduction, marriage, family life, and roles for men and women in the Church and in society."[38]

The Church's position on these issues is not likely to change in the foreseeable future. Someone once remarked that people would know that the Catholic Church had made progress when bishops were permitted to bring their wives to Church conferences. They would know that even more progress had occurred when bishops brought their husbands to these conferences.

All in all, it would seem that the Pope's stated goals of "discipline, order, commitment, and obedience" for the Catholic Church will not meet with easy acceptance in the United States. On the other hand, it must be noted that American Catholics, as they have always been, are loyal to the Church. They are a people of two clear loyalties, to their nation and to their Church. Neither has wavered over the course of Catholic presence in America.

We have seen that American Catholics share a great deal with Catholics around the world, as members of the one Catholic Church. They are also unique, and in many ways this uniqueness has come about as a direct result of the conditions under which American Catholicism has developed.

Historian Jay P. Dolan writes,

A new Catholicism is taking shape in the United States. Once again, people are asking what it means to be Catholic in modern America. Catholics have asked this question time and time again over the past two hundred years. This time the questioning is much more widespread, much more revolutionary. . . . In the United States, Catholics have accepted the challenge of fashioning a new Catholicism. . . . that is faithful to the Catholic tradition and at the same time is rooted in American culture.[39]

QUESTIONS AND ACTIVITIES FOR REVIEW, DISCUSSION, AND WRITING

1. If you are not Catholic, try to attend a Catholic Mass. If you are Catholic, try to attend a Protestant service. Notice both the similarities and the differences.
2. If you are not Catholic, talk with friends who are about what being Catholic means to them. If you are Catholic, talk with someone about what being a Protestant Christian means.

---

[37]Rose Solari, "In Her Own Image," *Common Boundary*, July/August 1995, pp. 18–27.
[38]Mary Jo Weaver and R. Scott Appleby, *Being Right: Conservative Catholics in America*, pp. 177–178.
[39]Jay P. Dolan, *In Search of an American Catholicism*, p. 197.

3. Look at a good road atlas of the United States. Note the prevalence of place names that reflect the Spanish and French Catholic influence in the Southwest, Florida, Louisiana, and the upper Midwest.
4. Are you aware of any anti-Catholic prejudice in your community? Elsewhere? Among other students? What forms does it take? Is it organized or informal? What might be done to end it?
5. In what ways is the Catholic Church distinctive?
6. Describe the Catholic sacramental system. In what way is it a "sacred materialism"?
7. Think about the issue of how much authority a community of faith ought to have over the lives of its members. Should it have a little or a lot? Are there things that you believe should be left up to the individual? What are the advantages and the disadvantages of a community of faith having great authority? Little authority? You might also discuss this issue with other people in your class.
8. In your opinion, should women be able to be ordained as priests in the Catholic Church? As permanent deacons? Why do you think the way you do on this issue?

FOR FURTHER READING

DOLAN, JAY, *In Search of an American Catholicism: A History of Religion and Culture in Tension.* New York: Oxford University Press, 2002. Dolan investigates the long-standing and still-present tension among Catholics in the United States between democratization and traditionalism in the Church. He gives thorough attention to popular devotion, a topic often obscured in other treatments.

GILLIS, CHESTER, *Roman Catholicism in America (The Columbia Contemporary American Religion Series).* New York: Columbia University Press, 2000. Gillis describes the distinctiveness of American Catholicism, the variety of viewpoints in today's Church, and Catholic views on contemporary social issues, as well as the influence of Catholicism on the larger culture of the United States.

GREELEY, ANDREW, *The Catholic Revolution: New Wine, Old Wineskins, and the Second Vatican Council.* Berkeley, CA: University of California Press, 2005. This seasoned Catholic novelist and sociologist has been a close observer of the Church in the decades following Vatican II. He cites a spirit of experimentation and reliance on personal choice among Catholic laity and lower clergy and calls on the hierarchy to respect that.

HELLWIG, MONIKA, *Understanding Catholicism, Second Edition.* Mahwah, NJ: Paulist Press, 2002. Dr. Hellwig's book has been a standard work in basic Catholic theology for years. This is a completely updated edition that is sensitive to the present situation within Catholicism in the United States.

ORSI, ROBERT, "Between Heaven and Earth," *The Religious Worlds People Make and the Scholars Who Study Them, New Edition.* Princeton, NJ: Princeton University Press, 2006. This leading contemporary scholar of American Catholicism explores the links between the study of Catholicism and the methods for studying it. His focus is popular or lived religion, the extraordinary meanings that run through people's ordinary, daily lives.

RELEVANT WORLD WIDE WEB SITES

Catholic.net Catholic.net: www.catholic.net

Catholic Online: www.catholic.org

Official Vatican Home page: www.vatican.va

Call To Action: www.cta-usa.org

National Conference of Catholic Bishops: www.usccb.org

CHAPTER 7

Ethnic Diversity in Christianity:
Two Examples

Since the late 1970s, Chicago's black inner city has become a harsher place to live. In the same period, storefront churches have flourished. . . .

In the storefront church, low-income blacks create ways of thinking about the world and acting in the world that reverse degrading public assumptions about inner-city blacks. . . .

Racist stereotypes about lazy, ineffective, immoral, and unresourceful blacks are contradicted by rigorous church protocols, steadfast commitment to work for the church, and creativity and skill on the part of the community of believers to maintain the storefront mission. . . . [Members] meaningfully address the problems they have securing work; the violence and crime they endure in their neighborhoods; the deprivation they see on the ghetto streets; and the hostility, indifference, and humiliation they suffer because they are poor and black.[1]

ETHNIC CHRISTIANITY

Ethnic Christian communities of faith are groups of people whose religion and ethnic, racial, or national identities are inextricably linked together. Eastern Orthodox Christians and black Christians in traditional black churches and black independent congregations are the two major representatives of ethnic Christianity in the United States. Although both of these groups include converts whose ethnic heritage differs from that most closely identified with the group—Eastern Orthodox of non-Eastern European descent and whites who are members of black churches—the ethnic identity of the group as a whole remains clear and important in its self-understanding.

These religious groups are important carriers of ethnic and cultural identity. For Eastern Orthodox Christians, the church often provides not only a place for

---

[1]Frances Kostarelos, *Feeling the Spirit: Faith and Hope in an Evangelical Black Storefront Church* (Columbia, SC: University of South Carolina Press, 1995), pp. 123–126.

worship, but a place in which native dress, language, food, and other cultural customs are preserved, understood, and appreciated. The church and its members become the primary social center for the group. Churches may also sponsor cultural festivals that help to bring the native culture of their members to the larger community. The church helps provide a link to "the old country," allowing its members to be both American and distinctively ethnic. By doing so, it plays an important role in easing the transition for new immigrants and in helping to keep the ethnic heritage from becoming lost in succeeding generations.

As you will learn, the black church played a central role in helping blacks become an integral part of American culture. At the same time, it helped to keep alive the traditions of distinctively black worship and religious life. It continues to do so today. The black churches provide a place in which black heritage and pride in blackness can be nurtured in an otherwise oppressively racist society. They also provide resources to help blacks advance in the predominantly white culture.

The ways in which religion and ethnicity are interrelated are too complex for full exploration here. Three important points can be noted, however, in addition to what has already been said. Religion is an important source of stability and comfort among immigrants and others who are not fully at home in American culture. Immigration—whether forced or undertaken by choice—means the loss of the familiar. Often it entails separation from not only friends but family as well. Although for many, coming to the United States has meant the hope of a new beginning, it has brought with it grief and a sense of loss. In the midst of such feelings, religion offers something of "home" that can come with the immigrant.

Another point at which religion and ethnicity intersect is in the role of religious leaders. The religious leaders are usually among the better-educated members of the ethnic community and are usually respected in this country simply because they are religious leaders. This puts them in an excellent position to serve as spokespersons for the ethnic, national, or racial group in question. This has been particularly evident in the role of articulate black ministers in the civil rights movement.

As the American Religious Identification Survey notes, social identity in the United States is "multilayered, an amalgam of religious, ethnic and cultural elements."[2] These elements have declined in social significance as diversity and pluralism have increased, although some individuals continue to assign great importance to them. Inherited identities often mean less socially than they have in the past. Intermarriage frequently weakens these ties even more. Religion is becoming more and more a matter of personal choice, and thus ethnicity is becoming less important as a factor in religious identity. This continuing trend will likely increase the cultural diversity of America's congregations. Becoming genuinely multicultural and multiethnic communities of faith will bring with it both new opportunities and new challenges.

[2]The American Religious Identification Survey, www.gc.cuny.edu/studies/religion_identity.htm

Eastern Orthodox Christianity

Some of you reading this book are undoubtedly Eastern Orthodox Christians. The majority of you are not. For those of you who are, this chapter is an invitation to see your church in a new way, from the point of view of the academic study of religion. For those of you who are not, I invite you to imagine yourselves in the world of an Eastern Orthodox service of worship. Bearded priests dressed in ornate vestments lead an impressive procession to the front of the church. The air is heavy with the smell of incense. Around the church are many icons—paintings of Jesus, Mary, and the saints done in glowing colors, embellished with gold. The priest and the people chant responsively in Greek, its measured cadences seeming to belong to the time that the Christian New Testament was written. An air of mystery makes you catch your breath.

The *Eastern Orthodox churches* are a group of churches whose members follow the teachings and practices of Christianity as it was practiced in the major cities of the Eastern Roman Empire in the first centuries of the Common Era. They include the Greek and Russian Orthodox Churches and churches with national ties to the former Yugoslavia, Ukraine, Serbia, Croatia, Armenia, Bulgaria, and Romania.

History

For the first ten centuries of its existence, the Christian church was essentially one and undivided, although there were certainly differences between churches in various geographical locations. Within a few years of the beginning of Christianity, there were communities of believers in all the major cities of the Roman Empire, one body of Christians with a diversity of beliefs and practices. There was as yet no central leadership, with the responsibility for guidance shared among the leaders in the different cities.

It is not necessary to trace the intricate political and religious differences that led up to the final division between Christianity in the West and in the East in order to understand American Orthodoxy. The political and economic factors were at least as important in bringing about the final division as were the religious ones. In 1054 C.E., an emissary of the Bishop of Rome excommunicated the Bishop of Constantinople, who, in turn, excommunicated the Bishop of Rome, making formal and official a division that had been growing for centuries. These mutual excommunications were formally lifted by the Second Vatican Council.

The first Orthodox church in the United States was a Greek Orthodox church in New Orleans in 1864, although there had been a colony of Greek Orthodox people at New Smyrna, Florida, a century earlier. Orthodox immigration into the United States came relatively late. The first significantly large numbers were not present until the nineteenth and twentieth centuries. The first archdiocese[3] in the United States was the Orthodox Archdiocese of North

---

[3]An *archdiocese* is a church governmental unit, usually a metropolitan center, headed by an archbishop.

and South America, incorporated in New York in 1921. Large numbers of Greek immigrants arrived in the United States at the turn of the century, bringing their Orthodox faith with them. Large numbers of Russians arrived after 1917, when the Bolshevik Revolution began in Russia.

Two other events played significant roles in Orthodox history in the United States. First, missionaries from the Russian Orthodox Church established missions in Alaska as early as 1794, providing a base from which Orthodoxy could enter the United States. The large number of Orthodox Christians in Alaska meant that when Alaska became a state in 1959, the number of Russian Orthodox in this country rose dramatically. Second, thousands of Orthodox immigrants came from Greece, Asia Minor, Russia, and Eastern Europe between the Civil War and World War I.

In spite of the close national connections of the Orthodox churches, early archdioceses often included all the national churches, because the total numbers were small. Such archdioceses were incorporated in New Orleans in 1864, in San Francisco in 1867, and in New York City in 1870. As the numbers increased, national churches were organized. A Serbian Orthodox church was incorporated in 1926, a Romanian church in 1935, Antiochene and Ukrainian churches in 1937, and a Bulgarian church in 1938. These churches still have a strong national consciousness that plays a major role in keeping them apart organizationally.

EASTERN ORTHODOX CHRISTIANITY IN THE UNITED STATES

About 1 percent of Americans are members of Orthodox churches. Most are members of either the Greek or Russian churches.[4] There are several monasteries, two schools of theology, a college, and several other institutions.

Belief

People of Orthodox Christian faith believe and practice in ways that are both like and unlike those of their Protestant and Catholic neighbors. Orthodox belief is based on the Bible and on the official teachings of the *seven ecumenical* ("of the whole church") councils of the Christian church, which took place during the first 1000 years of its history. Like Catholics but unlike Protestants, Orthodox Christians accept both the Bible and the church's tradition as genuine sources of revelation. Tradition is not found in a single document, but in many. The Nicene Creed is the principal creed. The creeds of the other councils are also believed to be true expressions of God's revelation. The Divine Liturgy (the principal act of worship) itself is an authoritative part of the tradition, as are the teachings of the early church Fathers. So is the Orthodox Churches' long history of *iconography*, the depiction of religious figures in special paintings. The veneration of icons will be discussed in the section on ritual.

[4]Greek Orthodox Archdiocese of America, www.goarch.org; Russian Orthodox Church in America, http://russianorthodox.org

The Christian belief that *God is a trinity* is very important to Orthodox Christians. They also give *great honor to Mary as the Mother of God*. Although she is not God, Orthodoxy teaches that at one time she contained God in the person of Jesus. She is called *Theotokos*, the bearer of God in God's human form, Jesus. With other Christians, the Orthodox affirm both Jesus's full divinity and humanity, and hold that he plays the essential role in the drama of human sin and redemption.

God, according to Orthodox thought, *is shrouded in holy mystery* and cannot be comprehended by human beings. Orthodox Christians believe that, because God is "absolutely incomprehensible and unknowable" (Saint John of Damascus, c. 675–749 C.E.), all that people can say about God is what God is not. Thus, God is *in*corporeal, *in*visible, and *in*tangible.

Like those of Catholic faith, Orthodox Christians believe that the grace of God is a divine, saving power available to persons through the sacraments of the church. *Divine grace requires human cooperation*. Salvation is not based on grace alone, as most Protestants affirm, but on both grace and human cooperation, another belief that the Orthodox share with their Catholic counterparts.

Orthodox Christians believe that the image of God in humanity is distorted and tarnished as a result of the disobedience of Adam and Eve that is recorded in Genesis. This ancestral sin continues to be transmitted to all people. Although the image of God is in each person, sin distorts it and makes it unclear. Orthodox Christians believe that by means of the cooperation between divine grace and human effort, the image of God can become clearer and clearer. By participating in the church as a worshiping community, human beings can become more and more like God. Although this process stops short of a full deification of humanity, the accent on the divine potential of human beings certainly tends in that direction in Orthodox thought and is an image of hope for all who follow it. God did not become human to satisfy the demands of divine justice, according to Orthodoxy, but to enable other human beings to become like God. *As people grow in God's grace, the image of God shines ever more brightly*.

Death means the separation of the soul or spirit from the body. Orthodox Christians believe that people immediately begin to experience something of heaven or hell—of being in communion with God or not. They also believe that there will be a final judgment. Based on the character of people's lives, their "resurrected existence will then live eternally in heaven in communion with God, or eternally in hell, out of communion with God."[5]

Ritual

While the Catholic Church emphasizes correct teaching and belief, Eastern Orthodox Christianity puts its greatest emphasis on worship and other ritual. Proper worship defines what it means to be Orthodox and links the various

---

[5]Stanley S. Harakas, *The Orthodox Church: 455 Questions and Answers* (Minneapolis, MN: Light and Life Publishing Company, 1988), p. 97.

national churches together in close communion. The central act of worship is called the *Divine Liturgy*. It is a solemn yet joyful act that is stylized and highly liturgical. Originally, the language of the Divine Liturgy was Greek. In most churches now, the custom is to use the language of the people for most of the service or to use a combination of the two. In some churches, a choir chants most of the congregational responses. The Sunday morning liturgy is usually based on an order of worship developed by Saint John Chrysostom (347–407 C.E.), or on one developed by Saint Basil the Great (c. 330–379 C.E.). It expresses the holy mystery of God without compromising it. In worship, the mysterious holiness of God is not so much to be understood as to be experienced and adored. The liturgy takes place in a church that is usually designed in the form of a cross, the arms of which project equally from the center, over which a dome is built (Figure 7-1). The Eastern arm of the cross is set apart by a richly decorated screen, the *iconostasis*, behind which the priest enacts the holy mysteries, shielded from the view of the congregation.

There are *three parts of the Orthodox liturgy*. The first, sometimes called the *morning service*, includes the preparation of the communion elements and recalls Jesus's birth and God's incarnation. The second, the *processions*, consists of responsive prayers, Bible readings, the sermon, and the Great Procession, in which the prepared communion elements are brought out. This symbolizes Jesus's coming to humankind to teach and to heal. The third part is the *communion* service itself. The priest goes behind the iconostasis, consecrates the elements, and places the bread into the chalice[6] of wine. The chalice is carried among the people, and all those who are prepared to do so partake. This third part of the liturgy symbolizes Christ's sacrifice for humankind. As do Catholic Christians, the Eastern Orthodox believe that the bread and wine actually

Figure 7-1   The drawing of an Eastern Orthodox Church showing typical architectural features including onion domes and crosses. *(Dorling Kindersley Media Library.)*

[6]A *chalice* is a special cup or glass, usually with a stem, used for the wine in the Eucharist.

become the body and blood of Christ. The entire service may last up to three hours. Not everyone attends for the full service, and it is not uncommon for people to leave the church and return during the service. It is customary for families to worship together, with even the youngest children present for much of the service. Orthodox Christians believe that it is beneficial even for children who are too young to grasp its meaning to be present for the Divine Liturgy.

In addition to the majestic Divine Liturgy on Sunday morning, there are various services throughout the day, marking out the passage of time into a holy cycle. Most people, of course, do not participate in all these services, but in the monasteries, these rites pace the monks throughout the day and night.

The Orthodox Churches celebrate the *seven traditional sacraments*, which are often called the *Holy Mysteries*. The sacraments are believed to convey grace by the presence of the Holy Spirit within them. "God touches, purifies, illumines, sanctifies and deifies human life through the mysteries. . . . In them, we encounter Christ in order to be Christ."[7] *People are baptized* by triple immersion, symbolizing both the three persons of the Trinity and the three days Jesus is said to have lain in the tomb. Infant baptism is the usual practice, in which case baptism may involve only partial immersion. Confirmation, or chrismation, in which the person is anointed with oil that has been blessed for that purpose, follows immediately. Newly baptized people, infants or adults, then receive their first communion.

Leavened bread and wine are used as the communion elements. As noted above, Orthodox Christians believe that the elements become the body and blood of Christ. It is expected that all Orthodox Christians who are baptized and confirmed will partake regularly, and participants often fast from the evening meal prior to the service. Only Orthodox Christians who are in good standing with the Church may receive communion. The laity usually receive the bread and the wine together in a small spoon made for that purpose; priests receive the elements separately. In some churches, Orthodox Christians who did not receive the communion elements, and non-Orthodox people as well, are offered the "bread of fellowship" after the communion as a way of sharing in the service more fully.

The rite of penance as practiced in Orthodoxy reflects a number of themes that have already been mentioned. Baptism is only the beginning of a lifelong process of healing and restoring the damaged image of God within each person. This process is carried out in part through the sacrament of penance. The priest stands with the penitent, approaching God on the penitent's behalf and pronouncing God's forgiveness. Penance, writes one Greek Orthodox scholar, "is essentially a healing mystery, since sin is viewed primarily as a disease that needs to be healed, rather than a crime that needs to be punished."[8] The Orthodox are not altogether different from their Protestant and Catholic neighbors in this interpretation, although non-Orthodox Christians (and especially some Protestants) are more

---

[7]Alciviadis C. Calivas, "Orthodox Worship," in *A Companion to the Greek Orthodox Church*, ed. Fotios K. Litsas (New York: Department of Communication, Greek Orthodox Archdiocese of North and South America, 1984), pp. 31–32.

[8]Ibid., p. 48.

likely to emphasize a juridical interpretation of sin and forgiveness. The Orthodox focus on healing the separation between people and God and the restoration of the divine image in people.

The sacrament of *ordination* sets men apart for the Orthodox priesthood. Married men may be ordained as priests, but priests are not permitted to marry after they are ordained. Bishops and other leaders in the hierarchy are always drawn from the ranks of the celibate monks. Priesthood is limited to men, because the ministry of Christ is carried out in the Church by the priests who are in Christ's image. Through the priest, Christ is present in and to the Church.

Marriage reflects the union of Christ with the faithful, of Christ and the Church. It is believed to be for life. However, because marriage involves human free will, there is always the possibility that a mistake will be made. When divorce happens, the Church usually holds that a true marriage did not occur. The marriage did not show its necessarily eternal character. The laity may have up to three attempts to establish a true and valid marriage. A fourth marriage is absolutely forbidden. The rites for marriages other than the first are subdued and have a penitential character. Clergy may marry only once, because they are expected to set a good example for the laity.

Customs surrounding Orthodox weddings vary from group to group, but two are widespread. At one point in the ceremony, crowns are placed on the heads of the bride and groom. The crowns are sometimes linked together with a ribbon. Although there are several meanings associated with the crowns, primarily they signify the new status of the couple as the king and queen of a new Christian household. Orthodox Christians traditionally wear their wedding rings on their right, rather than their left, hands. The rings signify the couple's solemn pledge to each other, and the right hand is associated with strength and authority.[9]

Ill persons are anointed with blessed oil. Like the Catholic sacrament for the sick, this special service is intended to assist in recovery if that be God's will or to ease the passage from earthly to eternal life.

Because the Orthodox churches follow the Julian rather than the Gregorian calendar, the dates of the major festivals differ from those celebrated by other Christians. For example, Holy Week (Palm Sunday through Easter) may be a week earlier or later than it is for Western Christians.

Orthodox ritual life, both in the church and in the home, is marked by the use of *icons*. Icons are special paintings that function as windows through which the sacred, without compromising its mystery, becomes visible. The painting of an icon is a devotional act carried out by a monk whose commitment to his work is not only artistic, but spiritual. According to Orthodox belief, icons are not to be worshiped; to do so is idolatry. Orthodox Christians worship only God, as do other Christians. But Orthodox Christians affirm the *veneration* of icons. In becoming human in Jesus, God accepted everything pertaining to humanity, including "being depictable." Thus, "to refuse to venerate an icon is . . . to deny

Figure 7-2   Icon painting is both an art and a devotional act. *(Andy Crawford/Dorling Kindersley Media Library.)*

the reality of the Incarnation."[10] Icons are carried in procession and venerated by bowing in front of them, kissing them, and lighting candles before them.

Lifestyle

The lifestyles of Eastern Orthodox Christians are determined as much by their national heritage and the extent of their accommodation to American culture as by their faith. Except for the celibate priests and monks, Eastern Orthodox Christians do not separate themselves from life in the secular world.

Marriage and family life are highly honored and respected. Deviations from this pattern, such as premarital or extramarital sex or active homosexuality, are regarded as inconsistent with a Christian life. Sexually abusive behavior is explicitly condemned.

Orthodox Christians may not marry non-Christians in the Church, but they may marry baptized non-Orthodox Christians. If married outside the Church, they may not participate in the Eucharist, nor may they serve as a godparent for an Orthodox infant or as a sponsor at an Orthodox wedding.

Abortion is not permissible except in cases in which the pregnancy or birth of the baby would gravely endanger the life of the mother. Although children are valued and seen as an important part of marriage, conception and birth are not regarded as the only reason for physical intimacy. Therefore, birth control is left up to the conscience of the couple.

Eastern Orthodox Christians are encouraged by their church to uphold all just laws. They may in good conscience break an unjust law. Orthodox

[10]Paul D. Garrett, "Eastern Christianity," in *Encyclopedia of the American Religious Experience: Studies of Traditions and Movements*, eds. Charles Lippy and Peter Williams (New York: Charles Scribner's Sons, 1988), vol. I, p. 328.

Christians, for example, participated in nonviolent civil disobedience during the civil rights marches of the 1960s. Involvement in public life is encouraged. Orthodox Christians support full human rights for all persons. Most churches officially supported the Equal Rights Amendment while simultaneously emphasizing the importance of the family. They remain, however, adamantly opposed to women being ordained to the priesthood, for the reasons noted in our discussion of ordination.

Organization

Organizationally, each of the nationally associated Orthodox churches is independent (the preferred word for this among the Orthodox is *autocephalous*, "self-headed"). Patriarchs lead the churches in each of the four ancient centers of Orthodoxy: Constantinople, Antioch, Alexandria, and Jerusalem. Among these four, the Patriarch of Constantinople is said to have primacy of honor and spiritual leadership. He is called first among equals but has no more authority than the rest. He is often referred to by the honorific title of His All Holiness Ecumenical Patriarch. The current Ecumenical Patriarch is Bartholomew I.

In addition to these four patriarchates, each of which has divisions within it, there are other major autonomous bodies of believers, such as those of Russia, Greece, and Serbia. Although they are independent in their organizational structure, they are united on important liturgical and theological points.

Orthodox Christians believe that the original Christian church was governed by bishops who presided over limited geographic areas. There was no one central authority. The Orthodox interpret the "rock" referred to in Matthew 16:18 ("upon this rock I will build my church") as Peter's faith rather than Peter himself, thus undercutting the primacy that the Catholic Church ascribes to the Bishop of Rome. This style of government has been maintained to the present time. Within each autonomous Church, government is hierarchical.

In practice, the American Orthodox churches operate with considerable autonomy. National consciousness notwithstanding, there is a degree of unity among Orthodox Christians in the United States. Particularly in the United States, most Orthodox Christians long for even greater unity:

> The more deeply the Orthodox strike roots in North America, the more they lament the ethnic foliage that conceals a united confession of faith. Immigration history, not theology, separates the Orthodox people. And in general they long for and anticipate their union in one organically Orthodox fellowship.[11]

The *Standing Conference of Canonical Orthodox Bishops in the Americas*[12] is one voice for American Orthodoxy. There are two views of how Orthodox unity in North America might come about. The *Orthodox Church in America*[13] was

---

[11]Anthony Ugolnik, "An Ecumenical Estrangement: Orthodoxy in America," *The Christian Century*, 109, No. 20 (June 17–24, 1992), p. 611.
[12]www.scoba.us/
[13]www.oca.org

formed in 1970 by the merger of several Russian churches. Its goal is to unite the Orthodox churches of the United States into a single body. It is headed by an archbishop who has the title, "Archbishop of Washington [D.C.], Metropolitan of All America and Canada." The fact that Russians were the first Orthodox Christians in the United States leads the Russian Orthodox Church to the belief that they have precedence in the United States. Greek Orthodox Christians, who far outnumber the Russians, however, have been reluctant to accept the Russian-founded group as representative. The *Greek Orthodox Archdiocese of North and South America* has become the center of the point of view that holds that all Orthodox Christians owe allegiance to the Patriarch of Constantinople (the Ecumenical Patriarch). In 1999, Archbishop Demetrios Trakatellis, born in Greece and educated at Harvard, was enthroned as Archbishop of America. In his inaugural speech, Archbishop Demetrios announced a "threefold plan" for Orthodoxy in the United States:

> (a) cultivating, nurturing, and sustaining of a vibrant and dynamic Orthodox faith in the Unites States, (b) teaching and practicing limitless love and philanthropy, and (c) emphasizing, pursuing, and enhancing the establishment of a strong and unbreakable unity within the Church and the human community in general.[14]

Saint Vladimir's Seminary (Russian) in New York state has become a training center for Orthodox clergy of many national backgrounds. There is also a Greek Orthodox seminary in the United States, the Holy Cross Greek Orthodox School of Theology in Boston. There is also an Orthodox Theological Society of America, which includes members of all groups, and an Orthodox Inter-Seminary Movement. In worship, pan-Orthodox liturgies on the first Sunday of Lent have become an American tradition.

Eastern Orthodoxy is an embodiment of Christian faith centered in a rich liturgical life that vibrates with the resonances of a tradition as old as the Christian Church itself. For a significant number of American citizens, it is the faith that provides the sacred meanings that make life good. It relates the passage of time throughout the year and the passage of life through its various stages to God, providing a context of holy mystery that transfigures the mundane world.

A Note on the Oriental Orthodox and Catholic Orthodox Churches

The term *Oriental Orthodox Churches* is now generally used to identify a group of six ancient Eastern churches. Their members are Christians who came to the United States from Egypt, Syria, Lebanon, Palestine, Iraq, and Ethiopia. Although they are in communion with one another, each is fully independent and possesses many distinctive traditions. While Eastern Orthodox Christians accept the authority of the first seven councils of the Christian church, as noted above, Christians in the Oriental Orthodox Churches embrace only those of the councils of Nicaea, Constantinople, and

[14]Athanasios Antonopoulos, "Biographical Sketch of His Eminence Professor Demetrios Trakatellis, Archbishop of America," www.goarch.org/en/archbishop/demetrios/biography/

Ephesus.[15] Members of the Catholic Orthodox Churches have come to the United States from various Middle Eastern nations. They differ from both the Eastern Orthodox Churches and the Oriental Orthodox Churches over the precise way in which the divine and human natures of Jesus coexist. Like the Eastern Orthodox Churches, however, membership in any of these churches is strongly linked with ethnicity and national background.

AFRICAN AMERICAN CHRISTIANITY

If you worship or have worshiped in a predominantly black congregation, you have an idea about what black Christianity is.[16] If you have not experienced it directly, you may not know much about it. In that case, have you seen black Christianity depicted in the movies or on television? How is it portrayed? In either case, what comes to mind when you think of African American Christianity and worship?

Whether they participate in a community of faith or not (although the vast majority do), spirituality is a "core value" for African Americans, and most are well aware of the spiritual influences that have come to them from previous generations. African American churches are extended families for their members, and the values and mores of church and family are deeply connected.[17] Religion has been "the one ongoing positive force" in their lives throughout their history, in large measure because "no other institution primarily served the good of the African American community."[18] Approximately 90 percent of all African Americans who participate in a community of faith do so in black-controlled churches.[19]

Data from surveys that include questions about frequency of attendance at worship, private prayer and Bible reading, strength of religious preference, and religious commitment typically show that blacks participate in both public worship and private religious acts more frequently than their white counterparts. Their religious preferences and commitments are stronger. They are more likely to consider religion a very important part of life and are more likely to believe that it can solve most or all of today's problems. Blacks are much more likely to be fundamentalist in their religious outlook, by about three to two, and are half as likely to be liberal.

---

[15]A good general description and links to each of these churches can be found at www.cnewa.org/ecc-bodypg-us.aspx?eccpageID=4&IndexView=toc

[16]Both the terms "black Christianity" and "African American Christianity" are current in literature written by African American Christians themselves. I will use the two interchangeably.

[17]Donelda A. Cook and Christine Y. Wiley, "Psychotherapy with Members of African American Churches and Spiritual Traditions," in *Handbook of Psychotherapy and Religious Diversity*, eds. P. Scott Richards and Allen E. Bergin (Washington, D.C.: American Psychological Association, 2000), pp. 369–370, 377.

[18]Peter J. Paris, "African American Religion," in *World Religions in America: An Introduction, Revised and Expanded*, ed. Jacob Neusner (Louisville, KY: Westminster John Knox Press, 2000), pp. 54 and 58.

[19]Hans A. Baer and Merrill Singer, *African American Religion: Varieties of Protest and Accommodation, Second Edition* (Knoxville, TN: University of Tennessee Press, 2002), p. 101.

The "Lost Third Theme" in the Religious History of the United States

One study of African American religion in the United States[20] advances the thesis that there have been two themes that have guided the interpretation of American religious history. One is pluralism—the existence of religious diversity and the extent to which it has been affirmed or at least tolerated. The other theme is Puritanism and the necessity that America have a collective purpose, a theme that appears to be fundamentally at odds with the first. These two, however can be seen as an evolving dialectic. As Puritanism and the sense of collective purpose and mission have lost ground, the affirmation of diversity has gained. When diversity has lessened, the sense of collective mission has gained.

There is, however, a third theme that cannot be subsumed under either of the other two: A major aspect of the religious history of the United States is the encounter between black and white. The Puritan theme has its primary locus in New England, and the pluralism and toleration theme begins in the middle colonies such as Pennsylvania, Delaware, and Rhode Island. The southern colonies and later southern states do not fit comfortably in with either of these.

> It is this problematic encounter of black and white—which tests the limits of all our views of pluralism and undermines every attempt to formulate a sense of collective purpose—that is the Southern theme in American religious history. . . . [And] it is not only a Southern theme.[21]

Although the religious history of the United States demonstrates a relatively steady increase in diversity and toleration, the black–white encounter is "the story of a persistent and seemingly intractable gap." In spite of efforts to overcome it, some of which will be described below, the gap endures and remains "one of the foundational realities of our national religious life."[22]

The Ambiguity of Christianity for African Americans

Christianity has always been ambiguous for the descendants of the African slaves brought to this country in the holds of ships. They were first introduced to Christianity by those who enslaved them, and it was usually used to undergird obedience to the slave masters. One author describes the beginning of this ambivalence dramatically:

> This ambivalence is not new. It was ours from the beginning. For we first met the American Christ on slave ships. We heard his name sung in hymns of praise while we died in our thousands, chained in stinking holds beneath the decks,

[20]David W. Wills, "The Central Themes of American Religious History: Pluralism, Puritanism, and the Encounter of Black and White," in *African American Religion: Interpretive Essays in History and Culture*, eds. Timothy E. Fulop and Albert J. Raboteau (New York: Routledge, 1997), pp. 9–10.

[21]Ibid., p. 15.

[22]Ibid., pp. 15 and 20.

locked in with terror and disease and sad memories of our families and homes. When we leaped from the decks to be seized by sharks we saw his name carved on the ships' solid sides. When our women were raped in the cabins they must have noticed the great and holy books on the shelves.[23]

On the other hand, Christianity provided benefits for the slaves. Some of the slaveholders allowed their slaves at least a measure of control over their religious expression, and patterns of worship developed that the slaves could claim as their own. Even being taken into town to the "white" church provided a social outing and some relief from the burdens of work. Later, especially as slaves and former slaves embraced the Exodus story of the Hebrews' escape from Egyptian slavery, Christianity provided a context for liberating action.

The Christian Churches and the Civil War

Religion figured prominently in the events that led up to the Civil War, in the war itself, and in the various attempts at interpreting its meaning that followed it. Both North and South looked to their faith, their churches, and their religious leaders to justify their position on the matter of slavery and to sustain them in the terrible bloodshed that pitted American against American and kin against kin. Both were certain that God was on their side, that theirs was the righteous cause, and that God would help them to prevail over their opposition. Both attempted to demonstrate support from the Christian scriptures. And, in both South and North, religious people sought to minister to those caught up in the war. There were chaplains with both armies, and aid societies assisted them in their work by providing reading materials, visitation, and facilitating communication between soldiers and the families they had left behind. It fell to these volunteers to deal as best they could with the grief of those from whom the war had taken family members, friends, and neighbors. The accounts of their work, along with that of the chaplains and medical personnel, are a stirring record of humanity amidst the inhumanity of war.

Religious perspectives gave rise to some of the most memorable literary and artistic responses to slavery and to the Civil War. Harriet Beecher Stowe's staunch and thoughtful Congregationalism led to her writing of *Uncle Tom's Cabin*. James Russell Lowell's stirring "Once to Every Man and Nation," familiar to most Protestant churchgoers, reminds us of the prophets of the Hebrews when they called on their people to make a decisive, once-and-for-all choice between good and evil. And Julia Ward Howe's "The Battle Hymn of the Republic," although it became an anthem of the North, spoke eloquently of God's judgment on any people who made the wrong choice in that decision.

After the guns of battle were silenced, the religious categories of divine wrath and punishment and the religious overtones of sacrifice were brought into play by both sides to interpret the meaning of the war and of victory gained or

---

[23]Vincent Harding, "Black Power and the American Christ," in *Black Theology: A Documentary History*, 1966–1979, eds. Gayraud S. Wilmore and James H. Cone (Maryknoll, NY: Orbis Books, 1979), p. 36.

defeat suffered. Others, keenly aware of the ambiguous nature of the entire situation, called for repentance on both sides and reconciliation of hearts as well as governments.

The Free Black Church

Emancipation led to the development of black religion in the context of official freedom coupled with social repression and oppression that continued long after the Emancipation Proclamation was signed.[24] This complex dialectic continues to influence African American Christianity.

The Baptist and Methodist churches carried out the most vigorous work among the blacks after emancipation. The vast majority of freed blacks were a part of one of these two communities of faith. A smaller, yet significant, number, especially in Maryland and Louisiana, were Catholic. Following the war years, the black church grew rapidly. Rejection or segregation of black members by historically white denominations (such as the Baptists' and Methodists' insistence on separate seating) led to the growth of all-black congregations within these denominations as well as to the formation of a number of black denominations. It was in these black denominations and in the all-black congregations within predominantly white denominations that black religion continued to evolve its distinctive style and message.

The black churches played a unique role in the developing black community, in the North and South, in rural areas, and in cities, to which increasingly large numbers of blacks were moving in search of work. The black churches were much, much more than simply religious institutions, although their primary identification as religious institutions influenced everything else in which they were involved. As a landmark study of the black church in the United States describes it:

> The black church has no challenger as the cultural womb of the black community. Not only did it give birth to new institutions such as schools, banks, insurance companies, and low income housing, it also provided an academy and an arena for political activities, and it nurtured young talent for musical, dramatic, and artistic development . . . in addition to the traditional concerns of worship, moral nurture, education, and social control. Much of black culture is heavily indebted to the black religious tradition, including most forms of black music, drama, literature, storytelling, and even humor.[25]

As historian Sydney Ahlstrom points out, black churches also served as a "surrogate for nationality" that substituted religious identification for the tribal identity that had been left behind.[26]

---

[24]The *Emancipation Proclamation* was a statement issued by President Abraham Lincoln on New Year's Day, 1863, that ended slavery throughout most of the South.

[25]C. Eric Lincoln and Lawrence H. Mamiya, *The Black Church in the African American Experience* (Durham, NC: Duke University Press, 1991), p. 8.

[26]Sydney E. Ahlstrom, *A Religious History of the American People* (New Haven, CT: Yale University Press, 1973), p. 710.

The Christian ministry was the only profession open to blacks, and the black churches were the only institution controlled by blacks. As such, they served as schools for leadership training and development. Most of the black political leaders in the United States trace their roots back to the church and many to the ministry itself. Frequently in the history of the black church, the minister, who was the most highly educated member of the black community, served as the liaison between the black community and that of the dominant whites. This function remains important, even though blacks have joined the ranks of the educated and the professionals in increasing numbers.

The Black Church and Civil Rights

Black religion was at the heart of the civil rights movement. It had helped the slaves maintain some sense of humanity and peoplehood. It had provided structure and organization in the years following emancipation. And it provided a framework in which hopes for civil rights could become political realities.

Too, *the civil rights movement became an integral part of black religion.* Most of the significant events of the civil rights movement occurred in the period that is centered on the turbulent decade of the 1960s and extends for a few years on either side of it. The black churches, their people, and their leaders were intimately involved.

Dr. Martin Luther King, Jr., pastor of the Dexter Avenue Baptist Church in Montgomery, Alabama, was the undisputed leader of the civil rights movement. He brought to the task his lifelong experience of the black church, the moving preaching style of the black minister, and a social conscience informed by the liberal Protestantism he had learned while obtaining his doctorate at Boston University. Dr. King advocated *nonviolent protest*. His reading of the lives and teachings of Jesus and of Mohandas Gandhi, the Indian Hindu political leader, convinced him that nonviolence was the morally right way to deal with the situation in which blacks found themselves. Nonviolence meant *civil disobedience* in the spirit of Christian love rather than hatred and revenge against whites. Civil disobedience meant deliberately breaking laws that were unjust but being willing to endure verbal and even physical abuse without fighting back and to go to jail if necessary for one's actions. It meant working for reconciliation, not encouraging separatism.

Within a few years, many blacks, especially students, had used King's nonviolent methods in sit-ins at segregated lunch counters throughout the South. Freedom rides began to protest segregation in interstate commerce facilities. Many blacks rode interstate buses and entered facilities, such as eating areas and restrooms that were reserved for whites. Such segregation was by that time illegal, but the laws were not enforced.

In January 1957, the *Southern Christian Leadership Conference* (popularly, SCLC) was formed, with Martin Luther King, Jr., as its founder. It proved to be one of the most effective black organizations throughout the 1960s and early 1970s. Protests in Birmingham, Alabama, were among the largest organized by the SCLC. King's *Letter from Birmingham Jail,* a classic of the movement, was written while he was jailed in Birmingham as a result of his participation in these efforts. In it, King distinguished between a just law and an unjust law. A just law is one that squares with the moral law or the law of God. An unjust law does not. Unjust laws also legalize inequality and difference and are inflicted upon a minority who, by reason of not being allowed to vote, had nothing to say about their passage. People should obey just laws. Unjust laws, on the other hand, should be broken, but in the spirit of nonviolence and love already indicated.[27]

In the late summer of 1963, a massive demonstration in Washington, D.C., focused on segregation in accommodations. The following summer, the *Civil Rights Act* was passed. This piece of legislation received strong support in Congress from leaders of Protestantism, Catholicism, Eastern Orthodoxy, and Judaism, and from blacks and whites alike.[28]

March 1965 saw the well-known march from Selma to Montgomery, Alabama. With King's able leadership, clergy and laity from all the major branches of Christendom and Judaism, along with humanists and free thinkers, marched and sang together in protest. Many went to jail. In August of the same year, the *Voting Rights Act*[29] was passed. When Martin Luther King, Jr., was assassinated in the spring of 1968, many of the goals of the early civil rights movement had been met. But there was much more to do.

Black Christian Militancy and Black Power

Gradually, the mood of the civil rights movement changed. Leaders arose who felt that these methods worked too slowly. They believed King was too willing to compromise, too moderate, too willing to work with whites. Why the change in mood? Black Presbyterian theologian Gayraud S. Wilmore puts it this way: By the mid-1960s, "many believed that following King meant to give more attention to loving the enemy than to doing something about the suffering of brothers and sisters."[30] In most respects, King was a moderate among Christian ministers. For many blacks, patience with moderation had worn thin. When it had been formed, the Student Nonviolent Coordinating Committee (SNCC) had been committed to King's nonviolent methods, but its early commitment to nonviolence had lessened. Its leaders and rank-and-file members alike were willing to accept and condone violence in the service of righting the wrongs of previous centuries. The passage of the Voting Rights Act in the summer of 1965 sparked an incident that drew national attention, and, in some quarters, outrage. There was a week of bloody and destructive race riots in several major American cities. The week of uprisings highlighted the great frustration of the black community and showed both whites and more moderate blacks how far the militants were willing to go to meet their goals.

---

[27]Martin Luther King, Jr., "Letter from Birmingham Jail," in *Why We Can't Wait* (New York: Harper & Row, Publishers, 1963). It can be read on line at www.mlkonline.net/jail.html

[28]The full text of the Civil Rights Act is available at www.usinfo.state.gov/usa/infousa/laws/majorlaw/civilr19.htm

[29]The Voting Act Rights text can be read at http://www.ourdocuments.gov/doc.php?doc=100&page=transcript

[30]Gayraud S. Wilmore and James H. Cone, eds., *Black Theology: A Documentary History*, 1966–1979 (Maryknoll, NY: Orbis Books, 1979), p. 16.

In the summer of 1966, *James Meredith* was shot and wounded while leading a 220-mile voting rights walk from Memphis, Tennessee, to Jackson, Mississippi. *Stokely Carmichael* and others who took over leadership on that march led the marchers in chants of "black power!" with clenched fists raised in what would become a nationally recognized symbol. The chants of "black power" were often led by church people, and they were accompanied by talk of God's judgment upon America for the injustices done to blacks and of coming retribution for oppression.

In 1967, the National Committee of Negro Churchmen became the National Committee of Black Churchmen. In 1969, the committee sponsored a conference on black economic development. Most of the key leaders of the black religious community had long since come to recognize that economic freedom was one of the main keys to ending oppression, a key without which no amount of good intention was enough. At that conference, James Forman read the "*Black Manifesto*." It is a document that "burns with anger and despair,"[31] as Forman said his brothers and sisters did. It made demands—demands that white Christian churches and Jewish synagogues pay reparations that would begin to offset the damage done by economic oppression. It explicitly accused these communities of faith of conscious and willing participation in the processes of slavery and oppression and of not moving nearly rapidly enough to bring about change. Specifically, it demanded $500 million. The money was to be spent in a variety of ways. Loans for land and homes were a main goal. Publishing, printing, and television networks were to be established. Training and skills centers were to be built. A National Black Labor Strike and Defense Fund was to be established. A black university was to be established in the South.

On May 4, 1969, Forman read the Manifesto, uninvited, to the congregation of New York's prestigious Riverside Church. The white churches and synagogues strongly resisted paying any money for reparations. Those that did discuss it seriously often found their congregations split. The Manifesto was an effective tool for drawing national attention to the economic problems that had not been solved. It also illustrated the distance that the civil rights movement had moved from King's style of leadership. No longer willing to work with white religious groups, the supporters of the Manifesto drew clear battle lines.

Not all black churches supported the black power movement, and the movement itself drew support from people and groups not associated with the churches. Nevertheless, the growing consciousness of Jesus as Liberator that would highlight black religious thought gave support and religious legitimation to a powerful new thrust in the ongoing struggle of the black community.

The Character of African American Spirituality and Christianity Today

We can identify at least three sources of African American Christianity. There are continuing influences from the tribal religions of Africa. It also has been influenced by patterns borrowed from white European American Christianity.

---

[31]James Forman, *Black Manifesto*.

Finally, it has developed a unique character as African Americans responded, first to slavery and then to their ongoing history of living in an oppressive and racist society.[32]

From its beginning, black religion in America has been affected by its context of "white racism and capitalist exploitation."[33] For this reason, the theme of freedom has been a paramount one:

> Throughout black history, the term "freedom" has found a deep religious resonance in the lives and hopes of African-Americans. . . . During slavery it meant release from bondage; after emancipation it meant the right to be educated, to be employed, and to move about freely from place to place. [Now], freedom means social, political, and economic justice. From the very beginning of the black experience in America, one critical denotation of freedom has remained constant: Freedom has always meant the absence of any restraint that might compromise one's responsibility to God. The notion has persisted that if God calls you to discipleship, God calls you to freedom. And that God wants you free because God made you for Himself and in His image.[34]

> Furthermore, there is a crucial difference in the connotations of freedom for black and for white Americans. While whites have characteristically interpreted freedom through the lens of individualism, African-Americans have seen it as communal in nature. No one is truly free until all are free.[35]

African American religion is Exodus religion. In coming to the New World, whites had drawn on the Exodus narrative in the Christian Old Testament. They saw themselves as the New Israel, the New World as the Promised Land, and their former life in Europe as bondage in Egypt. African Americans have of necessity given the Exodus story a different interpretation. They are the Old Israel, suffering in bondage to the new Pharoah of racism, in an American Egypt far short of the Promised Land. This American Egypt stands under God's judgment.[36]

The biblical Exodus remains a powerful metaphor. Exodus is not only an event that occurred long ago in Hebrew history. It occurs now, as well, every time God raises up a "new Moses" and rescues the captives from the new Egypt. It is not only the deliverance of the Hebrews, but the deliverance of American blacks. It calls contemporary African Americans to cooperate with the God of the Exodus to bring racial bondage to an end.

Along with the Exodus theme, Jesus is understood primarily as the Liberator, God as a human being who stands in solidarity with all those who are

---

[32]Baer and Singer, *African American Religion*, p. 1.
[33]Ibid., p. xxi.
[34]C. Eric Lincoln and Lawrence H. Mamiya, "The Religious Dimension: The Black Sacred Cosmos," in *Down by the Riverside: Readings in African American Religion*, ed. Larry G. Murphy (New York: New York University Press, 2000), pp. 33–34.
[35]Ibid., pp. 33–34.
[36]Albert J. Raboteau, "African Americans, Exodus, and the American Israel," in *Down by the Riverside*, pp. 20–23.

poor and oppressed. This is the Jesus of Luke's Gospel, who identifies himself as one sent to proclaim release to all in captivity of any sort and liberty to all who are oppressed (Luke 4:18–19). Jesus is the bringer of the age of liberation (Luke 7:22). Jesus, and hence God, is clearly and unambiguously on the side of the downtrodden and oppressed, and firmly against the oppressors, whomever they may be. The suffering of black people throughout their history finds "immediate resonance with the incarnational view of the suffering, humiliation, death, and eventual triumph of Jesus in the resurrection."[37]

Jesus as the liberator means liberation now, in this world, in terms of voting rights, jobs, equal access to good education, and adequate housing. The liberation that Jesus offers certainly includes freedom from the eternal punishment of unforgiven sin. It certainly includes a hoped-for future in which oppression and pain of every kind shall cease for all persons, and indeed for all creation. But first and foremost, Jesus means liberation now, sociopolitical and economic liberation. He means full humanity for people who have never had full humanity.

For some African Americans, Jesus the Liberator is also Jesus the black man. They point out that in a literal sense, Jesus "was a Palestinian Jew whose racial ancestry may have been partly African but definitely not European."[38] The traditional artistic portrayals of Jesus as a European simply are not true to the biblical account of who Jesus was. Moreover, on a symbolic level, Jesus's blackness demonstrates Jesus's solidarity with all oppressed blacks.

God is a God of justice who does not support the ruling class and the status quo but instead supports the attempt to bring about a more just and equal society. This, too, reflects the importance of the prophetic books of the Christian Old Testament in black religious thought. In a similar vein, the Kingdom of God is seen in terms of justice and equality in this world. People, with God's help and guidance, are responsible for bringing it about. While it may not come in its fullness until God intervenes decisively in human history, it can be greatly advanced. Black religious thought translates religion into political action; concepts such as the Kingdom of God are politicized and translated into concrete changes in how people live.

A recent study of African American religion notes that religion gives African Americans a voice, indeed multiple and variegated voices, to speak not only of their spiritual quest and fulfillment but of their earthly trials and social yearnings as well. In this interplay of worldly and otherworldly images and attributes, African Americans constructed their identity as a people. Consequently, African American politics has always had and continues to have a decidedly religious slant, while African American religion is deeply political.[39]

The interaction of Christianity with the diverse experiences of African Americans have given rise to a number of distinct types of African American churches.[40] There are the mainstream churches, the large black denominations.

---

[37]Lincoln and Mamiya, *The Black Church*, pp. 3–4.
[38]James H. Cone, "Black Theology as Liberation Theology," in *Down by the Riverside*, p. 397.
[39]Baer and Singer, *African American Christianity*, p. xvii.
[40]Ibid., Chapters 3–6.

The eight largest are the pentecostal Church of God in Christ (COGIC, which is the largest pentecostal denomination in the United States),[41] the African Methodist Episcopal Church,[42] the African Methodist Episcopal Zion Church, the Christian Methodist Episcopal Church, the National Baptist Convention, U.S.A.,[43] the National Baptist Convention of America, the National Missionary Baptist Convention of America, and the Progressive National Baptist Convention, U.S.A.[44] This category also includes predominantly black congregations within "white" denominations such as those described in Chapter 4, and Black Catholic congregations. The mainstream churches support a program of social reforms intended to integrate African Americans into American society and culture. While protesting racism, they do not usually challenge the underlying racist and classist structures of the culture, but rather focus on enabling African Americans to participate in the existing culture on parity with their white counterparts.

The *Congress of National Black Churches* was founded to promote unity, charity, and fellowship among member denominations. The Congress is a coalition of six major historic black denominations: African Methodist Episcopal; Church of God in Christ; National Baptist Convention of America, Inc.; National Missionary Baptist Convention of America; and the Progressive National Baptist Convention, Inc. It sponsors a number of programs, including programs for theological education, economic development, a black family program, and an anti-drug program, as well as facilitating unity among the nation's black churches.

Separatism and an overtly militaristic and nationalistic stance characterize the messianic-nationalist groups. They launch a "fundamental critique of the place and treatment of people of African heritage in American society." Their founders are often "charismatic individuals who are regarded as Messiahs who will deliver black people from white oppression."[45] They often are quite critical of the more integrationist stance of the mainstream black churches.

Conversionist groups, as their name suggests, emphasize the experience of conversion. Most are holiness and/or pentecostal. They emphasize strict personal morality and are often not deeply involved with either social action or politics. As with members of many other African American religious communities, members of conversionist or "sanctified" churches dedicate much of their Sunday to church activities:

> Sundays are extremely busy for Sanctified churches, beginning with Sunday school in the early morning and evolving into the Sunday worship service in the later morning and early afternoon. A special program . . . may occur in the

---

[41]www.cogic.org
[42]www.ame-church.com
[43]www.nationalbaptist.com
[44]www.pnbc.org
[45]Swatos, William H., Jr., ed., *Encyclopedia of Religion and Society* (Walnut Creek, CA: AltaMira Press, 1998), p. 9.

afternoon. Finally, an evening service of two hours or longer often brings to a close the most sacred day of the week. This round of religious activities may be punctuated by more profane affairs, such as a midday dinner or a picnic. Many Sanctified churches also conduct services on Friday nights as a way of making the transition between the profanity of life in the larger society and the sacredness of the Lord's Day.[46]

Finally, thaumaturgical [miracle-working] groups use religious ritual and esoteric knowledge to seek worldly prosperity, good health, and other benefits. Otherworldly dimensions take second place to their emphasis on improving life in their world. Thus, they promise benefits that their adherents have been denied or found difficult to obtain in the racist white culture. They offer a sharp contrast with the other types described above. They emphasize the individual over the group, embrace health and prosperity as an indicator of spiritual position, and do not seek to reform the larger culture.

Women in the Black Church

Like their predominantly white counterparts, black Christian churches have historically had a majority of female members and an almost exclusively male pastorate. This pattern continues in many black churches today. Women are attending and graduating from the seminaries of black Christian denominations in increasing numbers. However, "relatively few" are ordained and serving in formal ministerial soles in their denominations. One result of this is that they cross over into predominantly white denominations and serve churches there. This is especially true in the United Methodist Church.[47] Women do have many other leadership roles in the black churches, such as evangelists, deaconesses, lay readers, Sunday School teachers, counselors, and the like.

The black Methodist denominations were the first to ordain women as pastors. Congregational polity among the Baptist groups has limited the development of consistent policies on the ordination of women, but the tendency is for fewer women to be ordained there. While policy usually does not explicitly prohibit it, tradition does. Pentecostals remain firmly against it. Overall, the reluctance to grant full ordination to women has come under increasing criticism, and changes are coming about slowly.

There are at least two unique positions of honor for women in many black Christian churches. Women may be *Mothers of the church*, a position that derives from African-based kinship networks that carry over into the African American community. They are often given the honorific title "Lady." There is no parallel in white churches.[48]

---

[46]Baer and Singer, *African American Religion*, p. 170.
[47]Ronald L. Johnstone, *Religion in Society: A Sociology of Religion*, 8th ed. (Upper Saddle River, NJ: Prentice Hall, 2007), p. 323.
[48]Lincoln and Mamiya, *The Black Church*, p. 275.

Frances Kostarelos describes the role of church mothers in her ethnographic account of an inner city storefront church in Chicago:

> The Mothers Board . . . is . . . separated into junior and senior groups; the former includes women between fifty-five and sixty-five; the latter is for women who are over sixty-five. These women are also called church mothers. As church women approach their mid-fifties, they are expected to take their place on the Mothers Board. . . . Members of the Mothers Board say that through the good and evil they have known and a lifetime of serving God and their families, they have developed the personal qualities and habit of mind required for service on the Mothers Board. Church mothers are expected to be sober-minded, temperate at all times, and emotionally balanced. They are to avoid calling attention to themselves through their clothing and manners. They are to dress and comport themselves in a reserved and discreet manner. On Sundays they wear white dresses or suits, hats, stockings, and dress shoes. Their outfits represent their spiritual elevation and humility before God. At all times they avoid wearing striking outfits such as those worn by younger women in the church.

> It is the duty of the church mothers to be moral and spiritual guides to others in the congregation, especially to young women seeking to live in the Spirit. . . . Church mothers have the responsibility of counseling younger women. They are women who have been wife to one husband, good mothers and housekeepers, and in the church working for the Lord. The hardships they have endured as wives, mothers, and servants of God are believed to have strengthened them and brought them closer to the Spirit. The church mothers are highly respected and enjoy a great deal of deference from younger women. Church mothers have a significant spiritual role in worship services.[49]

Women may also serve as nurses in the church. Usually, the nurses are women younger than those on the Mothers Board. Dressed in a recognizable white uniform for church services and funerals, they are responsible for helping anyone in the congregation who needs assistance. They particularly help members overcome with emotion during services, and women with children who need to be taken out because they are fussing. Women on the Nurses Board achieve respect by consistently demonstrating their excellence in traditionally "female" qualities, such as compassion, helpfulness, and being good with children.[50]

It is clear that Mothers of the church and Nurses have positions of great power within their congregations. Equally clear is the fact that their respect and position comes from their manifestation of traditionally feminine qualities and upholding traditional female role models. It is also important to note that black culture has not always encouraged males to respect females. The black church has been a key element in encouraging black men to respect all black women as mothers, wives, and sisters. Some women, barred from ordination, also founded their own churches, becoming powerful preachers and leaders in their own right.

[49]Frances Kostarelos, *Feeling the Spirit: Faith and Hope in an Evangelical Black Storefront Church* (Columbia, SC: University of South Carolina Press, 1995), p. 51.
[50]Ibid., p. 49.

Black feminist theologians have articulated a bleak picture of the position of black women in American culture and in African American churches. They face "multiple jeopardy."[51] They are female, black, disproportionately in poverty and single mothers, and more often than their white counterparts the victims of physical, emotional, and sexual abuse. The *feminist* movement, including feminism in religion, has been largely white, middle to upper class, and educated. Black *theology* has been overwhelmingly male. Therefore, feminist theology has not usually addressed the concerns of *black* women (nor those of Latinas and other marginalized women), and black theology has usually failed to speak to the concerns of black *women*. Only recently has black feminist religious thought begun to find its own unique voice.

Womanist thought has grown out of the failure of white middle class feminism and black male theology to address the particular concerns of women of color:

> The term *womanist* was coined by Alice Walker in her work *In Search of Our Mothers' Garden: Womanist Prose* (San Diego: Harcourt Brace Jovanovich, 1983), xi–xii. The term is derived from the word *womanish* and refers to African American women as "courageous, audacious, concerned about family, community, and relationship with God." Walker calls the womanist "a black feminist, a feminist of color." Womanists are concerned about the multiple oppression . . . of African American women and women of color in general.[52]

Black Church Worship

The black church's worship is distinctive, with links back to the African and slave experiences of its members' ancestors. It is worship in which the Holy Spirit is encountered by the worshipers as an experiential reality, in which they are transformed by the presence of their God. Theologian James Cone has noted the *six main elements in black worship*, wherever it takes place.[53]

Preaching is the most important, because in the sermon, the preacher speaks the word of God to the people. The people in the congregation participate by their shouts or more subdued responses of "Yes, Jesus," "Say it, Brother," "Amen!" and the like. This congregational responsiveness pulls preacher and listeners together in a common act of worship.

Singing prepares for, and then intensifies, the experience of the Spirit. It sets the mood, although it cannot force the Spirit to come. Both choral and congregational singing take place, with the emphasis on the congregation's participation in hymns. For white Christians accustomed to two or at most three hymns during a worship service, the sheer number of hymns and religious songs

---

[51]Cheryl Townsend Gilkes, *"If It Wasn't for the Women . . . "*: *Black Women's Experience and Womanist Culture in Church and Community* (Maryknoll, NY: Orbis Books, 2001), p. 2.

[52]A. Elaine Brown Crawford, *Hope in the Holler: A Womanist Theology* (Louisville: Westminster John Knox Press, 2002), p. xi.

[53]James H. Cone, *Speaking the Truth* (Grand Rapids, MI: William B. Eerdmans Publishing Company, 1986), p. 22.

Figure 7-3   Easter Sunday service at Ebenezer Baptist Church, Poughkeepsie, NY. *(Kathy McLaughlin/The Image Works)*

in a black church service, as well as the hand-clapping, hand-waving enthusiasm with which they are sung, may come as a surprise.

Shouting and *conversion* are closely related. Shouting, sometimes referred to as "getting happy," is understood in the black church as a response to the action of the Holy Spirit, a form of religious ecstasy. It is not the same as similar phenomena in white pentecostal churches, because it grows out of an altogether different sociopolitical background and set of life experiences. The white pentecostal is a member of the dominant race, whereas the black is oppressed. As black theologian James Cone writes very pointedly, it is "absurd . . . to contend that the Ku Klux Klansman and the black person who escaped him are shouting for the same or similar reasons."[54] Blacks shout in joy over the authentic personhood given by Jesus and participation in his life and liberation, experienced as a present, here-and-now alternative to oppression and depersonalization. Shouting usually accompanies and is evidence of conversion and recurs when that experience is renewed. Conversion is, on the one hand, a one-time event, but on the other hand, it is an ongoing experience and process, and both events are signaled by shouting.

Prayer, free and spontaneous rather than formal and read from a book, is understood as communication with Jesus. Like so much else in black worship, it is rhythmic, with rhythms that echo the African past.

During *testimony*, people speak in front of the congregation about their determination to stay with their lives in Christ and in the church in spite of difficulties. They believe that they are called by God and testify to their intention to be worthy of that call. It is an encouragement both to the person testifying

[54]Ibid., p. 27.

and to those who hear it. The congregational responses of "Yes, Sister" or "Tell it, Brother" let the speakers know that the rest of the congregation is with them against the temptations that arise.

> People approach worship in black churches expecting to be changed. "There is an expectation that individuals will be different when they leave the worship experience. They will have received hope, healing, care, and empowerment to negotiate their daily lives."[55] In a social situation in which hope and empowerment are hard to come by, this is a great gift to the participants.

A Note on Black Spirituals and Gospel Music

The popularity of Gospel music has surged in recent years, and it is very much a part of what most people would consider mainstream music. Contemporary Gospel music has its roots in the spirituals of African slaves. Those spirituals, combined with the use of instruments such as drums and tambourines, were the beginning of Gospel. Black Gospel music was popularized by the Fisk University Jubilee Singers. Fisk is one of the historically black colleges and universities founded after the Civil War. Although there are similarities between black Gospel music and its white counterpart, its distinctive emphasis on hope in the face of suffering distinguishes it from the Gospel music of the white evangelical tradition.[56]

THE CHANGING FACE OF ETHNIC CHRISTIANITY

For many years, the term *ethnic Christian* referred to African American Christians, along with a very small proportion of Eastern Orthodox Christians. The latter increased dramatically when Alaska became a state and has increased with immigration from predominantly Eastern Orthodox countries in the former USSR. The portrait of ethnic Christianity has become far more complex in the decades since the passage of the Hart-Celler Immigration Act in 1965, which made it much easier for people from around the globe to immigrate to the United States. Consider the following:[57]

- Although only 15 percent of post-1965 immigrants are Europeans, about two-thirds are Christians.
- Many new immigrants come here from countries where Christianity is the predominant religion, with the majority coming from Mexico.

[55]Richards and Bergin, *Handbook of Psychotherapy and Religious Diversity*, p. 381.
[56]Peter W. Williams, *America's Religions from Their Origins to the Twenty-First Century* (Urbana, IL: University of Illinois Press, 2002), p. 444.
[57]R. Stephen Warner, "The De-Europeanization of American Christianity," in *A Nation of Religions: The Politics of Pluralism in Multireligious America*, ed. Stephen Prothero (Chapel Hill, NC: The University of North Carolina Press, 2006), pp. 233–241, and R. Stephen Warner, "Immigrants and the Faith They Bring," *Christian Century* (February 10, 2004), pp. 20–23.

- Some come from the Christian population in religiously mixed countries such as Korea and Jordan. Those who come from these countries are disproportionately Christian. For example, South Korea is about 25 percent Christian, yet half the Koreans who come to America are Christian, and overall, 75 percent of Korean Americans are Christians.
- Some come from countries where Christianity is growing rapidly, such as those of sub-Saharan Africa. Again, immigrants are disproportionately Christian.
- Many who arrive here without any religious affiliation become Christian after they arrive. For example, mainland Chinese who come to the United States typically profess no religious affiliation upon arrival, yet one-third of Chinese Americans are Christian.
- Those who come to the United States as spouses of citizens are most likely to be Christians because their spouses are Christians.
- The majority of Arab Americans are Christian, not Muslim as you might imagine.
- The largest of these new immigrant communities of Christian faith is that of Mexican American Catholics, who are as diverse in themselves as are the regions of Mexico from which they come. About 75 percent of Mexican Americans are Catholic. Of those who are Protestant, most are evangelicals or Pentecostals, and some are Mormons or Jehovah's Witnesses.
- Filipino Catholics are the largest Asian Christian group.
- Vietnamese Catholics practice a style of Catholicism that is blended with the ancient ideals of Confucianism.
- Cuban Catholics blend Afro-Caribbean elements with their Catholicism.

Overall, data indicate that two-thirds or more of these new immigrants are Christians. At the most, one-fifth follow any non-Christian faith, and perhaps one-sixth do not identify as religious at all.

> Thus, when Americans think of Christians, they will decreasingly be able to think simply of whites and the captive Africans they Christianized. They will also think of Asian students conducting Bible studies and witnessing for Christ on college campuses nationwide. They will think about Mexicans observing Holy Week with open-air passion plays known as Via Crucis and observing Christmas with the pageant known as Posada, about Haitian Catholics marching through the streets of New York to honor the Virgin Mary in July, and about Cuban Catholics gathering outdoors by the thousands to celebrate the feast of Our Lady of Charity in early September.[58]

QUESTIONS AND ACTIVITIES FOR REVIEW, DISCUSSION, AND WRITING

1. If there is an Eastern Orthodox church where you live or where you go to school, try to make an appointment to visit the church during the week. Notice particularly the architecture of the building, the icons, and the iconostasis. Most priests will be glad to have you visit and will be quite willing to answer your questions. You might also want to consider attending the Divine Liturgy on Sunday morning.

[58]Ibid., p. 247.

2. If you are accustomed to worshiping in a white congregation, attend a worship service at one of the historically black churches. If you worship in a mostly black congregation, attend a service in a mostly white congregation. Reflect on the differences you observe.
3. Get your class together in integrated groups of black and white students and discuss your perceptions of each other's worship.
4. In your opinion, what are the advantages and disadvantages of the nonviolent methods of Martin Luther King, Jr.?
5. Read and report on James Baldwin's autobiographical novel, *Go Tell It on the Mountain*.
6. If you can get a videotape of the movie *The Long Road Home*, with Whoopi Goldberg, view it and write a brief essay on the roles that the black church played in the civil rights movement, as depicted in the film.
7. In what ways do the roles of church mother and church nurse allow women honor and position within the black church while remaining within traditional gender roles?
8. What is *Womanist* theology and why did it develop?
9. How has increased immigration since the passage of the 1965 immigration act changed American Christianity?

FOR FURTHER READING

BAER, HANS A. AND MERRILL SINGER, *African American Religion: Varieties of Protest and Accommodation, Second Edition*. Knoxville, TN: University of Tennessee Press, 2002. This revision of an earlier work is an excellent analysis of African American religion in the context of the dominant white American culture.

CRAWFORD, A. ELAINE BROWN, *Hope in the Holler: A Womanist Theology*. Louisville, KY: Westminster John Knox Press, 2002. It is in hope, embodied in the "holler," a cry to God, that has enabled black women to survive despite being "permissible victims." This is an excellent introduction to womanist thought.

HARAKAS, STANLEY S., *The Orthodox Church: 455 Questions and Answers*. Brookline, MA: Holy Cross Orthodox Press, 1988. This older but concise and comprehensive handbook emphasizes Greek Orthodoxy but includes more general entries as well.

LITSAS, FOTIOS K., ed., *A Companion to the Greek Orthodox Church*. New York: Department of Communication, Greek Orthodox Archdiocese of North and South America, 1984. This is a good basic introduction to Eastern Orthodoxy in general.

MURPHY, LARRY G., ed., *Down By the Riverside: Readings in African American Religion*. New York: New York University Press, 2000. This is an outstanding collection of essays on a wide range of topics central to African American Christianity.

RELEVANT WORLD WIDE WEB SITES

The King Center: www.kingcenter.com

CHAPTER 8

American-Born Christianities

Days later, I found out that Aaron died. . . . We were all part of a community of devout Christian Scientists, a faith that shuns doctors and medicine and relies on prayer alone to cure the sick. . . . I thought of other deaths and suffering I'd witnessed over the years in the name of Christian Science. Most painful of all, I thought of the time seven years before when I'd almost let my own daughter die.[1]

I would like to thank God for a healing that occurred just after my husband and I got engaged. . . . And immediately all of the pain vanished—my understanding of the unreality of the accident was so powerful that it wiped out all illusion of pain. . . . I witnessed a complete and permanent healing of the skin, and there was no trace of scarring. I was in rehearsals for a musical two weeks later, dancing and singing without any hindrance. This healing has been an inspiration to me ever since.[2]

The first of the accounts above is by a former Christian Scientist, the other by a college student who is a follower of that faith. They typify the controversy that has characterized people's opinions of Christian Science, one of the American-born forms of Christianity to be discussed in this chapter.

The religious groups that are the spiritual home of the majority of America's population came to the United States from Europe. By contrast, the four religious groups discussed in this chapter began in the United States, and the nature of each bears the marks of that beginning. The four communities of faith described here include slightly less than 5 percent of Christians in the United States.

OVERVIEW

America was the "New World," a time and a place of new beginnings. There was a pervasive sense that anything was possible and that experimentation was desirable. In this climate, it is not surprising that new religious groups came into

[1]Suzanne Shepard, as told to Marti Attoun, "Suffer the Little Children," *Redbook*, October 1994, p. 66.
[2]Heidi Dittmar-Biever, "Reports of Healing," *The Christian Science Journal*, August 1994, pp. 54–55.

being. As historians of American religion Winthrop Hudson and John Corrigan point out, the entire area east of the Mississippi River had already seen many religious revivals. Scholars sometimes refer to this area as the "burnt over district" because so many revival fires had swept through it. Revival preaching typically had three emphases that contributed to the formation of new religious groups:

- Revival preachers demanded a direct encounter with God, not only an intellectual engagement but one that gripped the heart as well. This often led to visionary or mystical experiences that people took to be new revelations.
- Revivalists also called people to perfect holiness and a sin-free life. For many, this meant that life in a small, exclusive community of like-minded souls was preferable to life in the larger culture.
- Finally, they also preached that a new age was dawning, that the Second Coming of Christ on the earth and beginning of the Kingdom of God on earth, as described in the biblical Book of Revelation, was near at hand. Rather than simply wait for this greatly anticipated event, some people chose to band together in groups that tried to embody the Kingdom here and now.

As Hudson and Corrigan indicate, the new religious groups that formed during this time reflected at least one of these three perspectives and most incorporated elements of all three.[3]

The communities of faith to which you were introduced in the first part of this book fit in with the culture of which they are a part, so much so that they have tended to disappear into that culture. More important, their way of seeing the world has come to be regarded as the normal view in the culture. It is necessary to distinguish *majority view* from *normal view*, even though the two are often believed to coincide. The *majority view* is simply the opinions held by the majority of those in a given population. It takes on a different status when it comes to be thought of as the *normal*, correct, proper, or appropriate view. Then, it is the only one given full respect in a society. When this happens, it becomes a handicap for those whose views do not happen to be those of the majority. The indigenous American Christianities have much in common with traditional Christianity. In this, they are aligned with the majority culture. However, they interpret the tradition differently than do most Christians. The ways in which indigenous Christianities depart from more traditional teachings and practices usually result from the views of the founder of each group. They are the result of Christianity being passed through the lens of the unique vision of one person or a small group of people. It is changed in the process, although it retains clear and obvious links with more traditional groups. Participants in these communities of faith are Christians whose lives are centered in a faith that is different yet similar, clearly other and yet alike. The uniqueness of their insights and practices adds to the diversity and richness of religion in the United States. All of them, without exception, have been persecuted and looked down upon as a result of their nonconformity. Sometimes, they still are.

---

[3]Winthrop S. Hudson and John Corrigan, *Religion in America: An Historical Account of the Development of American Religious Life*, 5th ed. (New York: Macmillan Publishing Company, 1992), p. 181.

Have young Latter-day Saint (Mormon) missionaries ever come by your home asking to speak with you about their church? Have you perhaps seen them on your college campus? Have you seen a building in your community that is identified as a Kingdom Hall? It is the gathering place of Jehovah's Witnesses. Are you aware that Seventh-day Adventists worship on Saturday or that followers of Christian Science do not rely on doctors and hospitals for medical care? All these people are representatives of the religions that you will learn about in this chapter. Ask yourself how you feel about people whose religion makes them stand out from the rest of the culture. Are you interested in why they behave the way they do?

These communities of faith contrast with mainstream religion in several respects. Their members often have a sense of separation from the world. Although they may work very hard at making converts, their expectations for their members are high. The Mormons and the Jehovah's Witnesses are good examples of this. Members must be willing to accept more stringent rules and standards than those that apply outside the group. It is in this sense that they are somewhat exclusive. Their standards lead to a sense of separateness from the rest of the world, and members usually believe that they are following the one true way in religion while the rest of the world goes astray.

In addition to the Bible, other writings are often considered authoritative. They may be thought of as part of a group's scriptures or as interpretations of the Bible. These additional writings, usually those of the founder, may be regarded as new revelations or as interpretations inspired by God.

The material contained in the founder's writings gives rise to beliefs and practices that are different from those of more traditional Christianity. New revelations or new interpretations give rise to these new beliefs, rituals, and lifestyles and at the same time provide support for them.

A corollary of the sense of being set apart from the larger society is that these groups tend to be very close knit. Separation from those outside is complemented by closeness and community among those on the inside. They socialize together much more than they do with outsiders, and members of the group can count on strong support from other members in time of need. They often provide their members with a complete lifestyle and a full round of activities, not necessarily all of a religious nature. This reinforces the closeness of the community and limits contacts with outsiders.

Their lifestyles are frequently distinctive, making their separation from the culture somewhat obvious. There may be restrictions on dancing, gambling, and the use of alcohol and tobacco. There may be food regulations, and sometimes there are dress codes, especially for female members.

Authority in these religions is usually strictly enforced from the top down, with little room for innovation at the local or individual level. It would, however, be incorrect to conclude that members of these religious groups are blindly following their leader. For most, the acceptance of a strong religious authority and submission to that authority is in itself an important belief, one that has been consented to and taken as one's own.

The religions described below differ from traditional interpretations of Christianity in ways that are often quite noticeable and striking. For this reason, many Christians do not regard them as authentic embodiments of Christian faith. As you learned in Chapter 1, when we study religious groups and religious people from the standpoint of the humanities, we attempt to understand their beliefs and practices as they themselves do. We seek to enter empathically into their life and experience. Members of each of the communities of faith described in this chapter affirm their belief in Jesus as the Christ, as their Lord and Savior, and experience themselves as part of the Christian family of faiths. For this reason, we will do likewise.

We will focus on four groups in this category that still exist today. However, many of you may be familiar with two earlier groups, the Shakers and the Oneida Community.

The Shakers and the Oneida Community

The Shakers, whose proper name is the United Society of Believers in Christ's Second Coming, came to the United States from England in 1774, under the leadership of their founder, Mother Ann Lee. Mother Ann was believed by her followers to be the female, second incarnation of God, sent following God's first incarnation in Jesus. The Shakers lived communally and maintained strict celibacy in their quest for Christian perfection. They believed that procreation was unnecessary because the Second Coming of Christ was very near at hand. At the height of their movement, there were perhaps about 4,000 Shakers. There is still a very small community of Shakers at Sabbathday Lake in Maine.[4]

You may be familiar with the Shaker song "Simple Gifts." This song was composed in 1848 by Elder Joseph Brackett of the Sabbathday Lake community. The tune became well known after Aaron Copeland included it in his score for Martha Graham's ballet "Appalachian Spring." It was also adapted as the tune for the song, "Lord of the Dance."[5]

The Oneida Community existed from 1848 through 1880. It was founded in 1848 at Oneida, New York, by John Humphrey Noyes. At its peak, it had around three hundred members. At first glance, the community's practice of "complex marriage" seems to be the polar opposite of Shaker celibacy. In essence, Noyes taught that all the men of the community were linked in holy marriage with all its women. The community decided who would have children with whom, and the children of their unions were raised communally. Noyes' goal was "bringing together the best specimens of the human race to procreate and thereby to lift all humankind up to the level where a truly spiritual revolution could occur."[6] When the community disbanded, it formed a joint stock

[4]There are a number of Web sites for the Sabbathday Lake community. A good place to start is www.shaker. lib.me.us/index.html

[5]The lyrics and an interesting discussion of the Shaker hymn can be found at www.americanmusicpreservation. com/shakermusic4.htm. The tune and the words for Sydney Carter's "Lord of the Dance" can be heard at http://nethymnal.org/htm/l/o/r/lordoftd.htm

[6]Winthrop S. Hudson and John Corrigan, *Religion in America: An Historical Account of the Development of American Religious Life*, 5th ed. (New York: Macmillan Publishing Company, 1992), p. 136.

corporation that was the nucleus of what would become Oneida Silversmiths and Oneida Ltd., manufacturers of flatware and other tableware.

The Oneida Community and the Shakers, although they took very different approaches, were united in their quest for perfection, shared property and work, and established a community that would foreshadow the soon-to-come Kingdom of God on earth.[7]

LATTER-DAY SAINTS[8]

When most of us think of the Mormons, we probably think of neatly dressed, clean-cut young men, most likely on bicycles or walking, going from house to house talking about their faith with all who will listen, and hoping to make converts. Some may think of well-known U.S. citizens who are Mormon. Examples include the Osmonds; Ezra Taft Benson, former Secretary of Agriculture; and George Romney, former Governor of Michigan, or Mitt Romney, who entered the Republican primary for the 2008 presidential election. Others might well think of the world-famous Mormon Tabernacle Choir or Brigham Young University. Mormons have grown from a group whose numbers could be counted on the fingers of one's two hands to one of the larger and better-known communities of faith in this country. Yet many people still feel that the Mormons are not a part of mainstream America. In some ways, they *are* different and choose to stand outside the mainstream. In other ways, such as their involvement in public life, they have moved into the center. In this section, we will dispel some of the misconceptions that still surround this religious group. At the same time, some of the differences between their understanding of Christianity and that of their neighbors will be described. Some important ways in which their lives are different because of their faith will also be discussed.

The word *Mormon* itself is not the official name of the group. It is a nickname for members of *The Church of Jesus Christ of Latter-day Saints*. Mormon is believed by the church to have been a prophet in the area that would become the United States. In the concluding years of the fourth century C.E., Mormon compiled a book containing the records of the people of Lehi, a Hebrew who had led a colony of people from Jerusalem to America in about 600 B.C.E. Mormon's son Moroni added some information of his own, including a brief account of the people called Jaredites, who had come to North America at the time that the Tower of Babel was built. This record is preserved as the *Book of Mormon*.

The official name, *Church of Jesus Christ of Latter-day Saints*, tells us how this community of faith understands itself. They consider themselves to be Christians, members of the one true church that follows all the teachings of Jesus Christ.

---

[7]A very brief history, with photographs, can be read at www.oneidacommunity.org. A somewhat longer history can be read at http://www.oneida.com/about-oneida_history-of-community_learn-more
[8]www.lds.org

Figure 8-1   Salt Lake Temple of the Church of Jesus Christ of Latter-day Saints, Salt Lake City, Utah. Mormon temples are used only for special temple ordinances. Because they are regarded as sacred spaces, they are not open to the public. *(Photograph copyright LDS Church. Used by permission.)*

Although some more traditional Christian groups do not consider the Mormons to be fellow Christians, there is no doubt about their self-identification as Christians. They are neither Protestant nor Catholic nor Orthodox, however. The word *saint* is used in the Christian New Testament to mean "church members." *Latter-day* distinguishes this church from the church in the former days, which, according to Mormon teaching, fell away from the truth of Jesus Christ shortly after it was founded. About 2 percent of the population of the United States is Mormon.

The Latter-day Saints began in the first half of the nineteenth century. *Joseph Smith* (1805–1844), who would become the group's founder, grew up in the tumultuous burnt-over district mentioned above. Confused, he earnestly tried to discover which of the many religious groups in the area was correct, so that he might join it. One day in his reading of the Bible, he read, "If any of you is lacking in wisdom, ask God, who gives to all generously and ungrudgingly, and it will be given to you" (James 1:5, New Revised Standard Version). Taking these instructions to heart, the young man went and knelt in an isolated grove of trees to seek God's guidance. God spoke to Joseph Smith, according to Mormon belief, telling him that none of the available religious groups was the true church and that all had fallen away from the truth. Smith was to join none of them. Then, in 1823, the angelic messenger Moroni appeared to him and told him that he would be God's chosen servant to restore the church to the fullness of the Gospel. The restoration of the true church is an important Mormon belief. Mormons believe that the true church has been restored through the prophecy to Joseph Smith. This includes the restoration of true priestly authority so that sacred ordinances may again be rightly performed.[9]

Moroni appeared to Joseph Smith again in 1827 and revealed to him the location of golden plates upon which was written what would eventually become the *Book of Mormon*.[10] Because they were written in an unknown script, Smith was also provided with something to assist in the translation (identified as the Urim and Thummim mentioned in Exodus 28:30). The *Book of Mormon* was subsequently published in 1830. According to Mormon history, the golden plates were taken up into heaven after Smith had completed the translation. The Latter-day Saints believe that their church is founded not upon the human words and work of Joseph Smith, but on the direct revelation of God, as surely as the earlier Christian Church had been founded upon God's revelation in Jesus Christ.

The church was established in the spring of 1830, in Fayette, New York, shortly after the publication of the *Book of Mormon*. It began with only five people. They were persecuted almost immediately. Persecution led to the long westward trek that would eventually take them to Salt Lake City. They first moved from New York to Kirtland, Ohio, and then to a place near Independence, Missouri. From there, their travels took them to Nauvoo, Illinois. Trouble again broke out, and several of their number were jailed at Carthage, Illinois. Among those imprisoned were Joseph Smith and his brother Hyrum, both of whom were murdered by a local mob while in jail. Some of Smith's followers, led by Brigham Young, then began the journey to what would become Salt Lake City, in the Utah Territory. In this westward trek, the Saints echoed the westward movement of the American frontier itself. Salt Lake City became the world headquarters for the Church of Jesus Christ of Latter-day Saints in 1847. Some, including Smith's widow and young son, disputed Young's leadership and stayed

---

[9]Elder Charles Didier, "The Message of Restoration," *Ensign* on line edition (November, 2003), www.lds.org

[10]Both Old and New Testaments, the *Book of Mormon*, *Doctrine and Covenants*, and *Pearl of Great Price* are available on line at http://scriptures.lds.org/

in Illinois, forming the nucleus of what would become the second-largest Mormon group, the *Reorganized Church of Jesus Christ of Latter Day Saints* (now named the *Community of Christ*). The headquarters of this group is in Independence, Missouri.

One of the best-known and least-understood chapters of Latter-day Saints history is their practice of polygamy. For a time, men, although not women, were permitted to have more than one spouse. Some of the church's leaders believed that they had received a revelation from God in which God commanded this practice, which they began in 1843. It became public knowledge in 1852. It was met with public outrage, and the U.S. government moved quickly to undercut the power of the church in Utah and made the abandonment of multiple marriage a condition of statehood. In 1890, Mormon leaders announced that the practice was no longer approved. At any given time, probably less than 20 percent of the Church's leaders were actually involved in plural marriage. The only remaining polygynists are isolated in very small groups that are not recognized by the church. The era of plural marriage ended almost as quickly as it had begun.

Beliefs

Modern-day Mormons have beliefs that are similar to those of other Christians yet are in many ways distinctive. The *Book of Mormon* is considered to be scripture, alongside the Bible. In addition, new revelations were received at various times for specific purposes, and these were collected as the *Doctrine and Covenants*. A third book, *The Pearl of Great Price*, also contains revelations believed to have been received by Smith.

Latter-day Saints recognize four cornerstones of their faith. First among these is *Jesus Christ* himself. The *revelation to Joseph Smith* is the second. It is recorded in the *Book of Mormon*, which is the third cornerstone. The *Book of Mormon* is regarded as an additional Gospel. The fourth cornerstone is the *Mormon priesthood* that allows men to act with authority in the name of God.[11]

Mormons believe in God the Father, Jesus Christ the Son, and the Holy Ghost, as do most Christians. They are, however, believed to be separate individuals, united in purpose. Thus, their understanding of God as Father, Son, and Holy Ghost differs from the traditional Christian view that the Trinity is but one God. Mormons do not hold people accountable for the sin of Adam and Eve, as do some Christians. Being held responsible for a sin in which one had no part is repugnant to Mormon sensibilities. The concept of *free agency* is a central aspect of Mormon belief. Human beings have free will and therefore will be punished for their own sins, not those of Adam. Jesus' sacrificial death makes salvation available to all humankind, but may be lost through lack of human effort. There are also degrees of exaltation. Heaven is divided into various realms or states of being. Mormons teach that the highest of these

[11]Gordon B. Hinckley, "Four Cornerstones of Faith," *Ensign* (February, 2004) on line edition, www.lds.org

is available only to those who have followed all the laws and ordinances of the church. Those who attain this exalted status become gods, to whom all other things are subject, even the angels.[12]

A distinctive Latter-day Saints belief is that people have a premortal existence in the heavenly realm before birth. Being given a human body is a unique opportunity to carry out the actions necessary to return to God and achieve the higher degrees of exaltation. Mormons, along with other Christians, believe that people are created in God's image. People come to earth from existence in the premortal realm. Earthly life as lived by devout Mormons, including observance of the sacred ordinances, enables people to return to the kingdom of the Father upon earthly death. Individuals can return to the presence of God from whence they came, and families can remain together eternally.[13]

Latter-day Saints believe that God's will is revealed not only in the Bible, but to Joseph Smith, and, following Smith, to the leaders of the church throughout all the years of its existence. Revelation continues today. The concept of *continuous revelation* allows the church's leadership to be flexible in responding to issues and questions that are not dealt with directly in the Bible or the other Mormon scriptures. At the same time, the authority of divine revelation is maintained.

This is a distinctively American church. The *Book of Mormon* gives America a scriptural past. Many religious groups in this country have believed fervently that America has a special role to play in God's plans for the world, but none has expressed that belief as concretely as do the Latter-day Saints. They look forward to a literal regathering of Israel, restoration of the Ten Lost Tribes, and the building of the New Jerusalem, to which they refer as Zion, on the North American continent. Mormons affirm freedom of worship as a privilege for themselves and all other people and in obedience to the laws of the land and its leaders.

Lifestyle

If you are acquainted with many Latter-day Saints, you probably know them as people with an upbeat and healthful lifestyle. They participate wholeheartedly in the programs of their church. Saints strive to practice honesty and truthfulness, chastity, benevolence, and doing good to all. The body is given by God and is sacred, and taking good care of it is a religious act. This is the reason behind the *Word of Wisdom*, health guidance that Mormons teach was revealed to Smith in 1833. The code forbids smoking tobacco, drinking alcohol, drinking beverages with caffeine in them (such as coffee, tea, and many soft drinks), and taking drugs other than those prescribed by a physician for medical reasons. Meat is to be used sparingly, with the emphasis in the diet on grains, fruits, and

---

[12] *The Doctrine and Covenants of the Church of Jesus Christ of Latter-day Saints* (Salt Lake City, UT: Church of Jesus Christ of Latter-day Saints, 1982), 132:20.

[13] Gordon B. Hinckley, "The Family: A Proclamation to the World" (September 23, 1995), Latter-day Saints Web site (www.lds.org).

vegetables. Physical exercise is encouraged, as is good grooming. They teach that following the Word of Wisdom will lead to great wisdom and knowledge, as well as to good health that includes moral, emotional, and spiritual dimensions along with the physical aspects of health.[14]

As many of you probably know, *the family is absolutely central in Latter-day Saints' thought and practice.* It is the basic unit of church and society and is held to be sacred. Local churches provide many family-oriented activities throughout the week, of both a religious and a nonreligious nature. In addition, families have "family home evening" once a week, using materials provided by their church. This is a time for families to be together for study and for worship and discussion of religious matters. They also simply enjoy being together and benefit from the interaction of parents and children. Church members called home teachers visit members' homes frequently to bring messages of hope and goodwill. They are the representatives of the church leaders in helping the family to solve problems.

Latter-day Saints value marriage highly. Everyone is enjoined to marry, and requiring anyone to remain celibate is specifically forbidden. Adultery is grounds for dismissal from the Church, and premarital sex calls for severe repentance. Children are valued, and, however great a man's achievements, his highest goal and achievement is fathering children. The husband and father presides over the family. As a male member of the church, he holds a position within the priesthood. The family unit functions as a small church in and of itself. Traditional roles for men, women, and children are encouraged. The husband is the provider and leader for his family. His wife is the primary caregiver in the home and is the emotional heart of the family. Parents expect children to contribute as much as they possibly can by helping with chores and participating in family home evening programs. Through a special sealing ceremony that takes place in temples, husbands and wives, along with their children, may be joined for eternity.

The Mormon emphasis on the family involves the extended family through many generations, as well as the nuclear family of those presently living. The Church sponsors one of the largest genealogical libraries in the world and assists millions of people with research into their family backgrounds. Faithful Mormons engage in temple work on behalf of ancestors who died without being able to follow the ordinances for themselves. This is believed to be a great benefit to those who have died and confers a blessing on the living as well. The Latter-day Saints' extensive genealogical archives are available free of charge for anyone, Mormon or not, to use.

Latter-day Saints emphasize education for both men and women. Mormon children attend public and private schools but also participate in church educational programs that emphasize religious education. Home-study courses are available for those in isolated areas. A basic goal of the church is that every member will be able to read, write, do basic arithmetic, and study the scriptures and other uplifting books.

[14]*Doctrine and Covenants*, 89:19–20.

The Church sponsors several institutions of higher education, the best known of which is *Brigham Young University* (BYU) in Provo, Utah. BYU places education in the larger context of Latter-day Saints faith:

> A BYU education should be (1) spiritually strengthening, (2) intellectually enlarging, and (3) character building, leading to (4) lifelong learning and service. Because BYU is a large university with a complex curriculum, the intellectual aims are presented here in somewhat greater detail than the other aims. Yet they are deliberately placed within a larger context. The sequence flows from a conscious intent to envelop BYU's intellectual aims within a more complete, even eternal, perspective that begins with spiritual knowledge and ends with knowledge applied to the practical tasks of living and serving.[15]

In addition to studying a full range of course work, students are trained to become the type of people the Mormon tradition expects them to be. It may be of interest to many of you, because you are taking a religious studies class, to know that BYU students take at least one religious studies class every semester, ranging from world religions to Mormon theology.

Self-sufficiency is another trait encouraged by the Latter-day Saints. A detailed program of personal and family preparedness for self-sufficiency is spelled out, including education, career development, financial management, and home production and storage of necessities (sewing, gardening, food preservation, and the manufacture of some household items). These preparations will help individual families through hard times. The emphasis on self-sufficiency is balanced by readiness to help others who cannot help themselves. The church maintains storehouses that are used to help those who have exhausted their own resources. The church also sponsors an employment clearinghouse, social services, and other assistance programs that weave together into a comprehensive program of assistance for both members and nonmembers. Mormons who receive assistance through these services are expected to work to help earn what they need and to help others who are in need.

As with all religions, Mormons vary widely in their adherence to Mormon beliefs and their practice of the lifestyle that their church advocates. Some take it very seriously, while others pay little if any attention to it. Most come somewhere in between the two extremes.

Ritual

When Mormons gather for worship on Sunday morning in local churches or chapels, they do many of the same things that are done in Protestant Christian services. People sing hymns, pray, hear a sermon, and may have the opportunity to tell how God has been especially active in their lives during the past week. Concerns of the church family are shared. Men and women, boys and girls participate in their own study classes. In the weekly sacrament meeting,

[15]"Aims of a BYU Education," http://unicomm.byu.edu/president/aims.aspx

communion is observed, using bread and water, because the Mormons do not use alcohol. Other religious services take place during the week, and other activities at the church abound.

The Latter-day Saints distinguish between these local churches and their activities and temples. The *temples* and the rituals that take place in them are the most distinctive feature of Mormon ritual life. The first of these special buildings was built in Kirtland, Ohio, and dedicated in 1836. It was built following a pattern that Mormons believe God revealed to Joseph Smith. It was a temporary structure only, without all the features found in modern-day temples. Temples are reserved for the performance of special ordinances of the church. Many have been open to the public for tours for a time after they were completed, but after they are dedicated they are considered sacred space, and only worthy Mormons may enter.

Before Latter-day Saints can enter the temple, they must receive a *Temple Recommend* from the bishop. The bishop and the stake president, who is a local officer, conduct interviews to determine worthiness to enter the sacred place and to participate in its ordinances. Among other requirements, people must have "a testimony of the gospel," support the church and follow its programs and teachings, keep the Word of Wisdom, be morally pure, be members in good standing of the church, and be free of legal entanglements. Mormons who are judged worthy and go to the Temple change from street clothing to clean, white clothing provided at the Temple as a sign and symbol of purity. My descriptions of Temple ceremonies are of necessity rather brief and very general. The details are not made available to non-Mormons, and those who participate in the ceremonies promise not to reveal the details of their experience. This reticence to discuss details stems in part from the long history of misunderstanding that has marked the career of the Latter-day Saints. It also reflects the sacredness that Mormons attribute to these special observances.

The first temple ceremony is the *endowment*. This is a prerequisite for any of the other ceremonies. The endowment is said to confer the knowledge necessary for a person to return to God after death. The history of the human race as the Latter-day Saints understand it is retraced, emphasizing the importance of the present time. Covenants or promises are made and obligations conferred, along with their accompanying blessings.

Another very important Temple ceremony is *eternal marriage*. Marriage according to the laws of the world, even if the wedding is performed in a Mormon church, ends with the death of one of the spouses. Marriage and family ties can continue into eternity, according to Mormon belief. The marriage of husband and wife, and the relationship of parents and children, can be made eternal by participation in temple ceremonies. Temple marriage is also required for entrance into the highest degree of exaltation following death.[16]

Temple baptism is another temple ordinance. Temple baptismal fonts rest on the backs of twelve sculptured oxen that represent the twelve tribes of Israel. Mormons are baptized in fonts in their local churches or chapels in a service

[16]*Doctrine and Covenants*, 132:15–19 and 131:2–4.

very similar to that of other Christian churches. Baptism is by immersion and is restricted to those who are old enough to understand its meaning for themselves. Temple baptism is performed by the living on behalf of the dead. Many people die without hearing the teachings that Mormons believe are necessary for exaltation. Mormons believe that the opportunity to do so can be made available to them in the spirit world by a living member of their family who undergoes temple baptism on their behalf. Only these baptisms on behalf of another are performed in the temple. Part of the significance of tracing one's genealogy as far back as possible is to find those ancestors for whom temple work needs to be performed. Sealing ceremonies that join spouses, parents, and children for eternity can also be performed vicariously. In any case, the performance of a vicarious ceremony provides only the opportunity. The soul in the spirit world must give its voluntary consent. The concept of free agency applies even there.

Organization

There are several distinctive things about the institutional or organizational life of the Latter-day Saints. In many ways, the Church is a theocracy believed to be under the direct rule of God, because Mormons believe that the highest leaders of the Church continually receive revelations from God. No officer, however, serves without a sustaining vote from the people he serves, so that there are also democratic elements. There are no professional clergy, and lay members who serve as officers do so without pay. Now, however, both major branches of the church pay a living allowance to those people in the central administration. The Church has a president, considered to be a prophet of God. He is advised by two counselors who, along with the president, make up the First Presidency. There is a Quorum of Twelve Apostles that advises the First Presidency. The Church is highly organized along geographic lines, with no congregation being so large as to become impersonal.

Church President Gordon B. Hinckley died in January 2008. His successor is Thomas S. Monson, his long-time colleague and close friend. Two news items following President Hinckley's death give an indication of the affection and respect of Mormons for their living prophet. When asked why she had gotten up at four in the morning and skipped classes to be among the thousands of mourners who payed their respects in Salt Lake City, a college student named Michelle said simply, "He's been my prophet."[17] In response to e-mails and text messages notifying them of his death, thousands of Mormon high school students showed up for Monday morning classes wearing their "Sunday best."[18]

Priesthood in the Mormon church means the authority to act in the name of God. The priesthood is open to all worthy males, twelve years of age or older. There are two divisions, the Melchizedek (the higher order) and the Aaronic (the lower order). Each is further divided into three subdivisions. Specific responsibilities and privileges come with each designation, and a man moves

[17]Muncie, Indiana, StarPress, February 1, 2008, D-2.
[18]http://newsroom.lds.org/ldsnewsroom/eng/news-releases-stories/

through the designations in order as he studies and carries out the duties of his present designation. Women are not priests. They do, however, share in the blessings that are conferred by the priesthood through their husbands. The primary organization for women in the Church is the Relief Society. Women are eligible to serve on the governing councils of the Church. Mormons believe that the pattern of organization that they have is the same as that found in the primitive church before it fell away from the true Church of Jesus Christ.

Restricting the priesthood to men is only one of the ways the Latter-day Saints emphasize the importance of traditional roles for women. Although married women are not expected to work outside the home, many Mormon women do so, either out of choice or economic necessity. The role of women as wives and mothers is very highly respected. What distresses some Mormon women and angers the more militant among them is that this is the only approved role. Stepping outside it frequently leads to disapproval. Women who do so may be made to feel that they are endangering their eternal life with God. Speaking out publicly on feminist issues has occasionally resulted in dismissal from the Church. Mormons have also joined Catholics and conservative Protestants in their support of antiabortion legislation.

Another unique feature of the Latter-day Saints is their *emphasis on missionary work*. The rapid growth of this community of faith can be attributed largely to this energetic program. Thousands of young men and women and retired couples accept missionary assignments for up to two years, normally serving at their own expense, often receiving financial assistance from family and friends. The main work of these missionaries is going from house to house seeking converts to their way of life.

Music is an important part of Latter-day Saints culture. The *Mormon Tabernacle Choir* is a 325-voice group that began in the mid-1800s. Its "Music and the Spoken Word" program has been carried by many radio stations since 1929, making it the longest-running religious broadcast in the U.S. The choir's recording of "The Battle Hymn of the Republic" won a Grammy Award. There are also a Mormon youth symphony and a chorus, with 100 and 350 members, respectively. They, too, perform regularly.

The Saints' Conference Center, on the beautifully landscaped grounds of Temple Square in Salt Lake City, seats 21,000 people and has an electronic system to translate speakers' remarks into 100-plus languages simultaneously. It also houses an extensive collection of Latter-day Saints artwork.

The two major branches of the Mormon church grew out of a disagreement about who should be Joseph Smith's successor. The *Church of Jesus Christ of Latter-day Saints* (LDS) began with those who thought that Smith's successor should be a member of the Council of Twelve Apostles that advises the church president. This group chose Brigham Young as their leader. This branch is now based in Salt Lake City, Utah. The Reorganized Church of Jesus Christ of Latter Day Saints was founded by those who believed that Smith's successor should be his biological descendant. The RLDS changed their name to the *Community of Christ* in 2002.[19]

[19]www.cofchrist.org

The two groups are bound together by their shared commitment to the Christian Old and New Testaments, the *Book of Mormon*, and the *Doctrine and Covenants* as revealed scripture and the prophethood of Joseph Smith. They differ on several points. The Community of Christ has a core of salaried local ministers. Both women and men have been ordained to both orders of the priesthood since 1984. Two women were recently appointed to the Council of Twelve Apostles, a governing group second only to the three-member First Presidency in the church hierarchy. There is no baptism nor marriage of the dead by proxy, although those who die without hearing the Mormon gospel are believed to have the opportunity to do so after death. The single Community of Christ temple in Independence, Missouri, "is a house of public worship, and entrance to the temple or participation in its ministries is open to all."[20] There are numerous smaller points of difference, as well.

Mitt Romney and the "Religion Question" in American Politics

Former Massachusetts governor Mitt Romney's bid for the 2008 Republican presidential nomination marked the second time that a Latter-day Saint had been a contender for presidential candidacy. His father, George W. Romney, had made an unsuccessful bid for the Republican nomination against Richard Nixon in 1968. Mitt Romney's religious affiliation was clearly an issue. On the one hand, his prospective candidacy brought more attention to the church than at any time in recent history. On the other hand, Mormons and others were shocked by the negativity of that attention. A poll conducted by the *Wall Street Journal* and NBC News shortly before he withdrew indicated that half of Americans would have reservations or be "very uncomfortable" were a Mormon to become President. Armand Mauss, an LDS sociologist, observed that the response had been a "wake-up call" for the church. Romney's religious affiliation exposed more and more intense anti-Mormon prejudice than might have been expected. "I don't think that any of us had any idea how much anti-Mormon stuff was out there," Mauss said.

Although religion was not a stated reason for Romney's withdrawal from the campaign, it clearly contributed to his lack of support among voters. Nathan Oman, a Mormon law professor from Virginia, referred to Romney as a "member of the [Mormon] tribe" and said, "What happens to him is a test of whether or not our tribe gets included in the political universe." The reaction to Romney would seem to suggest that Mormons are not yet considered full players in the "political universe."[21] Full inclusion in public life is one key indicator of acceptance, and the Latter-day Saints have not yet found that acceptance in the United States.

Both Mormon churches offer their members a stirring vision of how life can be. They provide firm guidelines for life and a set of ritual ordinances that members believe will lead to a greatly enhanced quality of life now and eternal

[20]Community of Christ, www.cofchrist.org
[21]*Wall Street Journal*, February 8, 2008, A-1, 12.

life in the future. They embrace the vision of a coming Kingdom of God shared by most other Christians. At the same time, they interpret it in a uniquely American fashion, locating the coming kingdom in the United States. They offer a strong community and a full program of activities with other like-minded persons. Their emphasis on the family and on traditional morality offers a clear-cut alternative to the problems many people see besetting modern society.

CHRISTIAN SCIENTISTS[22]

Christian Scientists (members of the Church of Christ, Scientist) maintain a low public profile. They do not seek converts by missionary activity, but they do maintain Christian Science *Reading Rooms* where people can go and read the Bible as well as Christian Science literature. Christian Science is directly linked to the experiences of *Mary Baker Eddy*, its founder. In 1866, Mrs. Eddy reported a nearly instantaneous cure from a severe back injury after reading the account of one of Jesus' healings (Matthew 9:1–8). Along with the Bible, Eddy's *Science and Health with Key to the Scriptures* (first published in 1875) is the source of Christian Science teaching.[23]

Christian Scientists believe that all that God creates is good, because a good God would not create that which was not good. Therefore, the only reality that the evils of sin, sickness, and death have is that which we give them, when our erring human thought attributes to them a reality they do not have. Christian Scientists rely on the power of God for healing rather than on medical treatment, although this is always an individual choice. Reliance on Christian Science healing is a choice, just as relying on conventional medicine is a choice. A Christian Scientist who utilizes traditional medical care is not condemned or required to leave the church. They are however, strongly discouraged from mixing the two types of care. Christian Science is based on the belief that the cause and the cure of illness are spiritual. Medicine looks at both cause and cure as primarily material. Trying to use these incompatible systems together could compromise the healing process.[24]

Christian Science practitioners are specially trained by the church to assist those who seek Christian Science healing through prayer, and Christian Science in-patient facilities can provide supportive care to the seriously ill while treatment is given. Healing by prayer is believed to be divinely natural rather than supernatural, an integral part of the harmonious order of the created world as God means it to be. Christian Science healing is not limited to physical healing but extends to psychological, emotional, and other problems. Practitioners also offer their services to those who are not Christian Scientists.

Christian Scientists describe *God as divine Principle, Love, Mind, Spirit, Soul, Life, and Truth*, which are the seven synonyms for God.[25] God is understood to be

---

[22]www.tfccs.com

[23]This key scripture is available on line at www.spirituality.com/dt/toc_sh.jhtml

[24]The First Church of Christ, Scientist, www.tfccs.com

[25]Mary Baker Eddy, *Science and Health with Key to the Scriptures* (Boston: The First Church of Christ, Scientist, 1906), p. 465.

wholly spiritual and not personalized. God includes qualities associated with both genders, and there is a tradition of gender equality throughout the church's organization. There are no ordained ministers. Readers elected from the congregation serve for a period of three years, often without pay. It is preferred that one reader be female and the other male. Practitioners are more often female than male, and all church organizational offices are open to women.

The words *Christian* and *Science* in this church's name tell us something important about it. It is a church *focused on Jesus the Christ.* Christian Scientists believe people are saved through Jesus's atoning death on the cross.

Christian Scientists also believe that theirs is a *scientific religion. Science* is used to describe this religion because

> . . . it can be demonstrated. We see God as the universal, divine Principle underlying the life and healing work of Christ Jesus. God by His very nature must be unchanging Truth, invariable Love, operating through timeless spiritual laws rather than special miraculous acts. To understand these laws of absolute good is to find that Christianity can be scientifically applied to every human ill.[26]

The church meets for Sunday services that consist largely of readings from the Bible and *Science and Health*. Most of what takes place is determined by the Mother Church in Boston and is the same in all Christian Science churches. There is also music—organ music, hymns, and perhaps a vocal solo. Wednesday midweek meetings include readings from the Bible and from *Science and Health* and provide an opportunity for members and visitors to give and hear testimonies of healing. The First Reader chooses the subject and passages for the Wednesday evening meeting. One writer describes the two services this way:

> The Sunday service at a Christian Science church mingles something of the bare simplicity of the New England church services that Mrs. Eddy knew as a girl with a touch of the Quaker quietism and the Unitarian rationalism with which she came in friendly contact later. The midweek meeting . . . is chiefly known for the spontaneous "testimonies of healing" given by members of the congregation.[27]

Members of the Board of Lectureship are authorized to give public lectures explaining Christian Science and inviting further inquiry. They do not specifically invite people to join their church.

The Church of Christ, Scientist, has faced a number of challenges to its practices over the years. Currently, Christian Science healing is an accepted alternative to traditional medical treatment. Major insurance companies will usually reimburse those who receive Christian Science treatment. The Internal Revenue Service recognizes the cost of treatment as an income tax deduction, as it does medical fees. Christian Scientists do not claim that they have found the only way

---

[26]*Questions and Answers on Christian Science* (Boston: The Christian Science Publishing Society, 1974), p. 2.
[27]*Christian Science: A Sourcebook of Contemporary Materials* (Boston: The Christian Science Publishing Society, 1990), p. 51.

to God. They claim to have found a way that brings them peace and joy as well as physical healing, a way that they can recommend to others on that basis but that they do not ever attempt to force upon someone who is not interested.

Christian Science is also known to the public through its publication of the *Christian Science Monitor* newspaper, widely recognized as one of the best in the nation.[28] There are also Monitor radio and television networks. A religious magazine, the *Herald of Christian Science*, is published in a dozen languages plus Braille. Religious periodicals and the *Monitor* are a part of the church's missionary activity.

SEVENTH-DAY ADVENTISTS[29]

The Seventh-day Adventists are by far the largest single church within the group of churches that make up the adventist believers, a family that also includes the Latter-day Saints and the Jehovah's Witnesses. Adventism emphasizes the Christian belief, found especially in the biblical books of Daniel and Revelation, that the return of Christ to the world will be a literal, physical event. Most adventists believe that this will happen in the near future. Those who rebel against God will be destroyed, while true believers will be saved. The return of Christ is said to be the "grand climax of the gospel." The righteous, both living and dead, will be saved and taken into heaven, while the unrighteous will die. This will happen in fulfillment of prophecy, according to the Adventists. Since no one can know when this will occur, people must always be ready.[30]

Adventism began early in the nineteenth century. Soon the United States was the location where its tenets and practices were best defined. Like many other movements that eventually became separate organizations, most adventists had no intention of breaking off from the churches of which they were a part. They set out to be an emphasis within a church, not a separate body. The emphasis created conflict, however, and many did break away. Adventism is sometimes linked with holiness (see Chapter 5), as believers seek to be prepared on a daily basis for the return of Christ.

Most of the divisions within adventism occurred when people set dates for the second coming. These dates passed, and nothing happened. In the sharp disappointment that followed such events, differences of opinion led to separations. A second major point of disagreement concerned whether the Lord's Day or Sabbath was properly celebrated on Saturday or Sunday. This difference contributed to the formation of the Seventh-day Adventist Church.

William Miller (1782–1849) is perhaps the best known of the early Adventist preachers. Miller believed that the books of Daniel and Revelation were written in a numerical code whose message could be extracted by mathematical calculation. Miller initially put the date of the Second Coming in

---

[28]Available on line at http://www.csmonitor.com/
[29]www.adventist.org
[30]Seventh-day Adventist Web site (www.adventist.org.).

March, 1843. When that did not happen, he recalculated and predicted October of 1844. When this prediction proved incorrect (an event sometimes described as the Great Disappointment), some of the people whose hopes had been dashed began meeting together and continued the Adventist hope. Among them were *Ellen G. White* and her husband. Mrs. White began entering into trance states in which she experienced what she and her followers believed to be revelations, and she was soon accepted as a prophet by the group. Among the group's keystones was the *celebration of the Sabbath on Saturday rather than Sunday*. Mrs. White also confirmed the correctness of the 1844 date but redefined what happened on that date. Christ had not returned to the earth on that date, as was originally predicted, but had initiated the cleansing of the true, heavenly sanctuary described in Hebrews 8:1–2. This interpretation of the King James version of the text restored the adventist hope, and the effects of the Great Disappointment were at least partially overcome.

Seventh-day Adventists continue to celebrate the Sabbath on Saturday. "Seventh-day" in the group's name refers to this practice. Sometimes people who keep a Saturday Sabbath are called *Sabbatarians*. As they read the Bible, Seventh-day Adventists find nothing to warrant changing the Sabbath from the way it was commanded to be observed in the Hebrew Scriptures (Christian Old Testament). Proper observance remains from sundown Friday to sunset on Saturday. It is to be a day of rest and religious pursuits.[31]

Seventh-day Adventists believe that they are the "remnant church," a people called out in the last days to be the true church. Ellen G. White's gift of prophecy is recognized as a mark of such a remnant. Most of the church has fallen away from the truth, but this small remnant has been given the gift of true prophecy through the work of Ellen White in order to preserve the gospel and announce the second coming of Christ. Her words are regarded as authoritative and a source of truth, with the Bible being the standard by which all human words are judged.[32]

Like the Latter-day Saints, Seventh-day Adventists are known for their support of sound health practices, because they believe that the body is the temple of the Holy Ghost. Good health practices are a religious obligation. They abstain from the use of alcohol and tobacco as well as illicit drugs, and they advocate healthy habits such as exercise and proper nutrition. They encourage a positive mental outlook. Many are vegetarians. Seventh-day Adventists concentrate much of their missionary work, both in the United States and overseas, on hospitals and other medical missions. The following description sets their health practices in the context of their larger concern for holiness that relates them to the holiness movement described in Chapter 5:

> We are called to be a godly people who think, feel, and act in harmony with the principles of heaven. For the Spirit to recreate in us the character of our Lord we involve ourselves only in those things which will produce Christlike purity, health, and joy in our lives. This means that our amusement and entertainment

[31]Ibid.
[32]Ibid.

should meet the highest standards of Christian taste and beauty. While recognizing cultural differences, our dress is to be simple, modest, and neat, befitting those whose true beauty does not consist of outward adornment but in the imperishable ornament of a gentle and quiet spirit. It also means that because our bodies are the temples of the Holy Spirit, we are to care for them intelligently. Along with adequate exercise and rest, we are to adopt the most healthful diet possible and abstain from the unclean foods identified in the Scriptures. Since alcoholic beverages, tobacco, and the irresponsible use of drugs and narcotics are harmful to our bodies, we are to abstain from them as well. Instead, we are to engage in whatever brings our thoughts and bodies into the discipline of Christ, who desires our wholesomeness, joy, and goodness.[33]

Men's and women's roles emphasize the traditional over the innovative. Both genders are encouraged to dress modestly and to manifest a "gentle and quiet spirit" as you read above. Church and church-sponsored activities play a large role in most of their lives. Especially in some areas of the country, Seventh-day Adventist children may attend schools sponsored by their church.

JEHOVAH'S WITNESSES[34]

Many Americans have become acquainted with the Jehovah's Witnesses through their extensive program of *door-to-door evangelism*. All members are expected to participate in witnessing to people in this way. In addition, members may become Pioneers, full time preachers who donate at least ninety hours monthly, or special pioneers or missionaries who commit to spending 140 hours monthly evangelizing in remote locations with the intent to form new congregations.

The Witnesses believe that the world and its inhabitants are in a time of transition that will herald the coming reign of Christ on the Earth. Jesus predicted that wars, disease, famine, and natural disasters, as well as false prophets and false religions would precede his return to earth. We now live in such a time, say the Witnesses, and the second coming of Christ is near.[35]

Although most of us know them best as Jehovah's Witnesses, their official name is the *Watchtower Bible and Tract Society*. The name Jehovah's Witnesses comes from Isaiah 43:12, which, in some translations, has God saying to the people that God is named Jehovah and they are God's witnesses. They explain the name Jehovah's Witnesses this way:

It is a descriptive name, indicating that they bear witness concerning Jehovah, his Godship, and his purposes. "God," "Lord," and "Creator"—like "President," "King," and "General"—are titles and may be applied to several different personages. But "Jehovah" is a personal name and refers to the almighty God and

---

[33]Seventh-day Adventist Church, Fundamental Beliefs, http://www.adventist.org/beliefs/fundamental/index.htm
[34]The Witnesses' official Web site is http://www.watchtower.org/
[35]Watchtower Bible and Tract Society, www.watchtower.org

Creator of the universe. This is shown at Psalm 83:18, according to the King James version of the Bible: "That men may know that thou, whose name alone is JEHOVAH, art the most high over all the earth."[36]

Jehovah's Witnesses do not consider themselves to be a church, but rather a group of Bible students and publishers of God's Word. *Publishing* here has two meanings. They translate and publish Bibles and religious tracts, and they publish (in the sense of making public) their understanding of God's message for modern-day people by every means at their disposal.

The group was originally organized by Pastor Charles Taze Russell (1852–1916), who is thought of as an organizer and not the founder, because God alone is considered to be the founder. Unlike Joseph Smith and Ellen G. White, Russell disclaimed and condemned contemporary revelation, asserting that God's whole revelation was contained in the Bible. The Witnesses believe that theirs is the one true faith mentioned by Paul in Ephesians 4:5 (there is "one Lord, one faith, one baptism").

The group has never wavered from its focus on Bible study, and its teachings are supported by an elaborate system of references to scripture. When they meet, usually more than once a week, in Kingdom Halls (their meeting sites are not called churches), most of their time is spent in Bible study and discussion. They believe that the Bible was written by individuals who recorded God's message accurately. However, they hold that modern translations contain errors, and, in 1961, they published their own *New World Translation* of the Bible.[37] Witnesses believe that their translation corrects the errors of earlier translations.

God is presently gathering the righteous together, in order to spare them from the disaster that will take place in the universal battle of Armageddon described in the book of Revelation in the Christian New Testament. This cataclysmic battle will inaugurate the reign of Jehovah God on the earth. The Witnesses understand themselves as the forerunners of this new kingdom.

Witnesses believe that only a limited number of people—the 144,000 mentioned in the Book of Revelation 7 and 10—will live and reign with God in Heaven. The rest of the righteous will live in peace and harmony on an earth that has been restored to a paradisal state. Those saved to live on a restored earth vastly outnumber those whose eternal life will be in heaven. The Kingdom of God will come both on earth and in heaven, and saved human beings will be responsible for caring for the earthly Kingdom. This is one of the Witnesses' most distinctive beliefs.[38]

Those who are gathered out are called to separate themselves from the world and form a *theocracy*, a community under the rule of God. To maintain this separation insofar as possible, the Witnesses avoid involvement in the political process by neither voting nor running for public office. They do not serve in the military. Technically, they are not pacifists; they claim that they would fight

[36]www.watchtower.org
[37]Available on their Web site at http://www.watchtower.org/e/bible/index.htm
[38]Watchtower Bible and Tract Society, www.watchtower.org

in God's war. They do not salute the flag nor sing the national anthem. They believe that to do so is to worship the nation and make an idol of it. Oaths of any sort are forbidden. In an extension of the Christian Old Testament prohibition against drinking blood, they do not accept blood transfusions. Jehovah's Witness children do not participate in school celebrations of holidays such as Easter and Christmas, nor do their families celebrate these holidays. They also do not celebrate birthdays:

> Jesus never commanded Christians to celebrate his birth. Rather, he told his disciples to memorialize, or remember, his death. . . . Christmas and its customs come from ancient false religions. The same is true of Easter customs, such as the use of eggs and rabbits. The early Christians did not celebrate Christmas or Easter, nor do true Christians today. . . . The early Christians did not celebrate birthdays. The custom of celebrating birthdays comes from ancient false religions. True Christians give gifts and have good times together at other times during the year.[39]

Jehovah's Witnesses are particularly critical of what they regard as the three strongest allies of Satan in his plan to destroy the world. These three Satanic allies are the government, big business, and churches that teach false doctrines (i.e., all those except the Witnesses). They must be destroyed in the coming battle before God can recreate the world. Although their aggressive missionary tactics anger and put off many people, Witnesses have earned a reputation for being honest, courteous, and industrious. Their conservative lifestyle stresses traditional roles for men and women. However, women participate fully in the evangelistic efforts of this group, and many times children are taken along. By the time they are ten years old or so, many children are accomplished Witnesses.

AN AMERICAN INNOVATION

Three of the four contemporary groups described in this chapter—the Mormons, Seventh-day Adventists, and Jehovah's Witnesses—share a number of common characteristics. These features also describe the Shakers and the Oneida Community. Most basically, those who belong to them share a belief that something very significant is going on in the present time, something that means Christ can be expected to return to the earth soon. It is thus of great importance to be ready for that time. Being ready has not only spiritual, but mental, emotional, and physical dimensions. Part of being ready is being separated out from the larger culture into a small, select community that is often described as a remnant of true believers in a time of widespread apostasy.

These religious groups are, in important ways, truly an American innovation. They echo attitudes that characterized the founding of the New World. The New World was seen as a distinct innovation, as something clearly different from the ways of organizing society and politics that existed in Europe. Its

[39]Ibid.

significance was not only socio-political but religious as well. America was, in the words of American civil religion, to be a city set upon a hill, an example to the rest of the world. It offered the hope and the promise of being able to bring into being something genuinely different, genuinely better, than anything that had been known before.

These themes have continued to be important in American religiousness and in the larger culture as well. You read about the success of the *Left Behind* series of novels in Chapter 5. The premillennialist view that forms the framework for these novels is the same as the understanding of Christ's Second Coming that guides the groups discussed in this chapter. It also informs Hal Lindsay's earlier book *The Late, Great Planet Earth*.[40] It is reflected in bumper stickers that read, "In the event of the Rapture, this car will be unmanned." It is a belief that continues to capture the imagination of many in our culture. It is reflected in mainstream "secular" music, novels, and movies that make use, either explicitly or implicitly, of similar religious themes. The vision of the select community called to high purposes continues as well. It exists in the belief that America embodies a better way that offers hope and help to the rest of the world.

COMMUNITY AND REASSURANCE

What is it that motivates the members of these communities of faith to live a life that distinguishes them sharply from the culture of which they are a part? To be sure, there are many reasons. Many followers of these ways of life live with a keen sense that the world is a wicked and evil place and that only by separating themselves from it can they have any hope of salvation. They take the idea of God's last judgment literally and seriously. Many believe firmly that the time is near when Christ will return to earth to judge all persons and make a final separation of the saved from the condemned. Therefore, it is necessary to be ready at all times. They believe that they have increasing evidence of the work of the Holy Spirit in their lives and in the lives of their associates, and this helps to assure them that they will indeed be among the saved when that time comes.

Others have other reasons. For many, becoming a Mormon means joy and community in this life and the assurance that important family ties will remain intact on the other side of death. Christian Science offers not only an alternative to traditional medical care but an alternative way of understanding God and human nature. For many Scientists, their faith simply makes more sense out of their experience than do other alternatives.

These communities of faith offer their followers two very important things. They offer a strong sense of community that can be a refuge for those who are lonely and without other ties to the culture. It is a community of sharing among like-minded people whose goals and values are very similar. More

[40]Hal Lindsay, *The Late, Great Planet Earth* (Grand Rapids, MI: Zondervan, 1970).

important, many believe that they are called out of the world and into a small select community of faith. They believe that they are people who have heard and follow the message of the one true faith. The guidelines for life in this spiritual elite are clearly spelled out. The moral ambiguity that characterizes so much of contemporary society is absent.

Second, those who keep the faith and follow the guidelines are assured of salvation. Faith in justifying grace came as a great relief to Martin Luther, as it has to millions of other Protestants. It is nonetheless difficult to pin down. How does one know one is justified? How can one be absolutely certain of a place in heaven? These forms of Christianity emphasize true faith and an upright life. How to live an upright life is described in clear behavioral terms. This leads to a greater sense of security. They are high-demand communities of faith that offer the faithful even higher rewards. Thus, these American-born religions offer their followers answers to some of the deepest and most pressing problems of human life, answers with fewer ambiguities and uncertainties than those proposed by the religions of their neighbors in the religious consensus.

QUESTIONS AND ACTIVITIES FOR REVIEW, DISCUSSION, AND WRITING

1. Think about how you would feel if you were a part of a religion that set very different standards for you than those followed by your classmates. Don't make this exercise too simple by concentrating solely on being different. Remember that such religions also offer security and the assurance that one is on the right path.
2. Most Latter-day Saints are very willing to discuss their faith with non-Mormons, and Mormon churches welcome visitors eagerly. If possible, arrange to attend a service. You might also want to ask the missionaries to describe their experiences to you.
3. Visit a Christian Science Reading Room, and look over the literature. Report on what you find.
4. If you are not a member of one of the religions discussed in this chapter, write an essay about how your life would be different if you were a member. If you are a member, write about how your life would differ if you were not.
5. With a group, construct a chart that outlines the distinctive features of the communities of faith described in this chapter.
6. This chapter has touched on only the most central aspect of each of these groups. Visit the official Web site of each of these organizations to learn something that you did not learn from reading and discussing the chapter.

FOR FURTHER READING

ELIASON, ERIC A. ed., *Mormons and Mormonism: An Introduction to an American World Religion.* Urbana, IL: University of Illinois Press, 2001. This is a balanced collection by a Brigham Young University professor.

DRASHKE, DEREK AND W. MICHAEL ASHCRAFT, eds., *New Religious Movements: A Documentary Reader.* New York City: New York University Press, 2005. The editors have compiled a diverse collection of significant primary sources from many of the religious movements described in this chapter, as well as others.

STEIN, STEPHEN J. *Communities of Dissent: A History of Alternative Religion in America.* New York City: Oxford University Press, 2003. Professor Stein presents a fair and judicious overview of religious dissent in America that places it in the context of dissent throughout the culture.

ZELLNER, WILLIAM W. AND RICHARD T. SCHAEFER. *Extraordinary Groups: An Examination of Unconventional Lifestyles.* New York City: Worth Publishers, 2007. This is a nicely balanced study of extraordinary religious groups, including the Mormons and Jehovah's Witnesses as well as the Amish, Oneida Community, and the Father Divine movement, and the Jewish Hasidim. Although the book is written from a scholarly, sociological point of view, it reads almost like a novel. It is fascinating and very accessible.

RELEVANT WORLD WIDE WEB SITES

Communal Studies Association, www.communalstudies.info/

The Religious Movements Homepage Project, University of Virginia, http://etext.lib. virginia.edu/relmove/welcome/welcome.htm

CHAPTER 9

Living a Jewish Life in the United States

American Jews make their peace with lots of things; they are different in religion but the same as other people in most other ways of life. They are Jewish, but not so Jewish that they can't be as American as everybody else. In a country with a Christian majority, where the celebrations of Christianity divide the year, American Jews respect their neighbors and enjoy their goodwill as well. The secret of the Jews in America . . . is that, although they are different, they love being exactly what they are.[1]

WHO IS A JEW?

American Jewish Voices[2]

Dr. Ruth Westheimer, the grandmotherly and outspoken sex educator, looks into her grandchildren's faces and knows that Hitler did everything he could to prevent their generation of Jews from ever being born. There is, she says, a lesson for the world in the Jewish experience. Despite having been the victims of unspeakable horror, they held fast to their conviction that their mission was to help repair the world by responding to hatred with a commitment to justice, peace, and the repair of the world.

One of the blessings used in the synagogue in which *Leonard Nimoy* grew up was to divide the four fingers of one's hand into a "V," which created the Hebrew letter shin, symbolizing "Shah-dai," one of the names of God. "When we were creating the television program *Star Trek*," Nimoy says, "we needed a salute. I thought back to that hand symbol and proposed it. The rest, as they say, is history."

Who Is a Jew? An American Jew?

To a greater extent than any other religion in the United States, the term *Judaism* encompasses many different things, not all of them religious. Different aspects vary in their importance to individual Jews. One can, of

---

[1]Jacob Neusner, *World Religions in America, an Introduction, Revised and Expanded* (Louisville, KY: Westminster John Knox Press, 2000), p. 107.
[2]From the American Jewish Committee Web site, www.ajc.org/JewishLife/BeingJewish.asp

course, be a Jew *religiously*. In this sense, which will be the primary one for our purposes, a "Jew is one who seeks a spiritual base in the modern world by living the life of study, prayer, and daily routine dedicated to the proposition that Jewish wisdom through the ages will answer the big questions in life—questions like Why do people suffer? What is life's purpose? Is there a God?"[3]

The Jewish faith has given rise to literature, music, foods, folkways, and a rich and complex cultural heritage. To be a Jew *culturally* is to identify with this cultural heritage of Judaism, with or without claiming formal religious affiliation.

Judaism can also be *ethnicity*, people who have biological ties to Israel. Ethnicity and religion have in the past been closely tied together. Jewish ethnicity meant Jewish religion. Not all Jews share this ethnic link, because Judaism accepts Gentiles who want to convert to Judaism. About 10,000 Gentiles annually become "Jews by choice," which is the preferred term for those who choose Judaism rather than being born into the faith.[4] Once a person becomes a Jew, no distinction is made between Jews who are born Jewish and those who are not. In a sense, "all Jews are Jews by choice today, since even born Jews have to make the conscious decision that they will remain Jewish, rather than join another religion or become nothing in particular."[5]

Jews are not a race, because there are Jews of many races. Nor are they a nation, although early in their history they were identified with the nation of Israel.

Jews immigrated to the United States from many different Jewish cultures in Europe. This led to wide variations in Jewish practice and culture within the United States and set the stage for the development of the varied styles of Judaism that have remained important into the present.

Today, Jews continue to lead the nation in education, professionalization, and income and are a noteworthy presence in politics and culture. Most American Jews live in major cities and in the suburbs associated with them. Except for beliefs and practices specific to their religion, the lives of most Jews are very much like those of their Gentile (non-Jewish) counterparts.

One recent study notes that Jews in this country struggle to define what it means to be Jewish.[6] Synagogues must define who is a Jew as they decide whom to admit to membership. If their admission policy is very open, they must then decide who is eligible to read Torah in worship or to serve the congregation as an officer. Is the child of one Jewish and one Gentile parent Jewish? Questions like these bring up the issue of boundaries. In the face of declining numbers, it may be tempting to draw the boundaries very widely. This, however, raises the possibility of the loss of distinctive identity. American Jews are challenged by the need to find their way between clear identity and inclusiveness.

This is complicated by another factor. "No more than half the Jews in the United States consider themselves 'religious,' and less than half the Jews in

---

[3]Rabbi Morris N. Kertzer (revised by Rabbi Lawrence A. Hoffman), *What Is a Jew? New and Completely Revised Edition* (New York: Macmillan Publishing Company, 1993), p. 7.

[4]David C. Gross, *1,201 Questions and Answers about Judaism* (New York: Hippocrene Books, 1992), p. 277.

[5]Rabbi Morris N. Kertzer (revised by Rabbi Lawrence A. Hoffman), *What Is a Jew*, p. 8.

[6]Marc Lee Raphael, *Judaism in America, The Columbia Contemporary American Religion Series* (Irvington, NY: Columbia University Press, 2003), p. 2.

America are affiliated with a synagogue."[7] Because Judaism comprises much more than the Judaic religion, many persons who consider themselves Jewish do not participate in the institutional dimensions of the religion of Judaism:

> [Some] Jews affirm their Jewishness but not Judaism. They do not consider themselves Judaic. Born of Jewish parents and thus (even if only the mother is Jewish) considered Jewish according to those who observe Jewish law, they have abandoned anything connected to the synagogue or to religious ceremonies, customs, observances and rituals.[8]

A BRIEF HISTORICAL NOTE

Jews were the smallest religious minority in the colonies prior to the Revolutionary War, and their numbers did not increase significantly until the 1800s. The majority of Jews in colonial America were Sephardic Jews of Spanish origin who were thoroughly traditional in their religious beliefs and practices. They had distinctive ritual practices and a distinctive language that blended medieval Spanish with Hebrew and Arabic. They were localized along the eastern seaboard. A congregation formed at New Amsterdam, New York, where a synagogue was dedicated in 1730. An early Jewish community in Newport, Rhode Island, virtually disappeared but was revived in 1750. The classic Truro Synagogue in Newport, dedicated in 1763, remains an outstanding example of synagogue architecture. Synagogues were also dedicated at Savannah, Georgia, in 1733, in Philadelphia in 1747, and at Charleston, South Carolina, in 1749. The Sephardic Jews mainly kept to themselves, insulated by their language and the strictness of their orthodoxy from their non-Jewish neighbors. This, along with their small numbers, prevented their having much if any influence on the surrounding culture.

Beginning in the 1800s, two large waves of Jewish immigration came to America. The first, from approximately 1820 through 1870, brought many Jews of German origin. By and large, they were middle class and relatively well educated, with a strong interest in fitting into their adopted homeland. They were influenced by a very liberal current in German Judaism that came to be known as Reform, and they immigrated to the United States because they believed that its freedom of religion and democratic government offered an ideal environment for Reform Judaism. They spread out through the entire country, not desiring to remain in sheltered enclaves as had their Sephardic predecessors. By the mid-nineteenth century, they had become the largest group of American Jews.

An even larger immigration occurred from 1880 through 1914, and it was of a very different character. These were Jews from Eastern Europe, Russia, Rumania, Poland, and Austria. They fled their home countries in response to harsh persecutions and devastating attacks aimed at destroying the entire Jewish

[7]Marc Lee Raphael, *Judaism in America*, p. 3.
[8]Ibid., p. 10.

Figure 9-1   *The Magen David* (Star of David): The origin of the Star of David is lost in the mists of early history. It appears on synagogues as early as the second or third century C.E. In the early fourteenth century, it was used as a protective amulet or magical symbol. Apparently, it came into widespread usage as a symbol of Judaism (in the nineteenth century) because there was a desire to have a sign that would symbolize Judaism in the same way that the cross symbolizes Christianity.

population. Many were desperately poor, uneducated, and, for the most part, unskilled and did not speak English. They remained along the eastern seaboard, through which they had entered the country. They had reacted in two very different ways to the attacks they had endured in Europe. The majority retreated into a rigid and somewhat strident orthodoxy, whereas some had renounced religious Judaism altogether in favor of secular movements oriented around social reform. They brought both these attitudes with them to the United States. By 1914, the number of Jews in the United States had risen by more than tenfold, from a quarter of a million in 1870 to about three million.

JEWS AND CHRISTIANS

As many of you know already, Christianity began as a small sect within Judaism, as a variation on the teaching and practice of that ancient religion. The two thus share a common history, up to a point, and a common geography. The cultural conditions out of which Christianity was born were those of the Judaism of its time. It is not surprising, therefore, that Jewish and Christian members of the religious consensus have many things in common.

To begin with, they have some of the Scriptures in common. The Jewish Bible[9] and the Christian Old Testament are nearly the same in content,

[9]The preferred name among Jews themselves for the Jewish scriptures is "Tanakh," an acronym for the Hebrew names of its three major divisions: the Law (Torah), the Prophets (Nevi'im), and the Writings (Ketubim).

although the books are not in the same order. The history that is recounted and the religious teachings that are contained in both are quite similar. In most Christian churches today, the Christian Old Testament is used for one of the regular Bible readings during worship.

There are both similarities and differences between the Jewish and Christian Bibles. The Hebrew Bible is very similar to the Old Testament in the Christian Bible, containing the same books, although in a different order. However, it is inappropriate to refer to the Hebrew Bible as the Old Testament. That collection of writings is called the Old Testament by Christians because, for them, the New Testament is a part of the Bible. The Christian New Testament is not a part of the Jewish Bible. It has no authority and does not contain the revelation of the God of Abraham, Isaac, and Jacob. To refer to the Torah as the Old Testament is offensive to persons of Jewish faith, for whom the revelation of God recorded in the Hebrew Bible can never be superseded by another revelation such as Christians believe is contained in their New Testament.

These common scriptures tell of one God who commands that people worship no other gods. Judaism originated in an area in which it was most common for people to worship many gods and goddesses. The Jewish, and later the Christian, view held that there was but one God. This God is believed to be the creator of all that was, is, or ever will be. God is righteous and holy and acts in a just, upright, moral manner. God is personal; it is appropriate to talk of God's will, wrath, love, mercy, and judgment. God hears and responds to peoples' prayers, according to both Judaism and Christianity. Above all, God's character and will for people are shown to them by God's self-revelation.

History is important, because it is believed to be the record of God's continuing involvement with people. God is intimately involved in history, primarily through *covenants* with people. There are covenants with Noah and with Abraham, for example, described in Tanakh, and Jesus is referred to in the Christian New Testament as the bearer of a new covenant. These covenants define a people by their relationship with God. Judaism teaches that Israel was called into being as a people by God. Christianity teaches that the entire church is the Body of Christ, called into being by God.

The people who live in covenant with God are to live holy and righteous lives. Their special relationship with God is to be embodied in all that they do. The well-known Ten Commandments are revered in both Judaism and Christianity. Some of these commandments deal with people's actions with respect to God: having no other gods, keeping the Sabbath day holy, and not misusing God's name. Others have to do with relations between persons: not murdering or stealing, not lying, and not wanting what is not one's own, for example. In both Judaism and Christianity, the way people relate with God and the way they relate with each other cannot be separated.

Both Jews and Christians emphasize the importance of personal and congregational worship. Worship in each community of faith is both individual and corporate. Individual worship usually takes the form of prayer and devotional reading. Corporate worship provides time for the entire community of faith to focus on God. Prayers are said and praises given. Instruction is given to the faithful in a sermon. It is usually based on one or more readings from the Bible. The importance placed on history creates many holidays and festivals that recall and celebrate God's actions. Corporate worship also includes rites of passage. These are religious ceremonies that mark transitions from one stage of human life to another. Both faiths mark birth, coming of age, marriage, and death, for example.

There are many smaller points of agreement that could be discussed. These major points, however, clearly demonstrate that these two major religions—Judaism and Christianity—have a great deal in common. Their common heritage and devotion to the same God means that they are more alike than different. Yet the distinctiveness of Judaism is important as well.

PRINCIPAL BELIEFS AND PRACTICES OF JEWISH PEOPLE

Judaism in the United States has many variations in belief and practice. However, there are certain features that nearly all Jews share, in one way or another. Interpretations vary, but the basics are the same. Lists of what these basics are will be different from one author to another; what is included here is a minimal listing of fundamental points.

It should first be said that Judaism is primarily a religion of action; characteristically, it has emphasized proper *obedience* to the God of the covenant over proper beliefs *about* God. Samuel Belkin, President of Yeshiva University, the principal Orthodox Jewish educational institution in the United States, notes that "attempts . . . to formulate a coherent and systematic approach to Jewish theology" have not succeeded. Judaism is much more concerned with religious practice than it is with correct doctrine. Correct religious living takes precedence over doctrinally correct religious thinking.[10] Nevertheless, there are beliefs that can be identified as core in the Jewish way of thinking. Jewish theological thinking does not vary as much by Jewish subgroup as it does broadly between a traditional and a nontraditional interpretation. The discussion of beliefs below follows this distinction as delineated by Marc Lee Raphael.[11]

Beliefs

The first five books of the Bible—Genesis, Exodus, Leviticus, Numbers, and Deuteronomy—are considered by Jews to be the most important. These five books, which for Jews are the core of God's revelation, are believed by some Jews to have been revealed to Moses and are known as the *five Books of Moses*. They are also known as the *Pentateuch*, a Greek word that means "five books."

After the five Books of Moses are the Books of the Prophets. The rest of Tanakh is made up of the Writings and includes such well-known books as Psalms, Proverbs, Job, and Ecclesiastes, along with several others. In addition to the Tanakh itself, there is the *Talmud*, which is the written record of several

[10]Samuel Belkin, *In His Image* (New York: Abelard-Schuman, 1960), pp. 15–16.
[11]Marc Lee Raphael, *Judaism in America*, Chapter 2.

Figure 9-2 A Torah scroll is an important part of any synagogue or temple. *(Bill Aron/Photo Researchers, Inc.)*

centuries of discussion, interpretation, and commentary on Torah by the earliest rabbis, who were primarily scholars and teachers of Torah.

The cornerstone of the Torah is the *commandments* that Jews believe God gave to Moses at Mount Sinai. The commandments are found in the Book of the Exodus, Chapter 20 (paraphrased in Figure 9-3). The core commandments can be divided into two groups: The first four deal with how one ought to relate to God, and the latter six with how one is to relate with other persons. These commandments are the heart of the Torah and of Jewish life and living.

Jews are *monotheists*—persons who believe in one God, as are Christians, Muslims, and Baha'is. This central point is learned by Jewish children early in life and repeated daily by many Jews as the *Shema*: "Hear, O Israel! The Lord is our God, the Lord alone" (Deuteronomy 6:4, Tanakh). The passage goes on to prescribe that this God is to be loved with one's entire self, holding nothing back. Monotheism has been a part of Judaism from its beginning.

In his study of American Judaism, Marc Lee Raphael notes that American Jews can be divided into two very broad categories: those who are traditional and those who are better described as nontraditional. These distinctions cut across, rather than correlate with the various Jewish denominations in the United States. Many Jews embrace elements of both.[12]

- Traditional Jews hold to the attributes of God derived from Tanakh: omniscience, goodness, eternity, creatorship of the earth and of human beings, omnipotence. Those who are not traditional typically affirm belief in God but leave it up to the individual to ascertain the characteristics of God. In particular, since the Holocaust, many modify the traditional pairing of God's omnipotence and all-goodness.

[12]Ibid., pp. 17–27.

Figure 9-3

THE TEN COMMANDMENTS

1. You shall not worship any other gods.
2. Do not make images of God.
3. Do not take God's holy name in vain.
4. Remember to keep the Sabbath holy; in particular, you are not to work on this day.
5. Honor your parents.
6. Do not murder.
7. Do not commit adultery.
8. Do not steal.
9. Do not bear false witness against anyone.
10. Do not covet [i.e., be envious of] that which is your neighbor's.

- While traditionalists hold that the most important thing about Tanakh is that God revealed it, nontraditionalists offer a radical reinterpretation of the origin of their scriptures. Rather than a single event in which God revealed the Tanakh, nontraditionalists see revelation as the record of the ongoing process of human beings discovering the Holy.
- Traditionalists take the concept of the Jews as God's chosen people to refer to the special responsibility placed on the Jews as the elected servants of the Almighty. Their less traditional counterparts are more likely to interpret it in nonliteral ways, more focused on Israel's choosing of God.
- In worship, traditionalists use the full liturgy with little or no modification, while nontraditionalists feel free to modify and change it. As a result, there are widespread variations in worship among nontraditional Jews.
- Traditional Jews retain the Jewish belief in the coming of a Messiah, an individual person who will lead Israel and the world into a time of peace and prosperity and will restore the monarchy of the House of David. Those who are less traditional shift their focus from the coming of the Messiah to the attainment of a messianic age by human effort in cooperation with God.
- Traditional Jews struggle with the problem of evil in the world in the face of their belief in an all-powerful and all-good God. Nontraditionalists usually reject the ideas of God's omniscience, omnipotence, and unqualified goodness. The God of nontraditional Jews is often a God who is limited in some ways, not a God who is in complete control of the world.

Because the Jews are ever watchful to guard the uniqueness of God, they do not represent God in any material form; to do so would be idolatry. Nor is there any way, in the Jewish understanding of God, that any human being could ever be God. This is one reason that people of Jewish faith do not accept the Christian teaching that Jesus is the Messiah whose coming is foretold in Isaiah. The idea of a person who is at once divine and human is utterly repugnant to Jewish sensibility. We must remember that the link between the verses in Isaiah that speak of the coming of the Messiah and the person Jesus is found in the Christian New Testament and is not a part of Hebrew scripture. The Messiah as understood by those of Jewish faith will be a leader who will bring freedom and restoration to the entire people of Israel in more political than individual terms. Jesus as described by the early Christian church—the savior of individual person from sin and separation from God—is a different sort of savior than that expected in Judaism. According to most Jews, Jesus was a religious leader and teacher, perhaps a prophet, but not God.

Jews do not believe that God became human, nor that God had a son. They do not regard Jesus as a savior. These central Christian teachings are simply not a part of Judaism. The continued presence of suffering in the world leads Jews to believe that the Messiah has not yet come.[13]

The character of God has definite implications for how people treat each other. God is just, loving, holy, and righteous, according to the Hebrew Bible, and God's people must reflect these qualities in their lives and in their dealings with others. People's actions with other people must be characterized by an attitude reflective of God's own nature. Under the terms of the covenant, people are responsible to and for one another. Any human being is God's son or daughter and hence is ones brother or sister. Righteousness, love, and tolerance must be the rule, not only among Jews but with all persons. It extends to strangers, servants, and animals. Special concern is to be given to the less fortunate, such as widows, orphans, the poor, and the ill. Fair treatment is to be given even to one's enemies.

Jews are united in their understanding of themselves as a people. In spite of being scattered around the world, and, in spite of speaking many languages and following different practices and beliefs, *the people of Israel are one people*. They are linked by the love they have for each other, by their common tradition and history, and by their shared past and present experience.

The unity of the Jewish people takes on concrete form in widespread support for the state of Israel. Since the destruction of the Temple in Jerusalem in 70 C.E., the Jews have been a wandering people. But they have maintained the conviction of belonging to the land into which the Bible records they wandered under God's leading. For centuries, Jews have prayed for the restoration and rebuilding of Jerusalem. "Next year in Jerusalem!" is spoken at the end of the Seder meal every Passover. Land and covenant are linked; the people of the covenant are the people of the land. The founding of the state of Israel in 1948 is numbered among the most significant events of Jewish history.

Lifestyle

Especially in the United States, Jews' lifestyles vary as much as do those of their non-Jewish neighbors. Overall, survey data tell us two factors that are important in understanding what it means to be a person of Jewish faith in modern day America. Of all the religious preference groups, Jews lead the

[13]Rabbi Morris N. Kertzer (revised by Rabbi Lawrence A. Hoffman), *What Is a Jew*, pp. 275–276.

nation in both education and income. Judaism has always fostered a love of learning, and Jews believe that there is no conflict between faith and reason.

The second outstanding feature of the American Jewish population is that, across the board, Jews are more tolerant and broad-minded about moral issues, civil liberties, and nonbelievers than are their Christian neighbors.

Yet another general feature that can be mentioned is the extensive involvement of Jews in social reform and assistance programs and in occupations such as social work and professional psychology and psychiatry. Their belief in God's covenant with them and their responsibility for their neighbors translates into vocational terms, for both religious and nonreligious Jews.

Ritual

Judaism in its traditional form has a very rich ritual life. A set of rituals pace individual Jews through their lifetimes, and another set paces the community through its collective life. Differences in observance abound, but Judaism is united by these individual and collective religious practices. They are the people whose life, both corporate and private, is demarcated by these ritual observances. Here, I will note the principal ones.

I will first turn to those rituals that pace the individual through the life cycle. The circumcision of male babies and the Bar or Bat Mitzvah are two of the best-known. As is the case with every religion, birth is the first step of the life cycle to be ritually marked. After the birth of a girl, it is the father's responsibility and honor to read the Torah at the next synagogue service. He recites the usual benedictions before and after reading and officially announces his daughter's name. For a boy, it is more elaborate; *circumcision* is a major Jewish ceremony. Although other peoples circumcise infant boys, Judaism understands this as a visible sign of the covenant between Abraham and God, made again in each generation (Genesis 17:9–14). It takes place on the eighth day after birth. The ceremony involves both religious and surgical elements and may be performed by a physician or by a specially trained *Mohel* who has both the necessary medical and religious knowledge. A festive meal follows.

The next life-cycle rite in the life of a Jewish youngster is the *Bar Mitzvah*. Some Jews, although not all, celebrate the *Bat Mitzvah* for girls also. The words mean "son (daughter) of the commandment" and mark the religious coming of age of the child. The child is then considered to be an adult, responsible for observing the commandments and able to fill adult roles in the congregation, although the ceremony traditionally occurs on the Sabbath following the child's thirteenth birthday. The highlight of Jewish life for many, it is preceded by intensive study. The young person is called up to read Torah before the congregation for the first time. This is a great honor. The young person may also make a speech in which parents and teachers are thanked. Especially in the United States, this ceremony has grown in importance and is frequently the occasion for a lavish party with family and friends to recognize the person's new status. In some congregations that practice the Bat Mitzvah, the ceremony parallels that for boys, while other congregations have developed distinctive practices for it.

Some Jewish congregations have an additional ceremony of *confirmation* at about age fifteen or sixteen. Although originally intended as a replacement for the Bar or Bat Mitzvah, it is now a separate ceremony for Reform and Conservative Jews, in which the now somewhat older youths reaffirm their intention to live as Jews in the household of Israel.

Marriage is the next life-cycle ritual in the lives of most Jewish women and men. Judaism places a very high value on marriage and family, and celebrating the beginning of a new family unit in marriage is very important. The *Ketubah*, or marriage contract, which spells out the responsibilities of both spouses, is signed during the ceremony. It is a legally valid document as well as a religious one. The wedding ceremony itself is complex and reflects the sacred nature of marriage and family life. A celebration with family and friends follows. Although divorce is permitted by Jewish law, it is strongly discouraged. In practice, actual divorce statistics among Reform Jews differ little from those among their Gentile neighbors; for Conservative and, especially, Orthodox Jews, the rate is somewhat lower. To be recognized as valid among traditional Jews, there must be a religious divorce as well as a legal one.

At the end of life, many Jews follow distinctive customs associated with death and burial. Jews differ in the extent to which they follow tradition, but certain customs are very common. The body is carefully washed in preparation for burial, with men washing men and women, women. Specific prayers accompany this sacred act. People are buried in a simple white shroud symbolizing the equality of all before God. Men are buried with their prayer shawls. Elaborate and expensive caskets are not used; a simple wooden box suffices. A family member, a member of a sacred burial society, or someone else typically watches over the body from the moment of death until burial. The person watching over the deceased recites Psalms during this time.[14] Jews believe that burial as quickly as possible is most respectful of the deceased, and a viewing is not held. Both cremation and embalming are forbidden by Jewish law as disrespectful of the body.

Jews tend to focus more on life in the here and now, leaving what happens afterward in the hands of God. However, one common belief is that all Jews have a place in the *World to Come*. However, this will not be the same for each person. The World to Come can be compared with a theater. Each soul has a reserved seat in that theater. But, as in earthly theaters, some seats are better than others. Some are on the main floor, and some in the balcony. Some have a clear view of center stage, while others may need to peer around obstructions. The moral choices made during life determine the seat.[15]

Jewish mourning customs are carefully structured in three stages that facilitate the grieving process and then encourage the mourner's return to the fulness of life. The first stage is a seven-day period of intense mourning and seclusion from public life. This is observed only by those who have lost a parent, spouse, sibling, or child. Ideally it is observed in the home of the deceased and all the mourners' needs are cared for by others. Thus, mourners do not have to put on

[14]Plaza Jewish Community Chapel Web site, www.plazajewishcommunitychapel.org
[15]Jewish Literacy Web site, www.aish.com/literacy

a public face but may focus entirely on the needs of grieving. The second stage lasts for thirty days after the death and includes the first stage if observed. It is a time when people are still mourning but begin to return to normal life. Official mourning ends after this time except for the death of a parent. Mourning for the death of a parent lasts a full year after the death, including the first two stages. The longer time reflects a parent's formative influence on our lives.

As well as marking the stages in the individual's life with celebration and consolation, Judaism hallows time through a yearly cycle. This cycle lifts time out of the realm of a merely mechanical tracking of days and hours and uses it to keep history and tradition alive in the present.

The *Sabbath* is a high point in every week. In line with the accounts of creation in Genesis, the Jewish Sabbath is observed from sundown on Friday until nightfall on Saturday. The Sabbath is considered one sign of the covenant between God and Israel. God is said to have rested after the creation, and people, too, are to devote one day per week to rest. The Sabbath meal is prepared in advance. The Sabbath begins when the mother lights special Sabbath candles and recites the appointed blessings. There may be a synagogue service to welcome the Sabbath. The following morning, the family may attend the synagogue together, although in some congregations it is customary for the women to remain at home with the children.

A quiet day follows. Perhaps the best-known feature of the Jewish Sabbath is that any kind of work is strictly forbidden. To understand what it means to keep the Sabbath, however, we must see beyond the prohibition of work. The Sabbath is intended as a way of separating oneself from the cares and toils of everyday living to make time for what is truly important. It is a time to be with one's God, with one's family, and with oneself, and, for that to be possible in our busy world, a special effort must be made to make it so. Torah study is an important part of what may be done on the Sabbath. Prayer and meditation are encouraged. Taking moderate walks with the family, doing quiet family things together, and visiting friends who live close by are often done.

Like the individual life, the year is marked throughout with festivals and days of great significance. I describe some of the more important festivals, although there are many others as well. Although each of the festivals leads naturally into the one that follows it, the most reasonable place to begin is where the Jewish religious calendar (which differs from the one we use to mark secular time) itself begins, with the Jewish New Year.

Rosh Hashanah (literally, the "head of the year") takes place in early autumn (September or October). Preparation for it begins the month before, which is used as a time of contemplation and spiritual self-searching. The Jewish New Year is not a time of partying and rowdiness, as the secular New Year often is. Rather, it is a time for looking back over the past year, for reflecting on deeds done and left undone. Judaism emphasizes human beings' free choice in whether we will do good or evil and our responsibility for that choice. With responsibility comes accountability, and God is known as the judge of human actions. It is this sense of judgment that pervades the Jewish New Year and the period that follows it. The oldest and probably best-known of the rituals connected with this festival is the sounding of the *shofar*, an instrument made from the horn of a ram, which makes a sound some have likened to the wailing of the heart of the human race.

Rosh Hashanah is the beginning of a time of intense reflection. Taking stock of one's life and behavior over the preceding year is accompanied by the resolve to do better. Two types of sin must be dealt with: those against God and those against other people. People can be forgiven for those against God by the rituals of *Yom Kippur*, the Day of Atonement, which follows the days of penitence. For those sins in which one has wronged another person as well, forgiveness must be sought not only from God but from the person wronged, and one must seek to make amends if at all possible. There is no savior in Judaism except God and no mediator between God and people. Jews stand before God as individuals and as members of the household of Israel with their prayers for forgiveness and their resolve to live a better life. Given these factors, Judaism teaches, God will forgive the sincere penitent. The entire day of Yom Kippur is spent in fasting, prayer, and contemplation. Thus cleansed of previous sin and strengthened to live the Torah more fully, the Jew begins another year.

The next holiday is one that has come to be celebrated much more in the United States than it is elsewhere: *Hanukkah*, the Festival of Lights. It comes in November or December, and the increased emphasis it has received in the United States has come about in part because it is close to the time that the Christian majority and the culture in general celebrate Christmas. The word *Hanukkah* means "rededication" and refers to the rededication of the Temple after the Maccabean revolutionaries successfully recaptured it from the Greco-Syrians in approximately 160 B.C.E. Legend has it that only enough oil could be found to keep the Temple lamp burning for one day. Miraculously, the oil lasted for eight days, the time required to prepare and consecrate new oil. Thus, the Hanukkah candle holder, or *menorah*, has eight branches plus a ninth that holds the lighting candle, whereas the regular menorah holds seven candles (Figure 9-4). Another candle is lit every night of the eight-day celebration. There is another very beautiful Hanukkah story that the rabbis tell. When the Maccabees entered the Temple, they found that the menorah was not usable, having been destroyed by the raiding pagans. The Maccabees took their spears and used them to make a new menorah, turning the weapons of war into a symbol of peace.[16]

The Jewish holiday that Gentiles probably know best is *Passover*, which comes in the spring. It has both associations remaining from the early times when the Israelites were an agricultural people and the historical significance that was given to it later. It exemplifies the way that religious rituals keep the important stories of the faith alive and assist in transmitting them to each new generation. As an agricultural festival, it recalls the spring harvest. Its primary significance is now the historical one, however, in that it commemorates the exodus of the Hebrews out of slavery in Egypt. This is one of the two foundational events of Jewish history. It is sometimes called the Feast of Unleavened Bread, and *matzoh*, a crackerlike bread, is eaten. Unleavened bread is eaten

[16]Leo Trepp, *Judaism: Development and Life*, 3rd ed. (Belmont, CA: Wadsworth Publishing Company, 1982), p. 303.

Figure 9-4   An eight-armed menorah or Jewish ceremonial candle holder for Hanukkah. *(Dorling Kindersley.)*

because the hurried flight of the Hebrews left no time for bread to rise (Exodus 12:37–39, 13:3, 6–8, Deuteronomy 16:1–4). The name *Passover* comes from the biblical promise that the angel of death would pass over those houses marked on the doorpost with the blood of a sacrificial lamb (Exodus 12:12–14). The central ritual of Passover is the *Seder* meal, in which the story of the Exodus is retold. Special foods are eaten that help to bring the story alive. This ritual involves everyone present and uses virtually all the human senses, mixing food, fun, and serious intention to serve as an outstanding educational and community-reinforcing tool. Jews who must be away from home at this special time may count on being taken into the home of another Jewish family wherever they may be for the Seder.

Following Passover is another ritual calling to mind a founding event. The *Feast of Weeks (Shavuot)* has roots as a harvest festival, but its contemporary meaning is as a celebration of the giving of the Ten Commandments to Moses on Mount Sinai. Thus, the two interwoven themes of Jewish life, God-given freedom from slavery and the giving of the Torah, are celebrated

Figure 9-5   Seder plate used during the Jewish Passover. *(Dorling Kindersley.)*

and remembered. Either one without the other is incomplete and does not do justice to the fullness of Jewish understanding.

Yom Ha Shoah is a Jewish observance of more recent origin. It is also called Holocaust Remembrance Day and takes place in the spring. The activities on this solemn day focus on two things: It is a time to remember those people—both Jewish and Gentile—who died in the Holocaust, and is also a time for rededication to the principle that such a thing can never be allowed to happen again. In many communities, Jews and Christians sponsor joint Yom Ha Shoah observances.

ONE JUDAISM, SEVERAL EXPRESSIONS

Judaism in America is a single religious tradition that is spread across a wide range of practices and to a lesser extent beliefs. It remains, however, a "unified and unitary structure," and its varieties are "sectors of one tradition."[17] Due regard must be given to both the differences and the commonalities. Previous sections have described many of the commonalities, along with relevant differences. Here, we look at the differences.

For Jews, expressing a preference for one or another of the sectors of Judaism is one way to identify how they wish to live a Jewish life in the United States. In part, it involves what balance they choose to seek between the ways of the secular culture and the traditional religious ways. American Jewish scholar

[17]Jacob Neusner, ed., *Understanding American Judaism: Toward a Description of a Modern Religion, vol. II, Sectors of American Judaism: Reform, Orthodoxy, Conservatism, and Reconstructionism* (New York: KTAV Publishing House, 1975), p. xiii.

Jacob Neusner notes that in sorting out the various sectors of American Judaism, we need to begin with a fundamental question: "Should Jews live not only among gentiles, but also with them, or should Jews live all by themselves?"[18] The vast majority of American Jews believe that Jews can live a fully authentic Jewish life in interaction with Gentiles.

Among the minority who choose to remain apart from Gentiles, as well as from other Jews, are Hasidic and Yeshiva Jews. Hasidic Jews follow a tsaddiq, a holy man believed to bring God's special blessings to those who follow him. The Lubovitch Hasidim is the most important group of this type in the United States. Yeshiva Jews also keep largely to themselves. Their life focuses on intense Torah study in centers of scholarship called Yeshivas. Although they differ from each other, both groups believe that living an authentically Jewish life means living apart from others. They speak a distinctive language, wear distinctively Jewish clothing, adhere to a strictly kosher diet, and live mainly in Jewish neighborhoods.

In part, the division of American Judaism into its subgroups resulted from the multiple ethnicities of Jewish immigrants. In particular, however, it resulted from the mid-nineteenth-century growth of a style of Judaism informed by the European Enlightenment. This Reform Judaism, as it came to be known, "took the lead in developing an institutional infrastructure" for American Judaism. In doing so, it set the agenda that eventually led to the development of both Orthodoxy and Conservatism within American Judaism. Broadly speaking, Orthodoxy emerged in response to the modernizing, naturalistic, and liberalizing agenda of Reform Judaism. Conservatism developed as an alternative to both, an attempt to unify the divided factions by finding a middle ground.[19]

Orthodoxy[20]

We will begin with Jewish *Orthodoxy*. Orthodox Jews believe that their way of being Jewish embodies the authentic Jewish tradition that has existed since Judaism began. Their lives embody the style of Judaism of those Jews who wish to remain separate from Gentile culture, while living as a part of that culture.

Orthodox Jews emphasize very close observance of the commandments or mitzvot of God.[21] Orthodoxy, despite what the name and basic outlook might suggest, is not a monolith. There are vast variations in what Orthodox Jews actually believe and do. There are, however, factors that we can identify as clearly distinctive. Orthodox Jews agree that the entire Torah, in both its written and oral forms, comes from God, in the words in which it is now found. The ceremonial law is as binding as the ethical commandments, because both come from the same source and it is not for human beings to make distinctions among them. They are to be observed simply because they are commandments

[18]Jacob Neusner, *World Religions in America, an Introduction, Revised and Expanded* (Louisville, KY: Westminster John Knox Press, 2000), p. 117.
[19]Peter W. Williams, *America's Religions: From Their Origins to the Twenty-first Century* (Urbana, IL: University of Chicago Press, 2002), pp. 308–315.
[20]Orthodox Jewish Congregations of America, www.ou.org
[21]Ibid.

and because they were given to the people of Israel by God with the directive, "Do this." *Halakah*[22] is as authoritative as Torah itself, having sprung from the same source and having divine authority behind it. For most non-Jews, the two most distinctive things about Orthodoxy are the strict Sabbath observance (discussed below) and the keeping of the *kosher dietary laws*.

The kosher dietary laws are a collection of instructions regarding food, its preparation, and consumption. These regulations divide everything edible into three categories: edible or "kosher," things unfit for consumption, and neutral foods. The laws of *kashrut* or ritual purity are very complex, but they may be summarized this way: All fruits, vegetables, and nuts are kosher and may be eaten with anything else. Fish that have both fins and scales may be eaten. Meat from animals that have a split hoof and chew a cud may be used for food. Permitted animals must be ritually slaughtered and treated to remove as much of the blood as possible. Domesticated fowl may be eaten; wild birds and birds of prey may not. Fowl must be slaughtered and prepared ritually in the same ways as meat animals. All dairy products are permitted but may not be mixed with meat. This goes back to three different places in the Torah in which it is forbidden to cook a baby goat in its mother's milk (Exodus 23:19 and 34:25 and Deuteronomy 14:2). For example, cheeseburgers may not be eaten, and milk may not be drunk at a meal containing meat. In a fully kosher kitchen, the same set of cookware, utensils, and dishes would not be used for meat and dairy. Furthermore, a separate set of dishes is kept for Passover, necessitating a total of four completely different sets of dishes. Although they frown on drunkenness, Jews usually do not abstain from alcohol. Foods that are kosher have been prepared under close rabbinic supervision throughout. Foods so certified are marked, often with a "U" (for the Union of Orthodox Rabbis) or a "K" (for Kosher) on the container.

The overall effect of the kosher commandments, of which I have named only a few, is to keep the following of God's commandments uppermost in the minds of faithful Jews in matters as common as cooking and eating. In Judaism, the body is as holy as the soul and must be treated as such; keeping kosher is one way of doing so. The meaning of keeping kosher can be summarized by saying that Jews keep kosher because God commands them to do so, and that is reason enough. Over time, other interpretations have been added, amplifying the meaning. It is a way of hallowing everyday life in the very basic act of nourishing oneself and one's family. It helps teach reverence for life, particularly for animal life. It is a way of expressing connection to countless generations of Jews and of passing that connection on to one's children. It is part of the religious discipline that goes along with being Jewish.[23]

The other outstanding effect is to strengthen community among observant Jews and distinguish them from outsiders. Much of the time, they live close together because it is necessary to have ready access to a kosher butcher shop, bakery, and grocery. They socialize together, because full observance prohibits eating at the table of one who does not keep kosher.

[22]Halakah is the rabbinic record of the application of Torah law to specific circumstances through history.
[23]Anita Diamant and Howard Cooper. *Living a Jewish Life: Jewish Traditions, Customs, and Values for Today's Families* (New York: HarperCollins Publishers, 1996), pp. 98–100.

Other features also are common among Orthodox Jews. In synagogue, women and men sit separately, and in some communities it is not common for the women to attend. All of the service is in Hebrew, and the holidays and festivals are observed to their fullest. Men wear the *kippah,* or skullcap, at all times, out of respect for their always being under the watchful eye of God. They wear prayer shawls and *tefillin*[24] for formal daily prayer. Marriage to a non-Orthodox Jew is regarded as invalid even if performed by a rabbi, and Orthodox rabbis do not perform interfaith marriages.

Organizationally, Orthodoxy in the United States is represented by the Orthodox Jewish Congregations of America (commonly, "Orthodox Union"). Yeshiva University, founded in 1928, and the Rabbinical College of America, founded in 1915, are notable Orthodox educational institutions. Less than 10 percent of American Jews are Orthodox.

Reform Judaism[25]

Reform is the most modernized and liberal of the three main Jewish groups. According to Reform teaching, Judaism is a fully modern religion that must change to keep pace with changes in the rest of the culture. Monotheism and the moral law are constant. Everything else is conditioned by circumstances and therefore changes as circumstances change. Reform Jews make up between 40 and 45 percent of American Jews.

Reform Jews affirm the validity of Judaism and believe that Jews must study and know their tradition. They do, however, emphasize the importance of individual conscience in the interpretation and living out of that tradition. That interpretation may entail questioning practices and beliefs that seem inconsistent with modern life. They may reject teachings that run counter to the individual's conscience.[26] Hebrew Union College and seminary in Cincinnati, Ohio, is Reform's major educational institution. Its U.S. organization is the Union for Reform Judaism.

As with all the branches of Judaism, each Reform congregation is autonomous. However, they subscribe to a common set of core values:

- A God-centered Judaism that combines respect for Jewish law and Jewish tradition with a progressive religious outlook designed to remain relevant and meaningful to contemporary North American Jews.
- A commitment to *Torah* (lifelong Jewish learning), *Avodah* (worship of God through prayer and observance), and *G'milut Hasadim* (the pursuit of justice, peace, and deeds of loving kindness)—expressed in lifelong study of the sacred Jewish texts, creativity and spirituality in worship, and social action fulfilling the vision of the Prophets.

---

[24]*Tefillin* are small leather boxes containing Bible verses. Orthodox Jewish men wear them on their foreheads and left arms during prayer.
[25]www.urj.org
[26]Rabbi Morris N. Kertzer (revised by Rabbi Lawrence A. Hoffman), *What Is a Jew,* p. 10.

- A commitment to *klal Yisrael*, the entirety of the Jewish people, with special focus on the people and the state of Israel, and on world Jewry, particularly on the needs of Progressive congregations everywhere.
- A community-focused religion that honors the personal autonomy of the individual and the institutional autonomy of the congregation, within a framework of egalitarianism and inclusiveness.[27]

At the 2007 biennial convention of Reform Judaism, Rabbi Eric H. Yoffie, President of the Union, asked attendees to return home and focus on three things. This list illustrates the wide range of contemporary Reform concerns:

- He called for a renewal of Shabbat worship on the morning of Shabbat itself, rather than on Friday night as has been the Reform custom. He also encouraged a full 24-hour day of rest.
- He called for the establishment of state coalitions to work toward universal health care.
- Finally, he encouraged people to engage in dialogue with Muslims.[28]

Conservatism[29]

Conservative Judaism follows a middle road between Orthodoxy and Reform Judaism. It supports religious tradition more than do Reform Jews. But unlike Orthodox Judaism, it also supports the evolution and change of interpretation over time. Conservatives are passionate about Jewish law and at the same time willing to change it carefully and thoughtfully. Conservative Judaism supports both the extensive use of Hebrew in worship and English language sermons, as well as respect for traditional rites, rituals, and customs, including Sabbath and dietary observance, along with scientific training in biblical research for rabbis. Conservatism thus seeks to meld sensitivity to the evolution of human understanding and culture with genuine respect for Jewish tradition.[30]

The dietary laws illustrate the types of accommodation that Conservative Jews may make. Most do keep kosher at home. However, when eating with friends or in restaurants, they often do not insist on full observance. Thus, they can dine at the homes of nonkosher friends, and any Jew, even the most observant, can dine at their table.

The United Synagogue of Conservative Judaism is Conservatism's primary organizational embodiment. Its Executive Vice-President, Rabbi Jerome M. Epstein, has recently noted that large numbers of Conservative Jews do not live out their Jewish Conservatism very well. A relatively open membership policy has led to both growth and non-observance. He calls on Conservative Jews to restore meaningful observance to Jewish life. He notes that Conservative

[27]http://urj.org/about/
[28]http://urj.org/index
[29]www.uscj.org/
[30]Marc Lee Raphael, *Judaism in America*, pp. 83–84.

Judaism arose as "an approach that responded to the widespread disregard for Jewish living and the lack of Jewish practice shared by many Jews" at the time Conservatism began. He goes on to say that although there are variations of interpretation, Conservative Judaism shares "many beliefs and practices." These include daily prayer, keeping kosher, and keeping the Sabbath and other holidays. Conservatism advocates Jews marrying other Jews, and emphasizes the importance of "lifelong Jewish learning." There is also an emphasis on "ethical behavior and acts of kindness."[31] Conservative Jews account for between 30 and 40 percent of American Jews.

Reconstructionism[32]

Conservatism did not unify American Judaism as much as its proponents had hoped. The *Reconstructionist* movement was another attempt at unification. Reconstructionism's founder, Rabbi Mordecai Kaplan, was a teacher at the Jewish Theological Seminary. When he looked out over the whole of American Judaism, he saw two things. The House of Israel was in fact rather fragmented. More seriously, by 1920, those Jews not affiliated with any synagogue at all far outnumbered the total of Orthodox, Conservative, and Reform Jews combined. In 1934, Kaplan wrote a book entitled *Judaism as a Civilization*. In it, he said that Judaism should be thought of as a civilization that has evolved through the ages, based on the continuous life of the Jewish people themselves. While Reconstructionists regard religion as central, they also affirm that Jewish culture includes art and music, literature and drama, as well as the relationship with the historical land of Israel. Unlike Reform Jews, who emphasize the role of the individual, Reconstructionists emphasize the importance of community. They seek to develop living communities in which people can participate in all of Jewish life with heartfelt commitment. Freedom of choice in practice and observance is a hallmark of these groups, with group custom an important guideline.[33]

Reconstructionism is the only expression of Judaism that has been produced solely in America. It was a response to the situation of Jewish people in this country. Despite its small numbers (less than two percent of the total American Jewish population), it has had a large impact on Judaism in the United States.

We can summarize the range of American Judaism by looking at the approach these four groups take to tradition. Tradition is important to all four, but the way in which they regard it differs:

- Orthodoxy: The whole tradition must be adhered to.
- Conservatism: It's important to honor the tradition without being bound to or by it. Judaism's long tradition can be taken seriously without being taken literally.

---

[31]Rabbi Jerome M. Epstein, "Conserve Judaism—Live Jewishly," http://www.uscj.org/Conserve_Judaism__Li7461.html
[32]http://www.jrf.org/reconstructionism
[33]Jewish Reconstructionist Federation, "Is Reconstructionist Judaism for You?" www.jrf.org/recon

- Reform: Tradition can and should be followed as long as there are good reasons for doing so and as long as doing so does not pit religion and modernity or common sense against each other.
- Reconstructionism: Tradition includes religion, but includes far more as well, embracing the whole of Jewish culture and life.

Support for the State of Israel and for Peace in the Middle East

In 1896, Theodor Herzl, a Viennese reporter, wrote an impassioned pamphlet titled *The Jewish State*, in which he said that the only hope for the Jews was the establishment of a national homeland, preferably in Palestine itself. In 1897, the First World Zionist Congress met in Basel, Switzerland. The Zionist Movement had begun.

Although the leadership of the Zionist movement tended to be mainly nonreligious, Orthodox Jews supported it because it correlated with the Orthodox belief in the eventual restoration and rebuilding of Israel and the Holy City of Jerusalem. The Conservatives also were in favor of most points in the Zionist program. Reform Jews at first found little in it that was attractive because it conflicted with their teaching that Judaism was a religion that could be lived out authentically in any culture.

After the Holocaust, virtually all American Jews supported Zionism wholeheartedly. When the state of Israel was founded in 1948, American Jews raised huge sums of money via United Jewish Appeal to help resettle refugees. This focus on Israel remains a powerful unifying force for American Judaism. The Six Day War of 1967, with Israel seeming to be threatened with annihilation from its Arab neighbors, further mobilized Zionist sentiment and action, virtually eliminating any remaining questions about the necessity and appropriateness of Zionism's program.[34]

Hadassah, the Women's Zionist Organization of America, has been a primary way for Jewish women to be involved in support for the State of Israel. In Israel, Hadassah promotes education, health care, institutions for young people, and a workable land development policy. Its U.S. branch also supports educational and youth programs, health awareness, and promotes its members' religious and social enrichment.[35]

More recently, there has been a rise in Jewish organizations whose members actively seek a solution to the long-standing Israeli-Palestinian conflict, a solution that offers justice for both sides and recognizes the complexity and history of their ties to this contested land. Here are three examples:

- The Jewish Alliance for Justice and Peace supports a "negotiated two-state resolution of the Israeli-Palestinian conflict." Its goals include educating and mobilizing American Jews to work for such a resolution of the conflict.[36]

[34]Gerald Sorin, *Tradition Transformed: The Jewish Experience in America* (Baltimore, MD: The Johns Hopkins University Press, 1997), pp. 213–214.

[35]Hadassah.org/

[36]http://btvshalom.org/aboutus/

- Americans for Peace Now was founded to support the work of its sister organization in Israel. Its members seek "a comprehensive political settlement of the Arab-Israeli conflict consistent with Israel's long-term security needs and its Jewish and democratic values."[37]
- Jewish Voice for Peace supports the desire of Israelis and Palestinians to live in both security and freedom by advocating
  - A U.S. foreign policy based on promoting peace, democracy, human rights, and respect for international law
  - An end to the Israeli occupation of the West Bank, the Gaza Strip, and East Jerusalem
  - A resolution of the Palestinian refugee problem consistent with international law and equity
  - An end to all violence against civilians
  - Peace among the peoples of the Middle East.[38]

Judaism on Campus: Hillel International

The primary organization of Jewish students on United States college campuses is Hillel International. It is named after Rabbi Hillel, a noted Jewish rabbi who lived at about the same time as did Jesus. Founded at the University of Illinois in 1923, it has become the largest Jewish campus organization in the world. It reaches out to all Jewish students, whether they are religious or not. Its mission is

> to enrich the lives of Jewish undergraduate and graduate students so that they may enrich the Jewish people and the world. . . . Hillel helps students find a balance in being distinctively Jewish and universally human by encouraging them to pursue tzedek (social justice), tikkun olam (repairing the world) and Jewish learning, and to support Israel and global Jewish peoplehood.[39]

About 3,500 Hillel students went to Israel on mission trips over winter breaks. Its Steinhardt Jewish Campus Service Corps provides one- or two-year paid fellowships to recent college graduates to work with Jewish students on campuses across the country. Its Israel on Campus Coalition invited cyclists from all over the world to participate in a five-day bike tour of Israel to commemorate the 60th anniversary on Israeli statehood in 2008.[40]

JEWISH WOMEN

According to Tanakh, it was God's intention that men and women be equal. In the first account of creation, both are created in God's image. Woman is created from man in the second account, not as his subordinate but as one

---

[37]http://www.peacenow.org/about/index.asp
[38]http://jewishvoiceforpeace.org/publish/mission.shtml
[39]Hillel International, www.hillel.org
[40]These examples come from the organization's Web site, www.hillel.org

who is capable of fulfilling him. When Adam and Eve together violated God's commandments, however, their equality and mutuality was lost.[41] The Jewish tradition is characterized by a dialectical view of women. They are equal to men in essence, yet derivative in power and position.

The current status of women in Judaism, like women's status in Christianity and other major religions, is complex. Women's roles and status have changed dramatically in the twentieth century. Jewish women have responded to these changes in the same ways that other women have. Some have left Judaism as they have come to feel that the changes did not occur fast enough or go far enough. Some have remained within their synagogues to work for change. And some have chosen to fight against changes that threaten to make their familiar traditions less meaningful to them.

As you might expect, women's roles in Orthodox Judaism have changed the least. Even here, however, the situation is complex. On the one hand, Orthodox women's roles center on home and family, and the role of wife and mother is highly respected. Women are required to perform only three religious duties. One is to visit the ritual bath after her menstrual period. The other two, baking the Sabbath bread, or *challah*, and lighting the candles that officially begin the Sabbath observance are among the most important rituals in Judaism. Children are very important in Judaism and especially so in Orthodoxy. Women's role as the bearers and nurturers of children earn them great honor.

Women also play the central role in maintaining a kosher home. Following the kosher observances is complicated and time consuming. It is also considered one of the most important Orthodox observances because it serves to set the Orthodox apart from other people and reminds them on a daily basis of their life as the covenant people. The contribution of the wife and mother in the family is indispensable.

On the other hand, women cannot be ordained as Orthodox rabbis, nor can they serve as cantors.[42] Nonetheless, they can and do teach in Orthodox Jewish schools. Groups for women's study of both Tanakh and Talmud have increased rapidly. Women may lead prayer services for women's groups, services that differ little from those for men.

Ba'alat teshuvah are women who have returned to strict Orthodoxy. Most are of middle-class background, well educated, and had assimilated into the secular culture. For them, Orthodoxy provides meanings that they had been unable to find in the secular culture: a way of making moral sense of their lives, a hedge against relativism, boundaries where there had been none, valuation of the feminine virtues of nurturing, family, and motherhood, a sense of dignity and control.[43]

The attitude toward women in Reform and Reconstructionist Judaism is much more liberal by present-day standards. A significant number of women have been ordained as rabbis and as cantors. Women apply to their rabbinical

---

[41]William A. Young, *The World's Religions: Worldviews and Contemporary Issues* (Englewood Cliffs, NJ: Prentice Hall, 1995), p. 296.

[42]Cantors assist the rabbi by chanting some of the prayers.

[43]Debra Renee Kaufman, *Rachel's Daughters: Newly Orthodox Jewish Women* (New Brunswick, NJ: Rutgers University Press, 1991).

schools in numbers equal to those of men. Reform and Reconstructionism have eliminated the distinctions between men and women in synagogue seating and in the performance of religious ritual. Reform and Reconstructionist women have led in developing new forms of traditional rituals, such as the Passover ritual. The newer rituals include women's contributions to the story of Judaism in explicit ways. These branches of Judaism also pioneered the development and celebration of the Bat Mitzvah to mark a young girl's attainment of religious responsibility. The old ideas and practices concerning ritual impurity have been discarded. Women in these two branches of Judaism have been among the leaders of the women's rights movement in the United States. While motherhood remains important in the more modernized forms of Judaism, there is no bias against women holding jobs outside their homes.

Conservative Judaism has tried to maintain a middle-of-the-road position where women are concerned. Actual observance varies a good bit from family to family and from woman to woman. Men and women typically sit together in worship. Although the Conservative rabbis voted officially some time ago to ordain women to the rabbinate and as cantors, the actual practice varies from congregation to congregation, and the degree of acceptance of female rabbis is uneven. While many Conservative Jews welcomed the ordination of women as a needed step forward, a significant number refuse to recognize those women who have been ordained.

Observance of the kosher laws and the laws concerning ritual uncleanness varies considerably. While not required, it is strongly supported by many Conservative congregations. Freedom from compulsion makes it possible for some women to observe the tradition without experiencing it as an oppressive burden. For many, Conservatism has been a way to uphold aspects of the tradition that are meaningful while moving toward greater male–female equality.

HOLOCAUST, MEMORY, AND RELIGIOUSNESS

The **Holocaust**, as most of you know, refers to the genocidal German killing of over six million Jews during the Third Reich.[44] Many other people whom the Nazis deemed undesirable were killed by mass extermination methods as well, including Gypsies, homosexuals, and those with mental health problems. Contemporary Jews often refer to this almost unspeakable event by its Hebrew name, *Sho'ah*. Both Holocaust and Sho'ah mean the same thing— burnt sacrifice. Gentiles sometimes criticize Jews for what they regard as an unnecessary preoccupation with what Gentiles regard as a past event. Why set apart a day every year to remember? Why establish courses and centers and museums? Why keep references to Sho'ah in the words of the liturgy?

There are religious, practical, and moral reasons to remember. Religiously, it is important that the dead be remembered. By remembering the victims, they

---

[44]The Third Reich was the totalitarian dictatorship from 1933 through 1945 in Germany, under the leadership of Adolph Hitler and the National Socialist German Workers Party, also known as the Nazi Party.

are dignified. Practically, human beings tend to repress and conveniently "forget" that which is so horrible or to generalize it to make it easier to think about. Very specific remembrances counteract these tendencies. If Jews fail to remember the worst of what Hitler and those in agreement with him did, it increases the risk that it will happen again. Anti-Semitism still exists, and keeping its worst effects in mind may hasten the day when it will no longer do so.[45]

In many communities, Christians join with Jews in remembering in formal ceremonies and services on Holocaust Remembrance Day. While Hitler's motives were in no way Christian, many Christians nonetheless recognize the complicity of some Christian ways of thinking about Jews in the events that led to Sho'ah.

ANTI-SEMITISM

The Holocaust came about because of an especially virulent form of anti-Semitism. Anti-Semitism—dislike or hatred of and aggressive acts toward Jews simply because they are Jews, or the attribution of negative traits to all Jews—still exists in the United States. It seems unlikely that it will ever disappear completely. While there have never been pogroms nor respected anti-Semitic political parties here, Jews are still sometimes thought of as outsiders in a predominantly Christian land. However, the situation of Judaism as a religion and most Jews as individuals has been and is better in the United States than it was and is elsewhere.

One of the factors that led, and still leads, to anti-Semitism is the erroneous belief held by some Christians that Jews were responsible for Jesus's death. It is quite clear that Jesus was put to death by the Romans, not the Jews. Indeed, Jesus died because his intense Jewish patriotism made the Romans think he was disloyal. Nonetheless, this idea persists. Many Christians also find it very difficult to understand why Jews do not accept Jesus as the savior of humankind. This leads to both anti-Semitism and efforts to convert Jews to Christianity.

A second historical facet of Jewish-Christian relations is that the Christian church in medieval times did not permit charging interest on money loaned. European Jews thus became associated with money and banking, and many people came to feel that the Jews were prospering at the expense of the Christians. This historical fact gave rise to a distrust of Jews in financial matters and to the stereotypes that "all Jews are rich" and "all Jews are stingy."

The Sephardic Jews who settled in what was to become New York found in Peter Stuyvesant a governor who referred to them as a "deceitful race" who would "infest and trouble" his colony. Civil liberties and the vote were denied to any except Christians in many of the colonies and in some states for a time after the Revolution. In 1861, when Congress established a chaplain corps for the Union army, it was restricted to ministers of any Christian denomination. President Lincoln succeeded in securing an amendment to that action that allowed for Jewish chaplains, but damage had been done, nonetheless. The

[45]Rabbi Morris N. Kertzer (revised by Rabbi Lawrence A. Hoffman), *What Is a Jew*, pp. 159–162.

immigration bill adopted by Congress in 1924 was shamefully xenophobic, and that attitude was not eliminated until this bill was replaced by Lyndon Johnson's Immigration Measure. The Ku Klux Klan has been quite active throughout American history in anti-Semitic activities and diatribes. Henry Ford supported the publication of *The Protocols of Zion*. This classic piece of hate literature embodied an idea that also had currency elsewhere—that the Jews were engaged in a conspiracy to take over the world by overthrowing Christianity.

More general patterns of discrimination also occurred, such as quota systems that barred all but a few Jews from prestigious eastern colleges and restricted Jews to a handful of the professions. There are still private clubs that either restrict the number of Jewish members or do not admit them at all. Discrimination in housing has also been fairly commonplace. Synagogues have been defaced, frequently being spray-painted with Nazi swastikas, and crosses have been burned in the yards of synagogues and Jewish homes. Often, the attacks are verbal in nature, but there is also a pattern of physical attacks on Jewish property and Jewish people.

The Christian Identity Movement is staunchly anti-Semitic in its thinking, as well as advocating prejudice against Catholics, blacks, homosexuals, and various other people. People in the movement often describe the current situation as one in which a battle for the world is being fought under the direction of God, a battle between the whites whom God intends to inherit the earth and the Jews (and others) from whom they must wrest control of it. The close identification of some groups within this movement with the neo-Nazi movement is especially troublesome to Jews, as well as to other people.

Survey data demonstrate that anti-Semitism continues. A poll taken by the Jewish Anti-Defamation League in 2007 indicates that about 15 percent of American adults "hold views that are unquestionably anti-Semitic" (this adds up to almost 35 million people). Slightly under one-third of Americans believe that Jews are more loyal to Israel than they are to America and only slightly less than that hold the Jews responsible for Jesus' death. Fifteen percent believe that Jews have "too much power" in the United States, and 20 percent believe that Jews have "too much power" in the business world.[46]

These beliefs translate into action for some of those who hold them. A sampling of recent anti-Semitic incidents in the United States includes

- Vandalism of a Jewish cemetery in New Jersey
- Profanity and anti-Jewish statements scrawled on the homes of Jewish families and vandalism of Jewish homes, businesses, and synagogues
- Anti-Semitic graffiti, including a drawing of a burning cross, and a Ku Klux Klan hood in a restroom at the Saint Cloud University Student Center in Minnesota
- Verbal and physical assaults on Jewish people
- Vandalism at the Jewish Student Center at Indiana University in Bloomington and anti-Semitic graffiti at the Worcester Polytechnic Institute in Massachusetts, as well as a verbal and physical attack on a Jewish student at San Francisco State University
- A swastika on the hood of a car belonging to a Jewish high school student.[47]

[46]Anti-Defamation League, www.adl.org/Anti-semitic/poll_2007
[47]Examples provided by The Coordination Forum for Countering Antisemitism, www.antisemitism.org.il

The National Socialist Movement[48] is now the largest neo-Nazi group in the United States, with a full calendar of demonstrations, a presence on the Web, and a children's organization. It describes itself as "the political party for every patriotic American." The fourth of its "25 Points of American National Socialism" reads "Only those of pure White blood, . . . may be members of the nation. . . . Accordingly, no Jew or homosexual may be a member of the nation." Another states that "The Party combats the Jewish-materialistic spirit within and without us . . ."[49]

That there is less anti-Semitism now than at some other times in our history must not lull us into indifference. Remaining anti-Semitism, as well as other forms of discrimination, prejudice, and bigotry, whether religious or otherwise, must be addressed, and to whatever extent possible, eliminated.

Acceptance must not and cannot be contingent on differences being reduced to some sort of lowest common denominator or to minorities conforming to the majority opinion of how the minority ought to be. To do so dehumanizes the individuals in the minority and impoverishes the entire community, which is denied the richness of variety that healthy, culturally conscious minorities provide.

INTO THE FUTURE

We turn again to Jewish practitioner and scholar Marc Lee Raphael, who looks into the future of Judaism in the United States.[50] As the new century begins, people in the United States continue to seek *new spiritualities* that transcend, and sometimes ignore, institutional religion. This trend affects Judaism, too. As Jews look for new meaning in their Jewishness, both personal and internal as well as institutional, they also seek new institutional forms to support the new spiritualities.

There is greater interest in persons becoming "Jews by choice," converts to this ancient faith. Raphael records an increase in Judaism on the part of non-Jews and a corresponding effort by Jews to reach out to people with no religious affiliation.[51] There has been a rise in conversions as Jews and Gentiles intermarry. All of this has made and continues to make American Judaism more multicultural and ethically diverse.

There has also been an increase in gay and lesbian congregations and support groups within congregations, as well as in commitment ceremonies for same-sex partners. While Orthodox and Conservatives officially disallow homosexual behavior, Reform and Reconstructionist Jews accept gay and lesbian rabbinical students and perform commitment ceremonies. Dialogues were held, including some in Orthodox congregations, around the film *Trembling Before G-d*, in which gay Orthodox Jews try to reconcile these two aspects of their identity.

[48]www.nsm88.org
[49]"The 25 Points of American National Socialism," nsm88.org
[50]Marc Lee Raphael, *Judaism in America*, Chapter 6.
[51]Ibid., pp. 120–121.

Twenty-first century Judaism has also seen a surge in Jewish day schools and supplemental education, with most programs serving students from all denominations of Judaism. Jewish education has become a family matter, with children and parents both involved in study, often studying ages-old truths with the benefit of the latest in technology. Judaism also has a strong Internet presence, with all denominations represented.

Not only has Judaism been influenced by America, but it has influenced America, as well. The prophetic ideal of caring for those less able to care for themselves meant that Jews have strongly supported liberal social legislation. Jews have been in the forefront of support for individual civil liberties. The non-Orthodox have frequently led the women's movement. Avant-garde tendencies in the arts have benefitted from Jewish support. Popular culture has been receptive to Jewish popular culture, with its distinctive foods and language ("that isn't kosher" applied to actions that aren't right or the advice to "be a mensch!").[52]

QUESTIONS AND ACTIVITIES FOR REVIEW, DISCUSSION, AND WRITING

1. In what different ways may someone be Jewish?
2. What are the key similarities and differences between Jews and Christians?
3. Be sure that you know the basic beliefs and practices shared by most religious Jews.
4. If possible, attend a service at a temple or synagogue. This might be done by the entire class together. Write an essay in which you describe what you observed.
5. If possible, arrange to interview an Orthodox Jew about her or his Sabbath and kosher practices. Do the same with a Reform or a Conservative Jew.
6. If there is a kosher restaurant nearby, arrange a visit there. Talk with the owner(s)/employees about kosher dietary practices and what they mean to Jews in the United States.
7. In your own words, describe each of the expressions of Judaism. Of these, which seems the most attractive to you, and why?
8. Describe the attitude toward women in each of the major denominations of Judaism.
9. If possible, interview a Jewish woman about what being Jewish and female means to her.
10. Why is it important to Jews to remember the Holocaust?
11. What trends seem important as Judaism moves into the future in the United States?
12. Visit the Web site of Jews for Jesus, a Messianic Jewish organization (www.jewsforjesus.org). What is this group about? Visit the site of Jews for Judaism (www.jewsforjudaism.org). What is this group about? What is the issue between them?

FOR FURTHER READING

BRODY, LESLIE, ed., *Daughters of Kings: Growing Up as a Jewish Woman in America*. Boston: Faber and Faber, 1997. This is a collection of primarily first-person accounts from a variety of perspectives.

COHN-SHERBOK, DAN, AND LAVINA COHN-SHERBOK, *The American Jew: Voices from an American Jewish Community*. Grand Rapids, MI: William B. Eerdmans Publishing

---

[52]Robert M. Seltzer and Norman J. Cohen, eds., *The Americanization of the Jews*, p. 9.

Company, 1995. Like the previous book, this contains primarily first-person accounts. Both are highly recommended for this reason.

DINER, HASIA, *The Jews of the United States, 1654–2000.* Berkeley, CA: University of California Press, 2006. In this engaging chronicle of the Jewish experience in America, Diner thoroughly documents the Jewish determination to be both "good Jews" and "full Americans." She shows the constant process of negotiation necessary to achieve this goal in a setting in which it has not been a given.

HERTZBERG, ARTHUR, *A Jew in America: My Life and a People's Struggle for Identity.* San Francisco: HarperSanFrancisco, 2003. This is an engaging account of the interwoven identity of Jews as a people in the United States with one man's search for his own Judaic identity.

MORTON, KATHRYN, *Jewish Artisans Today: Contemporary Judaica and the Artists Who Created It.* Gaithersburg, MD: Flower Valley Press, 2000. This lavishly illustrated book includes not only the art itself, but describes the how, why, and what of Jewish ritual, along with the stories of the artists and the meaning they find in their work.

RELEVANT WORLD WIDE WEB SITES

Judaism and Jewish Resources: www.shamash.org/trb/judaism.html

Judaism 101: www.jewfaq.org

Jewish Feminist Resources: www.jew-feminist-resources.com

United States Holocaust Memorial Museum: www.ushmm.org

CHAPTER 10

Muslims in the United States: A Growing Minority

Imagine six million people who are Americans. Imagine that they believe in paying taxes and building community. Imagine that this group doesn't drink alcohol or consume drugs because of their beliefs in self-control. Imagine that they have to keep a schedule allotting time to pray five times in the day as well as time for work, family, and enjoying themselves. Imagine a group of six million who believe in respecting women, specifically their rights to education, to consent to marriage, to divorce, to vote, to hold political office, among other things. Too good to be true? You don't have to imagine—this group is real. They are the Muslims of America.[1]

Like Christians and Jews, Muslims are monotheists, people who believe in one God. Islam also began in the same general geographic area as did Judaism and Christianity and has much in common with them in addition to their shared commitment to monotheism.

ISLAM AND ISLAM IN THE UNITED STATES

Islam is the third of the major Abrahamic monotheistic religions, along with Judaism and Christianity. Abrahamic is a general term that refers to practitioners of religions who hold that Abraham is their common ancestor, and so includes Judaism, Christianity, and Islam, as well as others. People who practice Islam are properly called *Muslims*. The word *Islam* means the peace of one who submits wholly to God (or *Allah*, an Arabic name for God used by Arabic speaking Jews and Christians as well). A *Muslim* is one who submits to Allah. You may have heard Muslims referred to as "Muhammadans" or a similar term. This is incorrect and offensive to Muslims, because they are followers of Allah, not of Muhammad.

Before you read further, think about what your own opinion of Muslims and of Islam is. Do you know any Muslims personally? What kinds of things have you heard about Muslims, or about Islam as a religion?

[1]Asma Gull Hasan, *American Muslims: The New Generation* (New York: Continuum, 2001), p. 3.

222

Muslims are still regarded by many people in the United States as outside the religious mainstream. However, consider the following: Muslims outnumber Episcopalians, Lutherans, Presbyterians, and members of the United Church of Christ in the United States. The percentage of Muslims here is expected to exceed that of Jews soon, if it hasn't already done so. There are at least 3000 mosques, Islamic centers, and other prayer locations in the United States, along with perhaps 300 Muslim schools and six Muslim colleges. Americans are becoming Muslim in significant numbers.[2] Over 22 percent of American Muslims were born here. Nearly three-quarters of American Muslims believe strongly that they should participate fully in American institutional and political life, and they vote in greater numbers than does the non-Muslim population. And Suhail Khan, a congressional staffer, points out, "When people say we'll never have elected Muslim-American officials, I say, 'Hey, those are the same things they said about a Catholic named Kennedy running for president'."[3] The 110th Congress included one Muslim, Representative Keith Ellison, a Democrat from Minnesota. Over 60 percent of Muslims in this country are college graduates. And the United States Postal Service issued its first Eid Al-Fitr stamp in 2001.[4] By contrast, a Hanukkah stamp has been available since at least 1996, and Christmas stamps far earlier.

MUHAMMAD

The story of Islam begins with Muhammad, revered by Muslims as the "Seal of the Prophets," the last and final prophet in a long line of prophets sent by Allah to bring God's truth to humankind. He was born about 570 C.E. Forty years later, Muhammad had an experience in which Muslims believe the angel Gabriel spoke to him, conveying the actual words of Allah himself. He was told that he had been chosen as a prophet and that he must repeat the words that he would be given to all who would listen. The revelations continued until shortly before Muhammad's death in 632. Islam thus began as an oral tradition passed from Muhammad to a few close associates and, finally, to the world.

Muhammad, the Prophet, was a human being like all other human beings. The Christian identification of the person Jesus of Nazareth with God is blasphemous to Muslims because making a human being God's equal does not recognize the incomparable greatness and oneness of Allah. Muhammad is, however, regarded as the model for what an ideal person is, and the stories about his life are a source of inspiration for his followers. What Muhammad said and did, as recorded by his companions in the tradition (*Hadith*), provides a blueprint for the interpretation and application of the Qur'an to the various situations of life. Poetry in praise of the Prophet and his life exists in virtually every language spoken by Muslims, and love for him and for his family marks Muslim devotion. Standards for Muslim belief and action come not only from the Qur'an but from its application exemplified in the life and sayings of Muhammad.

[2]"Muslims in America: Profile 2001," http://www.soundvision.com/info/yearinreview/2001/profile.asp
[3]"Living in Two Cultures," http://usinfo.state.gov/products/pubs/muslimlife/living.htm
[4]"Facts About Muslims in America," www.opendialogue.com/english/facts.html

The Qur'an

The sacred scripture of Islam is called the *Qur'an*, or the *Holy Qur'an*. It was originally written in Arabic, and most Muslims believe that it is fully authentic only in that language. Because Islam is a missionary religion, however, the Qur'an has been translated into many languages, including English.

The first chapter is recited at the beginning of prayers. It summarizes many of the principal themes of Islam:

> All praise is due to Allah, the Lord of the Worlds.
> The Beneficent, the Merciful.
> Master of the Day of Judgment.
> Thee do we serve and Thee do we beseech for help.
> Keep us on the right path.
> The path of those upon whom Thou hast bestowed favors.
> Not (the path) of those upon whom Thy wrath is brought down, nor of those who go astray.[5]

Allah commanded that Muhammad *recite* the Qur'an, and reciting still plays an important part in Muslim devotion:

> Recitation of the Qur'an is thought to have a healing, soothing effect, but can also bring protection, miraculous signs, knowledge, and destruction, according to Muslim tradition. It is critical that one recite the Qur'an only in a purified state, for the words are so powerful that the one who recites it takes on a great responsibility. Ideally, one learns the Qur'an as a child, when memorization is easiest and when the power of the words will help to shape one's life.[6]

Beliefs

The core beliefs of Islam, from which all others arise, are the oneness and unity of Allah and the prophethood of Muhammad. There are two primary subgroups within Islam, the *Sunni* Muslims (by far the larger subgroup) and the *Shi'a* Muslims. There is a nucleus of beliefs that is widely shared among Muslims in North America, and these form the basis for our discussion here.

Muslims, as stated above, believe in *the oneness of Allah*. Oneness is not primarily a matter of arithmetic, of there being numerically only one God. Rather the emphasis is on the utter incomparability of Allah, there being nothing as great as Allah. It is also not simply an intellectual matter but requires trust in Allah, submission to the will of Allah, and reliance upon Allah for everything in life. These attitudes follow logically from Muslims' belief in the incomparable greatness of Allah.

They also believe in the *angels of Allah*. Angels are spiritual beings whose entire role is to serve Allah. Each has a specific duty to perform. This belief arises from the prior belief that knowledge cannot be limited to what can be perceived

---

[5]The *Holy Qur'an*, trans. M.H. Shakir (Tahrike Tarsile Qur'an, 1983), www.hti.umich.edu/relig/koran/
[6]Mary Pat Fisher and Robert Luyster, *Living Religions* (Englewood Cliffs, NJ: Prentice Hall, 1991), p. 275.

with the senses, that there are things we cannot know through the senses (Qur'an 16:49–50 and 21:19–20).

Muslims also believe in *all the books of Allah*, including the sacred writings of Judaism and Christianity, culminating in the Qur'an. There are specific references in the Qur'an to God's having given Torah to the House of Israel and the New Testament to Christians. The Qur'an is the standard by which the others

Figure 10-1   Calligraphy, as seen in this illuminated manuscript, is an important Islamic art form. *(Cecile Treal and Jean-Michel Ruiz © Dorling Kindersley.)*

are judged. Insofar as they agree with it, they are true and are to be accepted. When they differ from the Qur'an, it has precedence.

As a result of this, Muslims also believe in *all the prophets of Allah*. There are approving references to many of the Hebrew prophets (Abraham, Moses, and David among them) as well as to John the Baptist and Jesus. Each age and each nation is believed to have had its messenger from Allah. *Muhammad*, as stated before, *is the last and final Prophet* in this long succession. Allah entrusted him with the prophecy that completes and corrects those that have gone before.

Those of Islamic faith also affirm *life after death*. The Qur'an paints vivid pictures of both paradise and hell, as well as of a day of judgment in which all people will be called to account for their lives. Muslims believe that Allah keeps an accurate account of everything people do and think. Good deeds will be rewarded and evil ones punished.

Muslim morality is very similar to that of Christianity and Judaism. Marriage and family are very important; marriage is considered a duty and is based on a legal contract to which both husband and wife agree. Sexual relations outside marriage are strictly forbidden. Divorce is permitted but strongly discouraged. Anything injurious to oneself or to others—mentally, physically, or morally—is forbidden. Respect and care for the elderly is considered very important, and people are expected to care for their parents in their later years. The equality of all persons and dealing with others with respect and total honesty is a fundamental moral value.

This makes basic Muslim values very similar to those held by most non-Muslim Americans. As Shahed Amanullah, a Muslim engineer from San Francisco notes, " American values are, by and large, very consistent with Islamic values, with a focus on family, faith, hard work, and an obligation to better self and society."[7]

THE FIVE PILLARS OF ISLAM

Islam is second only to Christianity in its number of worldwide followers. Wherever they live, Muslims share five core practices, called the *Five Pillars of Islam*. The Five Pillars are *five specific acts required of all faithful Muslims*. Although they are classified as "required," their actual observance varies from one person to another, even in traditionally Muslim countries. There is tension between those who support strict observance as the only way to be a "good Muslim" and those who accept a wider range of observance. This tension is not unique to Islam but exists in all religions. Examples you have learned about so far include the tension between fundamentalist and more liberal Christians and between Orthodox and non-Orthodox Jews.

The first pillar is *faith*, shown in the *repetition of the creed* (*Shahadah*): "There is no God but Allah, and Muhammad is the Prophet of Allah." Devout Muslims repeat this affirmation of faith daily. Doing so helps keep the major principles of their faith at the center of their lives. These are often the first words

[7]"Muslim Life in America," http://usinfo.state.gov/products/pubs/muslimlife/

spoken to a newborn Muslim baby, and the last words spoken or heard by one who is dying. While saying the Shahadah is important, the faith which it expresses is the central concern.

The second pillar is *prayer five times daily*. Muslim life is based on consciousness of God at all times, and frequent prayer facilitates this. Ritual cleansing precedes the prayers, and each prayer is accompanied by specific ritual actions, such as sitting, standing, and prostrating oneself with the forehead touching the floor or ground. Muslims pray facing Mecca, the holy city of Islam, located in what is now Saudi Arabia. These are set, formal prayers. In addition, Muslims are encouraged to repeat these prayers more times than is required and to add their own personal prayers to the required ones. Prayers are said at dawn, at midday, midafternoon, dusk, and at night. There is some flexibility in the exact times; the idea is to have the prayers paced throughout the day. Doing so helps keep Muslims continually aware of Allah and of the need for submission to him. Those who can are encouraged to attend the *mosque (masjid)*, the Islamic place of worship (Figure 10-2) for the midday prayers on Fridays.

Islam does not have a weekly Sabbath, but the community of faith gathers at midday on Friday to pray these prayers together and usually to hear the Qur'an read and explained in a talk by the *imam* or prayer leader. While the Jewish Sabbath is a day of rest, and Christians have traditionally interpreted Sunday (the Lord's

Figure 10-2   The *Masjid*, or mosque, Islamic Center of Toledo, Ohio. The presence of Muslims, Hindus, Buddhists, and others of the less familiar religions in the United States expands the range of religious architecture, as well as of religious beliefs and practices. *(Photo courtesy of Richard J. Fears.)*

Day) similarly, Muslims are explicitly enjoined to attend to their work before and after Friday midday prayer. Whether individually or with others, Muslims pray as members of the community of faith and use "we" rather than "I" as they pray.

As you can imagine, the required prayers can be difficult for Muslims in the United States. Prayer times may conflict with work times, and there may not always be an appropriate place to pray in the workplace. Employers may not always want to make the slight accommodation necessary to allow time for prayers, and the curiosity of fellow workers can be embarrassing. On the other side, many Muslims appreciate the opportunity it gives for them to express their faith to non-Muslims.

The third pillar is the *giving of alms* to help those in need. This is not simply charity. It is more like a religious tax in that it is required. It amounts to about 2.5 percent, based on a person's net worth. Muslims in the United States select a Muslim organization to which they will pay the alms; for many, it is the Muslim Student Association. They are encouraged to make other charitable contributions, as they are able. Muslims do not look down on wealth, as long as it is gotten honestly; the honest earning of money and wise management of it is a tribute to Allah. But Allah must also be worshiped through one's wealth, and this is the point of almsgiving. Those who can also have an obligation to help those in need.

Fourth is *fasting during the month of Ramadan.* The Islamic religious calendar differs from the civil calendar, so Ramadan occurs at different times in different years. Ramadan is the month in which tradition holds that the revelation to Muhammad began. Fasting, in this instance, means complete abstention from eating, drinking, smoking, the use of tobacco, and sexual activity during daylight hours. A meal is eaten immediately before and immediately following the hours of fasting. This activity helps unite Muslims around the world, encourages empathy for those who are hungry or otherwise lacking, and reinforces submission to the will of Allah. Ramadan is also a time of increased spiritual awareness, when Muslims often spend extra time in reading and studying the Qur'an and in prayer. Many Muslims read the entire Qur'an during the month. Fasting is not required of young children, women who are pregnant or menstruating, travelers, the elderly, and those who are ill or frail, as well as others on whom it would impose an unreasonable burden.

The fast is followed by Eid Al-Fitr, the Festival of Fast-Breaking. This is a joyous time in which families and friends gather together to rejoice in the end of this strenuous time and to celebrate the spiritual benefits gained from it. For many Muslim families in the United States, it is a time to invite non-Muslim friends to join in the celebration and share special foods from their religious and national cultures. My own graduate school days were punctuated by Eids spent with the family of my daughter's Muslim elementary school classmate.

The last of the Pillars is the *hajj,* or *pilgrimage to Mecca,* a journey that Muslims are required to make at least once in their lives, as long as they are mentally, physically, and financially capable of doing so. Hajj brings Muslims from around the world together for a series of religious rituals in and around Mecca. Its center is the Grand Mosque and the Kabah, a large stone building that Muslims believe was built by Abraham and Ishmael for the worship of Allah. Most pilgrims also visit Medina, the city in which Muhammad found shelter after he was forced to flee Mecca because people there would not accept his teachings. After the Meccan tribes were defeated, Muhammad made a pilgrimage back to Mecca in 629 C.E. The rites that he performed then are the prototype for those carried out by Muslims today.

The pilgrimage is very demanding, both physically and emotionally. Huge numbers of people converge and emotions run very high. Nonetheless, Muslims regard it as a joyful occasion, not simply a duty. People stand before Allah as individuals in community, in the places where their spiritual history took root. Those who make hajj do not forget it, and they are privileged to use the title, *hajji*, designating one who has made hajj.[8]

MUSLIMS IN THE UNITED STATES

Estimates of the number of Muslims in the United States vary considerably. It is not necessary to be a member of a mosque to be a Muslim. Too, some Muslims remain hesitant to identify themselves as Muslims because prejudice still exists. Another possible source of inaccuracy in the data is that there may be Christians from Arab countries who identify culturally but not religiously with the Muslim community. Most nonimmigrant Muslims in the United States are black, although this accounts for only about 2 percent of the black population in the United States. Contrary to what you might expect, most Arab Americans are Christians, perhaps because Christians tend to emigrate to the United States from Muslim countries in greater numbers than do non-Christians.[9]

Muslims have come to the United States from virtually all of the Middle Eastern countries in which Islam is common, as well as from India, Pakistan, China, the former Soviet Union, and elsewhere. There have been Muslims in the United States for many generations, as well as a steady influx of recent immigrants. There are also American converts to Islam. Thus, on the one hand, there is an Islamic *community* here: a group of people united by a common religion. On the other hand, there are several *communities* of Muslims here: American-born, descendants of immigrants, and recent immigrants, as well as Muslims of various national and ethnic backgrounds.

As the Muslim community becomes more thoroughly integrated into the larger culture of the United States, distinctions such as "immigrant" and "indigenous" are becoming less useful to describe Islam in America as sociological changes occur over time:

> "Immigrant" communities are becoming "establishment," children are growing and intermarrying, foreign-born Muslims are becoming American citizens, demarcation between the "older" immigrants and the new African and Asian immigrants taking on racist overtones.[10]

[8]"Stoning the Devil," *The Wall Street Journal*, February 6, 2004, p. W23.
[9]*New York Times National*, April 10, 1991, p. 1.
[10]Gisela Webb, "Expressions of Islam in America," in *America's Alternative Religions*, ed. Timothy Miller (Albany, NY: State University of New York Press, 1995), pp. 240–241, n. 2.

Recent analyses of the Muslim experience in the United States indicate that the two key problems facing both immigrant and native-born Muslims are deciding how they will live an Islamic life in America and dealing with prejudice. Work schedules do not make daily prayers convenient, and it can be very difficult to follow Muslim dietary practices (which include a detailed list of permissible and forbidden foods) in institutions such as colleges, the military, and prisons. Many Muslims regard the pervasive use of alcohol, sexual permissiveness, and less than modest dress in the United States as problematic. American Muslims strive to be faithful to Muslim ideals in spite of these and other adverse circumstances.[11]

There is a growing subculture of young Islamic Americans, children of immigrant Muslims in the 1960s and 1970s, who are determined to forge an integrated identity that is both Muslim and American. Their doing so calls into question the usual stereotype of Islam as a "foreign" faith. They are also finding new ways to formulate that faith, ways that might well be unimaginable in the Muslim nations from which their parents came:

> American Muslims are experiencing both exhilaration at the opportunity to increase their numbers and develop their institutions and frustration and dismay as they continue to experience prejudice, intimidation, discrimination, misunderstanding, and even hatred. . . . [Muslims in the United States] have unprecedented freedom to experiment with forms and structures for the separation of religion and state away from the watchful eyes of wary governments and the criticism of traditionalists. At the same time, this freedom is fraught with the danger of innovation and deviance; the great range of options available in the American context carries the threat of sectarian division and fragmentation.[12]

Like members of most other religious groups, Muslims in the United States range from liberals who seek accommodation with the surrounding culture to the very conservative who seek to preserve the inherited tradition and advocate separation from those who do not agree. There are also differences of opinion between Muslims who want to convert non-Muslims and those who do not.

The Muslim mosque (*masjid* is being used increasingly) has changed character in the United States. In most traditionally Muslim countries, the mosque is simply a place in which the community of the faithful gathers for the Friday midday prayers. The *imam*, or prayer leader, is a member of the community who is skilled in Qur'anic recitation and perhaps exposition. There is no professional clergy in Islam, and usually the imam holds another job. In the United States, the mosque has become much more like a church or synagogue, and the imam has become a professional clergyman, in most instances. Mosques offer a full range of activities, both religious and cultural, for the Muslim community. Besides the traditional prayer service, there will often be women's groups, classes for all ages and both genders, social activities, and day care. The imam is expected to function as

[11]Webb, "Expressions of Islam in America," in *America's Alternative Religions*, p. 237.
[12]Yvonne Yazbeck Haddad, "Introduction: The Muslims of America," in *The Muslims of America*, ed. Yvonne Yazbeck Haddad (New York: Oxford University Press, 1991), pp. 3 and 5.

the leader of the congregation, a counselor, an administrator, and the representative of the Muslim community to the surrounding culture.[13]

As traditionally interpreted, Islamic law covers every aspect of life for Muslims: religious and secular (a distinction that is itself alien to Islam), private and public, extraordinary and mundane. Muslims who live in a non-Muslim culture must decide the extent to which full adherence to Islamic law is possible or desirable. As you might expect, individual Muslims vary in how carefully they keep all the details of Islamic law. There are two sources of variation: (1) different aspects of observance receive different degrees of attention and (2) different Muslim subpopulations vary in their observance.

In the first place, some regulations are kept much more fully than others. For example, Muslim law forbids the payment or receiving of interest on money. Using the American banking system makes this extremely difficult. Most Muslims in the United States do have bank accounts and do use credit when necessary. Muslim law also forbids the consumption of pork, pork products, and alcohol. The great majority of Muslims do not knowingly consume pork or pork products, and most Muslims make a conscientious effort to find out if prepared foods contain them. Fewer adhere absolutely to the alcohol prohibition, although a majority does. Whether or not Muslims themselves choose to use alcohol, they must decide whether to offer it to non-Muslim guests in their homes. Some do and some do not.

There is no consensus among Muslims in the United States about the application of Muslim laws and values. There is no doubt that observance declines with a number of factors. Less strict observance is associated with being in the United States for a longer time, with interacting with non-Muslim Americans, and "apparently as a general result of living in American culture."[14] Age is also a factor. While 70 percent of adults aged 18 and older surveyed in the Los Angeles area believe that Islamic values should be observed "strictly," among those under 18, only about half agreed.[15]

Muslims are discouraged or forbidden from dating as it is practiced in the United States. Youth meet prospective mates through their families and at activities at the mosque. Social interaction takes place only in well-chaperoned group settings. Marriages are usually arranged. Women especially, but men also, are discouraged from marrying outside the faith. If they do, they may marry only a Jew or a Christian (other "people of the Book"). This makes finding a suitable partner within such a small population difficult. Muslim magazines often carry matrimonial ads in which families invite correspondence from potential partners for a daughter, sister, son, or brother.

[13]For an ethnographic study of the changes that have occurred in one immigrant Muslim congregation, see Rogaia Mustafa Abusharaf, "Structural Adaptations in an Immigrant Muslim Congregation in New York," in *Gatherings in Diaspora: Religious Communities and the New Immigration*, ed. R. Stephen Warner and Judith G. Wittner (Philadelphia: Temple University Press, 1998), pp. 235–261.

[14]Yvonne Yazbeck Haddad and Adair T. Lummis, *Islamic Values in the United States: A Comparative Study* (New York: Oxford University Press, 1987), Chapters 3, 4, and 5.

[15]Kambiz GhaneaBassiri, *Competing Visions of Islam in the United States: A Study of Los Angeles* (Westport, CT: Greenwood Press, 1997), p. 49. This book provides considerable data on varying attitudes and degrees of observance among Muslims in the greater Los Angeles area.

An Islamic popular religion is also developing in the United States as more and more items become available as the market for them increases. There are Muslim Scout troops and compact disc Qur'ans and Islamic art screen savers for personal computers. An "I [heart] Allah" mug has been spotted, as well as a "Praise Allah" bumper sticker. Several companies cater to the clothing needs of Islamic women who wish to maintain traditional dress.[16]

MUSLIM COLLEGE STUDENTS

Muslim college students have come to study in the United States from nearly every country in the world where Muslims live. *The Muslim Student Association* was founded in 1963 to provide for the needs of Islamic students on American campuses and to help non-Muslim students come to know Islam and its followers better. It remains one of the largest and most active among Islamic organizations, appealing to both immigrant and American-born Muslims. It is an active and multi-faceted organization

> that serves Muslim students during their college and university careers by facilitating their efforts to establish, maintain, and develop chapters of Muslim Student Associations, Unions, Organizations, and Islamic Societies. Emphasis is placed on the learning and well-being of the individual Muslim student, as well as networking and growth of the chapter through sponsorship of educational programs, camps, zonal and annual conferences, and worker training programs. . . . MSA National strives to inform and mobilize students to respond to crises around North America and the world.[17]

There are very few specifically Muslim colleges or universities in the United States. The American Islamic College in Chicago was founded in 1983 and is the first school of its kind in the United States. It is "a bachelor of arts–granting institution approved by the Illinois Board of Higher Education and offers a range of studies in the social and physical sciences, computer science, economics, history, and other areas, as well as a number of courses in Arabic and Islamic studies."[18] The first Muslim graduate school was begun in 1996, the School of Islamic and Social Sciences in Virginia. It offers two programs of study, a master's program in Islamic studies and a program for training imams.[19]

A Web site offered "Top Ten Tips for Muslim College Students." Some of the tips are similar to those you might find on any similar site, such as advice to not skip classes and keep up with your reading assignments, remaining in contact with professors and fellow students, and taking classes in which you're genuinely interested. Others, however, focus specifically on being a *Muslim* college student:

[16]Using "Islamic clothing" or "Muslim clothing" as your search term will bring up several Internet sites offering this clothing.

[17]MSA of the United States and Canada, www.msanational.org/about/faq/

[18]Jane I. Smith, *Islam in America, Columbia Contemporary American Religion Series* (New York: Columbia University Press, 1999), p. 132.

[19]The URLs for these two institutions' Web sites are American Islamic College (www.aicusa.edu), and the School of Islamic and Social Sciences (www.siss.edu).

College is an excellent opportunity to introduce others to Islam. Hang out with others who help you to be a better Muslim rather than pulling you down. Stay away from situations that you think will compromise your faith and practice, such as social events at which alcohol is served. Be active in the Muslim Student Association. Balance college studies with Islamic studies.[20]

Many Muslim college students are international students, and their potential influence in the future can hardly be overestimated. Their experiences as students in American colleges will color their lifelong perception of the United States and how it relates to the Muslim world. This, in turn, will influence their nations' responses to America. Often, the most gifted students are the ones who come to the United States to study, and they will be their countries' future leaders. These students are "a hotbed of intellectual ferment about Islam and how it can and should respond to the challenges of the modern world."[21]

MUSLIM ORGANIZATIONS

There are a number of Muslim organizations in the United States. I will mention only a few of them. Most of you who are reading this book are college students. Some of you are members of or active in campus religious organizations sponsored by your community of faith. The Muslim Student Association, described above, is one of the constituent groups of *The Islamic Society of North America*,[22] an umbrella organization of several groups. It is generally considered to be the primary national Muslim organization, especially by immigrant Muslims. It publishes a journal, *Islamic Horizons*. The *American Muslim Mission* is the largest organization of American-born Muslims. It publishes *The Muslim Journal*.[23]

Recall that in the discussion of Muslim beliefs, we distinguished between Sunni and Shi'a Muslims. There is a third group of Muslims in the United States, the *Sufi Muslims*, or simply, Sufis. Sufism is the mystical branch of Islam, comparable in that respect to Hasidic Judaism and Christian mysticism. Sufism first came to the United States in 1910 with an Indian musician named Pir Hazrat Inayat Khan and his son, Pir Vilayat Khan. Indries Shah is another well-known figure in this movement, and many people in America have become acquainted with the poetry of the Sufi poet Rumi. There are now organizations throughout the United States. Their beliefs focus on the essential unity of all religions. They affirm that there is one God, one holy book, "the sacred manuscript of nature," one religion, one law, one human brotherhood, one moral principle, one truth, and one path.[24] Meditation and ecstatic dancing facilitate communion with God. The Order accepts individual students as initiates, sponsors worship as the Universal Worship of the Church of All, and also has a Healing Order that works with group healing rituals.

---

[20]University of Oklahoma Muslim Students Association Web site, www.ou.edu/student/oumsa/tips.doc
[21]Syed Dr. Yvonne Y. Haddad, "A Century of Islam in America," http://muslim-canada.org/HamdardCentury.html
[22]www.isna.com/
[23]www.muslimjournal.net
[24]"Sufi Thoughts," Sufi Order, Lebanon Springs, NY, n.d.

MUSLIMA: MUSLIM WOMEN IN AMERICA

Under Qur'anic law, women received more equal treatment than was otherwise common in Muhammad's lifetime. Religiously and legally, women and men were equals. It is also the case that, while having equal standing before Allah and before the law, women and men were thought to be different from each other, with different primary spheres of responsibility. Current research indicates that American Muslim women support equal rights and opportunities for women and men, while understanding their roles as complementary rather than identical.[25]

Figure 10-3   Muslim girl praying. *(Barnabas Kindersley © Dorling Kindersley.)*

[25]Jane I. Smith, *Islam in America, Columbia Contemporary American Religion Series* (New York: Columbia University Press, 1999), p. 105.

Many American Muslim women seek a path that allows for both fulfilling traditional Islamic expectations and exploring the new options and opportunities presented by life in American culture. What is distinctive in the United States is the individual choice that each woman can make, without interference, as she follows her own conscience in these matters.

Several issues are at the forefront of the discussion as women find their way in these new circumstances. While there is general agreement that working outside the home is acceptable and, for some, commendable, there is less disagreement on which occupations are preferable and how much interference with family life is allowable. There is agreement, too, that modesty in dress, especially by American standards, should be the norm, but what this means is less clear. In particular, whether it means covering the hair or not, and if so, to what extent, is debated. What it means to raise Muslim children, and the best ways to do this, are also matters that are discussed. Some women feel caught between the demands of their own increasingly complicated lives and the strong Muslim expectation that aging parents are to be cared for in the homes of their children.

Even as they are excited about new opportunities to study and interpret the Qur'an for themselves, some Muslim women are frustrated by the limits placed on the roles they can play in their masjids. Although leadership roles in education and fundraising are open to women, especially as American mosques become centers of religious and social life for the entire family, the key role of the imam is not. For some, not being allowed to sit with their husbands and older sons in prayer is frustrating, as well.

ISLAM AND BLACK AMERICANS

When Southern Blacks began migrating to the industrialized North, a new series of social-religious movements arose that often repudiated Christianity as the religion of slave holders. Black Americans were attracted to Islam by its message of complete racial equality. Muslim tradition holds that a daughter of Muhammad married a black man. Islam also offered belief in one God and a strong ethical code, as did Christianity, but it was not identified with the white oppressors. The story of Islam as it relates to the struggle for black freedom and self-definition is complex, as is the history of black Muslims in the United States. What is clear is that Islam offered American blacks an opportunity for a more positive self-identification:

> Although very few references explain how ideas about Islam became available in the black community, it is clear that this religion promised a new identity, a feeling of "somebodiness" denied by the dominant culture, a liberation from . . . relegation to insignificance. The new adherents shed Christianity, which they perceived as the root of their oppression in its glorification of suffering and promise of redemption in the hereafter.[26]

Islam was initially linked with the black power movement. Elijah Muhammad emerged in 1934 as the leader of what was then known as the

[26]Beverly Thomas McCloud, "African-American Muslim Women," in *The Muslims of America*, ed. Haddad, p. 178.

Nation of Islam. Elijah Muhammad's teachings contrasted sharply with those of mainstream Islam. He taught racial separatism and identified whites with Satan. The movement became known as the Nation of Islam.

In the 1960s, a group arose within the Nation of Islam who did not fully agree with Muhammad. This group was led by Malcolm X (born Malcolm Little in 1925). Malcolm X had earlier accepted Muhammad as a "divine leader." Especially later in his life, however, Malcolm X and his followers wanted to move the Nation closer to traditional Islam and away from complete separation from whites. They founded the Muslim Mosque, Incorporated, in 1964.

Elijah Muhammad died in 1975 and his son, Wallace (Warith) Deen Muhammad (b. 1933), assumed control of the Nation of Islam. Under his leadership, the Nation moved closer to the viewpoint of the Muslim Mosque. In 1980, the group became known as the American Muslim Mission. The official newspaper changed its name to *The American Muslim Journal* and later became the *Muslim Journal*. They retain a deep concern for the welfare of black Americans, but without the overtones of racial separatism and violence. Followers of W.D. Muhammad are now accepted by Muslims worldwide as followers of traditional Sunni Islam and are referred to simply as Muslims.

It is Malcolm X who has retained, even after his death, a hold on the imagination of American blacks, Muslim and non-Muslim alike. A poll done at the time that Spike Lee's controversial movie *Malcolm X* came out indicated that although only about half of American blacks really understood what Malcolm X stood for, a majority consider him a hero. Most rank him second only to Martin Luther King, Jr., in importance to contemporary blacks.[27]

Malcolm X was in prison at the time he became a Muslim. Muslims, primarily through the early Nation of Islam, had carried out an effective prison ministry for sometime and continue to do so even now. Many faith groups minister to those in prison. Muslims, however, have been especially effective with African American prisoners. Muslim prison chaplains counsel Muslims and non-Muslims alike, and non-Muslim chaplains counsel Muslims as well. Muslim prison chaplains—both paid and volunteer—provide for Friday midday prayer, counsel, lead Qur'anic studies, help with referrals to outside resources for support when someone is released, and help former prisoners reorient to life in free society and discontinue a criminal lifestyle. They also work with officials to make sure the religious rights of incarcerated Muslims are protected as required by the 2000 Religious Land Use and Institutionalized Persons Act.

The African American Muslim population is at high risk in American culture. As Aneesah Nadir, a Muslim prison chaplain says, the long list of challenges facing them includes poverty, plus

> unemployment and underemployment, residuals of alcoholism and sexual behaviors, marital and family issues, unequal justice in the court system, and interfaith conflicts with family members. The risk of ostracizing family members through conversion to Islam and difficulty socializing with immigrant Muslims, often put African American Muslims at great risk due to lack of

[27]*Newsweek*, November 16, 1992, p. 68.

support. Young African American men are especially prone to be estranged from community when they don't fit into the larger American society or into the immigrant Muslim community.[28]

In this setting, Muslim prison chaplains are uniquely positioned to be of help.

People who were dissatisfied with the emphasis on racial equality and the dignity and worth of people of all races in mainstream Islam came together around Louis Farrakhan in a movement to return to the separatist views and policies of the old Nation of Islam. Minister Farrakhan's followers have remained an outspoken minority among American Muslims.

The Nation of Islam[29] under Minister Farrakhan's leadership continues the themes of separatism and retribution that the Muslim Mosque, Incorporated, has muted or eliminated entirely. The Nation of Islam gives expression to the anger, bitterness, and resentment of a group of people so damaged in body, mind, and spirit by centuries of oppression that all talk of cooperation and "friendship" with the oppressors must ring hollow and hypocritical. While the American Muslim Mission branch attracts mainly middle-class blacks as well as other Muslims, membership in the Nation has continued to be comprised primarily of the under-employed and unemployed, who understandably see whites as the oppressors.

Although the themes of black power and separatism have been muted among most black Muslims, Islam remains a viable alternative for American blacks. It has important similarities with both Christianity and Judaism, while not being identified with slavery and oppression.

INTO THE FUTURE

Muslims see several issues as especially relevant as Islam in America moves into the twenty-first century. The degree of compromise and accommodation is a pervasive one, as Muslims seek to balance adherence to tradition with relevance to contemporary American life:

> Those who up to now have tried to lead lives of relative isolation, fearful that too much contact with America will compromise their own faith and culture, may have to question whether generations to come will find it necessary to be more open, more receptive to the culture of which they find themselves a part. Those who have opted for complete identification with America, abandoning many of the elements of Muslim observance, may find that they have lost some of the clarity and distinctiveness of what it means to be Muslim.[30]

Other nonmainstream religious groups (Orthodox Jews, for example, holiness Christians, Buddhists, and Hindus) face a similar necessity to balance tradition and modernization.

---

[28]www.isna.com/Leadership/pages/First-Annual-Muslim-Chaplain-Conference.aspx
[29]The Web site for the Nation of Islam is www.noi.org. The group publishes a newspaper known as *The Final Call*, www.finalcall.com
[30]Smith, *Islam in America*, p. 175.

There are several additional matters of concern. Who has the authority to determine what or who is a "good Muslim" when there are so many options and no central authority? What, if anything, unifies all American Muslims? Recruiting and training American-born imams and other leaders is crucial. In order to have their voices heard in the political arena, Muslims must learn ways to be effective in the political process. Political action committees (PACs) have been formed, and Muslim lobbyists work at the federal and state levels.[31]

QUESTIONS AND ACTIVITIES FOR REVIEW, DISCUSSION, AND WRITING

1. If you live or attend school close to an Islamic mosque (look in the yellow pages under "Religious Organizations," or perhaps "Churches"), make arrangements to attend the Friday midday prayer. Non-Muslims are welcome at mosques. There likely will be some dress requirements; inquire before you attend.
2. Especially if visiting a mosque is not possible, try to arrange for a Muslim student who attends your college or university to come and speak to your class.
3. If you are not a Muslim, pick one of the Five Pillars of Islam and discuss what it might mean to you if you were. You may want to do some additional reading on the Pillar that you choose. If you are a Muslim, discuss what one of the Pillars means to you.
4. If your library subscribes to any periodicals published by U.S. Muslims, read through two or three issues, and write about what impression you form of Islam.

FOR FURTHER READING

ABDO, GENEIVE, *Mecca and Main Street: Muslim Life in America after 9/11*. New York: Oxford University Press, 2007. Ms. Abdo clearly shows both the success story of immigrant American Muslims and the unprecedented challenges they have faced in the post-9/11 world. One strength of the book is her vivid descriptions of how American Muslims actually practice their faith, defining, as they do so, an Islam that is both truly Westernized and authentically Islamic.

BARRETT, PAUL, *American Islam: The Struggle for the Soul of a Religion*. New York: Picador, 2007. Barrett documents the racial and ideological diversity of American Islam. His portraits of individual American Muslims (e.g., *The Webmaster*, *The Scholar*, and *The Feminist*) put a human face on the religion.

HASAN, ASMA GULL, *American Muslims: The New Generation*. New York: The Continuum International Publishing Group, 2001. Hasan, a "self-proclaimed Muslim feminist cowgirl" (p. 3) writes about Muslims in the United States with warmth and humor, covering such issues as women, Jesus, jihad, militant black Islam, and Muslims in the media.

TURNER, RICHARD BRENT, *Islam in the African-American Experience*. Bloomington, IN: Indiana University Press, 2003. Turner describes the history and politics that led to the growth of Islam among African Americans and how this informs both the current leadership of W.D. Muhammad and Louis Farrakhan.

RELEVANT WORLD WIDE WEB SITES

Council on American-Islamic Relations: www.cair.com

The Islam Page: www.islamworld.net

Islam 101: www.islam101.com

Muslim Public Affairs Council: www.mpac.org

[31]Smith, *Islam in America*, Chapter 8.

CHAPTER 11

Humanism and the Unitarian
Universalists

The history of Western civilization shows us that most social and moral progress has been brought about by persons free from religion. In modern times the first to speak out for prison reform, for humane treatment of the mentally ill, for abolition of capital punishment, for women's right to vote, for death with dignity for the terminally ill, and for the right to choose contraception, sterilization, and abortion have been freethinkers, just as they were the first to call for an end to slavery.[1]

What associations, if any, does the word *humanism* bring to your mind? Does it have positive or negative connotations? What do you think about people who say that they are humanists? Do you think humanism necessarily excludes belief in God? Does your school have a college or department of humanities? Do you think these two words might be related? How?

There are many varieties of humanism. The group whose quotation appears above represents a thoroughly secular humanism, one that has no room for religion. Other forms of humanism are religious, as we will see.

WHAT IS HUMANISM?

Humanism can be defined briefly as a worldview or philosophy that derives its values from the experience of human life in this world, without reference to God as Jews, Christians, and Muslims understand God, or to anything else supernatural. In order to fill in this brief definition, we will look at some recent statements of the meaning of humanism. The American Humanist Association defines humanism as "a progressive philosophy of life that, without theism and other supernatural beliefs, affirms our ability and responsibility to lead ethical lives of personal fulfillment that aspire to the greater good of humanity."[2] A somewhat longer description focused strongly on the ethical dimension of humanism describes humanism as

---

[1]Freedom from Religion Foundation, www.ffrf.org
[2]American Humanist Association, www.americanhumanist.org/humanism

rational, scientific, and compassionate. It promotes the self-determination of each individual while affirming both individual and planetary responsibility. It affirms the democratic process, human rights, and social justice. It requires neither reference to nor support from anything supernatural. Values derive from human experience in this world rather than from theological beliefs.[3]

A review of these and other descriptions of humanism reveals several common themes:

- Humanism upholds human reason, compassion, responsibility, and the trust-worthiness of human experience.
- Humanism affirms the goodness and sufficiency of human life in this world, as a part of nature.
- It affirms the worth and dignity of each individual woman, man, and child, and the fundamental equality of all persons.
- It is possible for human beings to find meaning and fulfillment in life without recourse to the supernatural; people have the responsibility to engage in a search for meaning.
- Humanism supports the fullest development of democracy in all areas of life, human rights, social justice, and the expansion of individual rights to the fullest extent consonant with responsibility.
- Ethical and moral life is to be based on human experience, reason, and valuing.

Humanism, in other words, is based on the faith that people can live truly good lives in the here and now, that we have the capacity to cooperate to build a good society that balances out the needs of the individual and the larger group, and that we can find meaning and fulfillment without recourse to anything supernatural. Or, as one humanist puts it, humanism is "the use of reason in human affairs, applied in the service of compassion."[4]

Not all humanists are secularists, although many are. Jewish and Christian humanism also has a significant place in the story of American humanism. The humanist belief in the dignity and worth of every person, the emphasis on ethical conduct and human responsibility, and compassion in the context of human community are all shared by most religions. Liberal religion shares with humanism a belief in the basic goodness of human nature, its insistence that the context must be taken into account in making moral decisions, and its support for the use of reason and opposition to authoritarianism. Liberal religion often agrees with humanism that supernaturalism in religion is outdated and that scientific inquiry can and should be used to evaluate claims to religious truth. Humanism and liberal religion also share the belief that the sacred and secular worlds cannot, in the final analysis, be separated. Social justice, opposition to prejudice in all forms, and an interest in peacemaking also characterize both.

"The adventure of religion," writes one advocate of religious humanism, "is not in the discovery of Eternal Truth or Absolute Meaning—arenas in which

---

[3]The American Humanist Association, www.americanhumanist.org
[4]H.J. Eysenck, "Reason with Compassion," in *The Humanist Alternative*, ed. Paul Kurtz (Buffalo, NY: Prometheus Books, 1973), p. 91.

human beings do not and cannot deal—but in our individual and communal search for and creation of meanings and values that dignify and enhance life."[5]

HUMANISM IN THE UNITED STATES

The recent history of humanism in the United States is built on the foundation of centuries of earlier history, both in the United States and throughout the world. Rather than tracing this early history, however, we will look briefly at the more recent course of humanism in the United States. Humanism as a self-conscious movement began in the United States in 1933, when *Humanist Manifesto I* was written. There had been humanists and humanist philosophers in America as far back as the Declaration of Independence and even farther. Conscious attempts to articulate the principles of American humanism date from the first manifesto, however.

Four Humanist Statements

The first of these four statements is *Humanist Manifesto I*, written in 1933 by a group of humanists in the United States who set out to draft what they understood to be the basic principles of the movement. It is an optimistic and upbeat document that expresses great confidence in humanism as the wave of the future. "In every field of human activity," they wrote, "the vital movement is now in the direction of a candid and explicit humanism." The humanism of this document is explicitly religious humanism. Its authors wanted to separate religion from doctrines and from methods that they believed were "outmoded" and not workable in the twentieth century. They intended it to be a "new statement of the means and purposes of religion." It is written in the form of a series of fifteen brief statements with an introduction and conclusion and deals with those themes that we have already seen in connection with humanism. While the authors of the first major humanist statement were critical of the religious institutions of their day and regarded many religious beliefs and practices as unsuitable for life in the twentieth century, they were not, on the whole, hostile to religion.[6]

The authors of *Humanist Manifesto II* (1973) also expressed great confidence in people's ability to solve the problems that existed. It calls for people to "fuse reason with compassion in order to build constructive moral values." A major change from the first document is that this manifesto states that religion cannot be reinterpreted sufficiently to be made viable; something radically new is needed. It also has a much more clearly political tone than did its predecessor. Political and economic arrangements between nations receive more explicit attention.

---

[5]Kenneth W. Pfifer, *The Faith of a Humanist* (Boston, MA: Unitarian Universalist Association, n.d.).
[6]*Humanist Manifestos I* through *III* may be accessed on the American Humanist Association Web site, www.americanhumanist.org/about/

A Secular Humanist Declaration, written in 1980, is a very different sort of document. It outlines an explicitly secular humanism that clearly believes itself to be under attack and on the defensive. It names a variety of points of view and groups such as Christian fundamentalism, the Catholic papal hierarchy, Muslim clericalism, nationalistic Judaism, and many New Age beliefs and practices. It accuses them of promoting unthinking reliance on authority, restricting human freedom, and bypassing the use of reason and the scientific method to solve problems. It then moves on to a series of positive affirmations and calls for action that reflects the humanist values we have seen before.[7]

This document reflects a situation that had become more and more polarized. As Christian fundamentalism named secular humanism as the main focus of its attack, religious fundamentalism became the focus of secular humanism's attack. There can be no doubt that the views of fundamentalists and humanists are sharply different at almost every point. Fundamentalists tend to oppose both secular and religious humanism, believing that both are examples of human rebellion against God's authority. The kind of society envisioned by the one would have no room for the other. Each provides a framework within which significant numbers of Americans live and attempt to construct a meaningful life. If genuine dialogue between these distinctive points of view is to occur, the tendency of each to view the other as an obnoxious enemy must give way to an appreciation of what each provides for those who live their lives by it.

Humanists wrote *Humanism and Its Aspirations: Humanist Manifesto III, a successor to the Humanist Manifesto of 1933*, a fourth official statement of their position, in 2003, one which in many ways echoes the documents that preceded it.[8]

- Knowledge of the world is derived by observation, experimentation, and rational analysis.
- Life's fulfillment emerges from individual participation in the service of humane ideals.
- Humans are social by nature and find meaning in relationships.
- Working to benefit society maximizes individual happiness.
- Humans are an integral part of nature, the result of unguided evolutionary change.
- Ethical values are derived from human need and interest as tested by experience.[9]

HUMANIST ORGANIZATIONS

Humanist organizations are not nearly as well known as more traditional religious organizations, but there are several such groups in the United States. They are more common in major urban areas than in smaller communities and along the coasts than in the heartland.

---

[7]This document can be read on the Council for Secular Humanism Web site, http://www.secularhumanism.org/index.php?section=main&page=declaration
[8]Available at www.americanhumanist.org/3/HumandItsAspirations.htm
[9]The American Humanist Association, www.americanhumanist.org/3/HumandItsAspirations.htm

Felix Adler founded the *Ethical Culture Society* (now, the American Ethical Union) in 1876. He was trained as a rabbi but left Judaism in favor of ethical humanism based on the dignity and worth of every individual. The group is characterized by intense social activism in the areas of education, war and peace, and racism, among others. The American Ethical Union describes itself as "a humanistic religious and educational movement inspired by the ideal that the supreme aim of human life is working to create a more humane society."[10]

The *American Humanist Association*[11] was formed in 1941 as an effort to link the various humanist interests in the United States. Like the American Ethical Union, it supports an active program of social involvement that is based on the principles in the *Humanist Manifestos*. It publishes a periodical, *The Humanist*, and supports Prometheus Books, the largest American publisher of humanist literature.

HUUmanists publishes the journal *Religious Humanism*. It was founded in 1962 as the Fellowship of Religious Humanists. It is an affiliate of the Unitarian Universalist Association. It regards humanism as a religious way of approaching life, a philosophy that makes sense in religious terms. It emphasizes the inter-connection of all life. Its members participate in the human "search for the meaningful life without dogma and using the best tools of both mind and heart, both reason and compassion."[12]

The *Society for Humanistic Judaism* is a major Jewish humanist organization. It was founded by Rabbi Sherwin T. Wine in 1963 as a "nontheistic alternative in contemporary Jewish life." It "embraces a human-centered philosophy that combines the celebration of Jewish culture and identity with an adherence to humanistic values and ideas." It holds conferences and other educational events, assists humanistic Jewish congregations, and encourages nontheistic celebration of the traditional Jewish holidays and life-cycle rites.

The role of the black church has been central to the life of the African American community in the United States (see Chapter 7). However, there is also an association of *African Americans for Humanism*.[13] Although many of its goals are similar to those of the black Christian churches, its rationales and methods are those of humanism.

> Undoubtedly, the churches in America have played a positive role in the Black community, especially in the struggle for civil rights; and they have often provided the oppressed with consolation. But humanists believe that, in the last analysis, the only way to ameliorate the human condition is to overcome poverty and disease and to achieve the good life by human efforts. Humanists emphasize the importance of education, reason, and critical intelligence for understanding nature and solving human problems. Humanists wish to fulfill the highest human potentialities, to cultivate ethics, and to build a truly democratic world community.[14]

[10]The American Ethical Union, www.aeu.org
[11]www.americanhumanist.org
[12]www.huumanists.org, www.huumanists.org
[13]African Americans for Humanism, www.secularhumanism.org/aah
[14]Paul Kurtz, "The Importance of African Americans for Humanism," www.secularhumanism.org/index.php?
    section=aah&page=importance

The Center for Inquiry on Campus (formerly the Campus Freethought Alliance) began in 1996. The students who joined to form the Alliance were in search of a community for freethinkers among the college population. Its purpose is "to promote and defend reason, science, and freedom of inquiry in education, and to enhance the presence of freethought, skepticism, secularism, humanism, philosophical naturalism, rationalism, and atheism on college and high school campuses throughout North America and around the world." The group provides support for secular students and when necessary helps to defend their rights.[15]

These and other similar groups provide organizational cohesiveness to the humanist movement in America and provide a means by which people in agreement with this point of view can find fellowship and engage in social action. They also provide a means by which humanists can voice their concerns. Humanist organizations work to get legislation passed that reflects their viewpoint, just as do other political interest groups, including religious interest groups.

There can be no doubt that humanism serves many of the same functions for its adherents that traditional religions do for theirs. It has many of the same emotional dynamics. Like the religions, humanism has a place among the myriad ways that Americans organize their lives in a meaningful fashion. It is a continuing element in the American landscape, one that will interact with religion for a long time to come.

ATHEISM AND AGNOSTICISM

Before you read further, stop and ask yourself what might lead someone to be an atheist or agnostic. Do those views seem to you to be reasonable ones for someone to hold, whether or not you, yourself, do?

Atheism, agnosticism, and various other types of free thought not in accord with the Judeo-Christian and Muslim monotheistic perspectives have been a part of the religious and cultural mix ever since Europeans came to the New World. Atheism and agnosticism were included in the plurality of religious views held by the early colonists and by the framers of the Constitution. Most people in the United States do believe in the existence of God as commonly understood. However, current survey data indicate that around 16 percent of the population does not believe in some higher power. At the same time, over half of the population does not hold a favorable impression of those who do not believe.[16]

We'll begin with a brief definition of each word. In the United States, *atheism* usually means not believing in God as God is thought of in the Judeo-Christian-Islamic tradition. However, many atheists think that this definition is

[15]Center for Inquiry on Campus, www.campusfreethought.org
[16]The Association of Religion Data Archives, www.thearda.com

inadequate. While acknowledging that the word *atheist* is used to mean a person who *denies* the existence of God, they press for a distinction:

> [M]ost atheists . . . would hold that an atheist is a person *without* belief in God. The distinction is small but important. Denying something means that you have knowledge of what it is that you are being asked to affirm, but that you have rejected that particular concept. To be *without* belief in God merely means the term "God" has no importance or possibly no meaning to you.[17]

Agnosticism has a number of meanings. Some agnostics hold that they themselves simply do not know if God exists. Others believe that it is impossible for anyone to know if God exists. Some would put it in terms of the evidence being inconclusive. Others believe that, even if we can say with some degree of certainty that some sort of higher being or power does exist, we can have absolutely no knowledge of the nature or character of that being.

Reasons for Disbelief

There are a number of different themes that appear repeatedly in people's reasons for disavowing belief in a supreme being or higher power. Following psychiatrist Sigmund Freud, some atheists say that we as human beings want a father figure to protect us, to punish us when we deserve to be punished, and to reward us when we have been good. We want, in other words, to remain in a childlike relationship with a powerful father. Therefore, we create a God who is an omnipotent, all-knowing father. Alternatively, following Marx, people who are oppressed and mistreated project a God who will reward them in the future for present suffering and deprivation. This, then, invites abuse by the privileged and ruling classes, who can promise those they oppress future rewards in heaven for compliance and punishments in hell for disobedience. This dynamic was at work in some of the uses made of Christianity by slaveholders.

Another alternative of this type is more sociological. Following sociologist Emile Durkheim, this view holds that a society (rather than individuals) projects a God as the source of its dearest values and social norms. The social norms and cultural values gain authority and sanction by being attributed to the deity. A very similar dynamic can be seen when proponents of various (and often opposing!) social positions claim that "God is on their side," as has been done by both sides in the abortion rights debate and the homosexual rights debate.

Some atheists believe faith in God is simply not consistent with a scientific view of reality and the methods that such a view entails. In other words, "God" cannot be proven by the methods of science, especially as refined and practiced by the natural sciences. Furthermore, the concept of God may be used to fill in where knowledge does not exist, as a substitute for knowledge, thus hindering the development of knowledge. This is sometimes called a "God of the gaps" theology. Thus, as human knowledge grows, God must necessarily shrink.

---

[17]Gordon Stein, "Introduction," in *An Anthology of Atheism and Rationalism*, ed. Gordon Stein (Buffalo, NY: Prometheus Books, 1980), p. 3.

Although most theologians do not support the "God of the gaps" view, it is fairly common among believers generally.

Some people think that the word God simply does not have a clear, unambiguous meaning. Statements about God cannot be verified or falsified in the usual ways and thus are an unacceptable use of language.

A particularly troublesome problem for many people is that they cannot reconcile the existence of an all-powerful and loving God with the presence of so much human suffering. Catastrophic disasters, terror attacks, pain and suffering endured by innocent populations, and horrifying illnesses that afflict apparently good people all have led to questions about God's existence. Even if they do not question God's existence, people may question God's simultaneous goodness and power (cornerstones of the Judeo-Christian-Islamic view). If God is both all-good and all-powerful, the argument runs, why does God allow things like this to happen? These questions run the gamut from individuals asking "Why?" after the death of a parent, child, or spouse, to those of Jewish faith who asked and continue to ask "Why?" after the Holocaust.

Other atheists argue that God's existence is incompatible with the recognition of the autonomy and worth of humankind. The Christian claim that people need a savior or the Jewish and Muslim avowal that people need the guidance of God to live truly good lives seems to some people to contradict human autonomy, freedom, and worth.

Some people feel that belief in God takes away from people's proper focus, which is to work actively for positive change in the social order. In some instances, this is a response to the perceived social conservatism of religion, religion's tendency to maintain the status quo rather than support change. As you have seen, some women feel very strongly that their churches and synagogues have been on the side of female oppression rather than on the side of women's rights. In other cases, this view stems from the shift in focus that sometimes goes along with belief in God and life after death. For some, although certainly not for most, believers, life in this present world is greatly devalued compared with eternal life with God. This devaluation then undercuts any attempt to better this life.

Finally, some people simply point to the fact that, the world around, many people, including many who espouse very high ideals, do not believe. If the whole experience of humankind is taken into account, there are just too many people for whom God is not a fact of their experience.

While several of these views are most likely to lead a person to atheism, at least three of them might also lead to agnosticism. Many agnostics simply feel that there is not enough evidence either for or against God's existence to warrant certainty. Some are disturbed by the ambiguity and lack of clarity that surrounds our use of the word *God*. And certainly some point to how well people get along without such belief. Fewer agnostics than atheists tend to be militant about their position. For the most part, their "unknowing" makes them reluctant to try to make converts.

There are few atheist organizations in the United States. For most atheists, their atheism is a matter of private belief and conviction. Probably the best known is American Atheists,[18] founded in 1963 by *Madalyn Murray O'Hair*, the twentieth-century atheist whose name became, for a time, nearly synonymous with atheism itself. The organization publishes a magazine, *American Atheist*.

Most atheists do not try to persuade other people to join them in their denial of God. Most embrace positive, humanistically based moral values alongside their denial of the God of the believers. While they do not share the belief in God that most Americans have, they do share many of the same moral commitments.

Humanism, agnosticism, and atheism are some of the alternatives to participation in an organized community of faith. Woven into the tapestry of American religious life along with the mainstream alternatives, they help to make it a rich blend of colors and textures unrivaled anywhere else in the world.

UNITARIAN UNIVERSALISTS

Unitarian Universalism is an organizational embodiment of the very liberal religious tradition in the United States. The present Unitarian Universalist Association is the result of a merger between the Universalists and the Unitarians. We will first consider the two separately and then look at the Unitarian Universalist Association today.

The Universalists

Simply put, universalism is the belief that all persons will eventually be saved by God; in other words, salvation is universal, not limited to an elect number. This belief is suggested by certain Biblical passages. For example, Acts 3:21 speaks of a time of restoration or restitution of all things. John 1:29 refers to Jesus as the Lamb of God who takes away the sins of the [whole] world, and Romans 5:18 speaks of the righteousness of Jesus being imparted to all people. In Revelation 21:5, God is said to say, "I make all things new." Clearly, traditional Christian teaching has not taken these and other similar passages in this light, but this interpretation was seized upon by those who could not reconcile the concept of a God of love with the idea that such a God would condemn anyone to everlasting punishment. Nonetheless, universalism usually has been regarded as a heresy (erroneous and unacceptable belief) throughout Christian history.[19]

By the time of the American colonies, universalism was already present on the American religious scene and would remain there. English-born John Murray (1741–1815) is sometimes considered the father of American Universalism. In 1770, he preached what may well have been the first Universalist sermon in

---

[18]www.atheists.org
[19]*If Grace Is True: Why God Will Save Every Person*, written by Philip Gulley and James Mulholland (New York City: HarperCollins, 2003) is a very readable contemporary statement of this point of view.

America, in New England. The first covenant for a Universalist church was drawn up in Murray's church in Gloucester, Massachusetts, in 1779, and in 1780, he met with a group in Philadelphia to help draft a Universalist declaration of faith.

Elhanan Winchester (1751–1797) was another early leader, an intellectual and writer whose writing ability helped to spread the Universalist message and give it credibility. Both Murray and Winchester remained within the framework of trinitarian Christianity.

Hosea Ballou (1771–1852) was not a trinitarian, however, but a unitarian, who believed that God was one instead of three persons. Ballou's universalism was blended with his unitarianism in ways that prefigured the eventual merger of the two groups. Ballou's *Treatise on the Atonement* was the first American attempt to develop a coherent theology along Universalist lines. He became the pastor of the Second Universalist Church in Boston and held that post for over thirty years, becoming the chief spokesperson for Universalism in the new world. During part of his pastorate in Boston, he worked closely with William Ellery Channing, who would become known as the father of American Unitarianism.[20]

The denomination spread slowly in the nineteenth and twentieth centuries. It was especially successful in the rural and frontier areas, while the Unitarians were more concentrated in urban areas. By the mid-1900s, Universalism had become known as a liberalized and universalized form of Christianity, and it remained so until its union with Unitarianism.

The Unitarians

While the universalists were teaching universal salvation as a clearer expression of the will of an all-loving God, the Unitarians reacted to other elements in traditional Christian teaching. First among these was the doctrine that God is a trinity, formalized by the Council of Nicaea in 325 C.E. This doctrine, you will recall from the discussion of basic Christian beliefs, holds that God is three distinct persons with but one substance. The *Unitarians* taught the oneness of God, against the trinitarians. Although their name derives from this one teaching, there were other Christian doctrines to which they objected. Among these were the infallibility of the Bible, human depravity and the inheritance of original sin, and the doctrine that some will be damned eternally. This last point aligned them with the Universalists. The Unitarians also encouraged the use of reason as a way of determining religious truth, a theme that we saw in our discussion of humanism and one that remains a hallmark of modern-day Unitarianism.

The first church in the United States that took an explicitly Unitarian view of God did so in the late 1700s. In 1785, King's Chapel in Boston (Episcopal)

---

[20]A biography of Channing is available on the Dictionary of Unitarian and Universalist Biography Web site at www25.uua.org/uuhs/duub/articles/williamellerychanning.html. The site also has biographies of Ballou and Winchester.

appointed a young minister with Unitarian views, James Freeman. Freeman led his congregation in changing the Anglican Prayer Book to eliminate all references to the Trinity. The Episcopal Church refused to recognize the church as Episcopalian, and, in 1787, Freeman became the first American-ordained Unitarian minister. What had been the first Episcopal Church in Boston became the first Unitarian Church.

William Ellery Channing (1780–1842) is often said to be father of American Unitarianism. American religious historian Sydney Ahlstrom compares Channing's role in the Unitarian reformation in America to that of Martin Luther in the German reformation.[21] In 1819, Channing preached his famous sermon, "Unitarian Christianity," in which he defined the new movement. Channing's Unitarianism remained firmly Christian. In his interpretation, God the Father sent the Son and gives the Holy Spirit to those who seek it. These three are not to be considered three persons in one God, however. Six years later, Channing founded the American Unitarian Association. *Transcendentalism* played a large role in the early Unitarian movement. An American adaptation of English romanticism and German idealism, transcendentalism sought to refine Unitarianism and bring in into conformity with what it believed was the common substance of all the world's religions. Ralph Waldo Emerson (1803–1882) was the best-known leader of the Transcendentalist movement. Emerson preferred to be called a theist rather than a Christian, because the term was more general.[22]

Harvard Divinity School and College (later, Harvard University) became the intellectual stronghold of Unitarianism. Most faculty and students were consciously Unitarian in their outlook, and, especially in the decade between 1811 and 1820, Harvard became the leading Unitarian training center in the United States. Unitarianism remained strongest in New England and in the more urban areas of the growing nation. In rural areas and along the frontier, where Universalism was stronger, Unitarianism was looked upon as an elitist religion. It was that aspect of Unitarianism that led someone to remark that Unitarians believed in "the fatherhood of God, the brotherhood of man and the neighborhood of Boston."

Unitarianism gradually transformed itself from the distinctly Christian Unitarianism of Channing's sermon into an ethically oriented, pragmatic, humanistic, and sometimes theistic, religion. Along the way, and indicative of the changes that were taking place, American Unitarians played a dominant role in organizing and supporting the Parliament of Religions in Chicago in 1893. It was this transformed Unitarianism that carried over into the present-day Unitarian Universalist Association.

---

[21]Sydney E. Ahlstrom, *A Religious History of the American People* (New Haven, CT: Yale University Press, 1973), p. 398.

[22]Channing's "Unitarian Christianity" sermon can be read on the Channing Memorial Church Web site, www.channingmc.org/channingspeech.html. Emerson's Harvard Divinity School Address is available on the American Transcendentalism Web at www.vcu.edu/engweb/transcendentalism/authors/emerson/essays/dsa.html

The Unitarian Universalist Association[23]

As we have seen, the Universalists and the Unitarians shared both a dissatisfaction with the prevailing religious orthodoxies of their times and a substantial body of common beliefs and religious sensibilities. Nonetheless, despite Hosea Ballou's repeated calls for unity, there was almost no cooperation between them in the early years. They came from different social backgrounds, and, while many of their quarrels with traditional Christianity were similar, they arrived at their positions by different routes. The Universalists began with the conflict between the doctrine of God's love and the idea of eternal damnation. This gave their protest a different emotional quality than that of the more rational and intellectual Unitarian objection to what they saw as the illogic of belief in a trinitarian God.

However, as both groups changed, in many ways moving even closer together, interest in cooperative efforts grew, spurred by the fact that neither group was large. Their small size meant that they needed each other. The two groups merged in 1961, bringing into being the Unitarian Universalist Association, the national organization for the church today.

Unitarian Universalism Today

Many of us, when we encounter a community of faith with which we are unfamiliar, want to know, "What, exactly, do you believe?" Unitarian Universalism has no official creed. There is no statement of beliefs to which members must give assent. There is no confession of faith that is repeated regularly in Sunday services. Rather than having a set of firm beliefs worked out and handed to people, the Unitarian Universalists support a set of very broad operating principles that serve as guidelines for individual and community decision making.

Individual freedom of religious belief is perhaps the most fundamental of all these guidelines. All people, following the guidance of their own best understanding and informed by the community of faith as a whole, are responsible for working out their own beliefs. The emphasis is not on having a correct set of beliefs handed down from church authorities or from a sacred book but on responsibly working out one's own beliefs, subject to change as one's understanding grows. This understanding of how religious beliefs come about leads Unitarian Universalists to possess a large measure of tolerance for differences within their ranks, as well as appreciation for religious views other than Unitarian Universalism.

Unitarian Universalists believe that religious beliefs should change as people change throughout the course of their lives, rather than saying that there are beliefs that should be clung to throughout life. The process of arriving at religious beliefs is of central importance. For most, if not all, ethical action in the world, with and on behalf of other people, is of greater importance than belief.

[23]www.uua.org

A bookmark-sized pamphlet lists "Ten Good Reasons for Joining a Unitarian Universalist Congregation." Among the reasons given are that it's a place where people worship "with open hearts and minds, seeking what is sacred among us." Other reasons refer to the denomination's long tradition of tolerance and reasonableness, its honoring its Jewish and Christian roots while affirming truth in other religions as well, and Unitarian Universalists' belief that revelation is never finished and people are empowered to search for new truths. The denomination also encourages children's questions, welcomes diversity, works to bring about a more just society, respects the whole self, mind, body, and spirit, encourages its members and friends to be true to themselves and offers people a supportive community.[24]

These principles of belief lead most Unitarian Universalists to a lifestyle that includes engagement in social action. One notable characteristic of the members of this church is that they are, compared with their relatively small numbers in most areas, vastly overrepresented in those organizations that are identified with liberal social concerns. Organizations that work to make life better for all citizens can usually count on support from Unitarian Universalists. Groups that work on increasing civil liberties also attract Unitarian Universalists' interest. For most, political involvement, in the widest sense of that term, is a central way of working out their religious commitments in day-to-day life.

The freedom to work out one's own religious beliefs without pressure from any external authorities attracts the highly educated into Unitarian Universalism. They are the most highly educated, on the average, of any American church. This also means that this church includes many professional people among its members, both men and women. The freedom of religious belief that characterizes Unitarian Universalist churches also draws couples of mixed religious faith, because they can attend services at the same place without either of them compromising their own faith. People may also become part of a Unitarian Universalist congregation if they live too far from their own community of faith to participate in its activities.

Unitarian Universalists are also among the most culture-affirming people. They raise hard questions about the culture in which they live, especially when that culture seems less humane than it might be. Nonetheless, Unitarian Universalists believe in full participation in the life of the society of which they are a part. They believe in individual freedom regarding things like drinking alcohol, dress code, and sexual arrangements between consenting adults.

Unitarian Universalist congregations provide corporate ritual activity, but describing a "typical" service is difficult. The freedom that we have noted in belief translates into freedom in deciding what format religious meetings will take. Regular services usually occur on Sunday morning (Figure 11-1). It is not unheard of, however, for a church to hold services at some other time that suits the needs of the congregation better. In some churches, the service may be hard to distinguish from any other very liberal Protestant service. In others, greater

[24]Bill and Barbara Hamilton-Holway and Mark Harris, "Ten Good Reasons for Joining a Unitarian Universalist Congregation" (Boston, MA: Unitarian Universalist Association, 1995).

Figure 11-1   Unitarian Universalist services attract people seeking freedom of religious thought. *(Joe Traver/Liaison.)*

experimentation and innovation are the rule. There is a *hymnal*, or hymn book, that includes traditional hymns that are modified to eliminate gender-exclusive language. Other hymns specifically reflect the church's own teachings. Readings in a typical service might be taken from many sources. The Jewish and Christian scriptures, the sacred writings of other world religions, contemporary poetry, and novels are only a few possibilities. It is not unusual to find a reading from the Christian New Testament and a reading from a recent novel side by side. The minister or a guest speaker gives a sermon, talk, meditation, or commentary (some churches do not use the more distinctly religious word *sermon*). It may concern a matter of ethical importance, social involvement, self-development, or human relationships, to name but a few examples. An offering is usually received. A person expecting prayers might be surprised; Unitarian Universalist church services sometimes do not include them.

I have avoided using the word *worship* to describe the church services. *Worship* usually carries with it the idea that there is a god or supreme being that is being worshiped, an idea upon which not all Unitarian Universalists agree. There are no sacraments. Children are welcomed into the congregation and dedicated, at which time their parents and the congregation affirm their commitment to the child and celebrate the new life that has come into being. Other ceremonies, such as marriages and funerals, echo the liberal and humanistic perspective that is so much a part of the life of these communities of faith. Nearly all services include time for fellowship and refreshments before or after.

Fellowship is very important for the members of Unitarian Universalist congregations. Larger churches support a full range of activities from which members and friends can choose. Discussion, education, and debate characterize the life of these communities of faith. Education for adults, young people, and children is built into the Sunday morning activities, and other activities may occur during the week. Unitarian Universalist ministers often participate in interfaith groups.

Organizationally, each local church is fully autonomous. The Unitarian Universalist Association, with headquarters in Boston, takes care of many operational details and serves as the central offices for the group. Its statements have only an advisory function where local congregations are concerned. There is a national conference annually. Beacon Press is the church's publishing house. The Association also supports a unique outreach program. Called the *Church of the Larger Fellowship*, this program was designed especially for religious liberals who live too far from a Unitarian Universalist church to attend.[25] It makes available a news bulletin that contains sermons and inspirational writings, as well as reports on activities. A *Handbook of Services* for the major celebrations of life is provided for each member. A minister is available by mail or telephone. A religious education director provides parents with assistance in developing a religious education program for their children. There is also a lending library.

On some college campuses, there are organizations for Unitarian Universalist and other religiously liberal students, sponsored by a local Unitarian Universalist congregation.

Humanism and very liberal religion provide meaningful alternatives to traditional religion for significant numbers of Americans. They have influenced more traditional religion in the direction of increased social concern. Humanism and humanitarianism have been and continue to be very closely linked in the United States, and the presence of humanism has encouraged the society to be more humanitarian. Atheists and agnostics, too, have contributed to the American cultural landscape. All have a place at the table of religious diversity in the United States.

QUESTIONS AND ACTIVITIES FOR REVIEW, DISCUSSION, AND WRITING

1. Take a current ethical or moral problem of which you are aware. Think it through (1) beginning with the assumptions of Judaism or Christianity and (2) again from a humanistic viewpoint. What differences in the process and in the conclusions do you notice? You might want to organize this as a debate with a friend, each of you taking one point of view.
2. Humanism opposes all forms of authoritarianism. Do you agree, or do you feel that authoritarianism has a place in certain situations? Is it important to distinguish between authority and authoritarianism? For what reasons and in what circumstances might one person or group exercise authority over others?
3. In your opinion, is humanism a religion? Why or why not?
4. Which of the reasons given for atheism is most persuasive to you? Least convincing? Why? If you yourself are an atheist or an agnostic, why?
5. Visit a Unitarian Universalist Church or Fellowship if there is one in your community or close by. In what ways is the Sunday service similar to others with which you may be familiar? How is it different? Many members of these churches became Unitarian Universalists after having been part of other religious groups. If possible, make arrangements to speak with the minister about how some of the people in the congregation came to their present religious outlook.

[25]http://clf.uua.org/

6. What might be the advantages and disadvantages of being a part of a community of faith that expects that religious beliefs will change throughout people's lives, rather than offering a set of beliefs that are expected to remain constant?
7. Visit the Web sites of two of the organizations listed under "Relevant World Wide Web Sites" in order to learn something about each organization that goes beyond what is in this chapter.

FOR FURTHER READING

GRIGG, RICHARD, "To Re-Enchant the World," *A Philosophy of Unitarian Universalism.* Philadelphia, PA: XLibris Corporation, 2004. Grigg focuses on five strands of Unitarian Universalist thought: humanism, nature and ecology, engagement with the arts, commitment to social justice, and devotion to the sacred in its myriad forms. He relates the philosophy of Unitarian Universalism to important aspects of contemporary culture.

HERRICK, JIM, *Humanism: An Introduction.* Amherst, NY: Prometheus Books, 2005. This book covers the relationship of humanism to a host of other topics, including morality, religion, politics, the arts, and science, as well as humanist ethics and organizations.

HITCHENS, CHRISTOPHER, *The Portable Atheist: Essential Readings for the Nonbeliever.* Cambridge, MA: DeCapo Books, 2007. Although intended primarily for the nonbeliever, this book provides an around-the-world and through-the-ages tour of significant writings on atheism and agnosticism from both well-known and little-known authors.

KURTZ, PAUL, *What Is Secular Humanism?* Amherst, NY: Prometheus Books, 2007. Kurtz describes the influence of secular humanism on culture and advocates for its role in today's world.

SINKFORD, WILLIAM, *Unitarian Universalism Pocket Guide.* Boston: Skinner House Books, 2004. Barely over a hundred pages, the book covers the basics of Unitarian Universalism in a straightforward and easily read style.

RELEVANT WORLD WIDE WEB SITES

The Secular Web: www.infidels.org
Freedom from Religion Foundation: www.ffrf.org

CHAPTER 12

Hindus and Buddhists: Asia Comes to America

E pluribus unum, "From Many, One," could easily come from the ancient Rig Veda, with its affirmation: "Truth is One. People call it by many names." To be honest, the Vedas take the *unum* a giant step further. This affirmation of oneness is not sociological or political but theological; it is affirmation about the very nature of ultimate reality. God or Truth or Ultimate Reality is one, though people speak of that One in many ways and try to recognize it in their lives through many paths. On the face of it, Hindu immigrants would seem natural participants in the American project. . . . Hindus bring something unique to America—a theology of religious pluralism.[1]

Buddhist priests, classified by the Federal Bureau of Investigation (FBI) as potentially the most dangerous Japanese aliens, were among the first groups arrested by government officials following the bombing of Pearl Harbor on December 7, 1941. Shinobu Matsuura's husband, the Reverend Issei Matsuura, was one such Buddhist priest. He was taken by the FBI in the early hours of the morning and did not know if or when he would see his family again.[2]

Hinduism and Buddhism both began in India, a far different world than that which gave rise to Judaism, Christianity, and Islam. What we now call Hinduism began in India, sometime between 2,000 and 1,500 years before the lifetime of Jesus. Buddhism began later, in the fifth century B.C.E. Although Hinduism and Buddhism each account for less than 1 percent of the U.S. population, they are religious minorities whose visibility is increasing.

Hinduism and Buddhism are in many ways very different from the Abrahamic religions. I have kept the use of unfamiliar words to a minimum, instead using more familiar equivalents that convey the sense of what is meant.

---

[1]Diana Eck, *A New Religious America: How A "Christian Country" Has Now Become the World's Most Religiously Diverse Nation* (New York: HarperCollins, 2001), p. 80.

[2]Duncan Ryûken Williams, "From Pearl Harbor to 9/11: Lessons from the Internment of Japanese American Buddhists," in *A Nation of Religions: The Politics of Pluralism in Multireligious America*, ed. Stephen Prothero (Chapel Hill, NC: The University of North Carolina Press, 2006), p. 63.

I have used less familiar terms when doing so seemed warranted because (1) they are used often in discussing a particular religion, (2) you would be likely to encounter them in other reading or experience, or (3) they are often used and/or greatly preferred by followers of the religions.

The history of Asia's religions in the United States is too extensive and too complex to delineate here. Suffice it to say that by the time widespread immigration from Asia to the United States became viable in 1965 with the Hart-Celler Immigration Act, Asia's religions were already present here in significant ways.[3]

- Systematic trade with Asia had begun in 1784, bringing with it cultural artifacts, ideas, and sometimes people.
- Magazines and books began to pay more attention to Asian religions around the same time.
- In the 1800s, the Transcendentalists, such as writers Emerson and Thoreau, provided a scholarly introduction to Asian religious ideas in ways accessible by non-Asians.
- Spiritualism and the Theosophical Society continued this trend, depicting Asian religious ideas in a distinctively American idiom.
- In 1893 the first World's Parliament of Religion, held in conjunction with the World's Columbian Exposition in Chicago, brought notable Hindu and Buddhist speakers to the United States. Some of them stayed on as teachers.
- In short, there has been a third strand of religion in the United States that has not always been recognized. Alongside the evangelical and mainstream Protestant hegemony, there has been "metaphysical religion," defined in part by its "openness to Asia and an embrace of South and East Asian religious ideas and practices." It has been "a normal, recurring, and pervasive feature of the American religious landscape."[4]

We will concentrate on Hinduism and Buddhism, the two Asian religions with the largest numbers and highest public profiles in this country. There are, as well, significant numbers of Sikhs, Jains, and followers of other Asian traditions in the United States. Also, as with all the previous religions you have studied, Hindus and Buddhists in the United States live out their religion in widely varying ways that stem from such things as their country of origin, current culture, and personal preference.

HINDUISM AND HINDUS IN THE UNITED STATES

Unlike the religions you have studied so far, Hinduism has no single founder. The word *Hinduism* itself is an umbrella term for a vast collection of religious beliefs and practices that nonetheless have enough in common to warrant grouping them

---

[3]For more detailed yet brief and accessible accounts of this topic, see Thomas A. Tweed and Stephen Prothero, eds., *Asian Religion in America: A Documentary History* (New York: Oxford University Press, 1999), General Introduction, and Catherine L. Albanese, *A Republic of Mind and Spirit: A Cultural History of American Metaphysical Religion* (New Haven, CT: Yale University Press, 2007), especially the Introduction.

[4]Albanese, *A Republic of Mind and Spirit*, pp. 12 and 16.

together. It is also a term coined by non-Hindu Westerners. Hindus themselves often use the term *Sanatana Dharma* for their religion. It means original religion, and Indians believe that theirs is one form of the religion that has existed since the dawn of humanity. This religion is not Hindu, nor Buddhist, nor Muslim, nor any particular religion. It is simply *human* religion, and Hinduism is but one embodiment of it. Hinduism differs dramatically in many respects from the religions you have learned about thus far. Religion in the United States tends to be about belief, or doctrine. Hinduism, on the other hand, is much more concerned with practice. You have seen this orientation toward practice in Judaism, particularly Orthodox Judaism, as well.

There is no one worldview or set of beliefs that is required of Hindus, nor any to which all hold without exception. What follows here is an outline of what most Hindus in the United States would agree on, at least in principle.

Most Hindus regard the *Vedas* with reverence and many hold them as a defining feature of authentic Hinduism. The Vedas are the oldest of the sacred writings and have influenced the entire development of Hinduism. The *Bhagavad-Gita*, a section of a much longer epic work called the Mahabharata, is an important devotional classic.

The sacred, while One, is known in many forms and by many names. Whereas the Semitic religions clearly distinguish between God as Crea*tor* and everything else as crea*tion*, Hindus do not make this distinction. Rather, *every living thing is a manifestation of the sacred.* The divine can be seen and known in everything that is, and everything that is can be seen as a part of the divine. This also means there can be no sharp separation between things—between the divine and the human, or between people and all other beings. In the innermost core of our being, myself, my cat, and the fly my cat is chasing are one. This divine One is both immanent and transcendent, knowable both as personal and suprapersonal. Rather than being a creation from nothing by the will of God, Hindus believe that the *universe goes through endless cycles* that have no absolute beginning or end. The current universe is one of countless numbers that have evolved over time, eternally.

Karma is the moral law of cause and effect through which our actions create our destiny. The principle of karma states that every action has a reaction. In our own culture, even if we ourselves are not a part of the Judeo-Christian-Islamic tradition, most of us are accustomed to thinking in terms of rewards and punishments: Good deeds will be rewarded and evil ones punished. Karma, by contrast, is a moral law that operates analogously to natural laws such as gravity. Certain results inevitably follow certain actions.

Reincarnation is widely believed throughout India, and this belief is widely shared among American Hindus and Buddhists as well. Reincarnation means (1) that a person's present life was preceded by other lives and will likewise be followed by other lives. It also means (2) that these lifetimes do not happen randomly but are connected. The way that life is lived in one lifetime determines the quality of the next incarnation. Karma is in effect the engine that drives the process of reincarnation.

Belief in reincarnation brings up the question of what it means to be a person, according to Hindus. Our empirical self is what we think we are, what ordinary experience tells us we are. According to most Hindus, there is more. The *Real Self*, or *Atman*, is the divine within each and every person. This is what carries on from lifetime to lifetime throughout successive incarnations.

The ultimate goal of human life is escape from this cycle of death and rebirth. Throughout however many lifetimes it requires, a person comes increasingly closer to grasping the unity of all things, including the self and divine. Eventually, when that unity is fully grasped, incarnation ceases and the real self is reunited with the divine, which, of course, it never really left. Most Hindus describe this as an uninterrupted communion between the real self and the divine, in which the distinction between the two is preserved while the separation is overcome. Others, however, prefer to picture it as a complete merger between the real self and the divine, in which both separation and distinction are overcome. For the majority of Hindus, this is a far-distant goal. Most simply look forward to living better lives throughout successive reincarnations. Hindus believe that all persons, without exception, will eventually reach a state of liberation.

Hindus recognize *many divine beings*, gods and goddesses as well as other spiritual beings. Worship and ritual, both personal and corporate, can bring people into communion with these beings. Hindu worship life revolves around the home altar, which is an important part of most Hindus' homes. The altar will probably have a statue or statues of the chosen deity or deities. After ceremonial cleansing, people make offerings of fruit, incense, or flowers to their deities. They see the deity in the image and in return are seen by the deity. The food offered to the deity may then be eaten by the worshiper as a part of the deity's blessing. Some people perform this ritual, or *puja*, twice daily, while some perform it only in the mornings. While approximately 75 percent of Hindu women perform daily devotions for the benefit of their families, only about half of Hindu men do so. Puja is also performed in *temples*, where it is more elaborate.

Each god and goddess has a festival day, and these are celebrated with worship at the temple. Other religious holidays are celebrated as well. Often, weekly worship is also held, usually fitted into the common Sunday morning time period. This is a distinctive feature of Hinduism in America, a key aspect of its accommodation to the non-Hindu culture. It resembles worship at the home altar, with the addition of readings from sacred texts, a sermon or lecture, and devotional songs. Many temples in the United States have become social centers for the Indian community, as well, and sponsor a number of social events, in addition to holding classes for children and adults.

Priests associated with the temple—who may hold other jobs as well—also perform life-cycle rites such as birth rituals, weddings, and funerals for Hindu families. Hindus who do not live close enough to attend a temple regularly can request that puja or other services be performed at a distant temple in return for a financial contribution. While most temples in India are dedicated to one primary deity, those in the United States are often dedicated to several. Many deities may share space on an altar, or there may be different altars dedicated to different deities.

The moral life is one that coincides with the natural order of the universe. What it means to live by the dharma differs, depending on a person's place in the society, stage in life, and gender. There are also ethical prescriptions and proscriptions that are constant.

Hinduism recognizes four goals of human life, all consistent with the living of an ethical life. These goals pull together diverse elements of life into a unified whole. Each is appropriate in its place, as long as we recognize that only the last one can provide ultimate satisfaction. They are the

> *joy* cluster (sensual, sexual, artistic, aesthetic joys, compatible with ethics), the *economic and social fulfillment* cluster, the *morality* cluster (duties, obligations, right action, law, righteousness, general virtues and supreme ethical virtues . . .), and the *spiritual goal of salvation/liberation* (union and oneness with God).[5]

Because all *life is sacred*, noninjury or nonharming, *ahimsa*, is a central moral virtue. This is why most Hindus refrain from eating meat or eat it very sparingly. Many avoid fish and eggs as well. Noninjury is practiced because there is the divine in everything and also because harm done to another returns to oneself by the law of karma.

Hinduism provides other moral guidelines for its adherents. Traditionally these largely have been determined by the caste structure. The role of caste is very much muted for American Hindus. One summary statement of Hindu morality specifically for American Hindus gives this guidance, understood to apply to everyone:

> We should be uplifting to our fellow man, not critical or injurious. We should be loving and kind, not hateful or mean. We should express the soul's beautiful qualities of self-control, modesty and honesty. We should be a good example to others and a joy to be around, not a person to be avoided.[6]

Hindu morality has also been spelled out traditionally in ten things to be avoided and ten things to be practiced. The ten things from which people should abstain include injuring any living being, lying, stealing, misuse of the senses, impatience and intolerance, lack of steadfastness and perseverance, insensitivity, dishonesty and deception, overeating and eating meat, fish, and eggs,[7] and impurity. The ten practices to be observed include modesty, contentment, giving, faith, devotion, the study of scripture, spiritual development, fulfilling religious observances, especially life-cycle rites, the chanting of mantras or sacred sounds, and austerity. As with other religious peoples, Hindus vary widely in the extent to which they observe these moral guidelines and which ones they consider most important for their own life.

[5]Dr. T.K. Venkateswaran, "A Portrait of Hinduism," in Joel Beversluis, ed. *A Sourcebook for the Community of Religions* (Chicago: The Council for a Parliament of the World's Religions, 1993), pp. 62–66 (italics in original).

[6]Satguru Sivaya Subramuniyaswami, *Dancing with Śiva: Hinduism's Contemporary Catechism* (Concord, CA: Himalayan Academy, 1993), p. 181.

[7]Hindus do use dairy products. Clarified butter, called ghee, is important not only in Indian cooking but in rituals. Meat, fish, and eggs are held to contain the life force in a way that dairy does not.

No one religion embodies the only way to salvation or liberation. As there are any number of ways to climb a mountain, say most Hindus, so there are many paths to reunite with the divine. Such a view does not rule out having personal preferences among these ways, nor does it necessitate approval of them all. Most Hindus believe all sincere seekers, by whatever path or paths they choose, will in time arrive at their destination.

The Diversity of Hinduism: Ways of Liberation

Within itself as well, Hinduism offers people more than one way to seek release and liberation. These ways are not exclusive; people usually follow more than one, accenting one over the others and perhaps changing emphases during a lifetime. People differ in their personalities, in their stage and station in life, and no one method will be best for all. Finding the *appropriate* path for the individual is more important than following a single path believed to be correct. This multiplicity of paths accounts for a lot of the manifold variation in how Hindus live out their faith on a day-to-day basis.

One very popular way is *devotion to a god or goddess.* By increasingly identifying with their chosen god or goddess, people increase their intuitive grasp of the oneness of themselves and the divine. Many Hindus worship *Shiva,* and many others are devotees of *Vishnu or of Krishna or Rama, both his avatars or manifestations,* gods whose concern for human beings is paramount. Others are devotees of the *Great Goddess,* who takes many forms. Deities are worshiped by prayer and offerings to their images at home altars and in temples. Deity worship personalizes the divine, giving the devotee the opportunity for a warmly emotional relationship with the sacred. It satisfies the human longing for knowing and being known by the sacred just as we know and are known by a lover, close friend, or family member.

Hindu religious art abounds with images of deities, both pictures and statues. Statues are especially important. It may be difficult for you to understand the role that images of gods and goddesses play in Hinduism. For Hindus, *seeing the divine* is a basic way of experiencing communion with the sacred. The divine is present precisely *as* the image, giving itself for worship. These are not idols. The clay or the brass of the statue is not worshiped; rather the deity whom it portrays and makes present to the devotee is worshiped.

A second popular way to seek liberation is through *work* or *action.* To follow this way means to do what is called for by one's position in life, without allowing oneself to become attached to the results of the action. Neither hope of reward nor fear of punishment is the motivation here, but simply the presence of a duty to be done. Scripture says that people have a right to their actions but not to the fruits of those actions. Attachment to the results of what we do binds us in the cycle of reincarnation. To whatever extent our action is selfless, without thought of "what's in it for me?" we lessen the grip of karma, according to Hindu belief. This path makes the ongoing flow of daily life the way to liberation.

For countless generations of Indian Hindus, for whom survival in the face of extreme poverty and climatic conditions is problematic, this allows for religious

Figure 12-1   This "dancing Shiva" statue represents the Hindu God as both creator and destroyer. *(Photo by the author.)*

fulfillment without having to do something additional. For contemporary American Hindus caught up in the realities of professional and business life combined with family and community responsibilities, it offers the same hope. Beyond that, it affords the opportunity to transform the dailyness of life into something sacred and meaningful.

For students, this would mean, for example, studying, attending class, and doing homework simply because they are students, rather than in order to get a good grade on the test and succeed in the class. For professors, it would mean carrying out the tasks expected of us without having an eye on the next promotion or other professional recognition. Making daily life the focus of spiritual liberation calls for acting rightly *because* it is right, not because it will produce beneficial results.

Other, less widely practiced, ways of liberation include intense study and *contemplation* of sacred writings, the physical disciplines of *yoga*, and the intensive practice of *meditation*.

Women in Hinduism

Hinduism's attitude toward women has always been highly ambivalent. On the one hand, the Great Goddess is worshiped and adored in all her manifestations. The major gods have their female consorts. Female energy is important in the attainment of liberation in certain approaches to meditation. In Vedic times, women were educated, participated in religious rituals, and were recognized as scholars, poets, and teachers.

On the other hand, women have been relegated to second-class citizenship throughout most of the Hindu world. Arranged marriages often took place when a girl was very young, and submission to one's husband has often been considered a woman's paramount virtue. The practice of a widow burning herself on her husband's funeral pyre (now outlawed in India) highlights the dreadful situation of a woman without a man.

Hindu women in the United States are primarily cosmopolitan and educated. They move in social circles that include professionals, administrators, and managers. Their lives are less determined by the Hindu tradition regarding women than by their position in American society. However, temple leadership is usually limited to male priests, with women having a role to play as teachers of children. Typically, women are the ones who maintain the tradition of worship at their home altar for the benefit of their families.

Hinduism in the United States

The number of Hindus in the United States is small—less than 0.5 percent of the population. Nearly all Hindus are either Asian immigrants or their descendants; fewer Westerners have become Hindus than have embraced either Islam or Buddhism. As you saw with Arab Americans, most Asian Americans are Christians. With a few exceptions, Hindus have not sought converts. The largest concentrations are in the Los Angeles, San Francisco, New York City, and Chicago metropolitan areas. Many Hindus now living in the United States are professionals, intellectuals, and upper-level management personnel. Many have come here to work in the technology or medical fields.

The variety of Hindu groups in the United States reflects the many forms in which Hinduism has taken root here. Some offer Indian Hindus the opportunity to maintain community and culture. Others are primarily ways for non-Indians to become involved with Hinduism. Many now serve both functions.

The *Vedanta Society*[8] was founded in 1894 by Swami Vivekananda. He came to the United States for the 1893 Parliament of the World's Religions and remained here. It was the first Hindu organization in the United States and is arguably the most influential on an intellectual level, although it is neither the largest nor the best known. Each Vedanta Center in the United States is a branch of the Ramakrishna Order, the monastic organization that Vivekananda founded in India. Although it initially appealed primarily to Euro-Americans with its "Protestantized" form of Hinduism, many Indian Hindu immigrants now find a spiritual home in Vedanta as well. It offers immigrant Hindus a highly assimilated form of Indian religion that emphasizes the universal over the ethnic.

---

[8]There is no national organization Web site for the Vedanta Society. One of the best is that of the Vedanta Society of New York, www.vedanta-newyork.org/

Vedanta seeks to incorporate the methods and ideals of all Hindu movements. It describes itself as "a federation of faiths and a commonwealth of spiritual concepts." It focuses on a core of essential truths:

- God is one; people worship him in different forms.
- Humanity, in its essential nature, is divine.
- The goal of humanity is to realize this divinity.
- The ways to realize this divinity are innumerable.[9]

Vedanta centers usually offer weekly worship that is similar to that already described for Hindu temples. They usually offer classes in various aspects of Hinduism as well. The leader, or *swami*, who is invited by a local Board of Trustees to come from the Ramakrishna Order in India, also gives private instruction to students. The organization also operates Vedanta Press, a source for Hindu religious literature and other relevant books.

As Diana Eck points out, Vedanta has become very American in some ways. Its Sunday morning services take place in rooms called *chapels* with chairs to sit on. It has weekday study classes. On the other hand, leadership has remained in the hands of Ramakrishna monks from India, without an indigenous American leadership developing.[10]

The primary embodiment of Hindu devotionalism in the United States is the daily and weekly worship that Hindus perform in their homes and in temples. The *International Society for Krishna Consciousness*[11] (also known as ISKCON or the *Hare Krishna Movement*) is an organizational embodiment of Hindu devotionalism. It was founded in the United States by His Divine Grace A. C. Bhaktivedanta Swami Prabhupada (1896–1977) in 1965. The Krishna Consciousness movement emphasizes union with the divine attained through ecstatic devotion to Krishna. The Movement describes its mission as promoting

> the well being of society by teaching the science of Krishna consciousness according to the *Bhagavad-Gita* and other ancient Vedic scriptures of India.[12]

Members follow five rules of conduct: (1) They do not eat meat, fish, or eggs. (2) They do not use intoxicating drinks or plants, including tobacco, alcohol, coffee, and tea. (3) They may not gamble. (4) Any sexual activity between people who are not married to each other or marital sex except for procreation is prohibited. Finally, (5) the name of Krishna is to be chanted daily in a prescribed ritual.

Devotees who choose to devote full time to the movement and live in the temples follow a rigid schedule of devotion and work. There are also opportunities for those who cannot or do not wish to enter this fully into the community. Devotees, whether living in the temple or not, give very high priority to

---

[9]Diana Eck, *A New Religious America*, p.102.
[10]Ibid., p. 104.
[11]www.iskcon.com/
[12]"International Society for Krishna Consciousness Fact Sheet," (Alachua, FL: ISKCON Foundation, 1990).

Figure 12-2 Congregational members of the International Society for Krishna Consciousness live and work in the general community, practicing Krishna consciousness in their own homes and attending the temple on a regular basis. *(Photo courtesy of the International Society for Krishna Consciousness.)*

sankirtan, daily chanting of the *mantra*. Mantra chanting has been a part of Hindu religious practice since its earliest times. Mantras—spiritual phrases—help to focus the mind and are believed to have power in and of themselves to align the devotee's consciousness with the deity.

Krishna Consciousness members practice chanting the Hare Krishna mantra, a song of praise to the Lord Krishna, as the best way to find union with the divine (the *a* in Rama is soft, as *ah*, and *hare* is pronounced *ha-ray*):

> Hare Krishna, Hare Krishna (Praise to Krishna, Praise to Krishna)
> Krishna Krishna, Hare Hare (Krishna, Krishna, Praise, Praise)
> Hare Rama, Hare Rama (Praise to Rama, Praise to Rama)
> Rama Rama, Hare Hare! (Rama, Rama, Praise, Praise!)

The Krishna Consciousness Movement teaches that this one mantra is the mantra for everyone in this present age, rather than following the more traditional practice that requires that mantras be given individually by gurus and kept secret.

Temples are always open to visitors, who are welcomed into a world that may make them feel as if they have been magically transported to India itself. There are about fifty ISKCON temples in the United States, as well as six farm communities and six vegetarian restaurants. The organization claims about 3,000 fully initiated members and an additional 500,000 lay members who participate in temple activities at least monthly.

Besides the temples, farm communities, and restaurants, the Society operates the Bhaktivedanta Book Trust for the publication of literature on Indian philosophy and religion. It also publishes *Back to Godhead: The Magazine of the Hare Krishna Movement*. Its "Food for Life" program distributes meals at no cost to those who are in need of food. This program is an outgrowth of the custom of sponsoring a free meal every Sunday at the temples, which began in the very early days of the movement.

The rigorous monastic life and the sometimes aggressive solicitation of Krishna's American devotees have marked them off as distinctive and unusual. There can be little doubt, however, about the sincerity and devotion of these followers of an Indian deity whose main attribute is his desire to help struggling human beings attain release from spiritual suffering.

There are many different Hindu groups in the United States that are based on some form of yoga. The *Self-Realization Fellowship*[13] is typical of these. It was founded by a Bengali Indian, Paramahansa Yogananda, in 1925. Yogananda (1893–1952) taught in this country for more than thirty years. It was the most popular Hindu movement in the United States for nearly forty years.

Yogananda taught the classical form of yogic meditation outlined in the *Yoga Sutras* of Patanjali. His teaching and the practices that he developed are based on the traditional Hindu belief that the divine is within each person and can be experienced directly through meditation. Having experienced it in meditation, people can come to manifest it increasingly in everyday life. According to the Self-Realization Fellowship:

> The science of Yoga offers a direct means of stilling the natural turbulence of thoughts and restlessness of body which prevent us from knowing what we really are. By practicing the step-by-step methods of Yoga . . . we come to know our oneness with the Infinite Intelligence, Power, and Joy which gives life to all and which is the essence of our own Self. . . . [The] inner fulfillment we seek *does* exist and *can* be attained. In actuality, all the knowledge, creativity, love, joy, and peace we are looking for are right within us, the very essence of our beings. All we have to do is realize this.[14]

The Self-Realization Fellowship emphasizes that the techniques they teach and practice do not have to be accepted on authority or faith but can be tested in the life of each person. It is a scientific method for self-discovery and realization. Awareness and consciousness, that is, energy, are withdrawn from outward concerns and redirected inward toward the goal of self-realization. There are several temples and many more meditation centers in the United States, as well as a program of correspondence study. The centers offer classes, workshops, and weekly devotional experiences. Besides laypeople who participate in the centers' activities, there are renunciants who have chosen to pursue liberation more arduously and remain celibate, spending extensive time in meditation and study.

[13]www.yogananda-srf.org
[14]*Undreamed-of Possibilities: An Introduction to Self-Realization: The Teachings of Paramahansa Yogananda* (Los Angeles: Self-Realization Fellowship, 1982), pp. 5 and 3 (italics in original).

There are several umbrella organizations of Hindus in the United States. The oldest is likely the VHPA, the Vishwa Hindu Parishad of America.[15] Its efforts include promoting Hindu unity and representing Hindu organizations and institutions in the United States, raising awareness of Hinduism, providing community service, and making Hindu values available. The Hindu Student Council,[16] an organization specifically for college students and other young people, is a spin-off of VHPA. It also gave rise to American Hindus Against Defamation, modeled on the Jewish B'nai B'rith Anti-Defamation League. These and similar organizations attempt to articulate what it means to be both American and Hindu and to correct the widespread misperceptions of Hinduism that still exist in the United States. They help immigrant American Hindus become full participants in American society, while maintaining their religious and cultural distinctiveness.

AMERICAN BUDDHISTS AND BUDDHISM

Buddhism has made its way into American culture to a greater extent than has Hinduism, and in general it is better known among non-Asian Americans. As with Hinduism, I will outline the basics of Buddhism, with the understanding

Figure 12-3   Buddhist Temple on Oahu, Hawaii. *(Photo by the author.)*

[15]www.vhp-america.org
[16]http://www.hscnet.org/

that interpretation and practice among individual Buddhists and Buddhist groups can be quite variable.

As a young man, the Hindu prince Siddhartha Gautama became very distressed over the inevitable suffering of human life—aging, sickness, and death, among other things. Although born to a noble life, he renounced his life of privilege and set out in search of a resolution to the spiritual unrest that plagued him. According to Buddhist tradition, he found what he sought during meditation, discovering the way to freedom from the burden of suffering. He then went about teaching what he had learned to other people and founded an organization based on his teachings. His followers called him *the Buddha*, which means *the awakened* (or *enlightened*) *one*.

The New England Transcendentalists, with their interest in things oriental, helped prepare the way for Buddhism in the United States on an intellectual level, as they did for Hinduism. Sir Edwin Arnold's poetic account of the life of the Buddha, *The Light of Asia* (1879), was one early way in which Euro-Americans became acquainted with Buddhism.

Like Hinduism, Buddhism has a number of different sacred writings. The *Pali Canon* records what Buddhists take to be the teachings of the Buddha himself after his Enlightenment. Its importance is agreed upon by the great majority of Buddhists. Beyond that, various Buddhist subgroups rely on several additional scriptures.

Basic Buddhist Teachings

The Buddhist worldview is different from that of Hinduism in important respects, although there are similarities as well. Impermanence and the connectedness of all things are the central attributes of everything that is. *Impermanence* points to the Buddhist belief that everything changes. Everything in the universe, including ourselves, is part of a vast, interconnected process. What underlies the universe as we observe it is not the eternal, changeless absolute of Hinduism, but constant change, constant becoming. Connectedness points to the belief that nothing exists in and of itself. Everything that exists does so with endless connections to all other things.

Buddhist beliefs about the nature of reality and of ourselves lead to a reinterpretation of rebirth, because there is no eternal self that goes through the rebirth process. Buddhists simply say that each lifetime is connected to the ones before it and will be connected to those that come after it in a chain of causation. What continues through the rebirth process are the habitual energies that have characterized the person's lifetime. The analogy of lighting the wick of one candle from the flame on another is often used. Nothing is transmitted from candle to candle, but the flame of the second is unarguably connected to the flame of the first.

The *Four Noble Truths* is a basic statement of Buddhist belief, attributed to the Buddha himself. It is an application of the Buddhist vision of the world to human life and the human problem. My interpretation loosely follows *The*

Heart of the Buddha's Teaching,[17] a contemporary interpretation of basic Buddhist teachings by Thich Nhat Hanh, a Vietnamese Buddhist monk whose work is widely appreciated in the United States.

1. All of life is marked by suffering. The Buddha was not, and Buddhists today are not, long-faced pessimists without joy and happiness. Quite the contrary! What the Buddha had in mind here is that, no matter how good life is, there is always an element of dissatisfaction about it. We feel things are not quite right. Birth and death, he said, cause suffering on either end of the life cycle. In between, there is illness, having to deal with things we do not like, and being separated from things that we do like. There is wanting more than we have or wanting something different than what we have. Pain in life is inevitable. However, suffering is not necessary. It is our response to pain, not something basic to existence, and it can be transformed.

2. We can know the causes of our suffering. The traditional interpretation holds that all suffering comes from inappropriately holding onto things that inevitably slip from our grasp. However, we can also see that there are other causes, such as anger, ignorance, suspicion, false pride, and various misunderstandings. The secret is to identify the cause of suffering clearly so that we can eliminate or at least modify it.

3. We can end our suffering. While we cannot avoid life's inevitable challenges and problems, we can limit their tendency to make us miserable. Healing is possible.

4. The Buddha proposed a method for accomplishing this goal. Buddhists call it the *Noble Eightfold Path*, sometimes called *the Path of Eight Right Practices*. It is a set of guidelines for living in a way that lessens suffering. Because the Buddha became enlightened by his own efforts, traditional Buddhists teach that people are responsible for bringing about their own liberation from suffering.

   • Right view is our ability to see things as they really are, changing and impermanent. It is also to have confidence that transformation is possible.
   • Right thinking is correct thinking, based on a sound understanding of reality.
   • Right mindfulness is living fully in the present moment without judging or reacting. It simply means appropriate awareness.
   • Right speech is to speak truthfully and compassionately, without exaggeration, harshness, or rudeness of speech.
   • Right action is observing the basics of Buddhist morality. Beyond that, it means acting with a balance of wisdom and compassion, always seeking the good.
   • Right effort is steady attention to weeding out negative and unhelpful ways of thinking and acting and replacing them with positive and helpful ways.
   • Right concentration deals directly with meditation techniques. Different schools of thought teach somewhat different techniques. What unites them is that meditation is used as a way of being fully aware in every moment, then letting that moment go, as a way of calming and focusing the mind and bringing home the fleeting nature of everything.
   • Right occupation says that one's occupation (which takes up a significant part of one's time) should not involve violating the moral precepts and should be such that it encourages peace and harmony, again striving for the good of all beings.

---

[17]Thich Nhat Hanh, *The Heart of the Buddha's Teaching: Transforming Suffering into Peace, Joy, and Liberation* (Berkeley, CA: Parallax Press, 1998), pp. 131–132, 21–22, and Chapters 9 through 16.

Like Hindus, Buddhists believe that there can be an end to the cycle of death and rebirth. This is the ultimate goal of the Eightfold Path. The Buddhist word for that goal is *Nirvana*. The Buddha did not speak very much about Nirvana, believing that doing so was not useful in the search for liberation. It certainly means living without dissatisfaction and thus with complete peace. It means the elimination of anything that separates the individual from everything else, that is, the end of the illusion of isolated existence. When someone who has reached this advanced state of spiritual awareness dies, he or she escapes from rebirth.

The *Three Treasures* (also, *Three Refuges*, or *Three Jewels*) is another way Buddhists summarize what is important in their faith. Although there is no affirmation of faith that is required to become a Buddhist nor any set formula that makes a person a Buddhist, the Refuges help to define what being a Buddhist means. Usually, when someone becomes a Buddhist by choice, they formally take the Three Refuges and the Five Precepts in the setting of a Buddhist community, or *Sangha*.

"I take refuge in the *Buddha*." To take refuge in the Buddha means to place one's trust and confidence in the Buddha having become the Enlightened One. For traditional Buddhists, especially, the Buddha is a human being, nothing more. That he, through his own effort and determination, was able to achieve liberation means that *any* person can do so, provided they are willing to make the effort.

"I take refuge in the Dharma." Buddhists use the word *Dharma* to refer primarily to the Buddha's teaching. To take refuge in the Dharma, then, means to have confidence in the Buddha's teachings as a true analysis of reality and as a way to accomplish what he accomplished. Many Buddhists also interpret it as a vote of confidence in our own capacity as human beings to comprehend reality as it truly is.

"I take refuge in the *Sangha*." Sangha has two levels of meaning. Narrowly, it is the community of Buddhist monks. For traditional Buddhists, liberation is possible only after one has become a monk. On a broader level, the *sangha* means the entire community of people, living and dead, who have walked the path to enlightenment mapped out by Gautama. Buddhists live in the certainty that they are not alone in their quest for enlightenment. Others walk with them on their journey.

Lama Surya Das, an American lama whose affiliation is with the Tibetan Dzogchen lineage, translates the Three Refuges in a way that links the traditional understanding with the practitioner's vow to practice:

> I go for refuge in the Buddha, the enlightened teacher;
> I commit myself to enlightenment;
> I go for refuge in the Dharma, the spiritual teachings;
> I commit myself to the truth as it is;
> I go for refuge in the Sangha, the spiritual community;
> I commit myself to living the enlightened life.[18]

---

[18]Lama Surya Das, *Awakening the Buddha Within: Eight Steps to Enlightenment: Tibetan Wisdom for the Western World* (New York: Broadway Books, 1997), p. 56.

Buddhist Morality and Ritual

Buddhist morality has already been mentioned as one of the steps on the Eightfold Path. One standard statement of Buddhist morality is the *Five Precepts*.

- Do not kill. Buddhists expand this precept to include not harming any living being, insofar as it is possible to avoid such harm. Positively, it means doing all that one can for the good of all beings on the earth. Nonviolence and noninjury are central in Buddhist ethics. Stated positively, the precept enjoins compassion for all beings.
- Do not steal. Again, Buddhists understand this as going beyond outright stealing. It also means not taking advantage, not appropriating anything that is not ours. Avoiding paying legitimate taxes is another example, as is borrowing and not returning an item. Positively, the precept urges an attitude of generosity with our time, resources, and talents.
- Refrain from wrongful sexual behavior. Complete abstinence outside of marriage has been the traditional rule. Buddhist monks and nuns are celibate. Sexual activity is regarded as appropriate only for committed couples. Buddhists disagree among themselves on the morality of same-sex relationships. Wrongful sexual behavior includes any behavior that degrades another person, as well as sexual behavior that might spread disease. This precept is about practicing loving, responsible relationships.
- Do not lie. Expanded, this includes refraining from saying anything that is hurtful, such as slander and gossip, rude and harsh speech, impolite language, running down other people, as well as idle chatter when silence would be better. Speak the truth with care, lovingly.
- Finally, Buddhists *avoid the use of intoxicants* of all kinds, such as alcohol and intoxicating drugs. Not all Buddhists take this as an absolute prohibition on an occasional drink, interpreting the precept as a ban on *intoxication* rather than on intoxicants. However one interprets this precept, its point is to keep a clear and sober mind.

The American Buddhist Sangha interprets the Precepts in language that reflects American concerns and ways of thinking: Respect for life, for personal property, for personal relationships, for truth, and for mental and physical well-being.[19]

Buddhism presses home the importance of cultivating proper attitudes and a proper frame of mind, so that outward actions flow freely from internal dispositions. Four attitudes are especially valued. Buddhists strive to cultivate loving-kindness and friendliness, compassion and empathy, joy and rejoicing, and equanimity and peace of mind.[20]

As do Hindus, Buddhists often have a small altar or shrine in their homes. A Buddha statue represents the historical Buddha and helps devotees focus on the Buddha nature within themselves, as well. Flowers symbolize enlightenment and a candle or altar light symbolizes the light of wisdom. Incense is often offered

[19]American Buddhist Sangha, www.awakeningthedragon.com
[20]This particular translation of the "four noblest qualities of mind" comes from Das, *Awakening the Buddha Within*, p. 292.

Figure 12-4   Meditation at the Ball State University Museum of Art. Many Buddhists in the United States meditate regularly. *(Photo courtesy of the Ball State University Recreation Services, and photographer Kevin Mealy.)*

in gratitude for the Three Refuges and other blessings. An offering of water represents cleansing and a food offering represents giving and the willingness to share what one has with other beings. As with their Hindu counterparts, individual Buddhists vary considerably in how much time they spend in meditation, chanting, prayer, and other personal or family devotional activities.

Meditation is central to Buddhist practice, and is one main focus of practice for many Buddhists in the United States. There are three aspects to Buddhist meditation. The first is developing one-pointed *concentration*, the ability to truly focus on or do one thing at a time. To do this, people often practice by concentrating on their breathing. The second is the development of *insight* into the true nature of reality. This facilitates experiencing reality as it is, without getting caught up in conceptualizations of it. The third is the extension of these attitudes into daily living as *mindfulness* in everyday life. Put simply, although it is far from simple to attain, this means being fully present in whatever one is doing in the present moment.

Buddhists who live where they can go to a temple may participate in activities that center around the natural rhythms of the lunar calendar. The holy days occur at the new moon, the full moon, and eight days after each, making them about a week apart. Many American temples have services for chanting and meditation every Sunday. Attendance at the temple is not required, and some Buddhists participate much more than others. There is a religious new year festival in the spring, and the Buddha's birthday is widely celebrated. Temples also offer classes, conduct special rituals for the passages of life, and serve as social centers. Like Hindu temples, they help immigrant Buddhists to assimilate to American culture while preserving their unique heritage too.

Women and Buddhism

Traditional ideas about women and women's capabilities persisted in Buddhism even as in Hinduism. At the same time, Buddhism allowed for the establishment of orders of nuns. The rules established for nuns, however, guaranteed submission of nuns to monks and ensured that their number would remain small. That they existed and continue to exist, however, is significant.

One of the ways that Buddhism has changed as it has come West has been that greater gender equality in the West has forced the issue within the Buddhist community. American women have been and continue to be interested in Buddhism, and their increased participation, especially in leadership positions, contributes distinctive accents to the practice of American Buddhism.

Specific changes that can be traced to the influence of women include greater egalitarianism and warmth in relationships between teachers and students, increased emphasis on working with the emotions and with the body, emphasis on sharing and openness, downplaying of traditional themes such as effort and striving in favor of themes of healing and openness, and a strongly activist orientation.[21]

Buddhist theologian Rita Gross describes some of the ways in which American Buddhist women have changed and continue to change the face of American Buddhism.[22]

- American Buddhist women are highly active in meditation and teaching centers, providing perhaps the most noticeable evidence of these evolving changes. Women practice side by side with men, and frequently they are the majority of practitioners.
- As a result, male-dominated language in readings and chants is becoming more gender-inclusive.

[21]Joseph B. Tamney, *American Society in the Buddhist Mirror* (New York: Garland Publishing, 1992), p. 95.
[22]Rita Gross, "How American Women Are Changing Buddhism," Shambhala Sun (July, 2005), available on the Shambhala Sun Web site, www.shambhalasun.com.

- The number of fully trained and authorized female Dharma teachers has increased.
- The notable female practitioners in Buddhist history are being honored. Written records of the accomplishments of early Buddhist women are being tapped as a resource for Buddhist women.
- Accounts of sexual scandals between male teachers and female students in the 1960s and 1970s have resulted in nearly all Buddhist communities developing guidelines to prevent abuses.
- To allow female practitioners the same opportunities as men, meditation centers have developed childcare facilities, and Buddhist fathers are taking on childcare responsibilities so that their wives can practice.
- Increasing attention is being paid to how to raise Buddhist children in a non-Buddhist culture.

The Diversity of Buddhism in the United States

Three distinctive strands of Buddhism—Theravada, Mahayana, and Tibetan—evolved in Asia, and all three of these forms have a significant presence in the United States. As with other religions, these diverse strands of Buddhism share a common core of basic understanding but interpret it differently and practice in different ways. Each of these three major groups has subgroups within it, as well. The scriptural base of all three is the Pali Canon, also called the *Tripitaka* or Three Baskets, consisting of sayings of the Buddha, monastic discipline, and basic Buddhist teachings.

The oldest form of Buddhism is the *Theravada* or tradition of the elders, sometimes called *monastic* or *foundational Buddhism*. It adheres strictly to the Tripitaka, without using additional scriptures. Theravada Buddhism focuses on the Buddha as a human, historical figure, and its adherents believe there is only one Buddha in any given age. Enlightenment, liberation, or Nirvana is believed to be a plane of existence vastly different from the daily round of life, called *samsara*, attainable only after many lifetimes of strenuous self-effort. The necessary focus and effort to finally attain the wisdom that brings enlightenment are possible only for monks in a monastery. Laypeople have their own path, no less important than the monastic life, but distinctively different. They support the monks, receive teachings from them, and participate in important life-cycle rituals to mark the turning points in their lives.

Theravada is the Buddhism of Southeast Asia, in countries such as Sri Lanka, Myanmar, Laos, Thailand, Cambodia, and Vietnam. In the United States, Theravada Buddhism is largely practiced by immigrant communities from these Southeast Asia nations, many of whom have come here as refugees because of the political turmoil in that area.

The Theravada community in the United States grew rapidly with the influx of immigrants from nations torn by the military conflict in Southeast Asia. However, there was already a small Theravada presence in the United States. A small number of Euro-Americans visited Asian Buddhist temples in the 1960s and 1970s, and some came back committed to practicing meditation in the *Vipassana* or insight tradition of Theravada.

The predominantly Vietnamese Phap Luan Buddhist Culture Center[23] in Houston, Texas, can serve as an example of Theravada in the United States. Phap Luan was founded in 1993 and now has eight resident monks and about 800 members. It draws as many as 1,500 people for major festivals, although average attendance at weekly events is about 150. The center provides rituals for life's transitions and for Buddhist festival days. The monks conduct classes on Buddhism and on meditation and offer a meditation retreat four times annually for those who wish to engage in intensive meditation. Chanted weekend services are done in much the same way as in Southeast Asia. The chanting is followed by silent meditation and a Dharma talk. Other activities round out the morning, and many people bring lunch and stay for meetings or work in the afternoon. There are evidences of Phap Luan's adaptation to American culture, especially as the proportion of second-generation Vietnamese born in this country increases. English is used more, and the congregation sits on pews rather than on mats or cushions on the floor. Some wear their shoes in the shrine room. Although in Vietnam people tended to consider meditation something to be done by the monks, laypeople in America are more interested in learning to meditate themselves.[24]

Translating Asian monasticism into the American context, in which there is no widespread monastic tradition, is difficult. So far, even in traditional Theravada communities, very few of the second generation choose to be ordained as monks. Leadership must come from Asia. Monks, too, find they must adapt the letter of the monastic code to the realities of life in the United States. It is often necessary to drive, for example, and many have adopted the custom of shaking hands with women and men alike, while traditionally, touching women in any way is forbidden by the monastic code.[25]

The insight meditation practice of Theravada Buddhism has also appealed to Euro-Americans, and centers have been founded to accommodate those who want to engage in serious Buddhist study and meditation. The Insight Meditation Society and Barre Center for Buddhist Studies is one of the largest and best-known centers. The Insight Meditation Society describes Vipassana or insight meditation as

> the simple and direct practice of moment-to-moment mindfulness. Through careful and sustained observation, we experience for ourselves the ever-changing flow of the mind/body process. This awareness leads us to accept more fully the pleasure and pain, fear and joy, sadness and happiness that life inevitably brings. As insight deepens, we develop greater equanimity and peace in the face of change, and wisdom and compassion increasingly become the guiding principles of our lives.[26]

[23]Phap Luan does have a Web site, but as of this writing, it is only in Vietnamese.
[24]Robert Wuthnow, *America and the Challenges of Religious Diversity* (Princeton, NJ: Princeton University Press, 2005), pp. 47–49.
[25]Diana L. Eck, *A New Religious America: How a "Christian Country" Has Become the World's Most Religiously Diverse Nation* (New York: HarperSanFrancisco, 2001), p. 161.
[26]Insight Meditation Society, www.dharma.org.

There are perhaps around 150 insight meditation centers in the United States. Books, tapes, and CDs have helped bring this form of meditation to a wider audience as well.

Mahayana Buddhism, also known as the "Greater Vehicle," is a more liberalized form of Buddhism. It uses additional scriptures, called *sutras*, alongside the Tripitaka. For Mahayanists, the Buddha is not only a human, historical figure but is a transcendent being who has taken many forms. Further, every living being has Buddha nature and thus is capable of becoming a Buddha. Bodhisattvas are the ideal figures in this tradition, compassionate beings who delay their own liberation in order to work toward the liberation of all. For Mahayanists, all human beings are moving together toward enlightenment, and liberation is an appropriate goal for all persons, not only for monks. Mahayana also has orders of nuns and an ordained priesthood. Nirvana and the daily round of life are not different planes of existence, but are one and the same. How we experience it depends on our own attitude. Mahayana Buddhists use meditation and study as tools on the spiritual path, as do Theravadins. Additionally, however, they emphasize faith and devotion to the Buddha and to bodhisattvas, who are active helpers in the quest for enlightenment and freedom. Of the twin Buddhist virtues of wisdom and compassion, Mahayanists emphasize compassion, whereas Theravadins emphasize wisdom. According to Mahayana, compassion can lead one to freedom as surely as, and perhaps more so than, can wisdom.

Mahayana Buddhism is found in China and Japan, as well as in Korea, and to a lesser extent in Southeast Asia. It has come to the United States with immigrants from these Asian nations. It first arrived on American soil with Chinese people who were brought here to work in the late 1700s through the 1850s on the west coast. Early temples were built in Chinatown in San Francisco, and others followed up and down the west coast and into the Rocky Mountain region. Now such temples can be found across the nation. These temples still play a large role in the life of immigrant communities, serving not only religious but social needs as well. Many are small, with some in converted houses and storefronts; others are large and elaborate temple complexes.

Immigration increased dramatically during the Gold Rush in California, and soon thereafter the Chinese Exclusion Act of 1882 was passed. Although the Chinese Exclusion Act was repealed in 1943, broader legislation that prohibited Asians from entering the United States took effect in 1924. It was not, however, until the passage of the Hart-Celler Act of 1965 that Asians again came to the United States in significant numbers. This, coupled with an already-existing interest in Asian religions greatly strengthened the presence and visibility of Buddhism in America.

The Hsi Lai Temple near Los Angeles is a distinctively Chinese American Buddhist institution. Built by Buddhists from Taiwan, it is reputed to be the largest Buddhist temple in the Western hemisphere. The name *Hsi Lai* itself means "coming to the West." It is related to the Fo Kuang Shan temple complex in Taiwan, which advocates humanistic Buddhism, which is clearly described on the Web site:

> Humanistic Buddhism . . . embraces all traditions and schools and stresses the salient teachings of the Buddha, which are relevant to and essential for the well being and progress of humanity in modern times. We at Hsi Lai are committed to serving as a bridge between East and West so that the Buddha's teachings of kindness, compassion, joyfulness, and equanimity might be integrated into our lives and of those around us to the benefit of all and that we might learn the ways to cultivate the wisdom to clearly understand the true nature of all things.[27]

Hsi Lai has a membership of over 20,000, most of whom are immigrants from Taiwan, and houses nearly one hundred monastics, most of whom are nuns. Other facilities include a conference center whose auditorium has state-of-the-art translation capability, a museum, a library, bookstore, and a cafeteria. Its many social service activities include food baskets at Thanksgiving and Christmas for those in need, community dinners, meditation classes at a drug dependency center, visitation with prisoners, weekend classes for children, and meditation retreats for non-Chinese people. Its high altar has three large Buddhas. Shakyamuni, the historical Buddha, is in the center. Flanking him are statues of Amida Buddha, the Buddha of the Pure Land tradition, and the Medicine Buddha, who promises healing of body and mind.[28]

Jodo Shinshu (often called simply *Shin*) or Pure Land Buddhism is an especially interesting example of Buddhist adaptation to American culture because it has been deeply affected by the internment of Japanese citizens during World War II. Shin is lay-oriented, devotional Buddhism and is the predominant form of Buddhism among Japanese Americans.

Even before anti-Japanese sentiment led to significant changes, this form of Buddhism already bore a striking resemblance to Protestant Christianity, although there are important differences as well. Shin Buddhists believe that we are incapable of bringing about our own liberation. It is only by faith in Amida Buddha that people can be reborn in his Pure Land, from which enlightenment and liberation are easily attained. There are significant differences, however. Shin Buddhists do not believe in a God as do Jews, Christians, and Muslims, nor do they believe that human beings have eternal souls. The human problem is considered to be ignorance rather than sin. Nor is there any absolute, divinely revealed scripture.

Diana Eck describes this juxtaposition of Protestant form and Buddhist content in her visit to a Shin temple:

> The ritual idiom reminded me of my hometown Methodist Church in Bozeman, Montana. We stood for a hymn, sat for a scripture reading, stood for a responsive reading, just as I had all my life. And yet the content was Buddhist, and the overall feeling I had as a worshiper was of a Methodist-Buddhist blend.[29]

---

[27]http://www.hsilai.org/english/index.htm. The site also offers a virtual tour of the temple complex.
[28]Diana Eck, *A New Religious America*, pp. 143–147.
[29]Diana Eck, *A New Religious America*, pp. 172–173.

The organization changed its name to the Buddhist Churches of America[30] in 1944. Churches often have pews on either side of a center aisle leading up to the altar. Sunday morning services are frequently in English or in a combination of English and Japanese. There may be chanting, but there will probably also be hymns. The priest usually gives a sermon, and people of all ages can attend Dharma school classes. Shin Buddhists have taken the lead in developing educational materials for children, as they have been in the United States for four or even five generations. After the service, the congregation gathers in the fellowship hall for refreshments and conversation. Many Shin congregations offer weekday and weeknight activities for the congregation and reach out into their communities with a range of social service projects.

When Euro-Americans in the United States think of Buddhism, they think of the Zen tradition (*Ch'an* in Chinese). It is in many ways a quite different style of being Buddhist than Shin and has appealed more to Westerners. Zen Buddhists were among the representatives at the World's Parliament of Religion in 1893, and travelers had been bringing back their impressions of Zen before that. Like Shin, Zen is one form of the great Mahayana tradition in Buddhism. Its focus, however, is different in that it focuses on the practice of *Zazen*, or sitting meditation. Meditation is deemed a more reliable means to come to the direct experience of reality than is scripture study or any other form of theoretical understanding.

Eido Tai Shimano Roshi, Abbot of the Zen Studies Society, describes Zen in a way that helps us understand its appeal to Euro-Americans:

The special transmission of Zen is the realization of the Buddha's enlightenment itself, in one's own life, in one's own time. . . .

In ordinary experience, being and doing are separated: what one does is cut off from what one is, and conversely. Such separation leads inevitably to the condition of self-alienation. Particularly in this century, this condition has become acute. With time and sincere effort in Zazen practice, mind and body, inside and outside, self and other are experienced as one. . . .

The second and more difficult aim is the actualization of the Bodhisattva (Enlightened Being) ideal. As one's practice ripens, one becomes more alive, more creative; filled with the longing to actualize the Bodhisattva spirit in every moment and every aspect of daily life.[31]

There are many Zen centers for meditation and study throughout the United States, some quite small and some vast and complex. The Indianapolis Zen Center[32] in Indiana is part of the Korean Kwan Um school of Zen, although the vast majority of its members are not Koreans. The Center offers a five-days-per-week schedule of chanting, sitting, and walking mediation, with a Dharma talk and fellowship time added on Sunday mornings. It also has a

[30]www.buddhistchurchesofamerica.com
[31]www.amacord.com/taste/essays/zen.html
[32]www.indyzen.org/

Foundations of Zen class, monthly open houses, and one-day, weekend, and weeklong retreats for the intensive practice of meditation.

The Zen Community of New York (ZCNY) is one among the better-known Zen centers in the United States. ZCNY exemplifies engaged Buddhism, an expression of the Buddhist tradition that has had widespread interest in the United States. It blends rigorous Zen Buddhism with social activism that reflects the bodhisattva vow to help save all sentient beings. In addition to a full schedule of meditation, classes, interviews with leading teachers, and retreats, some of its social action initiatives include employment initiatives for those who are often deemed unemployable, eighteen apartments for homeless families, with childcare and other tenant-support services, and Maitri Center, a medical center for persons with HIV/AIDS, for whom Issan House provides a place to live. The Zen Mountains and Rivers Order, of which it is a part, also sponsors a Zen Environmental Studies Institute and the National Buddhist Prison Sangha.

A brief consideration of *Soka Gakkai* will round out our discussion of some of the ways in which Mahayana Buddhism is present in the United States. What distinguishes Soka Gakkai among American Buddhisms is that it has the most diverse membership in terms of ethnicity and class than any other convert-centered form of American Buddhism. Most Euro-American Buddhist groups are predominantly white and upper middle to upper class, well educated, and in professional or managerial occupations. There are two groups within this tradition in the United States: Soka Gakkai International(SGI)-USA,[33] with a greater number of centers and followers, and Nichiren Shoshu,[34] which is considerably smaller. They divided in 1991 over disagreements about religious authority. Both stem from the interpretation of Buddhism taught by Nichiren Daishonin, a thirteenth-century Japanese priest, and honor the Lotus Sutra as the preeminent Buddhist scripture.

Members of SGI-USA practice for both their own happiness and the well-being of others, emphasizing the importance of creating a peaceful society. The Preamble to the SGI International charter states:

> We believe that Nichiren Daishonin's Buddhism, a humanistic philosophy of infinite respect for the sanctity of life and all-encompassing compassion, enables individuals to cultivate and bring forth their inherent wisdom and, nurturing the creativity of the human spirit, to surmount the difficulties and crises facing humankind and realize a society of peaceful and prosperous coexistence.[35]

The major practice of Soka Gakkai Buddhists is daily chanting of the name of the Lotus Sutra (Nam Myoho Renge Kyo), parts of the Sutra and other ritual chants, along with prayers, before a home altar. Along with this, faith in the practice and working to study and spread their faith are the cornerstones of this form of Buddhism.

---

[33]www.sgi-usa.org
[34]www.nst.org
[35]www.sgi-usa.org

Soka Gakkai began as the largest lay affiliate within Nichiren Shoshu Buddhism. When the two groups went their separate ways, Soka Gakkai developed along egalitarian lines and evolved further into social engagement based on the bodhisattva ideal of compassionate concern for all living beings. Nichiren Shoshu retained its focus on priestly authority and the preservation of ritual practice. Soka Gakkai also moved in the direction of ecumenical dialogue with other Buddhist groups and interfaith dialogue with other religions. Nichiren Shoshu has resisted such dialogue, holding that their version of Buddhism is the one true faith to which all should adhere.

The last major form of Buddhism is that found in Tibet. It is often called Tibetan Buddhism, but is also called Tantrayana because it recognizes additional sacred writings called *Tantras*. Tantrayana brings a heightened ritualistic dimension to Buddhism. Tibetan Buddhists use precise hand gestures called *mudras*, specific vocal sounds or words called *mantras*, and ritual diagrams called *mandalas* done in many different media. Like Mahayanists, Tibetan Buddhists believe that enlightenment is possible within this lifetime, on this earth, as well as on a completely different plane of existence. Lamas are distinctive figures within Tibetan Buddhism. They are believed to be incarnate bodhisattvas, the very power of enlightenment in human form. The Dalai Lama, the world leader of the Tibetan nation in exile in India, has become a well-known and revered figure worldwide. He is believed to be an incarnation of the Bodhisattva of Infinite Compassion who is known as Avalokita or Avalokiteshvara in India, Guan-Yin in China, Kannon in Japan, and Kwan-Um in Korea.

In addition to the distinctiveness contributed by Tibetan Buddhism's tantric dimension, both Theravada and Mahayana were present in Tibet. Tibetan monks and nuns took monastic vows that differed only in slight detail from those of the Theravada tradition. They also studied, debated, and contemplated the sutras of the Mahayana tradition. Within this context, some adherents also practiced tantric ritual and studied tantric texts. As a result, when Tibetan Buddhism came to the United States, it was the first time Americans encountered the full range of the Asian Buddhist tradition. Further, the multivalent Buddhism of Tibet had been finely tuned to become an instrument to foster the development within everyone of the Buddhahood promised by the Mahayana tradition. As such, it posed an alternative to Western culture that addressed not only religion but psychology, philosophy, science, medicine, government, ethics, and the arts.[36]

The Dalai Lama helped popularize Tibetan Buddhism in the United States as well. His writing and his frequent speaking tours engendered both curiosity and respect for the faith he lived. His book, *The Art of Happiness*,[37] spent nearly one hundred weeks on the *New York Times* bestseller list. Shambhala Publications, a major publisher of Tibetan Buddhist literature, has grown from a small bookstore to a widely recognized and respected publishing house.

[36]Prothero, *A Nation of Religions*, pp. 97–101.
[37]His Holiness the Dalai Lama and Howard C. Cutler, M.D., *The Art of Happiness* (New York: Riverhead Books, 1998).

Naropa University in Boulder, Colorado, is the only fully accredited university in the United States that is based on Buddhist principles. It translates these principles into what it calls contemplative education:

> Contemplative education is learning infused with the experience of awareness, insight and compassion for oneself and others, honed through the practice of sitting meditation and other contemplative disciplines. The rigor of these disciplined practices prepares the mind to process information in new and perhaps unexpected ways. Contemplative practice unlocks the power of deep inward observation, enabling the learner to tap into a wellspring of knowledge about the nature of mind, self and other that has been largely overlooked by traditional, Western-oriented liberal education.[38]

There is also a group of Euro-American lamas who are interpreting the Tibetan traditions in distinctively American forms. Lama Surya Das, born Jeffrey Miller in New York City, is one such figure.[39] He is a popular teacher and best-selling author who also leads rigorous meditation retreats.

The Karma Thegsum Choling Meditation Center in Columbus, Ohio, founded in 1997, exemplifies how the Tibetan tradition is both being preserved and adapted to its new American context. The group meets in a building that was formerly a church and follows a Sunday morning schedule that resembles that of Columbus' many Christian churches. Colorful prayer flags adorn the front of the small building that is close to one of Columbus' busiest interstate highway junctions. An early service for more experienced practitioners involves chanting, meditation, reading from transliterated Tibetan texts, and mantra recitation. A later, more general service follows, in which participants may either sit on chairs and engage in silent meditation or practice in walking meditation. Afterward, an adult Dharma school class focuses on Buddhist teachings. Refreshments are available in the fellowship hall. In addition to these Sunday morning activities, the center has meditation practice on Tuesdays and Thursdays, classes for those who are not members but are interested in learning more about Buddhism, and an Alcoholics Anonymous group.[40]

THE CALL OF THE ORIENT

Why do some Euro-Americans look to the East for inspiration and spiritual sustenance? The question is a complex one, without any easy answers. The "turn East" is often associated with the 1960s counterculture, and correctly so. However, it has shown its staying power into the opening decade of the twenty-first century, as interest in serious study and practice has grown.

[38]Naropa University, www.naropa.edu. There is a more extensive discussion of contemplative education on their site.
[39]www.surya.org/
[40]Karma Thegsum Choling Meditation Center, www.columbusktc.org

Certainly some are drawn by the lure of the exotic, by the undeniable "otherness" of Asia that E. M. Forster portrayed so well in *A Passage to India* (originally published in 1924). This is the lure of the soaring Himalayas and of the Orient Express. That is, to an extent, Euro-Americans check out the new in religion and spirituality in much the same way that we check out new car models.

But what of the serious seekers? They are drawn both by the ways in which Asian religions are similar to what has been more common in the United States and by the ways in which they are different.

As Hinduism and Buddhism have developed in the United States, they have important similarities to the predominant religious culture and to themes found in the larger culture. At the same time, some characteristics also provide alternatives to how many experience contemporary culture.

- Both provide opportunities for person-to-person contact and offer small groups that allow for the development of greater closeness among participants. Such opportunities are a boon to many people struggling with the impersonality of today's fast-moving and technologically based culture.
- They emphasize self-effort, discovering one's own spiritual truth and working diligently toward one's own enlightenment or liberation. "Pulling oneself up by one's own bootstraps" is a theme that echoes throughout American culture.
- Some forms of these religions are compatible with science and even emphasize that compatibility, as do the Self-Realization Fellowship and many Buddhist groups. Most teach that religious truth should be tested out in one's own experience rather than be accepted on the basis of faith. This practical empiricism is also a theme that runs through American culture generally.
- The fervent devotion of the Krishna Consciousness Movement or the faith of the follower of Amida Buddha is not all that different from that of the evangelical Protestant Christian.
- Many have fit their major weekly activities into the typical Sunday morning time slot.
- Both have developed forms suitable for those with jobs, homes, and families, while also offering more intensive periods of semi-monastic retreat or even long-term monastic commitment for those who desire them.
- While both Hinduism and Buddhism offer their followers congregational activities, there is greater emphasis on individual spirituality than what many have found in more traditional American religions. This appeal to the individual runs through contemporary culture.

Hinduism and Buddhism also appeal to Americans by their differences, some of which have already been noted in passing above.

- They are frequently more accepting of multiple paths to liberation or enlightenment and are less inclined to believe there is a single correct teaching or practice.
- The Hindu teaching that the Atman is the divine at the heart of all and the Buddhist belief that all beings share Buddha's nature is a more positive view of human nature, in contrast with the prevailing emphasis on human sinfulness and willful disobedience.
- Also, both Hinduism and Buddhism do not see the human being as an isolated, separate self, but describe each as connected with all, another antidote to the perceived isolation many experience.

- Some variations emphasize a close relationship with a guru or religious and spiritual mentor, guaranteeing personal attention and guidance.
- For many, the belief that all persons are evolving toward liberation through multiple lifetimes governed by karma as a moral law of cause and effect is more attractive than the idea of one lifetime followed by an irreversible final judgment.
- Their practice often focuses on functional techniques that lead to greater calmness and equanimity in the face of life's inevitable ups and downs. They spell out these techniques clearly, encourage their diligent practice, and frequently promise results if they are followed.
- For many, these techniques become valuable tools for stress reduction and improved physical and mental well-being alongside their spiritual benefit. They seem to many to hold out hope for genuine personal transformation.
- In addition to these benefits, many people find these techniques facilitate direct experience of the sacred.
- To many people, the Asian religions seem to be less "religious" and more "spiritual," less beset by the foibles that plague many religious institutions. Although data indicate this is probably an incorrect perception, it remains an attractive one for many people.

These elements are obviously not entirely lacking in Christianity and Judaism, and have received more attention recently, in part, I think, as a result of the continuing interest in Asian religions. Christians have embraced centering prayer or contemplative prayer. Labyrinth walks are a form of walking meditation. Modern-day Jews are becoming acquainted with their own mystical and meditative traditions. Both Jews and Christians encourage individual religious practice. In the dance of adaptation, each has influenced the other.

QUESTIONS AND ACTIVITIES FOR REVIEW, DISCUSSION, AND WRITING

1. If you are fortunate enough to live or attend school close to a Hindu or Buddhist temple, arrange to visit, and write an essay on what you observe and your response to it.
2. Especially if attending a temple is not possible, try to arrange for a Hindu or Buddhist student who attends your college or university to come and speak to your class.
3. If your library subscribes to any periodicals published by U.S. Hindus or Buddhists, read through two or three issues, and write about what impression you form of the religion. Two to check are *Hinduism Today* and *Tricycle: The Buddhist Review*.
4. Yoga as a form of physical exercise and relaxation is taught in many physical education departments. If your school has such a class, invite the instructor to demonstrate some of the basic postures with class participation.
5. Discuss with a group of your classmates the ways in which the Four Noble Truths might apply in (1) your own lives and (2) American culture in general.
6. What are some practical, concrete applications of the Hindu and Buddhist ideal of noninjury or nonviolence in our own culture? How could you as an individual put this ideal into practice?

7. How would your life as a college student be different than it is now if you attended Naropa University? Visit their Web site for additional information that you can use to help you understand what being a student at Naropa might be like.
8. Visit the Web site of the American Buddhist Congress. In what ways does it reflect a specifically American interpretation of Buddhism?
9. How do you respond to the reasons given for interest in Asian religions?

FOR FURTHER READING

ECK, DIANA L., *A New Religious America: How A "Christian Country" Has Now Become the World's Most Religiously Diverse Nation.* New York: HarperSanFrancisco, 2001. This book by the founder and director of Harvard University's Pluralism Project has chapters on Hinduism and Buddhism, as well as on Islam and more general chapters on pluralism. Her accounts of individual congregations make this an especially readable resource.

PROTHERO, STEPHEN, ed., *A Nation of Religions: The Politics of Pluralism in Multireligious America.* Chapel Hill, NC: The University of North Carolina Press, 2006. Like Eck's book, this is a more general work, with excellent chapters on Buddhism and Hinduism. It also has a chapter on Sikhs and discussions of pluralism and its challenges.

RELEVANT WORLD WIDE WEB SITES

Hinduism Today (journal): www.hinduismtoday.com

The Hindu Universe: www.hindunet.org

Tricycle: The Buddhist Review: www.tricycle.com

The American Buddhist Congress: www.americanbuddhistcongress.org

CHAPTER 13

Other Religious and Spiritual Movements

A long line of scholars from Emile Durkheim to Mary Douglas has shown that societies are, among other things, commonly held ways of ordering reality. . . . Defining these bounds of inclusion and exclusion takes on an urgency disproportionate to their practical significance. Through this process of excluding outsiders, the shared order of a society is clarified and social solidarity is reinforced. . . . In such conflicts, the dominant culture typically maintains its status precisely by keeping a new minority faith marginal.[1]

In what ways are we . . . creating a new infrastructure for a society in which religious difference is just a part of the traffic of a creative democracy? From the Brooklyn Bridge to the Golden Gate, civic and religious bridge building is our greatest challenge today. Without bridges and traffic, we will allow ourselves to be fragmented into a multitude of separate religious, ethnic, and cultural enclaves.[2]

This chapter draws together several diverse movements. They include the New Age Movement, the self-help movement and twelve-step programs, feminist Wicca, the Fellowship of Metropolitan Community Churches, and religion on the Internet. The self-help movement and twelve-step programs have become an accepted feature of the American landscape. Others are controversial. The groups and movements reviewed in this chapter help demonstrate the expanding diversity of religion in the United States. The controversy surrounding some of them illustrates the dissention that may come with that diversity.

THE RELIGIONS OF THE NATIVE AMERICANS

Describing the religions of the original inhabitants of what we now call the United States is marked by several difficulties. To begin with, there is even controversy over how to refer to these peoples collectively. *Native Americans?*

---

[1]James Davison Hunter and David Franz, "Religious Pluralism and Civil Society," in *A Nation of Religions: The Politics of Pluralism in Multireligious America*, ed. Stephen Prothero (Chapel Hill, NC: The University of North Carolina Press, 2006), pp. 258–259.

[2]Diana Eck, *A New Religious America: How a "Christian Country" Has Now Become the World's Most Religiously Diverse Nation* (New York: HarperCollins Publishers, Inc., 2002), p. 335.

American Indians? Traditional peoples? Tribal cultures? Indigenous peoples? All these terms have their proponents and their detractors. The people to whom they refer have been stereotyped as barbaric and as noble savages, both of which miss the mark. They have been described as "primitive," a term sometimes used to denigrate and other times to glorify. However, all these terms are Euro-American constructs.

Native Americans constitute a small proportion of the population. The 2008 Pew Religious Landscape Survey[3] includes Native American religion in a category that also includes Unitarian Universalists, New Age followers, and others. The category as a whole accounts for only 1.2 percent of the population.

Then there is their diversity. More than 500 different languages and native cultures have existed in North America at one time or another. Native Americans lived throughout what is now the United States, and regional differences, related to other differences such as culture and sustenance, were pronounced.

This diversity makes it difficult to give any kind of general description of Native American religion that is at the same time meaningful. However, in a very brief survey such as this, it is necessary to do so. The following general features of Native American religion are widely accepted by native and non-native scholars alike.[4]

Although Native American spirituality is often depicted as the antithesis of Euro-American culture, American religious historian Peter W. Williams notes that in some ways, the earliest Americans were quintessentially American. Like all subsequent Americans, they were immigrants, having come probably from Siberia originally. They were also mobile, remaining on the move after their original immigration. Third, their history is one of great adaptability and adjustment to varying circumstances. Finally, their diversity itself fits into this category.[5]

One way to bring some order to the diversity of Native American religions is to note that there are four main categories of such religion today.[6]

- Tribal traditions are practiced within the context of particular tribes, each of which has a distinctive language and a distinctive culture. They tell their own mythic stories and perform distinctive rituals. They are based on the oral transmission of accumulated tribal lore and wisdom. Over one hundred of these traditions exist today.

---

[3]www.religion.pewforum.org

[4]See, for example, Sam Gill, "Native Americans and Their Religions," in *World Religions in America: An Introduction*, ed. Jacob Neusner (Louisville, KY: Westminster/John Knox Press, 2003), pp. 8–23; Joseph Epes Brown with Emily Cousins, *Teaching Spirits: Understanding Native American Religious Traditions* (New York: Oxford University Press, 2001); Vine Deloria, Jr., *God Is Red: A Native View of Religion* (Golden, CO: Fulcrum Publishing, 1992); and John G. Neihardt, *Black Elk Speaks* (Lincoln, NE: University of Nebraska Press/Bison Books, 2004).

[5]Peter W. Williams, *America's Religions From Their Origins To the Twenty-First Century* (Urbana, IL: University of Illinois Press, 2002), p. 13.

[6]Sam Gill, "Native Americans and Their Religions," in *World Religions in America: An Introduction*, ed. Jacob Neusner (Louisville, KY: Westminster/John Knox Press, 2003), pp. 8–21.

- Native American Christianity is now the most widely practiced religion among native peoples. Some Native American communities are almost exclusively Christian, while others have incorporated extensive elements of Christianity within their own traditions. Although such traditions were usually begun by non-native missionaries, Native American clergy have increasingly assumed leadership. These communities are most often evangelical and conservative/fundamentalist in orientation.
- New religious movements have occurred in response to stresses that have impacted the Native American community. Some have been crisis cults, movements begun by visionaries who sought to renew native culture and promised the return of the world to the way it was before the arrival of the Europeans. The Native American Church is another of the new religious movements. Although it incorporates elements of Christianity along with the sacramental use of peyote, it originates with Native Americans themselves, unlike Native American Christianity.
- Native American spirituality encompasses those characteristics and sensitivities in which native religion contrasts most sharply with the Euro-American culture. It is this dimension of Native American religion that has received the greatest interest in the last several decades, not only from Euro-Americans, but from Native Americans as well. We'll focus on this dimension below.

Native American Religion: An Overview

An interesting place to begin is that most native languages have no word that corresponds to the term *religion* (a bit disconcerting, perhaps, to those of us who have made a career of studying it!). While non-Native Americans tend to isolate religion in terms of specific activities such as prayer, other rituals, or attendance at services, and specific places such as temples, mosques, or churches, Native Americans do not. Religion and everyday life are inextricably woven together. Even the smallest details of daily life are experienced as significant and as having religious meaning. Thus, to even label it as religion is to make of it something it isn't. When we would use the word *religion*, Native Americans might simply say *life*.

As you learned in Chapter 2, having options in religion is an important factor in the religious landscape of the United States. Americans can practice whatever religion they wish, or none at all. Religion relates to the social order quite differently in Native American cultures. Their religion envelops everyone within the social group and tends not to extend beyond that group. For example, it would be very unlikely for a Sioux to take on the religious practices of a Cherokee, although some cross-fertilization does occur at times.

Euro-American culture is permeated by a specific experience of time. Usually described as linear time, this is time that has a beginning, an end, and does not double back on itself. Many monotheists think of it as beginning with God's creation of the world and culminating at whatever point this creation is brought to its final fulfillment. The idea of progress goes along with this view of time. Although there are high points and low points, the general trend is expected to be upward toward greater and greater advancement, and newer is regarded as better. It is also clock and calendar time, measured by the human conventions of hours and days stretching into months and years.

Native Americans, on the other hand, experience time as cyclic. This is reflected in language, in that many tribal languages have neither past nor future tense. Both are taken up into the present. This does not mean that nothing changes. If we were to picture this type of time, it would have to be more like a three-dimensional spiral rather than a flat drawing, circling back upon itself but with a vertical dimension as well that connotes change within the context of the cycles. It is not measured by the clock and the calendar, but by the markers of the natural world, such as the phases of the moon, the seasons of the year, planting and harvest, and the cycles of human life.

When I lived in the country on several acres of land with a river running through it, I often thought of it as "our land" and "our river." Such thinking would be almost nonsensical to a Native American. The land is there for human use, given to humans in the beginning times. Its use must be guided by respect and a lively awareness of its sacredness, but it cannot be owned by anyone.

Native Americans experience their individual lives as enmeshed in an extensive web of relationships that stretches far beyond the nuclear family and is replete with religious significance. It extends outward through all the various circles of extended family, tribe, clan, and all human beings. But beyond that, it reaches animals, spirit beings, and ultimately to the universe itself. Many Euro-Americans experience a three-story universe, in which God, people, and everything else are sharply differentiated. This sharp distinction is foreign to the Native American experience. Everything is related, and everything is holy because everything is suffused with spirit. This is reflected in the way in which tribal economies, although they vary somewhat, are based on cooperation and sharing rather than on competition. When game is killed for food, what is not needed immediately is not preserved for one's own immediate family but rather is shared widely with others in the group.

Ritual is perhaps the key component of Native American religious life. It is the means by which people align themselves with the sacred powers. Music, dance, sacred actions, and the retelling of significant myths all combine to bring participants into keenly felt connection with the spiritual dimension. The word *myth* is used here in a very specific way; it does not mean a false or fictitious story. Rather, it points to a traditional account of how things are, that is, the proper relationship between people and the divine. To tell the story is not just to entertain people with an account of something that happened long, long ago in a faraway land, but to make that power effectively present again. This in turn reflects the power of oral communication that is characteristic of native cultures. Stories and songs have power when told or sung, prayers when prayed aloud, and names when uttered with respect and care.

Many ritual actions revolve around the need for sustenance or around the human life cycle. Well-known examples of the former include dancing for rain and a variety of rituals that surround hunting for food. Hunters usually must avoid intimate contact with women immediately prior to the hunt and often ritually apologize and make an offering to the animal they have killed. This is done both out of respect for the spirit of the animal and because of the belief that not doing so will threaten the success of future hunts. The human life cycle as well is marked by a series of rituals. Conception and birth, coming of age both physically and socially, marriage and setting up a new household, and finally death all have their ritual recognition. Some such rituals define the transition for the person undergoing them, making it clear, for example, that someone is now an adult woman in the eyes of the group, with new privileges and responsibilities. Others highlight the change for the group itself, as do those surrounding death.

Healing and curing rituals are also common among native tribes. Whereas most Western medicine attributes illness to a variety of physical causes such as viruses or out-of-control cell growth, native healers look for personal, social, or spiritual causes. The ill person might, for example, have offended the elders, acted in a way that was outside the boundaries of moral behavior, or run afoul of spirits. Thus, the appropriate cure is ritual, because the causes of illness are at root religious.

Native American Religion: Restriction and Freedom

This very brief listing will give you some idea of how the religious practices of Native Americans have fared in the courts and in legislation. Most of the cases have revolved around interpretations of the free exercise clause. It has been a mixed history, to be sure. In recent years, the tendency has been toward greater freedom of practice and restoration of at least some of the freedoms lost earlier.

- In 1887 Congress enacted the Dawes Act (also referred to as the Allotment Act) that required breaking up tribal lands into private areas for cultivation. The intent behind this act was clearly to eliminate what was distinctively Native American. The Wheeler-Howard Act (also, the Indian Reorganization Act) rescinded the Dawes Act in 1934, but not before tremendous damage had been done to the entire native way of life.
- The American Indian Religious Freedom Act[7] was passed in 1978, signed by President Jimmy Carter. This legislation holds that "it shall be the policy of the United States to protect and preserve for American Indians their inherent right of freedom to believe, express, and exercise the traditional religions of the American Indian, Eskimo, Aleut, and Native Hawaiians, including but not limited to access to sites, use and possession of sacred objects and the freedom of worship through ceremonials and traditional rites." A previously defeated act, the Native American Free Exercise of Religion Act of 1993 was passed as the American Indian Religious Freedom Act Amendments of 1994.[8] This set of amendments further clarifies what is covered by the 1978 Act.
- In *Lyng* v. *The Northwest Indian Cemetery Association* (1988), the Supreme Court held that the U.S. Forest Service could allow roads to be made through Forest Service land that was sacred to Native Americans in the Northwest. In an earlier case (*Wilson* v. *Block*, 1983) the Court held that the Forest Service had not

---

[7]This Act can be accessed at http://www.cr.nps.gov/local-law/FHPL_IndianRelFreAct.pdf
[8]Links to the original Act and the amendments can be found at http://www.erowid.org/freedom/ civil_rights/religion/religion.shtml

infringed on the religious rights of Native Americans by allowing commercial development of an area sacred to the Navajo and Hopi because they had not denied them access to the area. To prevent Native Americans from performing ceremonies at sacred sites, or to allow tourist access to them, is to desecrate the site, according to native belief, much as allowing such restriction or access to a church, mosque, or synagogue would be for followers of the monotheistic faiths.

- Congress passed the Native American Graves and Repatriation Act in 1990. The act requires that federally funded universities and museums give an inventory of all human remains and sacred materials in their collections to the tribe or tribes from which they came and to return such materials to the appropriate tribes.
- President Bill Clinton signed an executive order in 1994 permitting Native Americans to have eagle feathers (otherwise prohibited because the eagle is protected).
- In 1995 Congress legalized the use of peyote by the Native American Church. Earlier, the Court had upheld the denial of unemployment benefits to two Native Americans because they had been fired for "drug use" because they used peyote in their church (*Employment Division, Department of Human Resources of Oregon* v. *Smith*, 1990). Prior to *Smith*, the Supreme Court had reversed a California court decision that convicted members of the church on possession of narcotics charges (1964).

THE NEW AGE MOVEMENT

Most of you have probably come across the term *New Age*. Although it began as such in the 1960s counterculture, its roots go back much deeper, into the metaphysical religion also reflected in Transcendentalism and Theosophy, New Thought and Spiritualism. Its focal point has been the belief in wide-reaching personal and planetary transformation, with personal spiritual transformation seen as a groundswell whose culmination will be a sweeping planetary renewal. It includes interests and practices such as environmentalism and ecology, holistic healing, alternative dietary practices such as vegetarianism and macrobiotics, feminism, astrology, karma and reincarnation, peace activism, and the cultivation of paranormal powers.

Beliefs

The teachings and practices of the New Age movement are diverse. There are, however, several major themes that stand out because they recur frequently in New Age literature. We can begin with the major beliefs and attitudes that characterize New Age thinking.

Dualistic ways of thinking have become part of how we view the world and ourselves. We experience and understand things in terms of religion or science, spirit or matter, mind or body, male or female. Virtually without exception, New Age thinkers believe that dualism must be replaced with a *holistic vision* of the world and ourselves that overcomes dualism while including legitimate differences.

An important corollary of this view is the belief that the divine is immanent within all things. New Agers believe that there is a single life force that is inherent in all living things. The New Age philosophy is thus *monistic*. The same universal energy animates everything.

This means that *all things are interrelated*. The entire universe is a seamless web of life. Nothing happens in isolation, and anything that happens has an impact on the whole. Because all things are interrelated, the fate of each hinges upon the fate of all. Everyone is responsible for the preservation of the earth's resources and species. Thus, *cooperation is more important than competition* and much more desirable. If everything is indeed interconnected, competition is simply the various parts working against the whole. Cooperation benefits the whole by eliminating conflicting actions of the parts.

Individuals have a responsibility to work to transform themselves in order to bring about planetary transformation. No one is exempt from this responsibility, and everyone can do something about the fate of the whole by working on themselves. Most of those who identify themselves as a part of the New Age movement share a nearly boundless optimism about the possibilities for both personal and communal transformation.

Compassionate service to individual people, to one's community, and on wider levels is a prominent theme, although one that receives relatively little attention from outside the movement. Through such service, people can have a dramatic impact on universal transformation.

Although religion takes many forms in different cultures, beneath the differences is a universal religion that will eventually be recognized by all people. This universal religion is grounded in the cycle of the changing seasons and the cycle of human lifetime. It understands life as a continual process of transformation through which people grow into greater consciousness. Inner exploration, psychic development, and self-awareness are valued highly.

This is one dimension of the *belief that the development of a planetary culture is both possible and desirable*. This worldwide culture will *not* replace the distinctive cultures that now exist. It will complement them, both enhancing them and being enriched by them. New Age believers look forward to a time when there will be one world government and a world language that is spoken and understood by all, facilitating communication and greater understanding among nations. Some favor the development of a worldwide monetary system to facilitate trade and a world court system as well.

Most followers of the New Age believe in some form of the Asian teachings of *karma* and *reincarnation*. They often emphasize the karmic effects of actions in the present lifetime. They often believe that people can become aware of past lives through meditation, hypnosis, or past-life regression therapy. Doing so is held to be an important way of resolving present problems.

Practices

Several key practices are shared by many within the New Age movement. Most try out a variety of spiritual disciplines and combining them into a uniquely personal synthesis. Many draw on Hindu or Buddhist practices, especially meditation and yoga. For some Americans, the importance of finding a compatible spiritual path has led to the study and practice of Native American spirituality. Most believe the goal of union with the mysterious reality that is both within and beyond can be attained more quickly if an intentional path is taken, rather than leaving it to chance.

Meditation is a central practice for many in the movement. People meditate for many reasons and by many specific means. Meditators seek to quiet and focus their minds, to bring a sense of peace and focus to all of life, to cultivate a kind of heightened awareness and perspective that extends to all activities and relationships. Many people believe that it also has significant health benefits. It is a primary way of being in touch with the sacred life energy.

Rituals of many kinds are also important elements of New Age practice. Meditation is itself a ritual. Rituals may be done to celebrate the changing seasons and the phases of the moon. The New Age movement offers the opportunity for people to construct their own rituals to mark events and occasions for which the larger culture does not have rituals or to develop creative, more personalized rituals to be used instead of more common ones. Many individuals develop private rituals for themselves.

Holistic health and *alternative healing* are important dimensions of the New Age movement. The underlying philosophical and religious assumptions of the movement lead people both to question standard medicine and to seek out alternatives to it. Chiropractic, herbal medicine, traditional systems of healing such as those of China and India, and nutritional approaches to healing are all part of the New Age healing repertoire. So are many kinds of body work and massage.

Figure 13-1 Incense, essential oils, candles, water, and flowers are used in many New Age ceremonies and rituals. *(Mark Harwood/Dorling Kindersley Media Library.)*

Aromatherapy makes use of the effects attributed to specific scents, and color ther-apy does the same with color. Healing through the use of crystals is popular with some. As with nearly everything in the New Age movement, there is a wide-ranging pragmatism in its approach to healing—try it and see if it works. Different things work for different people and in different situations. *Complementary medicine* is an approach that combines standard medical approaches with alternative ones.

Many advocates of the New Age try to follow what they describe as a *simple, natural lifestyle.* This means different things to different people but often includes a preference for clothing made from natural fibers such as cotton and wool over synthetics, natural cosmetics and household products, organic food and growing food at home, and limits on participation in America's consumer-based culture.

This description of the beliefs and practices makes clear that the influence of New Age thinking and practice has extended beyond the movement itself. The soothing qualities of New Age music make it popular with many who do not consider themselves part of the movement. Complementary medicine combines traditional medical methods with alternative healing practices. Yoga and meditation classes fill up almost as soon as they are announced, and massage therapists' calendars are full. Cities encourage people to recycle by offering curbside pick-up of recyclables. Major manufacturers have discovered that "natural" sells and are developing products that meet those guidelines. Many more people in the United States believe in karma and reincarnation than consider themselves part of the New Age. Service vacations, in which people use vacation time to be involved in a service project, have become popular. One specific variation on this theme is the alternative Spring break, in which college students use their Spring break not to party but to perform service to others.

Organization

There is *vast diversity* within the New Age movement. Beliefs and, especially, prac-tices range from the serious and thoughtful to the frivolous and mercenary. Merchants have discovered that New Age sells and do not hesitate to take advantage of that fact. Most of the publicity surrounding the New Age movement has focused on many highly publicized teachers and adepts, a renewed interest in angels, chan-nelers, and popular self-help books and tapes. The requirement for inclusion at this level seems to be that some glitzy aspect of the movement catches public interest.

Other followers of the New Age movement are genuinely committed to dramatic change in themselves and in their culture. They challenge themselves and their peers to help bring it about. They speak about becoming able to see everything that is as holy, a reintegration of the human with the sacred and with the earth conceived as a living being. In one author's words, it is "a deepening into the sacramental nature of everyday life, an awakening of the consciousness that can celebrate divinity within the ordinary and, in this celebration, bring to life a sacred civilization."[9]

[9]David Spangler, *Emergence: The Rebirth of the Sacred* (New York: Dell Publishing Company, 1984). Spangler's analysis still seems correct today.

A group of *journals and magazines* makes new information available and facilitates communication among New Age believers. Titles include *Spirituality & Health*, *Yoga Journal*, *Body and Soul*, *Vegetarian Times*, and *Mother Earth News*.[10] There are also organizations, most of which sponsor conferences, and retreat centers and programs, that serve the same organizing function.

New Age followers are a diverse group of people for whom an authentic spiritual search has led generally eastward and inward. Their affiliation with the movement varies from being at its center to barely touching its edges. They are among those whose religious needs have not been met in the more common religions. New Age believers do not meet in church buildings or have an organized hierarchy of leadership. For most of its followers, it provides the four elements of belief, lifestyle, ritual, and organizations in a way that helps to make life meaningful and good.

The movement has its detractors, however. Fundamentalist, conservative, and evangelical Christians criticize it for its rejection of moral and theological absolutes, its blurring or erasing of the distinction between human beings and God, and its hope for a global world order undergirded by a global religion. It has been called "a false religious system authored by the evil one" that must be "avoided, guarded against, and . . . destroyed."[11] Those who are rationally and scientifically minded critique it for its reliance on a worldview they deem irrational and antiscientific and for thinking that seems to them generally fuzzy.

The New Age movement is not something wholly alien to American culture. It integrates themes and basic ways of approaching religion that have been a part of our culture almost from the beginning. Nor is it new. It is another instance of the metaphysical strand in religion that also includes Theosophy and the transcendentalists (see Chapter 12). The viewpoints and methods it offers extend beyond the movement to the larger culture, as well.

THE SELF-HELP MOVEMENT AND TWELVE-STEP PROGRAMS

Twelve-step programs such as *Alcoholics Anonymous* are only part of a larger movement that we can call the self-help movement. The founding of Alcoholics Anonymous marked the beginning of a new era in self-help movements. Its twelve steps to recovery provide the blueprint for many such programs today.

The approach that AA takes to recovery from alcoholism is that it is a disease that has physical, mental, and spiritual dimensions. It can be best treated through its spiritual dimension. When alcoholics work on their spiritual lives, physical and mental recovery will follow as well. This is best done, say AA members, in the context of supportive groups of fellow sufferers. The strategy is summarized in

---

[10]www.spiritualityhealth.com, www.yogajournal.com, www.bodyandsoulmag.com, www.vegetariantimes.com, and www.motherearthnews.com. All have archives of noncurrent articles. Any of these will give you a much fuller idea of what the New Age movement is than can be done in this brief review.

[11]One of the better critiques of the New Age Movement from this perspective is that of the Christian Apologetics and Research Ministries, www.carm.org/newage.htm. The quote is from this site.

the famous Twelve Steps.[12] Several of these steps mark the movement as one that is essentially spiritual in nature.

- Step 2 affirms belief in a "Power greater than ourselves" which can "restore us to sanity."
- Step 3 refers to turning one's will and lives over to God however the individual understands God.
- Steps 4 through 7 call for a "searching and fearless moral inventory" and the admission of wrongs to oneself, to another person, and to God, then asking God to remove "all these defects of character."
- Step 11 calls for prayer and meditation to improve intentional contact with God.
- Step 12 encourages outreach to others with the message of hope and salvation from alcohol abuse.

This analysis of the twelve steps clearly delineates the spiritual character of the movement. Like organized religions, twelve-step and other self-help programs offer their followers something from each of the four dimensions of religion. Perhaps the most important belief is that human beings *can* transform their lives. This belief is widely shared among nearly all self-help programs. Some programs, like AA, advocate reliance on a power outside oneself. Other programs focus on self-effort. Certainly the reliance on an outside power is more in tune with the predominance of Christianity in this country. Reliance on self-effort, however, echoes a theme as old as the beginning of the United States: the self-reliant frontiersman or frontierswoman setting out to conquer the wilderness. Self-effort and individualism, although not always highlighted in American religion, are significant parts of the larger American cultural story. The importance of working on oneself and bettering oneself goes back as far as the Puritans, for whom growth in personal character was a highly prized goal. Taking responsibility for one's actions and their results is also a theme that is written large in both religion and secular culture in the United States.

There is yet another presupposition of the self-help movement that draws on an important feature of American religion. In self-help groups, people are aided in their own efforts by their peers. While a few groups have a professional leader or counselor, many do not. Even in those that do, the professional is there primarily as a facilitator, not as a person whose responsibility it is to fix everything. Democracy in government in the United States has spilled over into many areas of life. We noted that even those communities of faith that are primarily hierarchical in their organization are usually less so in their American embodiments. There is a tendency to see the leaders as leading their congregations in ministry, rather than being the only ones involved in ministry. Many alternative popular spiritual groups are very democratic in their structure. Especially in recent years, trust in professionals has declined, and many people have sought to take a larger role in their religion, health care, education, or

---

[12]The Twelve Steps are listed in nearly every Alcoholics Anonymous publication. They are also available on the organization Web site, www.alcoholics-anonymous.org (use the search function to search for "twelve steps").

automobile repair. Many people no longer think that calling in a professional is the only or the best solution.

Alcoholics Anonymous teaches the importance of changing one's lifestyle if one is to stay sober. Lasting sobriety is not likely to be achieved if recovering alcoholics continue to go to bars, socialize with former drinking buddies, and engage in whatever other behaviors were associated with their drinking. Most self-help groups emphasize changes in lifestyle. The details of these changes depend upon the goal of the particular group, but lifestyle is a focus for nearly all. New habits must replace old, and new rewards must supplant old, negative ones. This reflects the importance that lifestyle and morality in general have for American religion.

The ritual dimension is there as well. Meeting together for mutual support and fellowship is central for the self-help movement. It is customarily believed that the best context for making important changes is a fairly small, supportive group of people who know what each other are going through because they're all in the same boat. Some groups help people develop rituals to mark important changes of life, recognizing that rituals simply do not exist for many contemporary occasions that nonetheless need rituals. Alcoholics Anonymous groups celebrate the anniversaries of their members' sobriety, for example.

Certainly the organizational dimension is present. Alcoholics Anonymous itself spawned a number of other organizations such as Al-Anon (for families of alcoholics) and Alateen (specifically for teenagers), and, most recently, groups for adult children of alcoholics. Twelve-step groups have been formed to help people recover from other compulsive behaviors, including drug addiction, gambling, overeating, uncontrolled spending, and spouse and child abuse. These organizations have then developed groups for spouses and other family members of the recovering person.

A nearly limitless number of other kinds of support groups have formed, all based on the premise that the best support in a crisis comes from other people who have been through similar experiences. Some direct all their energies toward helping the people involved. Weight Watchers is one example. There are also support groups for people with cancer (and for their families and friends), and those who are divorcing, chronically ill, or in chronic pain. Your campus may have a variety of support groups for students, such as a group for students who suffer test anxiety.

Other support groups have also developed a political dimension that complements their supportive function. Mothers Against Drunk Driving (MADD) began as a support group for parents whose children had been killed or injured in an alcohol-related accident. They soon began working actively to reduce the number of such accidents. Support groups for people who are HIV-positive or who have AIDS (and their families and friends) often undertake political activity on behalf of affected people.

As we have seen, the self-help movement, exemplified by Alcoholics Anonymous and other similar groups, is clearly a spiritual movement. For some people, it is an adjunct to participation in a community of faith. For others, it is a substitute for such participation. The specific format, and certainly the proliferation of these groups, is relatively new on the American scene. On the other hand, as we have seen, some of the themes and presuppositions are as old as the United States itself.

Feminist Wicca

Most—although not all—religious groups and organizations in the United States share at least some of the patriarchal viewpoints and practices that continue to mark American culture in general. This has created concern for many women in these communities of faith. We can describe the responses that women make to this situation in terms of a continuum. At one end are those many women for whom traditional structures, views, and rituals are meaningful and fulfilling. Survey data strongly indicate that women are more traditionally religious than are men. Many women, perhaps the majority, are not disturbed by references to God as "He" and to humanity as "man." These women can and do remain within their traditional communities of faith and find meaning there, without seeking or desiring change.

Most women choose to stay in their communities of faith, either accepting things as they are or working actively to change the things with which they disagree. But some women choose not to remain in their churches, temples, or synagogues and found or join groups specifically based on women's spirituality. Wicca is one form of feminist spirituality.

Women and men who consider themselves to be followers of Wicca do not agree completely on how their religion should be named. Some prefer *Wicca* (practitioners are *Wiccans*), a word meaning "Wise Ones." It has the same root as the word *wisdom*. Some of its advocates believe that using this less familiar word helps overcome the negative connotations often associated with the word *witch*. Others deliberately use *Witchcraft* and *Witch* in a bold move to reclaim the word from its detractors. Others prefer *the Craft*, with its emphasis on the ritual work that Wiccans do. For still others, *the old religion* signifies the ancient roots of this worldview. I will use these terms interchangeably.

Most Wicca in the United States traces its roots back to British author and lecturer Gerald B. Gardner (1884–1964) and therefore it is called *Gardnerian Wicca*. Although there are various accounts of exactly how Gardner developed his religious thought and practice, it blended together elements from Western occult and magickal traditions with various pieces of Eastern religions that he picked up while living in India and Southeast Asia. The Gardnerian tradition came to the United States with Raymond and Rosemary Buckland in the mid-1960s. The Bucklands formed a coven on Long Island, and Gardnerian thought and practice spread from there. Although there are many variations within the American Wiccan community, most of them retain at least the outlines of Gardner's worldview and ritual. Among the most closely related schools is the Alexandrian, formed by Alexander Sanders (1926–1988).

Criticism of Wicca and Wiccans often comes from the same points of view that criticize the New Age movement. Scientists and rationalists say its reliance on a magickal and fundamentally irrational worldview is mistaken. Conservative Christians, while acknowledging that Wiccans do not recognize the existence of the devil as portrayed by Christianity, nonetheless hold that "the theology behind Wicca is not from God and that it is ultimately authored from Satan." Thus, "the God and Goddess worship offered by Wiccans is really an offering to the devil himself."[13]

Beliefs and Practices

Attempts to develop an agreed-upon statement of Wiccan belief have fallen far short of universal acceptance among actual Wiccans. Decentralization and the autonomy of individuals and groups is a primary organizing principle. However, it is possible to describe certain basic beliefs that are widely shared among Wiccans. In a similar fashion, I will describe common ritual practices.

Wicca is one form of a larger worldview, that of *magick*. When used this way, magick is spelled with a *k* to distinguish it from stage magic. Sybil Leek, a contemporary American witch, defines magick as "the art of producing a desired effect or result through the use of various techniques such as incantations and presumably assuring human control of supernatural agencies or the forces of nature."[14] Ritual is the primary tool for working with these forces. In a nation in love with technology (although perhaps less enamored of its promises than we once were), Witchcraft offers a spiritual technology with which to interact with unseen forces.

The way in which the sacred or holy is thought about and spoken about, addressed in prayer and celebration, is one of the most central beliefs in any religion. Instead of the traditional habit of thinking and speaking of God in the Judeo-Christian-Islamic tradition as if God were male, Wiccans focus on the Goddess, often paired with a god as the male principle. Some women have turned to belief in and worship of the goddess instead. Followers of the goddess look back to religions that predate Judaism and Christianity, in which the goddess was very important. Worshiping both a god and a goddess, with the emphasis placed on the goddess, restores a balanced view of ultimate reality or the holy for her followers, in ways that simply altering traditional language cannot. Not all followers of the Goddess are Wiccans, but virtually all Wiccans are worshipers of the Goddess. For followers of the Goddess, she provides a strong affirmation of the female in a way they do not find elsewhere.

For many goddess worshipers, *the goddess is a way to the recognition and celebration of the divinity within themselves*. They experience the entire world as one divine whole and see themselves as a divine part of it.

Wiccans usually worship the Goddess in her threefold form, sometimes referred to as the *Triple Goddess*. She is *maiden*, *mother*, and *crone*, signifying the various ages of woman. She is frequently symbolized by the phases of the moon— the waxing or rising crescent, the full moon, and the waning or subsiding moon.

[13]www.carm.org/wicca/satanists.htm
[14]Sybil Leek, *Diary of a Witch* (Englewood Cliffs, NJ: Prentice Hall, 1968), p. 4.

Figure 13-2   Wiccans worship the Goddess in many forms; here, a representation of Astarte.
(Man Hills and Barbara Winter © The British Museum.)

Wiccans draw on the goddess traditions of many times and cultures, believing that all the names of the goddess are equally valid.

Wiccans also *affirm the divinity and holiness of all living beings and of the earth itself* (or, as many would put it, herself). They experience the sacred in the changing seasons and in the constant rhythms of life. All aspects of the cycle of life and death are sacred.

Witches do not worship Satan or the Christian devil. The beginnings of Wicca predate Christianity, while Satanism relies on the development of the idea of Satan within the Christian tradition. Although they are often carelessly lumped together, there is no relationship between them aside from the underlying magickal worldview they share.

Nor do witches try to put evil spells and curses or hexes on people. They consider this sort of behavior unethical. Most witches feel that it is unethical even to work a spell for someone's benefit without their knowledge and agreement. There are two basic principles that guide behavior. One is the "Wiccan Rede," *An ye harm none, do what ye will.* (*An* is an ancient use of the word that means as long as.) The second is the principle that what people do returns to them. Many put this in terms of the *Threefold Law*: Whatever we do returns to us three times over, be it good or ill.

Witches often organize into *covens or small groups* of three to twenty people to perform rituals and enjoy fellowship. There are also solitaries, witches who, through personal choice or circumstances, practice alone. Some covens are all female (and a few are all male), and some are mixed. Although there are traditional rituals that have been handed down, most feel very free to improvise and create new rituals as occasions call for them.

Casting a circle is a fundamental ritual. The circle thus marked off becomes a sacred space. Wherever it is, indoors or out, city or farm, it becomes a place in which the sacred can be contacted and interacted with. Ritual purification of the circle removes negative energy from it, protects those within it, and helps to concentrate their own spiritual energies on the task at hand. This is most often done using the traditional elements of air, earth, fire, and water. Often, gods and goddesses are called upon to be present alongside the human participants.

The circle having been cast and purified, participants often *raise a cone of power* by chanting or dancing (or both) or running around the circle. The cone of power represents and taps the power of the combined wills of the group, intensified and focused through ritual and meditative techniques.

The focus can be any of a number of things. Healing can be directed toward individuals (within the circle or outside it), groups, or the earth itself. Sometimes the focus is simply to raise positive energy. Coven work often centers around directing positive energy toward the goals of the members and others— be it finding a job, a love relationship, overcoming a crisis, or simply living with grace and joy in everyday life. This type of work is done in *esbats*, coven meetings that are held traditionally at the time of the full and new moons, although they may be held at other times as well. Some covens, for example, meet weekly. The ritual work is most often followed by sharing a meal or at least refreshments and a time of fellowship.

Witches celebrate *seasonal festivals or Sabbats* that reflect the natural cycle of the seasons and the positions of the sun and earth relative to each other. There are *four Great Sabbats*:

- *Samhain* or the Celtic New Year on October 31
- *Candlemas* on February 2, a winter festival that focuses on purification and the beginning of spring
- *Beltane*, May 1, the great spring festival of fertility and renewal symbolized by the marriage of the god and goddess and
- *Lughnasadh* (in some accounts, *Lammas*), the August 1 festival of the first fruits of harvest that also looks toward the seasonal decline of winter.

Four Lesser Sabbats celebrate the summer and winter solstices (June and December) and the spring and fall equinoxes (March and September).

Initiation is an important ritual for individual witches. Although some witches believe that a person must be initiated by another witch, others support self-initiation, especially if the opportunity for initiation by a practicing witch is not available. However it is carried out, it is a rite of beginning, of accepting and celebrating one's status, and of becoming a part of the Wiccan community of faith and agreeing to live by its norms.

Organizations

Most Wiccan covens are small, and there is no central organization. The *Church and School of Wicca*[15] in New Bern, North Carolina, is one of the most accessible of the witchcraft groups. Its members have campaigned energetically to promote what they believe is a correct understanding of the meaning of the craft and to help overcome centuries of prejudice and misunderstanding. In 1972, it became the first Wiccan group to be granted federal tax-exempt status as a religious organization.

The *Covenant of the Goddess*[16] is "an international organization of cooperating, autonomous Wiccan congregations and solitary practitioners." They sponsor many events for the Wiccan community and interested others, as well as providing information and advocating for the rights of Wiccans and Pagans in special situations such as the military.

The *Covenant of Unitarian Universalist Pagans* (CUUPS)[17] is a network of pagan- and Wiccan-identified Unitarian Universalists. It is formally acknowledged and supported by the denomination, which also lists earth-centered spirituality among its sources of belief and practice. CUUPS is the first such recognition of the goddess tradition within a mainstream American denomination.

One indication of the evolution of the Wiccan movement in the United States is that the well-known Wiccan practitioner and author Starhawk

---

[15]www.wicca.org
[16]www.cog.org
[17]www.cuups.org

(Miriam Samos) has written a book titled *Circle Round: Raising Children in Goddess Traditions*.[18] This indicates that Wicca in the United States is no longer just a movement of converts, or of first-generation practitioners, but that a need has developed to address the issue of raising up the next generations.

Wiccans and the Military

The U.S. military is frequently seen as one of the most conservative organizations in the nation, and in some respects it is. However, it has often led the way in diversity issues. For example, there were racially integrated units in the Army at a time when drinking fountains and public toilets were still labeled "whites" and "coloreds." Women became military pilots before they flew commercial airliners. Military chaplains are trained to minister equally to those of any and all faiths, and of none.

However, in the first decade of the new century, it came to light that the military would not accept Wiccans as chaplains, nor could the five-pointed star or pentacle, symbol of Wiccan faith, be placed on the grave markers of Wiccan veterans in veterans' cemeteries. Although the issue about chaplains has yet to be resolved, the Department of Veterans Affairs has added the five-pointed star to the official list of emblems permitted in national cemeteries and on government-issued headstones for soldiers.

THE UNIVERSAL FELLOWSHIP OF METROPOLITAN COMMUNITY CHURCHES

The Universal Fellowship of Metropolitan Community Churches is a Christian community of faith for lesbian, gay, bisexual, and transgendered persons. Homosexuality has been and continues to be thought of as sinful by a significant proportion of Christian churches. As a result, gays, lesbians, and transgendered people, and sometimes their straight allies, have often felt unwelcome in these churches. The Universal Fellowship of Metropolitan Community Churches provides a place that is welcoming, and gives people a way to openly affirm both their Christianity and their sexual orientation.[19] The founder and moderator of the Universal Fellowship of Metropolitan Community Churches is Troy Perry, author of *The Lord Is My Shepherd and He Knows I'm Gay*.[20]

Solidly within the mainstream Christian tradition as far as belief and worship are concerned, the Fellowship teaches that God's promises of salvation and fellowship are offered to all persons, without regard to sexual orientation. Homosexuality is regarded as neither a sin nor an illness, but as something natural and God-given that neither can nor should be changed. As God creates

[18]Starhawk, Anne Hill, and Diane Baker. *Circle Round: Raising Children in Goddess Traditions* (New York: Bantam Doubleday Dell, 1998).
[19]Fellowship of Metropolitan Community Churches World Wide Web site, www.ufmcc.com
[20]Troy D. Perry, *The Lord Is My Shepherd and He Knows I'm Gay* (Kalamazoo, MI: Steven J. Nash Publishing, 1972).

some people heterosexual, others are created homosexual. The Bible does not condemn "loving, responsible homosexual relationships," and therefore these relationships should be encouraged, affirmed, and celebrated.

The Fellowship is the largest and probably the most widely known religious organization for gays, lesbians, and transgendered persons. It is not the only one. There is also a Gay Buddhist Fellowship, an organization of Gay and Lesbian Atheists and Humanists (GALAH), and a National Gay Pentecostal Alliance.

RELIGION ON THE WEB

We have already seen that many religious groups have pages or sites on the World Wide Web. Religious organizations have found the Web a useful place on which to present their views to others and to keep their own constituencies informed. Individuals motivated by religious concerns maintain sites and pages to present their views.

When I use the term *religion on the Web*, I have something else in mind. There are manifestations of religion that have developed specifically on and for the Internet or World Wide Web. Unlike "bricks and mortar" religion in the United States, which is increasingly diverse, Internet-based churches are predominantly Christian and more often than not, conservative in their theology.

One example is the First International Church of the Web, founded by the Reverend Dr. David M. Ford.[21] It is a conservative and evangelical group that describes itself as Christ-centered, non-denominational, and Web-based. Its founder also founded the *International Alliance of Web-Based Churches.*[22] The Alliance links online churches together in a shared commitment "to bringing the Word of God to all the nations through the internet."

The Church of Virus is a serious attempt at creating a very different style of Internet religion, although with an unlikely name. It is an atheistic religion with a scientific emphasis. It intends to provide people with a "conceptual framework for leading a truly meaningful life and attaining immortality" without reference to anything supernatural. Its founders chose the name "Church of Virus" because the word *virus* has such a negative connotation, particularly among computer users acquainted with the havoc that computer viruses can cause. It was chosen to "deliberately antagonize" people and to warn people that it might "infect" them with the truth.[23]

What are we to make of religion in cyberspace? It would seem to be very difficult to replicate some of the features of real-world religion in virtual religion. There is communication, to be sure, some of it very personal, in cyberspace. However, it is not face-to-face. People and groups can easily deceive others about their identity when the only connection is through words on a

[21]The First International Church of the Web, www.ficotw.org
[22]http://www.ficotw.org/Alliance.html
[23]Church of Virus, http://virus.lucifer.com/about.html

computer monitor. Accountability is seriously lacking, or wholly absent. Despite the development of emoticons to indicate emotions, these fall far short of a real human hug or smile. A virtual congregation cannot come sit with you while your partner or child has surgery.

One of the things that is most often used as a marker for something being religious is the presence of ritual. In spite of some few attempts, ritual has shown itself to be hard to do in cyberspace. So much of ritual is about embodiment—about bread and wine as the body and blood of Jesus in the Christian Eucharist, for example, or about offerings of flowers or fruit or rice. And virtual reality is very much *dis*embodied reality.

That having been said, if virtual religion seems to be a questionable matter at this time, the role of the Internet—the Web, bulletin boards, chat rooms, newsgroups—in providing a forum for people to share their religious views, to advocate for their particular community of faith, to learn about religions other than their own, to find support among those with similar views has become an important part of religion in the United States.

In February, 1998, three Tibetan Buddhist monks at the Namgyal Monastery in New York State prayed for a half-hour, conducting a formal Buddhist blessing of cyberspace:

> In the monks' view, cyberspace resembles space in general, which Tibetan Buddhists characterize more as the absence of obstructions than as a distance between two points. . . . Where there is an absence of obstructions, there is the potential for something to arise, the nature of which depends on the motivation of those who use it. In blessing cyberspace, the monks reasoned, they could offer prayers that the motivation of Internet users become more positive and that the benefits of using the Internet become more positive.[24]

The monks chanted a traditional Buddhist prayer for the welfare of all, in the hope that the positive potentials of cyberspace would develop in such a way that they would outweigh the negative ones.

SATANISM

Students are often curious about *Satanism*. We can distinguish between two types of Satanism. Anton LaVey (1930–1997) founded the Church of Satan in 1966. He collected standard occult and magickal teachings around the motif of the worship of Satan. Secrecy is part and parcel of this perspective. It is a defense against hostility and misunderstanding, as well as against those who are merely curious. More important, Satanists feel their rituals are very powerful tools that would be dangerous in the hands of most people.

---

[24]This rationale for the blessing, along with an audio clip of the blessing itself, comes from the Web site of the Namgyal Monastery in New York, www.namgyal.org/blessings/cyberspace.cfm

The Church of Satan teaches that those things that Christianity has usually condemned as sins (such as pleasure seeking, vengeance, and pride) are actually virtues. Logically, the Church of Satan is dependent on Christianity; it is a reaction to it. LaVey's teachings are contained in three books: *The Satanic Bible* (1969), *The Compleat Witch* (1970), and *The Satanic Rituals* (1972). A list of Nine Satanic Statements at the beginning of *The Satanic Bible* summarizes LaVey's teachings:

- Satan means indulgence, not abstinence.
- Satan means living fully now, not vague spiritual aspirations for a future life.
- Satan means self-knowledge, not hypocrisy and self-deceit.
- Satan stands for kindness to those who deserve it, not love for the unworthy.
- Satan stands for vengeance, not forgiveness.
- Satan means responsibility for those who are responsible, not misplaced concern for "psychic vampires."
- Satanism teaches that humans are simply animals, animals whose intellectual and spiritual development can make them more vicious than the other animals.
- Satan encourages gratification of physical and mental desires.
- "Satan has been the best friend the church has ever had, as He has kept it in business all these years!"[25]

The Church of Satan, in other words, encourages individuals to seek the greatest gratification of their desires and feel free to practice "selfish virtues." The followers of Satan developed a religious framework for a pleasure-seeking life, without violating laws. For the most part, they maintain a very low profile in society. The shock value of something that calls itself Satanism has made its members the target of persecution. At the same time, it has been an ideal vehicle for those who wish to rebel against the predominant culture. (Remember that one of the characteristics attributed to Satan is that he is the arch-rebel.) Although membership figures are not made public and members are often understandably reluctant to reveal their affiliation, membership in the Church of Satan is not widespread.

The individual's birthday is the most important holiday celebrated. Walpurgisnacht (April 30) marks the rebirth of nature in the spring, and Halloween is celebrated as well. Various other magickal and celebratory rituals round out the ritual calendar. In line with its orientation to magick, ritual is the central focus of Satanism in any of its forms.

The second form of Satanism consists of small and loosely organized groups not connected with the Church of Satan. Participating in these groups is often a way that their members act out psychological and emotional disturbances. It is important to distinguish cause and effect here. One model depicts Satanism itself as leading to violent, criminal, and antisocial behavior. Another, more accurate model, posits a prior cause—anger and rage, alienation, social maladaptation—that leads both to membership in a Satanic group and to the violent, criminal, and antisocial behavior.

[25]Church of Satan Web site, www.churchofsatan.com; click on the link for theory and practice.

It is important to put concern about Satanism in perspective. The presence of Satanic symbols and motifs in the youth culture, especially in music, the fantasy game *Dungeons and Dragons* along with similar games, and the high-profile accounts of evangelical Christians describing their former involvement with Satanism may make it seem as if there are far more Satanists than can actually be documented. As one author notes, "their numbers have been few, their activities mostly innocuous, and their influence vastly exaggerated."[26]

CHRISTIAN IDENTITY

The term *Christian Identity* has two meanings. (1) Its earlier meaning refers to Anglo-Israelism or British-Israelism, the belief that white Anglo-Saxons, Germanic peoples, Scandinavians, Celts, and similar cultures are the true descendants of the biblical Israel. Americans and Canadians who are descendants of these groups are a part of this true Israel as well. (2) The meaning that is more commonly used in the United States refers to a number of faith groups whose members accept British-Isrealism and combine it with beliefs that are intensely homophobic, racist, sexist, and anti-Communist. These very conservative and fundamentalist Christians believe Jews are descended from Satan. They usually oppose equal rights for homosexuals, gun control, and any control over militia movements.[27]

There is no national structure to the movement. It is more a collection of independent groups united by their loathing of all persons of non–northern European descent, homophobia, embrace of paramilitary activity, and their belief that the present age will soon end in a cataclysmic battle which will result in their victory as God's "elect."

Many Americans feel threatened by the problems that confront us all: inadequate healthcare funding, AIDS, terrorism at home and abroad, economic problems, unemployment and underemployment, homelessness, and discipline problems among youth, to name but a few. In this situation, it is easy to look for a scapegoat. Christian Identity focuses this scapegoating and gives it a violent edge, at the same time assuring its followers that they are the only ones who are truly doing God's will.

The movement has been criticized on several grounds. Biblical scholars point out that its theology cannot be supported by any evidence. More pointed criticism has been directed against the racial views and policies of its constituent groups. Because the movement's theology inherently contains the potential for violence, its activities are closely monitored in areas where such groups exist. Some members have been indicted on charges ranging from murder to burglary and conspiracy, with some convictions resulting from the charges.

[26]Peter W. Williams, America's Religions from Their Origins To the Twenty-First Century (Urbana, IL: University of Illinois Press, 2002), p. 496.
[27]Ontario Consultants on Religious Tolerance Web site, www.religioustolerance.org

QUESTIONS AND ACTIVITIES FOR REVIEW, DISCUSSION, AND WRITING

1. In what ways does Native American spirituality seem similar to that of mainstream religion in America? Different from it?
2. If there is a New Age bookstore in your community, visit it and note the types of literature, music, and other items that are available. If you can, speak with the owner, manager, or someone who works there about their clientele and the purpose that they believe the store serves.
3. Compare and contrast Native American and New Age spirituality.
4. If you have been a part of a twelve-step or self-help group, reflect on the extent to which it was based on spiritual presuppositions or had a spiritual impact on you.
5. If you can locate one in your community, attend a Wiccan ritual or meeting. Write an essay on what you observe and how you respond to it. If this is not possible, try to find a Wiccan who is willing to come and speak to your class.
6. What effect do you think that ritual observance of the changing seasons and phases of the moon would have on you?
7. Briefly identify in your own words each of the following faith topics discussed in this chapter: Native American spirituality, the New Age movement, self-help movement, twelve-step movement, Wicca, Universal Fellowship of Metropolitan Community Churches, Internet religion, and Christian Identity.

FOR FURTHER READING

GILL, SAM, *Native American Religions: An Introduction*. Belmont, CA: Wadsworth Publishing, 2004. Professor Gill's is an accessible, empathic overview. He also looks at the sources of widespread Euro-American, misunderstanding of Native traditions.

PIKE, SARAH M., *New Age and Neopagan Religions in America*. New York City: Columbia University Press, 2004. Pike focuses on the "main concerns and daily lives" of followers of this diffuse religious tradition in the United States. Early chapters provide historical background, including the early history of metaphysical religion and the "watershed years" of the 1960s.

DAWSON, LORNE L., *Religion Online: Finding Faith on the Internet*. New York: Routledge, 2004. This edited collection of essays covers both mainstream and new or emerging religions on the Internet.

DASCHKE, DERECK and MICHAEL ASHCRAFT, *New Religious Movements: A Documentary History*. New York City: New York University Press, 2005. This book covers a very wide range of new and not-so-new religious movements, most of which either are or have been controversial. It offers an excellent combination of documents in which the religions' followers can speak for themselves with careful contexting and commentary.

Nova Religio: The Journal of Alternative and Emergent Religions. This journal is devoted solely to the examination of new religious movements from a variety of academic perspectives. Its cross-cultural and interdisciplinary approach makes it highly recommended.

RELEVANT WORLD WIDE WEB SITES

The Religious Movements Homepage at the University of Virginia, http://etext.lib.virginia.edu/relmove/welcome/welcome.htm

Community and Communication

In the Introduction to this book, I described the affirmation of religious diversity as an active and open engagement with diversity, a commitment to dialogue in order to understand difference, not to reach agreement. The affirmation of religious diversity calls on all of us to join in the dialogue with our religious commitments and our deeply felt sense that our religious truths are true in a uniquely compelling way for us.

To be truly present with an open mind and an open heart, to listen carefully and thoughtfully, and to speak truthfully and with respect, is the first step in building a community in which people of all faiths and those of none are truly welcome for who they are.

The affirmation of religious diversity—or of diversity in any area—calls for the creation of genuine community. It is no accident that the words *community* and *communicate* stem from the same root. Community is made up of those who can and do communicate with each other. Communication in community must be based on several things. There must be the *willingness* to communicate—to share ideas, beliefs, and feelings openly. There must be *openness* to receive what is shared. This requires an open space, as it were, free of prejudice and preconceptions. There must be *accurate information*, in order for communication to be meaningful. And, there must be genuine *difference*. Community is not based on uniformity. It is based on respect for and affirmation of difference. It cannot be based on an attitude of weighing differences to see who is right and who is wrong. People in the community, although committed to their own communities of faith and the values they uphold, are also committed to the larger endeavor of understanding, not to judgment.

This survey of the religious beliefs and practices of people in the United States has been largely descriptive. I have not assessed the truth or falsity of any religion, belief or practice. Chapter 3, "Conflict and Controversy," has, however, suggested that another dimension must be present in the dialogue. Religion is not and cannot be above criticism. Some religious practices and beliefs, like those in any other area of life, may tend to produce undesirable outcomes. As I was finishing this manuscript, the news was full of accounts of a fundamentalist Mormon compound in Texas in which young girls were spiritually married to much older men and were subject to physical and sexual abuse. This group was not affiliated with either of the two large Mormon churches described in Chapter 8. Neither the Latter-day Saints nor the Community of Christ supports their practices.

In the Texas group, isolation and an authoritarian power structure, combined with belief in and the practice of multiple marriages, helped to bring about a very negative situation. Those things are not exempt from criticism. We must be prepared to ask the hard questions, and in the community of dialogue, we must listen when others ask hard questions about our own points of view. Only so can wrongs be righted and progress be made.

Index

Note: page references with f and n notations refer to a figure or note on that page.

Sessions, Jeff, 40
Seton, Mother Elizabeth
    Bayley, 136
Seven ecumenical councils, 143
Seven synonyms for God, 183
Seventh-day Adventists,
    185–187
Sex education
    fundamentalist view, 81
    holiness movement, 110
    religious-political right view
        of, 102, 104, 107
Sexism, 305
Sexual misconduct
    by clergy, 36–38
    of televangelists, 95
Sexual morality
    Buddhism, 270
    Catholic Christianity,
        126–127, 137
    Hindu, 259
    Islamic, 226, 228
    Latter-day Saints, 177
    Orthodox Christianity, 148
    religious-political right view,
        102, 103
    of Unitarian Universalists, 251
Seymour, William Joseph, 114
Shahadah, 226, 227
Shakarian, Demos, 94
Shambhala Press, 279
Shavuot, 206
Shema, 199
Shia Muslims, 224
Shin Buddhist White Path
    Temple, 276
Shiva, 260, 261f
Sho'ah, 216, 217
Shofar, 205
Shorter Catechism, 77
Shouting, in black churches,
    163–164
Sikhs, religious violence, 45
"Simple Gifts" (song), 171
Sin
    Eastern Orthodox Christian
        view, 144, 147
    Jewish view, 205
    Latter-day Saints
        view, 175
Singing. *See* Hymns; Music
Sisters of Charity, 136
Six Day Arab-Israeli War,
    48, 213
Skullcaps, 210

Slavery
    and Christianity,
        153–154, 158
    exodus out of Egypt, 206
    identified with
        Christianity, 237
    obedience of Christianity, 235
Smart, Ninian, 12
*Smith, Employment Division
    of the State of Oregon* v., 22
Smith, Hyrum, 174
Smith, Joseph, 174–175, 176,
    179, 182, 188
Snake handling, pente-
    costalism, 113
Sobriety groups, 295
Social activism
    atheist view of religion, 245
    of humanists, 240, 242
    influenced by Buddhist
        women, 272
    of Jews, 202, 209
    of Methodists, 73
    of Unitarian Universalists,
        240, 242
    of United Church
        of Christ, 80
Social conservatives, 30
Social institutions,
    and religion, 13
Social justice, 214, 240
Social order upheld by Supreme
    Court, 21
Social progress and
    freethinkers, 244
Social-scientific study
    of religion, 11
Social service activities
    Catholic, 135–136
    Friends, 82
    holiness movement, 110
Social services, faith-based
    initiatives, 33, 53–54
Social traditionalists, 101
Society for Humanistic
    Judaism, 243
Sociological view of religion, 229
Sociopolitical involvement
    of evangelicals, 85
Solar Temple, 45
Sola Scriptura, 62
Solitaries, Wiccan, 299
Solstices, 300
Soon-to-come Kingdom of God
    Shakers and Oneida, 171

Soul freedom (soul
    competency), 70
Southern Baptist Convention,
    69, 71, 76
    interfaith broadcasting
        alliance, 97
    and marriage amendment,
        39–40
Southern Christian Leadership
    Conference, 155–156
Southern Methodist Church, 74
Southern religious history, 152
Soviet Union, 229
Spangler, David, 292 n
Spanish-American War, Catholic
    nurses, 135–136
Speaking in tongues, 113,
    115, 116
Special interest religious
    groups, 16
Spiritual goal of
    salvation/liberation,
    Hindu, 259
Spirituality of black Christians,
    157–161
Spiritual technology, 297
Sports leagues, 23
Stake president, 179
Standing Conference
    of Orthodox Bishops
    in America, 149
Starhawk, 300–301
Star of David, 196f
Star Trek TV show, 193
State governments, 21, 101
Statistical data. *See also*
    Survey data
    Catholic marriage
        and divorce, 126
Statues
    of Buddha, 276
    Catholic religious
        artifacts, 133
    in commercial culture, 17
    Hindu gods and
        goddesses, 260
Stealing, Buddhist precept, 270
Storefront churches
    in Chicago, 140
Storehouses of Latter-day
    Saints, 178
Stowe, Harriet Beecher, 153
Strangers, 201
Stress-reduction
    techniques, 282